BLACKS AND REDS

BLACKS AND REDS

RACE AND CLASS IN CONFLICT
1919-1990

EARL OFARI HUTCHINSON

Michigan State University Press
East Lansing
1995

All Michigan State University Press books are produced on paper which meets the requirements of American National Standard of Information Sciences— Permanence of paper for printed materials ANSI Z39.48-1984.

Michigan State University Press
East Lansing, Michigan 48823-5202

03 02 01 00 99 98 97 96 95 1 2 3 4 5 6 7 8 9

Library of Congress Cataloging-in-Publication Data

Hutchinson, Earl Ofari.
Blacks and reds: race and class conflict, 1919-1990 / Earl Ofari Hutchinson.
        p.   cm.
Includes bibliographical references and index.
ISBN 0-87013-361-6 (alk. paper)
1. Communism—United States—History. 2. Afro-American commu-nists—History. 3. Afro-Americans—Politics and government. 4. Afro-Americans—Civil rights. 5. Black power—United States. 6. Racism—United States. I. Title.
HX86.035 1995
335.43'089'96073—dc20
                                                        94-45031
                                                        CIP

Contents

Preface/Acknowledgements

In November 1967, I attended a black student conference in Los Angeles. The conference was called to plan a series of militant protest demonstrations by black student groups on college campuses in Southern California. The conference had barely gotten underway when a small band of white Communists began picketing in front of the church where the conference was held. Many of the blacks were enraged. Some charged from the building and began pummeling the picketers. As the picketers fled, the black students shouted at them, "We don't want any white communists here, they're the enemy, too." A few years later, I talked with an older acquaintance who had been active in the Communist Party during the 1940s. He praised the communists, "they were the only whites who ever fought for blacks."

Was he right? Or were the black students right? Were the communists friends or enemies of African-Americans. I was determined to find out. For five years I examined the personal correspondence of party members, party documents, private papers of party activists and sympathizers, and the exhaustive FBI files on the Communist Party. I talked with party activists, organizers, and critics. Were they friends or foes of blacks? The truth is at various times during the past half century they were both.

I am deeply grateful to John Henrik Clarke, John Shannon, William L. Patterson, Bill Taylor, Dorothy Healey, Jacqueline Tunberg, Dorothy Healey, Gerald Horne and Martin Duberman for helping me discover that truth. Their suggestions and criticisms were crucially important. I must give special thanks to my wife Barbara Bramwell. She believed in the importance of this project and never let me quit. My thanks also to the staff at Michigan State University Press for their belief in the importance of *Blacks and Reds*.

Finally, a project of this scope would have been impossible without the kind assistance of the staff of the following research collections: Southern California Research Library; Amistad Research Library, Tulane University; Special Collections Library, California State University, Los Angeles; Schomberg Research Library, New York Public Library; Library of Congress; Black Resource Center, Los Angeles County Bilbrew Library; University Research Library, UCLA; Moorland Collection, Howard University; Labadie Collection, University of Michigan; Graduate Research Library, University of Massachusetts; and the Graduate Research Library, Columbia University.

Any mistakes are mine.

1 Introduction

In 1990, millions of Americans watched with fascination and hope the battle between democracy and communism in Eastern Europe and the Soviet Union. But few Americans know that Communists fought another battle here at home. It was an intense battle in which the American Communist Party used all of its organizational and propaganda weapons. At stake was the allegiance of black Americans.

During the Depression years, Communists achieved some success in influencing black leaders and their organizations, but as they soon discovered, race and class in America are complex and thorny issues that do not lend themselves to easy solutions. Like its counterparts in Eastern Europe, the American Communist Party discovered that its policies and practices, despite the idealism of many of its members, could not withstand the challenge of American democracy.

Founded in 1919, the American Communist Party was modeled on Lenin's Bolshevik Party in the Soviet Union. Following the lead of the Bolsheviks, American Communists set out to organize American workers into a powerful movement to overthrow capitalism and establish an American Soviet state. Communist leaders were dimly aware that they could not attain their goals without attracting sizable numbers of black workers to their banner. But how?

Party leaders spent the better part of the first decade of their existence trying to decide whether blacks were simply economically exploited workers, as they considered whites. If so, they did not need to formulate any special programs to appeal to them. They would simply exhort them to join with their white labor comrades and fight as "exploited proletarians" against capitalism. But was this enough?

1

White workers were not lynched, denied the right to vote, required to live in segregated neighborhoods and attend segregated schools, excluded from trade unions, and relegated to the dirtiest and lowest-paying jobs simply because of their color. Yet, blacks were.

By 1928, the Communist Party leaders realized that if they were to have any impact on blacks they would have to change their approach. Acting under orders from the Soviet-controlled Communist International, the Party began an intense drive for economic and racial justice for blacks. They scored their biggest gains among blacks during the Depression.

Communist Party members could rightfully boast that they broke American racial taboos by supporting social equality and mounting national campaigns against Jim Crow laws and lynching, as well as running black candidates for every office from Vice President to city council. With their unemployment councils, rent strike committees, tenant councils, and prisoner defense committees, Communists cast a long shadow over the political life of America during the Great Depression.

The next decade brought war, prosperity, and world-power to America. For Communists it brought division, near collapse, and the abandonment of their lofty pronouncements on civil rights. The hey-day of the Communist Party was over. The 1950s brought the bleak years of McCarthyite political repression and disarray. In the 1960s, the Communist Party searched for ways to become an effective player in the civil rights movement and the black power movements, but the doors were closed and their decline accelerated.

Even the world-wide campaign the Party directed to free Angela Davis in 1971 could not halt the slide. The 1980s, which ushered in the era of Reagan conservatism and pro-democracy movements in Eastern Europe, nearly brought the curtain down on the Party.

But throughout their *Sturm und Drang* years, Communists would always claim that their fight for black rights sprang from the purest of motives. In turn, blacks would repeatedly ask which meant more to them: defense of Soviet policies or social justice in America? Communists could not serve two masters. If they did indeed take their marching orders from the Soviets, their intentions toward blacks would always be suspect.[1]

Yet there was more to the picture. Blacks hardly sat patiently waiting for deliverance by the Marxists. The unrelenting hostility of white workers produced a powerful counter reaction in blacks. Since the

2

labor unions would not admit them as equals, many blacks got their revenge by breaking strikes and taking "white jobs."

Black leaders from Marcus Garvey to the Black Power advocates of the 1960s argued that the Marxists were guilty of perpetuating illusions about the common interests of black and white workers. During the 1920s, Garvey even contended that since the capitalists employed blacks, they were better friends than the labor movement.

Many blacks were more afraid of the Communists than of white conservatives. Black businessmen, ministers, and professionals did not want radical change. They were native sons and daughters who believed deeply that loyalty, patriotism, hard work, and individual achievement were the keys to success.

They saw America as a land of opportunity, where enterprising men and women could pull themselves up by their bootstraps. They were hard-headed realists who figured that for better or worse America was their home too, and Communists had nothing to offer them.

Other blacks sharply criticized both capitalism and socialism. They viewed them as European political and economic systems intended for whites only. Black leaders from A. Phillip Randolph to Malcolm X implored blacks to be their own advocates. They urged them to form their own organizations and devise their own programs and philosophy. No matter what differences they had among themselves, they agreed on one thing: whites, especially Marxists, could not do it for them.

Former black Communists such as writers Richard Wright and George Padmore believed that the final conflict would not be between capitalists and proletarians, but rather between non-whites and the rich white West. American Marxists challenged them. They claimed it was suicidal for blacks to go it alone. Only the unity of black and white workers could defeat capitalism and implement socialism.

How realistic was this, black scholar W.E.B. DuBois asked? Was not America a nation whose very premise was built on ethnic pride (and division)? Did not white ethnics doggedly use their culture, traditions, history, and values as a ladder to march out of the ghettos, shanty-towns, and Little Italies of America?

More than a few blacks noted that Communist Party members as late as the 1930s bragged about being Finns, Germans, Italians, or Irish before being Marxists. Black newspaperman Cyril Briggs, who joined the Communist Party in 1921 and stuck it out for more then forty years, constantly picked and nagged at his Party comrades to see

3

race as important as class. In later years, the struggle for racial justice would have the same meaning for Communists like James Ford, Harry Haywood, Angelo Herndon, Ben Davis, and Angela Davis. Thousands of blacks would admire them as individuals and support them as leaders.

Impressed by what the Reds said and often did in the battle against racial oppression, many blacks would wear the Red label with pride. In time, many more would discard it. They would become casualties to the Red dream deferred.[2]

In a century of bittersweet relations between blacks and Reds, there is room for many views of what went right and what went wrong. Marxists put their spin on history. They see the 1930s as the first time since the Reconstruction era in the South that they were able to make white Americans face up to their racism. Communists take credit for putting the issues of segregation and racial violence firmly on the nation's agenda. Old-timers who fought in the Communist Party battles of the 1930s always speak fondly of the days when Reds did make a difference. They have every right to be proud of their contributions. They were real.

But they are also viewing the past through an idyllic prism. They do not mention the 1940s and the downplaying of civil rights by Communists. Nor are they willing to reflect on why they failed to influence black groups from Marcus Garvey's Universal Negro Improvement Association to the National Urban League and the National Association for the Advancement of Colored People.

They also do not admit they erred badly when they branded black leaders and organizations that did not agree with their aims and tactics as traitors, lackeys, and "Uncle Toms." The Communist Party made enemies of many blacks who were not Socialists, but who also were neutral toward Communists.

In fact, during the 1930s, the NAACP and the National Urban League worked with the Communists on campaigns to get Congressional anti-lynching legislation, freedom for the Scottsboro Boys, and the National Negro Congress. As always, the success was short-lived. It took little time for relations between the Communists and the black moderates to degenerate into name-calling and finger-pointing.[3]

It was a pattern that would be repeated again and again over the next forty years. Why it did is the story of *Blacks and Reds*.

Notes

1. David A. Shannon, *The Decline of American Communism* (New York: Harcourt, Brace and Co., 1959), 58-67; Nathan Glazer, *The Social Basis of American Communism* (New York: Harcourt Brace and World, Inc., 1961), 169-84; William Z. Foster, *History of the Communist Party of the United States* (New York: International Publishers, 1952), 226-34, 266-68 and 444-46; Robert L. Allen, *Reluctant Reformers* (Washington, D.C.: Howard University Press, 1974), 207-47.
2. For a broad view of the roots of the cleavage between blacks, whites, and the Marxist left, see Tony Martin, *Race First* (Westport, Connecticut: Greenwood Press, 1976); Sterling Stuckey, *Slave Culture* (New York: Oxford University Press, 1986); Theodore G. Vincent, ed., *Voices of a Black Nation* (Berkeley: Ramparts Press, 1973); Edward Peeks, *The Long Struggle for Black Power* (New York: Charles Scribner's Sons, 1971).
3. James W. Ford, *The Negro and the Democratic Front* (New York: International Publishers, 1938),19-28; Wilson Record, *Race and Radicalism* (Ithaca: Cornell University Press, 1964), 84-131.

1 "On with the Dance"

"The Soviet government proceeds apace. It bids fair to sweep over the whole world. The sooner the better. On with the dance!" In May 1919, A. Phillip Randolph could barely contain his excitement over the triumph of the Russian Communists. He wanted the same for America. "What we really need is a patriotism of liberty, justice and joy," he wrote, "that is Bolshevik patriotism."

Randolph spoke for a small but effective band of black radicals. They believed that socialism and labor radicalism held the promise of a bright future for blacks. Randolph and Chandler Owens, styling themselves "The New Negroes," had founded the *Messenger* magazine in Harlem 1917 as a forum for their radical politics. Although Randolph did not know it when he praised Bolshevism, and despite his later disillusionment with it, his dream of communism coming to America was only months away.[1]

The Founding of the Party

On September 27, 1919, 128 dissident Socialists gathered at the Russian Federation hall in Chicago for the founding convention of the Communist Party of America. There were Hungarians, Poles, Latvians, Lithuanians, and Czechs at the convention. Very few of the delegates spoke any English. Most of the convention business was carried on in the mother tongues of the delegates. There were few "native" whites, and no blacks present.

The delegates were a tight-knit, clannish group who figured to play it safe by hewing close to the standard Marxist prescription for fighting the class struggle. It was, as one observer said, "the Russian expression of Marxism which predominated this convention, the Marxism of Lenin and the party traditions of the Bolsheviki."

The new Communist Party platform attempted to cover the same bases as the Bolsheviks. It called for workers' political power, workers' control of industry, industrial union organizing, and international revolution. To the mainly Slavic delegates, their platform was a sufficient blueprint for the seizure of state power. They felt their program was pragmatic enough to attract workers of all races to communism. The delegates believed that revolution was near and that class antagonisms between the bourgeoisie and the proletariat were acute enough for the working class to overcome any racial animosities.

They did not trouble themselves with prolonged debate or devise any elaborate political formulas for blacks since Marxism had already provided answer enough. They kept their resolution brief: "The Racial oppression of the Negro is simply the expression of his economic bondage and oppression, each intensifying the other." Communists, they agreed, need only agitate "among the Negro workers to unite them with all class conscious workers."[2] Communists routinely blamed all racial strife on the capitalists. During the bloody summer riots in Chicago in 1919, *The Communist* admonished blacks and whites to "realize that their misery is not due to race antagonisms, but to CLASS ANTAGONISMS." *The Communist* assured blacks that the capitalists and not white workers were the instigators of the violence: "The cry of the negro worker should not be 'Down with the whites.'"

Since the ethnic federations were the ones who made the new Party go, it was no surprise that the Central Executive Committee at the Communist's First Party Council in 1921 designated the East European ethnics as the workers most isolated and removed from the labor movement: "The position of the foreign born in the basic industries of America entitles them to this position."

At its December convention, the Communist Party (now renamed the Workers Party) apparently saw nothing incongruous in singling out the Italian Socialist Federation, the Bohemian Socialists, and the Jewish Labor movement for special commendation. The Party's Executive Council boasted that the Czech-Slovak Marxist Federation had established their own educational and political program. They also praised the "Jewish comrades" for the "success of their drive for a daily paper in their language." The Council did not consider the separate language papers, ethnic schools, and ethnic bloc politics they engaged in a violation of Communist principles.[3]

The racial blindspot also touched the Party's short-lived rival for power. The Communist Labor Party was formed the same month and its best known convert was John Reed—a romantic and an adventurer who brought dash and passion to his Marxism. Reed's faction believed that it could lead the working class more effectively because its members were the English-speaking "nativist" Marxists.

But with blacks it was the same story. At the Second Congress of the Communist International in Moscow in July 1920, Reed told the delegates, "The only proper policy for the American Communists to follow is to consider the Negro first as a laborer." With Reed the class struggle was everything, and anything else, including racial problems, was incidental to him: "The Negro does not demand national independence. Every movement which has thus far been carried on among them with the aim of establishing a separate national resistance has met with little, if any, success." Reed further assured the Congress delegates that blacks were only important as part of "a strong proletarian labor movement."

In a well-intentioned but even more atrocious reading of the black experience, the Communist Party's *Workers Council* magazine condemned the vigilante attacks on Tulsa blacks in 1921: "The Negro of the Southern states to-day, fifty years after the civil war, is still virtually the slave of the rich white employing class." The paper scolded blacks for being "too ignorant to know the nation guarantees him rights he has never been strong enough to defend. "The *Workers Council* noted that blacks "lacked self-confidence" and grimly concluded, "Let the Negro once again become conscious of his own manhood, and he will force the white man to see in the black neighbor a human being."

Did Workers Party leaders honestly think that blacks had developed no concrete programs, formed no organizations, nor produced any competent and "self-assured" leaders for a century?

Because they did indeed think this, Workers Party leaders were trapped in a political never-never land. They either ignored or did not understand that times were changing, and a new black political awareness was growing.[4]

The New Awareness

In the North, thousands of black migrants found jobs in the packing houses, auto and steel plants, and the coal mines. A 1920 Department of Labor survey of the steel industry revealed that 11.8 percent of the employees at the United States Steel Homestead plant in Pittsburgh were black. Black women had begun to abandon their traditional jobs as domestics and sewing operators and move into major industry. More than 100,000 black women worked in manufacturing and mechanical service jobs. By 1920 the black industrial work force had increased more than 150 percent, while the percentage of black farmers and sharecroppers had decreased thirty percent. Workers Party leaders certainly could see that the skin complexion of workers in northern factories was changing.

The mechanic or the assembler next to a white worker was just as likely to speak with a Mississippi or Alabama drawl as with a Yiddish, Ukrainian, or German accent. The decade promised to be one of intense struggle by both blacks and Communists to gain a real foothold in unions and industry.[5]

The harsh experience in northern factories, and the continued exclusion from the craft unions, had already turned many blacks into racially militant workers who demanded decent jobs, fair pay, and full admission to unions. The twenty-three black delegates that showed up at the American Federation of Labor's 1919 convention were the largest group of blacks that had ever attended a labor conference. They were prepared to challenge the AFL's policy of permitting local affiliates to maintain whites-only exclusionary clauses in their charters.

The delegates submitted five resolutions to the AFL's Executive Council, demanding an end to job bias, union exclusion, the revoking of the charters of lily-white unions, the granting of charters for black trade organizations, and recognition of an International Union of Organized Colored Labor. The Executive Council tried to dodge the resolutions and in the end voted against four of them.

The delegates did not come away completely empty handed. The Council recommended that the AFL "give particular attention to the organization of colored workers everywhere and assign organizers for that purpose whenever possible." Yet the recommendation was purely symbolic. There was no mechanism of enforcement. AFL officials could not compel local affiliates to amend their charters.

While the AFL was forced to go on record against union discrimination, the black press did not attribute the Council's decision to altruism. It was a pragmatic step, as the *Amsterdam News* correctly observed, taken to head off the "concerted movement of Afro-Americans to form labor organizations of their own."

The Crisis, the monthly publication of the National Association of Colored People, also attributed the AFL action to self-interest: "When black and cracker are kept apart despotism is at its height." But *New York Age* editor Fred Moore perhaps came closest to the truth: "With the large influx of colored labor into the Northern states during the last three years there was danger to the Federation of Labor from colored strike breakers."[6]

If a mainstream labor organization could grant concessions to black labor, it seemed unlikely that revolutionary Communists could ignore them. But given the racial blindfold that Marxists wore in 1920, it was still a distinct possibility they would miss the cues. However, now there were the Bolsheviks.

Lenin and the Bolsheviks had defied the classic Marxist prescription that revolution would come first in an industrially advanced capitalist country. Russia was a rural, semi-feudal nation that in some ways more closely resembled the colonial Asian and African nations than a Western European nation. Lenin understood that the Bolsheviks could not rely solely on the European working class to free the colonies. The Bolsheviks saw the colonial people as a tremendous, untapped source of revolutionary power.

The Soviets were determined to make Europeans and American Marxists shed their color phobia and organize non-white workers and peasants on a program of equality. In March 1919 the Soviets organized the Third International to unite Communist Parties worldwide to overthrow "imperialist rule." They made it clear that no Communist party or organization could join the Third International unless it agreed to support "not only in words but practically, all movements of liberation in the colonies."

The Soviets were growing impatient with their American comrades. A particular sore point with Moscow was the seeming unwillingness of the Americans to break out of their narrow ethnic shell. Three years after the American Communist Party was formed there were still dozens of clannish federations. This only reinforced ethnic exclusion and spawned political and personal rivalries.

Native whites, much less blacks, could scarcely feel comfortable joining the ethnic cliques, particularly when they could not speak Hungarian or Polish. The word from the Soviets in 1922 was break up the shop, street, and geographic units the ethnic federations maintained and recruit more blacks.[7]

Search For a New Direction

A few American Communists, however, did heed the racial signs. They knew it was foolish for Communists to pretend that black workers either did not exist or had the same interests as white workers. They even had some ideas on how blacks should be recruited. At least that is what government officials claimed in August 1922, after they raided an outdoor meeting of Communists at Bridgeman, Michigan.

At the time, Communists still considered themselves in their "underground" stage and were trying to decide whether to become a fully legal party. Government officials captured documents that purportedly proved that the Communists had a "Negro Program." Based on the documents, the press fed the public sensational tales of Communist plots to foment race riots, infiltrate established black organizations, and spread Red insurrectionary propaganda among blacks.[8]

Government officials dug deep to make their case that a Communist-led black uprising was imminent: "The entire program is intended to incite the negroes to attain by violence the ends specified." The press added a little spice to the sinister dealings when it revealed that the document was smuggled into the country by an "authorized Soviet courier." The program allegedly was sanctioned by high Kremlin officials and bore the signatures of Nikolai Bukharin, Karl Radek, and Otto Kusinen, all high-ranking members of the Executive Committee of the Communist International.

Was any of this true? Historians are divided on it. The government permitted the documents to be viewed only by carefully selected, friendly reporters. None of the Communist leaders who were at the Bridgeman meeting ever mentioned the" Negro program." Joseph Cannon, William Foster, and Jay Lovestone—men who soon would become major leaders in the Communist movement, said nothing about the program in accounts they wrote of the Bridgeman raid. Rose Pastor Stokes, a prominent Communist organizer who also was there, ridiculed the meeting as a farce. She told black writer Claude McKay at a meeting of the Communist International in Moscow in 1924 that the Communists were silly in thinking that they could actually evade the "iron heel of the capitalists."

A healthy dose of skepticism is in order for another compelling reason. In 1922, blacks were hardly a priority for the Workers Party. It would have taken an enormous leap in imagination to believe that

Party leaders could formulate a sweeping program for blacks. But the Bridgeman raid made good copy.[9]

The Soviets could set conditions for the Americans but they could not force their American comrades to change their attitudes overnight. The Soviets simply had no experience with American racism. The mix of abuse, indifference, and paternalism that characterized white treatment of blacks was deep and pervasive. Marxists had not escaped the effects of stereotyped racial thinking. However, the Russian pressure remained intense.

The Workers Party tried to respond. At their second convention in 1922, the Party admitted that blacks were "exploited and oppressed more ruthlessly" than white workers. The resolution also confirmed that blacks had reacted to the oppression by developing "purely racial aims." This was a bow to the impact that Marcus Garvey's Black Nationalist movement was having among blacks.

Party leaders gave only a vaguely condescending promise "to help" blacks fight for economic, political, and educational—but not social— equality. The program did single out hotels, restaurants, theaters, and public places as targets for protest. That was just enough to interest some blacks. The *Amsterdam News* was happy that the Communists would "support the Negroes in their struggle for liberation."[10]

The Soviets were prepared to do their part to help the Americans "recruit more blacks." They even made a believer out of a doubting Claude McKay. Shortly before his departure for the Soviet Union in the summer of 1924, McKay told a reporter for the *Afro-American* that the Marxists had no idea how to relate to the black experience. Once in the Soviet Union, he sang a different tune. Russian leaders gave him the red carpet treatment during his country-wide tour. The poet visited factories, schools, stores. He was "tossed in the air" by exuberant crowds. He was the subject of admiring conversations "until my face flamed." Everywhere he was in demand "at the lectures of poets and journalists, the meetings of soldiers and factory workers." The Soviets almost made a true believer of him: "I was welcomed thus as a symbol of the great American Negro group."[11]

Although the Soviet leaders made him feel like an insider, he discovered that they had some murky ideas on the role of American blacks. In a private meeting at the Kremlin, Leon Trotsky told McKay that blacks were "Negro slaves of American capitalism" who in time could be "politically educated." The Red Army commander, said McKay, believed that black troops should stay out of European wars. However, if they wanted to fight, Trotsky said that he would be delighted to train some blacks as officers in the Red Army. He did not ask Trotsky which Red Army—Soviet or American—he meant. In time, Trotsky might laugh at his ideas too. In talks with black Socialists during the 1930s, Trotsky recognized that blacks were not just exploited workers, and that color oppression was more severe than economic exploitation. He implored Marxists to support self-determination for blacks.[12]

Fortunately, The Chairman of the Communist International was a little more realistic than Trotsky. Gregori Zinoviev realized that blacks had their own aims, programs, and organizations. He did not regard this as a threat to Marxist goals. In a letter to the "American Negro Guest," his term for McKay, Zinoviev suggested that "Negro workers organize their own circles" to later "link up with the proletariat." Zinoviev cautioned McKay that blacks should not be tempted to go it alone. They could solve their problems, Zinoviev assured him, if they "put themselves under the red banner of internationalism."

McKay's seeming coziness with the Soviet leaders evidently convinced W. L. Hurley, an American consular official, that McKay had become a threat. Hurley tracked McKay's activities in the Soviet Union for William J. Burns, director of the State Department's Bureau of Information. He claimed that the C.I. Executive Committee hired McKay "to organize Communist propaganda among North American Negroes."[13]

Before he left the Soviet Union, McKay also sat in the conference hall in the Kremlin and listened attentively to a speech by Rose Stokes. The first lady of the Workers Party was in Moscow as an official delegate to the Fourth World Congress of the Communist International.

In her Congress address, Stokes delivered the new revolutionary "Thesis on the Negro Question," which reflected the latest Kremlin thinking on blacks. Stokes declared that blacks were "a vital question of the world revolution." The C.I., she announced, would launch "a special campaign" to "compel admission" of blacks into "the unions of the white man."

Stokes threw in a few new wrinkles. If the unions would not admit them, she said, the C.I. would organize blacks "into unions of their own." The C.I. pledged to convene an international black workers conference in Moscow. She confidently told C.I. delegates that the Workers Party was making the new thrust among blacks because "their movement tends to undermine or weaken capitalism." It probably sounded to McKay like blacks were important to Communists only if they could be useful to their purposes.

14

Without questioning the motives of the C.I. too closely, it appeared Moscow had made its point with the Americans. The Workers Party had a clear mandate to move blacks from bit players to lead actors in their scheme to organize American workers.

McKay left Moscow feeling that a new day was at hand. In a glowing report on his trip in *The Crisis*, he confidently predicted that more blacks would travel to the Soviet Union and would be impressed with a land apparently free of racism.[14]

The Soviets had only begun their campaign to control and pressure their comrades in the West to accept their policies. The C.I. planned to turn the world of American Marxists upside down with a big ideological assault on two of their oldest tenets.

It was hard for many Party leaders to swallow Israel Amter's explanation that blacks cross picket lines not because they love or are duped by the capitalists but because white workers "refuse to admit the negro into their unions." Yet he was a high-ranking official of the C.I., so the Americans had to listen. Amter told them that white workers were as much to blame as the capitalists for perpetuating racism: "The white workers assist the capitalists in this prejudice, helping to keep the Negro on a lower plane."[15]

The Workers Party was not starting totally from scratch in adopting Moscow's racial line. They had successfully recruited a small but politically astute cadre of astute black radicals who believed in Marxism and would follow Party dictates. They included Cyril Briggs, Otto Huiswood, Lovett Fort-Whiteman, and Otto Hall and Harry Haywood.

Huiswood had already attained some distinction when he was selected by the leadership as the first (and only) black to attend the Fourth Communist International Congress in Moscow as an official delegate. Probably because of the small number of blacks in the Party, the government watched the Communists even closer for signs of racial agitation. The Senate Foreign Relations Subcommittee which held hearings in 1924 on Communist influence among blacks alleged that the Workers Party had black organizers in major northern cities.[16]

The Senators were partially right. They had one major organizer in one northern city. Lovett Fort-Whiteman was making the rounds in New York City for the Workers Party. The Texas-born Fort-Whiteman came to New York in 1916 as a nineteen-year-old with dreams of becoming a professional Shakespearean actor.

As a member of the Shakespeare Negro Players, he actually did get to play in their production of Othello. He might have continued his

15

acting career if he had stayed off the street corners of Harlem. But after listening to Randolph, Chandler Owen, and black socialist Hubert Harrison, Fort-Whiteman shed the acting bug for socialism.

In quick succession in 1918, he became drama editor of the *Messenger*, joined the Socialist Party, and enrolled at the Socialist Rand School. His next stop was the Workers Party, where he was assigned the job of recruiting black members. Fort-Whiteman took his role as the nation's top black Red so seriously that Haywood later remembered him parading down the streets of southside Chicago dressed Russian style with fur hat, belted shirt, and high boots.

After the Fourth Congress, Fort-Whiteman, Briggs, and the others became even more important in the Workers Party plan to bring in more blacks. Acting on Moscow's orders, Party leaders decided the best way to get more black recruits was to go straight to the source, namely, the established black organizations.

It required some fast shifts. They had scorned the black middle class as "petty-bourgeois compromisers" who hated labor and embraced capitalism. Briggs and Fort-Whiteman would have to either modify or conceal their antipathy to moderate black leaders if they expected to work with them.[17]

The Sanhedrin

The first opportunity for them to test their new approach came when they learned that a preliminary planning meeting would be held to plan an "All Race Assembly." Six black organizations, led by the NAACP and the National Equal Rights League, planned the assembly for March 1923 in New York.

NAACP executive secretary James Weldon Johnson and *Boston Guardian* editor William Monroe Trotter agreed to take part in the assembly. Briggs and Fort-Whiteman saw that as a plus since both men in the past had been relatively open-minded toward the radicals.

Johnson did not seem to have any problems serving with Foster and Elizabeth Gurley Flynn, both prominent Communist leaders, on the Board of Directors of the liberal Garland Fund. The fund had approved substantial grants to leftist organizations the year before. The outspoken Trotter, meanwhile, had occasionally said a complimentary word or two about socialism. They were not as thrilled when they found out that Howard University Dean Kelly Miller was also going to participate. An unabashed black conservative, he was deeply suspicious of the Reds.[18]

With men like Miller around, Fort-Whiteman chose to play it cautious and stay in the background. The low-key strategy yielded immediate results when Domingo, Huiswood, and Richard Moore, a recent Communist convert, were invited to sign the "Call" for a conference. Moore and Domingo were not officially linked with the Workers Party.[19]

The planning meeting came off in March as scheduled. Sixteen delegates spent a day making preparations for the giant assembly. In a speech opening the meeting, Briggs tried to soothe the fears of the black moderates that the radicals were out to dominate the assembly. He insisted that the leaders present "a united front on the interests of the race." He was elected secretary.

Richard Moore also spoke. The light-complexioned, slightly built young Communist was rapidly making a name for himself in Harlem radical circles. A polished speaker, Moore sought to give the delegates a broader world vision of the struggle: "Hindus, Turks, Russians, South Africans are in the grip of reconstruction, the Negro can't lag behind." Briggs and Moore with their carefully tailored remarks got the Workers Party in the door; now the question was, could they stay in? They would find out in Chicago.

In February 1924, two-hundred and fifty official delegates gathered in the auditorium of the Wendell Phillps High School for the opening of the "Negro Sanhedrin." The delegates had earlier agreed to call the conference Sanhedrin after the legendary ruling council of the Hebrew nation of biblical times.

The delegates came from twenty states, and represented sixty-one black organizations. The roster of delegates read like a who's who of black America. The NAACP, Urban League, and National Negro Business League sent their top officials. The editors of the *Pittsburgh Courier, Chicago Defender,* and *Baltimore Afro-American*, the three major black newspapers, were present.

The noted deans of Morehouse, Wilberforce, and Howard universities discussed political strategy with students. Black businessmen rubbed shoulders with black unionists. Fraternity and sorority members dined with janitors, while black ministers huddled with Communists.[20]

But one notable black leader was conspicuous by his absence. The militant black nationalist Marcus Garvey was not at Chicago. The delegates, bitterly hostile to the black nationalist leader for his flamboyant style, mass following, and emphasis on exclusive black organizing, did not invite him. They preferred anyone—even Communists—to him.

The only dissent came from the Communist delegates. They demanded that the Sanhedrin send a telegram inviting Garvey to come to Chicago. In turn, they suggested that the conference send their own delegates to the convention of Garvey's Universal Negro Improvement Association in August. Whether they expected anything to come of it is a matter of conjecture. It was probably more a case of political showmanship, since the Workers Party already was eyeing a possible future alliance with Garvey.

The Sanhedrin shrugged off the proposals and Fort-Whiteman, Gordon Owens, S. V. Phillips, Ethel Hall, P. Eugene Burton, and Otto Huiswood claimed their own small victory when they took their places as official delegates. No one opposed them when they listed their affiliation as representatives of the Workers Party.

Black leaders took Briggs' at his word that the Sanhedrin would be a united front of all black organizations, and that the Communists were not out to dictate policies. As most of the delegates understood it, they were there not to debate communism or trade union policies but to develop a militant program for civil rights and equal opportunity. The *Chicago Defender* was optimistic that "such organizations as the Blood Brotherhood and the NAACP with such widely different philosophies of life shall be able to work with harmony and zeal."

It was a naive hope. The delegates were barely in their seats when the issue of communism was thrown to the front of the program. Chicago Mayor William Dever, in his welcoming address, warned the delegates not to listen "to the colored and white demagogues. Your salvation rests within yourself." The Workers Party delegates ignored Dever.

When the *Daily Worker* extended its "greetings" to the Sanhedrin it provided the first hint of what the Communists wanted: "We hope that the All-Race Congress will unite with the left-wing of the American labor movement and give added strength to the revolutionary forces striving to unite the workers of America." The *Daily Worker* proclaimed that "the Russian Revolution brought new hope to the subject peoples."

The Communists also wanted the Sanhedrin to endorse the demand to recognize the Soviet Union. This was a doubtful proposition. The Workers Party was asking the Sanhedrin to do what the U.S. government refused to do. The Bolsheviks were still very much anathema to Washington policymakers. President Woodrow Wilson had provided active support to the anti-Bolshevik armies during the Russian civil war by dispatching American troops to occupy the Russian Pacific port city of Vladivostok.

The delegates listened courteously as the Communist delegates demanded that the Sanhedrin not only recognize Russia but send a delegation "to make an impartial study of the situation there." They got a boost from a Chicago minister who claimed that the Soviets had treated him with "cordiality" during his recent visit to the country. The Sanhedrin delegates thanked the minister for his remarks and promptly forgot about the resolution.[21]

The Communists were not through. They submitted a lengthy package of resolutions that included condemnation of the League of Nations, government ownership of the railroads, constitutional amendments for government takeover of the schools to promote integration, and outlawing all bans on intermarriage. These resolutions were also ignored.

Labor issues, however, could not be dismissed. As a member of the Sanhedrin's Labor Commission, Fort-Whiteman was in a good position to influence the delegates. The Communists introduced two resolutions. The first attacked the AFL for refusing to organize unskilled black workers into craft unions. Most delegates had no trouble with this. For two decades, the NAACP had fought for these rights.

The second resolution was questionable. Fort-Whiteman demanded that the Sanhedrin send delegates to the May convention of the Communist-sponsored Farmer-Labor Party in St. Paul, Minnesota. If the delegates had gone along with this they would have committed the Sanhedrin to partisan recognition of a third party with open Communist ties.

The delegates were not about to do that. The final resolution on labor had very little of the Workers Party imprint on it. It basically reaffirmed "that Negroes be welcomed into all unions on the basis of equality."

Fort-Whiteman was not going to let the matter go at that. At the next to last session, he and Huiswood challenged the chair to reopen the labor question. Fort-Whiteman claimed that there were "eighteen representatives of labor whose rights must be respected." When the chair ruled him out of order, Huiswood shouted: "I see that labor is an outcast here as it is outside."[22]

Huiswood's diatribe was directed at Kelly Miller, who had lobbied hardest against the labor resolution. Miller knew that nothing short of a full-blown denunciation of capitalism would satisfy the Communists and he was not about to give them that satisfaction. He fished around for a way out while Fort-Whiteman and Huiswood fumed.

Finally, he agreed to raise the labor question at the last session. Fort-Whiteman and Huiswood were ready. They packed the session with their most vocal supporters, who clapped and stomped at every word that they said. Desperate to end the session, Miller invited them to adjourn to a side room away from the main auditorium to continue the discussion.

Huiswood recognized Miller's ploy and immediately leaped to his feet, screaming at Miller: "You have been sabotaging this convention from the first day. You promised labor a hearing. "It worked. There were more shouts, hisses, and boos from the audience. Miller gave up. The Workers Party delegates and their supporters stayed in the auditorium and spent the rest of the day venting their anger at Miller and the capitalists. But it was a Pyrrhic victory. The final resolution on labor stood.

It was left to Workers Party leader Robert Minor to give the Party's gloomy assessment of the outcome: "The Sanhedrin flatly and cold-bloodedly rejected the proposal to organize the millions of Negro industrial workers."

The *Defender* was also miffed that "the question of labor was given no place on the agenda." The paper likened the omission to "attempting to build a house before laying a foundation." The final rebuke came when Miller was elected to the seven-member governing committee. The committee was assigned to formulate the assembly's constitution to be presented at the next year's Sanhedrin.[23]

It was never held. Chicago was the first and last such meeting. Fort-Whiteman, Briggs, and Huiswood had scared off many of the moderates whom they desperately needed to give them credibility with blacks. Black conservatives like Miller became even more vehemently anti-Communist. In November 1925, he warned blacks that "joining the restless ranks which threaten industrial ruin would be fatuous suicide." Two months later, he told the *New York Times* that blacks should "stand with capital" and forget unionism.

Newspaper columnist George Schuyler wrote the final epitaph for the Sanhedrin: "These people with such disparate interests and views, and a pompous pretension of representing significant memberships, made me dubious about the outcome of these deliberations." The same year Schuyler would aim his sharpest barbs at the Communists in a debate with Otto Hall.[24]

A New Leader Emerges

Workers Party leaders gamely pushed forward. They had no alternative: the Soviets continued to press them for results in organizing black workers. So far, outside of Briggs, Fort-Whiteman, and Moore, few blacks had shown any real interest in joining the Party. So the Communists devised another plan.

This time they would target one black organization and try to bore hard from within. There was not much doubt which one that would be. The NAACP had no peer among the black organizations. It had political influence, a vast membership, and a stable core of chapters nation-wide.

Since its founding in 1909, the NAACP had been the most consistent fighter for civil rights. The campaign it waged against lynching was even beginning to pay dividends. In 1922 the House passed the Dyer anti-lynching bill, which would have made lynching a federal crime. Although the bill was defeated in the Senate, the NAACP had shown its clout. Also, many of the early founders of the organization were men and women who were Socialists and political rebels.[25]

It seemed to the Communists that the possibilities for a working relationship with the organization were there. Party leaders viewed the 1926 NAACP national conference as their first testing ground. In August 1925 they drew up a plan for "selected Communists to enter NAACP conventions and to make proposals calculated to enlighten the Negro masses under its influence as to the nature of the class struggle."

Workers Party leaders needed someone fresh and politically untainted to work with the cautious business and professional leaders who sat on the NAACP's Board of Directors. Briggs and Fort-Whiteman were already too compromised by the fiasco at Chicago to be of any use. Fortunately, a newcomer to their ranks looked like he might fit the bill.[26]

His college chums at Fisk University called him "Rabbit Ford" because of the speed and shifty moves he displayed on the football field. James Ford was such an outstanding athlete that he could have had a lucrative career barnstorming in the semi-professional Negro baseball leagues. For a time he did earn a living playing semi-pro ball in Chicago. But Ford had ambitions for more than glory days on the playing field. He had shown that early in his life when he overcame the tragedy of his grandfather's murder in Alabama, a murder some said was committed by whites jealous of his farm holdings.

The young Ford put the tragedy behind him, left his rural home in Pratt City, Alabama, and headed for Fisk, where he enjoyed life as a campus bigwig, star athlete, honor student, and member of Omega Psi Phi fraternity. When World War I broke out, Ford eagerly enlisted in the army to serve his country. He shipped out to France with the famed all-black 92nd Division. A grateful French nation bestowed many battlefield decorations on the black soldiers for their heroism against German attacks. As a member of the signal corps, Ford was sheltered from the rigors of combat. At his segregated training school, he received valuable instruction in radio, electricity, and telephone communication. These were skills that Ford believed would enable him to find a well-paid professional job after the war. With training and an honorable discharge in hand, he returned to Chicago fully expecting to prosper in his trade. It did not work out that way.

After months of futility searching for jobs with government agencies, Ford settled for a job as a parcel post dispatcher at the post office in 1921. Ford soon found that, despite his education and skills, he was hardly an exception at the post office. During the 1920s, there were large numbers of black men with college degrees who worked there because they could not find jobs anywhere else. He was disturbed by this.[27] He was even more perturbed when he saw that black postal workers were refused promotions, confined to segregated offices, and relegated to menial positions. He joined the Postal Workers Union and began to agitate for changes. Shortly afterward, he was chosen as the postal union's representative to the Chicago Federation of Labor.

When he heard that a group of militant black trade unionists planned to hold a convention of the newly formed American Negro Labor Congress in Chicago in October 1925, he immediately made plans to attend. The eager Ford left the convention of the American Negro Labor Congress inspired by the militant speeches against the capitalists and labor exploiters. Ford was now committed to working for communism. The post office decided that he could not serve Communists and the government too. He was fired.[28]

Party leaders were delighted. They had found an educated black who could serve the Communist cause well. Ford was groomed as an organizer and future leader. Although those who knew him would never regard him as a critical thinker, his ability to impress audiences while doggedly following Communist directives would keep him in good stead in the Party.

In 1926 he got his first big Party assignment. He did not know it then, but when he spoke at the NAACP's annual conference he would become the first and the last Communist in history to have the honor. Ford was listed as the official delegate to the NAACP conference from the American Negro Labor Congress. His job was to secure the "cooperation" of the NAACP in "a campaign for the organization of the Negro wage earner in industrial pursuits." He wanted the NAACP to form inter-racial labor commissions, organize relief and legal aid departments for workers, and send a questionnaire to all international unions to find out whether they discriminated against black workers.

Ford was given his allotted time to speak. The delegates listened attentively, applauded respectfully, and then moved on to the next speaker. The resolution was rejected. The problem was not with the proposals Ford put forth. Most delegates privately did not find anything objectionable in supporting labor unions.

The problem was with the group that offered the proposals. NAACP officials did not want to be accused of being openly supportive of proposals put forth by Communists—even if they agreed with them. Workers Party leader William F. Dunne accused the organization of "placing the whole struggle of the Negro masses at the mercy of the AFL officialdom."[29]

Quite the contrary, the NAACP had fought a ferocious fight against the AFL to break down union Jim Crow. In January 1918 the organization sent a tough memorandum to Sam Gompers urging the AFL Executive Committee to drop craft union organizing and to broaden its membership to include Southern workers, women, the unskilled, and government employees. The NAACP had no illusions about the AFL. They recognized that AFL officials were a clubby group of labor conservatives who would not force equality on their affiliates.

Abram Harris, a Howard University professor and NAACP researcher, confirmed that AFL leaders were possessed of an "overwhelming desire for craft autonomy and business unionism devoid of industrial or idealistic purposes. " Harris said that AFL officials were tied to the "bitch goddess" of American individualism.

The NAACP demanded that the AFL promote democracy in the ranks of American labor and represent the interests of all workers. If it would, the NAACP would "urge Negro workingmen to seek the advantages of sympathetic cooperation between men who work."[30]

For years, the NAACP national headquarters was deluged with appeals for help from black postal and customs employees, railroad

23

porters, domestics, foundry workers, carpenters, and trainmen. The petitioners usually got an encouraging response from either Johnson or his assistant, Walter White.

Communists also did not understand that the NAACP was a multi-dimensional organization. It used an array of tactics and approaches in the wide-ranging battle against American Jim Crow. NAACP officials worked through the courts, applied the picket and boycott, and engaged in political lobbying. The organization's goal was to win justice for blacks within the system.[31]

The NAACP did not operate through a monolithic structure. It was a flexible coalition of individuals and groups who held diverse opinions and philosophies and represented often competing interests. There were businessmen, farmers, professionals, and blue-collar workers in the nationwide chapters. As its name suggested, it was an association, not a party. Ford was simply asking the NAACP to be something they were not.

The Communists did not seem to understand that NAACP leaders, particularly James Weldon Johnson and W.E.B. DuBois, were visionaries as well as pragmatic organization men. They kept their sights on the main goal of racial justice. The two newcomers in the NAACP hierarchy, William Pickens, NAACP Field Secretary, and Walter White, who succeeded Johnson as Executive Secretary in 1931, also shared the same capacity for idealism, tempered by businesslike practicality.[32] They saw themselves locked in prolonged combat for black rights in an era when there were no civil rights laws, no equal opportunity commissions, voting rights, or federal statutes to protect blacks from mob violence.

Ford, Briggs, and Fort-Whiteman simply did not have the program or organization to match the NAACP's appeal. The Communists had utterly failed to define a coherent racial policy or to win the good graces of black moderates. If they had been more flexible and worked with NAACP leaders—and indeed other black moderate leaders—on their terms, they may have played a greater role in the battle against segregation. As a result, they found themselves isolated and attacked by black leaders.

Despite the rebuff, the eagerness of Communists to recruit black organizers, attack racism head-on, and court black organizations during their maiden years was a major step forward. Now they were poised to go further. The year before Ford spoke at the NAACP conference, Party leaders had devised yet another plan to prove that they could

24

organize black workers. They banked their hopes on the organization which, the *Workers Monthly* happily noted, had sent Ford to the NAACP convention: the American Negro Labor Congress.[33]

Notes

1. *Messenger* 3 (May-June 1919): 8-9; *Messenger* 6 (August 1923): 784. The best accounts of Randolph and Owen's early radical years are found in Jervis Anderson, *A. Phillip Randolph* (New York: Harcourt, Brace, Jovanovich, 1972), 85-109; Theodore Kornweibel Jr., *No Crystal Stair* (Westport, Connecticut: Greenwood Press, 1975), 66-69; William H. Harris, *Keeping the Faith* (Urbana: University of Illinois Press, 1991), 26-59; Manning Marable, "A. Phillip Randolph and the Foundations of Black American Socialism," *Radical America* 14 (March-April 1980): 7-13; and George Schuyler, *Black and Conservative* (New Rochelle, New York: Arlington House, 1966), 133-49.
2. Theodore Draper, *The Roots of American Communism* (New York: Viking Press, 1957), 181-84; *The Communist* 1 (27 September 1919): 9; Anthony Bimba, *History of the American Working Class* (New York: International Publishers, 1927), 285-87; *The American Labor Year Book* (New York: Rand School, 1920), 419. For a firsthand account by a founding member see Ella Reeve Bloor, *We Are Many* (New York: International Publishers, 1940), 158-65.
3. *The Communist* 1 (9 August 1919): 1-2; *The Communist* 2 (1922): 1 and 8; *Workers Council* 1 (15 December 1921).
4. *Proceedings of the 2nd Congress of the Communist International* (Washington, D.C.: Government Printing Office, 1920), 151-54. In May 1920 the two rival Communist Parties merged (Draper, *The Roots of American Communism*, 218-22; *The Workers Council* 1 [15 June 1921]). Although Communist organizer E. T. Allison acknowledged the racial nature of the Tulsa violence, he still fell back on the standard Marxist conclusion: "It was white business interests which fomented the Tulsa riot. Whatever differences there may have been between white workers and black workers were because of the undercutting of wages by the Negroes because of unemployment" (*The Toiler*, 18 June 1921).
5. Abram L. Harris, "Negro Labor's Quarrel With White Workingmen," *Current History* 21 (September 1926): 903; Elizabeth Ross Haynes, "Two Million Negro Women at Work," *The Southern Workman* 51 (February 1922): 64-72.
6. Phillip Foner, *Organized Labor and the Black Worker, 1619-1973* (New York: Praeger, 1974), 154-56; *The Crisis* 20 (September 1919): 239-41. The reaction of black publishers to the AFL convention is recapped in the *Literary Digest*, 28 June 1919.

7. N. N. Agarwal presents a cogent summary of Lenin's voluminous writings on the colonial world in *Soviet Nationalities Policy* (Agra, India: Sri Ram Mehra and Co., 1969), 148-77; also see Bohdan Nahaylo and Victor Swoboda, *Soviet Disunion* (New York: The Free Press, 1989); *The Communist International* 1 (March 1919): 175-77; Theodore Draper, *American Communism and Soviet Russia* (New York: Viking Press), 18-22.

8. R. M. Whitney, *Reds in America* (New York: Beckwith Press, 1924), 20-35. The Program of the left-leaning African Blood Brotherhood is reprinted in *The Communist Review* 2 (April 1922): 448-54; *The Crusader* and *Messenger,* between 1917 and 1921.

9. Whitney, *Reds in America,* 192-95 and 205; Draper, *The Roots of American Communism,* 361-72; Foster, *History of the Communist Party of the United States,* 194-95; Claude McKay, *A Long Way From Home* (New York: Lee Furman, 1937), 160; Manning Johnson Color, *Communism and Common Sense* (New York: Alliance, Inc., 1958), 21.

10. *The Worker,* 2 December 1922; *Amsterdam News,* 3 January 1923.

11. *Afro-American,* 11 August 1922; McKay, *The Crisis* 23 (December 1922): 65; McKay, *A Long Way From Home,* 167-71.

12. McKay, *A Long Way From Home,* 208; *International Press Correspondence,* 15 March 1923. Trotsky had a series of conversations with a group of American Marxists led by the West Indian historian C. L. R. James, who used the pseudonym J. R. Johnson. The talks took place on 4, 5 and 11 April 1939 in Coyoacan, Mexico, where Trotsky was then living in exile (*Leon Trotsky on Black nationalism and Self-Determination* [New York: Merit Publishers, 1967], 20-48; *SWP Internal Bulletin* 9 [June 1939]).

13. Gregori Zinoviev to Claude McKay, 8 May 1923, NAACP Papers; William J. Burns to W. L. Hurley, 10 April 1923 and 13 April 1923, Dept. of Justice Records Group 60, case file 61-23.

14. McKay, *A Long Way From Home,* 160-62; *The Worker,* 10 March 1923; *The Crisis* 22 (December 1922): 64-65.

15. Israel Amter, "Black Victims of Imperialism," *The Communist International* 26 and 27 (1922); Draper, *American Communism and Soviet Russia,* 327-28.

16. Cyril Briggs to Pat Alexander, 15 August 1956 Briggs Papers, Southern California Research Library; *Hearings, United States Senate Foreign Relations Subcommittee,* 68th Cong., pt. 1, 1st sess., 135 (Washington, D.C., 1924).

17. *Messenger* 1 (January 1918): 22. Fort-Whiteman was listed on the editorial masthead of the *Messenger* as an assistant editor from 1921 to 1923. Haywood, *Black Bolshevik: Autobiography of an American Communist* (Chicago: Liberator Press, 1978), 144; *Daily Worker,* 9 February 1924; *Daily Worker,* 24 March 1924.

18. Kelly Miller, "The Negro Sanhedrin: A Call for a Conference" (Washington, D.C., 1923), Kelly Miller Papers, Library of Congress. The annual prospectus of the Garland Fund for 1923 and 1924 is reprinted in Elizabeth Dilling, *The Red Network* (Chicago: Elizabeth Dilling, 1934), 163-64; Cyril Briggs to J. W. Johnson, 18 July 1923, NAACP Papers, Library of Congress; Stephen R. Fox, *The Guardian of Boston*, 277; *Boston Guardian*, 11 March 1911. Miller spells out his pro-Booker T. Washington conservative economic and social views in essays collected in *Race Adjustment* (1908); this has been reprinted as *Radicals and Conservatives* (New York: Schocken, 1968).

19. *The Worker*, 14 April 1923; Schuyler, *Black and Conservative*, 150.

20. *Amsterdam News*, 28 March 1923. For background on Moore's political career see "Richard Moore," *Caribbean Studies* 15 (April 1975): 135-45; *Defender*, 12 January 1924.

21. *Daily Worker*, 13 February 1924; *Defender*, 19 January 1924; *Defender*, 2 February 1924; *Daily Worker*, 11 February 1924; *Resolutions, Workers Party*, 12 February 1924, 3, 8, 12, 16, 20, Robert Minor Papers, Columbia University. For an account of America's role in the civil war against the Bolsheviks see William Appelman Williams, "American Intervention in Russia, 1917-1920," in *Containment and Revolution*, edited by David Horowitz (Boston: Beacon Press, 1967), 26-69; *Daily Worker*, 15 February 1924.

22. *Resolutions, Workers Party*, 10; *Daily Worker*, 13 February 1924; *Daily Worker*, 15 February 1924.

23. *Daily Worker*, 16 February 1924; Robert Minor, "The Black Ten Millions," *Liberator* 7 (March 1924): 15; *The Defender*, 8 March 1924.

24. Kelly Miller, "The Negro as a Workingman," *American Mercury* 10 (November 1925): 313; *New York Times*, 17 January 1926; Schuyler, *Black and Conservative*, 151.

25. *Daily Worker*, 28 June 1925; *Daily Worker*, 13 August 1925. The NAACP managed to get House approval for the Dyer anti-lynching bill despite the lukewarm support of the Harding administration (Mary Francis Berry, *Black Resistance/White Law* [New York: Merdeity Corp., 1971], 158).

26. *Daily Worker*, 28 June 1925; Wilson Record, *Race and Radicalism* (Ithaca: Cornell University Press, 1964), 37-40.

27. Interview with Don Wheeldin, 2 December 1989; Interview with Charles Morgan, 13 December 1989; Ben Davis Jr., *James W. Ford* (New York: Workers Library Publishers, 1936) 16-17; James Ford, *The Negro and the Democratic Front* (New York: International Publishers, 1938), 13-14.

28. Interview with Earl Hutchinson Sr., 18 December 1989; Davis, *James W. Ford*, 18-19.

29. William F. Dunne, "The NAACP Takes a Step Backward," *Workers Monthly* 5 (August 1926): 460; Record, *Race and Radicalism*, 40.

30. Charles Wesley, *Negro Labor in the United States* (New York: Vanguard, 1927), 276-77; *The Crisis* 20 (September 1919): 239-41; Ray Marshall, *The Negro Worker* (New York: Random House, 1967), 19-21; Abram L. Harris, "The Negro and Economic Radicalism," *Modern Quarterly* 2 (February 1925): 206.

31. Bernard Eisenberg, "Only for the Bourgeois? James Weldon Johnson and the NAACP, 1916-1930," *Phylon* 60 (June 1982): 116 and 118; NAACP Annual Report, 1917 and 1918 (New York: NAACP, 1919).

32. See Charles F. Kellogg, *NAACP, a History of the National Association for the Advancement of Colored People 1, 1909-1920* (Baltimore: Johns Hopkins Press, 1967). Pickens and DuBois amply laid out their Socialist views in early editions of *The Crisis*, *New Review*, and *Liberator*. Eisenberg discusses Johnson and White's pro-labor leanings in "Only for the Bourgeous?" 120-24.

33. *Workers Monthly* 5 (August 1926): 30.

2 The American Negro Labor Congress

The five-hundred men and women who came to Chicago in late-October 1925 were there to build a militant black workers organization that could break down the racial barrier in labor unions. They were delegates and observers attending the American Negro Labor Congress, an event that *Daily Worker* editor Robert Minor mistakenly dubbed the "first" black labor gathering. Since 1830, blacks had convened dozens of labor congresses, trade associations, and union meetings.[1]

The initial Call for the Congress went out in the spring of 1925. There was no hint of political compromise in the tone: "The American Negro Labor Congress will fight for the abolition of industrial discrimination in factories, mills, mines, on the railroads, and in all places where labor is employed." Of the seventeen blacks who signed the Call, six of them—including Hall, Huiswood, and Fort-Whiteman—were members of the Workers Party.

The Communists had some hope that the ANLC might draw enough support from black workers to allow it to challenge the NAACP and Marcus Garvey's UNIA for leadership supremacy. Communists considered both groups hopelessly anti-Communist and hostile to trade union organizing.

To be credible and effective, Workers Party leaders shrewdly realized that the ANLC must not be seen by the public as merely an insular gathering of black Communists. Opponents could then easily dismiss them as just another disgruntled group of radical troublemakers. The ANLC's Call stipulated that the delegates must represent independent black unions, interracial unions, farm workers, or unorganized factory workers, or be "individual advocates" promoting "the cause of the Negro working class."[2]

The First Congress

The opening-day crowd included forty official delegates and hundreds of observers. The excitement and anticipation was contagious. Harry Haywood left the meeting hall after the first day's session on a cloud: "I was literally walking on air. At last, I felt, we were about to get somewhere in our work among blacks."

Haywood and the other Workers Party members were particularly delighted with the type of delegates that turned up. They were not middle-class professionals but men and women who represented black labor associations, union locals, and grass-roots community organizations. There were waiters, cooks, farmers, domestics, pullman porters, longshoremen, janitors, and steel and mine workers. They were the sorts of blacks the Communists felt the NAACP and Urban League forgot.

The ANLC also had an international touch to it. There were representatives from labor movements in Ethiopia, Mexico, South Africa, and West Africa. The Congress received telegrams from the Defense League of Italian Peasants and striking Polish miners in Pennsylvania praising the event.[3] The delegates gave a rousing cheer to the representatives from the Negro Press Association and a black attorneys' organization. Both men read telegrams of support from their memberships.

Suspended over the stage was a giant portrait of a black farmer and laborer with clasped hands and the hammer and sickle. The hall was decorated with bright red banners exhorting the workers to revolution. A huge sign that stretched across the front of the hall read "Organization is the first step to freedom."

George Wells Parker had a unique way to get the attention of the audience. He read part of the ritual of the Ku Klux Klan, which stressed the inferiority of blacks. After the shock passed, Parker made a plea for the black man to "rid himself of the inferiority complex" and unite with workers worldwide.[4] A parade of speakers took the podium to attack union racism, the capitalists and middle-class black leaders for "betraying" the black workers. The audience reserved their biggest roar for the man *Time* Magazine called the "Reddest of the blacks."

Fort-Whiteman had labored hard to pull the ANLC together. As head of the ANLC's provisional organizing committee, he traveled to cities in the South and Northeast trying to sell the idea of a Congress to black groups. Fort-Whiteman was determined that the Congress would successfully "present the cause of the Negro worker."[5] Now, with the months of hard work behind him and the ANLC a reality, Fort-Whiteman took the podium and read a telegram to the delegates: "We, Dr. Ossian H. Sweet and ten co-defendants, thank you for your sympathy and support." The audience burst into applause.

Dr. Sweet was currently on trial in Detroit for defending his home against the attacks of a white mob. For weeks the trial was headline news nationally. Sweet was being defended by Clarence Darrow. The first day of the Congress the delegates had sent Dr. Sweet a telegram congratulating him for "defending the whole race from the brutal savagery of segregation and lynching." The telegram from Sweet was a welcome treat and strengthened the delegate's conviction that the ANLC was already having an effect on blacks.

Fort-Whiteman then announced that ten blacks, seven of them women, were undergoing three years of intensive training for the Russian "diplomatic services." It was not exactly true. The ten were enrolled as students at the School of the Toilers East, a Party-run training school for African and Asian Communist recruits in Moscow.[6]

The Congress also heard from Bishop William M. Brown, who mixed Christianity with Marx to condemn all capitalists to eternal hell-fire: "No religion has any right to be called holy which does not lead to a freer life for the masses who toil." The good bishop told the delegates, "the Christian church was started by workers, and you workers must take it back." Later the *Chicago Defender*, in a headline on the Congress, proclaimed, "Bishop flays Capitalist Religion."[7]

The main resolution gave the obligatory salute to solidarity between black and white workers. Congress delegates absolved the white worker of any responsibility for racism. He was just a victim of capitalist manipulation: "This discrimination against the Negro worker comes back against him." Other resolutions called for heavy penalties against landlords, hotel owners, theaters, and restaurants that excluded blacks, and attacked the notion of black inferiority: "We declare that all claims of inferiority are ignorant and unscientific."[8]

And then there was one surprise. The delegates were explicit that race, not class, was the overriding cause of black oppression. They wanted full equality not because blacks were exploited workers but because the "whole caste system" had made them pariahs. The ANLC's National Executive Committee was "instructed" to convene a world race congress. This was a repeat of the proposal made by the

31

Communist International in 1922. The race congress would "lay the foundation" for a world organization of black workers and farmers to "liberate the darker-skinned people in the colonies" from imperialism.[9]

Anticipating that the ANLC would need a publication to promote its program among the black masses, Party leaders over the previous summer distributed two issues of the *Negro Champion* in Harlem. The paper actually sold well, probably because the Party focused on news of black events and pictorial spreads on black life. Encouraged by the paper's reception, Party leaders began putting out two editions a month. It continued to sell well enough for the *Amsterdam News* to remark that its pictures and cartoons "hit the spot." The *Negro Champion* was designated by the delegates as "the official organ of the ANLC."[10]

The Congress closed with a greeting to Soviet Russia as "the friend and ally of the oppressed of all races." After making so many weighty decisions, the delegates wound down and let the corks fly at a Halloween masked ball. The costumes they wore were so outrageous and brightly colored that a cynical reporter for the *Defender* quipped they were "about the only outward evidence of the 'red' terror alleged to have dominated the convention."

The mainstream press was not as amused as the *Defender*. The staid magazine *The Independent* was appalled that blacks should entertain the thought of casting their lot with the reds: "It will be hard for a Communistic agitator to fool them into taking part in an adventure in which they have everything to lose and nothing to gain." The *Chicago Tribune* played hard on the theme of red conspiracy, calling the Congress "a plot of Red Russia to spread Communism among the colored people of the entire world."[11]

For a few weeks the *New York Times* kept out of the fray. When it finally spoke in January, the *Times* opened with a fairly restrained report on the developments that led to the Congress. It accurately traced Fort-Whiteman's background and presented an extensive summary of the Congress resolutions. But the tone of the report quickly changed.

The *Times* scored the Congress for being "Moscow controlled" and "Moscow financed." Noting that the *Daily Worker* "enthusiastically welcomed" the delegates, the *Times* cautioned labor to be on guard against the Communists trying to use the ANLC to "influence the Negro labor movement along radical lines."

After sounding out James Weldon Johnson, Kelly Miller, and W.E.B. DuBois for their views on the Communists, the *Times* concluded that the three men, in varying degrees, "regard the Communist propaganda among the Negroes as a potential source of trouble." However, DuBois was not totally hostile. He tempered his criticism with the sober observation that "Communists have gone out of their way to express sympathy with Negro and colored workers all over the world."

DuBois refused to comment on the merits of the ANLC since he "did not know the persons back of the Chicago convention." But he defended the right of blacks "to investigate and sympathize with any industrial reform whether it springs from Russia, China or the South Seas."[12]

A. Phillip Randolph was not as charitable. By now he was thoroughly disillusioned with the Communists for what he considered their efforts to "manipulate" black organizations. He agreed that black workers were most in need of industrial reform and economic justice, but not if there was a red string tied to it: "The American Negro Labor Congress is certainly not representative of the American Negro worker because its seat of control is in Moscow." If some blacks were drifting toward the Communists, AFL officials had no one to blame but themselves, Randolph said. "The AFL has been inexcusably indifferent to the entreaties of the Negro workers."

Fort-Whiteman may have frowned at the reports in the *New York Times*, the *Independent*, and the *Messenger*, but the comments from the black press generally brought smiles. Black editors were willing to look beyond the ANLC's "red taint." The *Defender* and the *Pittsburgh Courier* gave full coverage to ANLC activities. The *Courier* accurately summarized the resolutions passed. When the Congress ended, the paper made only a noncommittal comment that "the congress decided to spread Communistic doctrines among Negro workers."[13]

Other reports were equally favorable. Howard University professor Abram Harris liked the ANLC enough to take on the critics. "Not Soviet gold but social facts furnish the explanation for the convention's radicalism." Harris stole Randolph's line that if organized labor cleaned up its own racial house it would have nothing to fear from the Communists: "The American Negro Labor Congress appears to me to be, fundamentally, a revolt against the color psychology in the labor movement."

The ANLC helped its own cause with the black press by sticking with racial issues. Few black editors could find fault with the Congress' demands for abolition of Jim Crow in housing, the military, courts, education, and voting. They were fighting for the same goals. They regarded communism as a bogeyman, but the editors did not forget

33

that black readers paid the bills that kept their papers and magazines circulating. They would take a dim view of an editorial that attacked a group who proclaimed, "We demand the full equality of the Negro in the social system of the United States." Black readers would have found it "peculiar"—as *Opportunity*, the Urban League's monthly magazine, tactfully put it—to be told to "keep away" from someone who called them "brother." William N. Jones was not about to tell his readers to keep away. The *Afro-American* editor did not care what the critics said about the ANLC. He was for it. "It may be red Bolshevism but stripped of all propaganda, it is the Naked Truth." Jones devoted his weekly "Day by Day" column to a glowing paean to "Lovett Fort-Whiteman's New Philosophy."

The Congress was over. Now Fort-Whiteman faced the real test. Would black workers work with Communists? Could the Workers Party put aside its doctrinaire sectarianism and work in a cooperative movement with non-Communist black organizations? And could the Congress make good its promise to crack the rigid color barriers of many trade unions? The future of the ANLC rested on how the organizers handled these questions.

The ANLC Organizes

Fort-Whiteman did not stop to ponder these intangibles. He was on the road again. His first stop was Pittsburgh, where he made the rounds of the city's black Baptist churches. Again, he played the role of the racial moderate patiently explaining to the attentive worshippers that the aim of the Congress was "to battle race discrimination."

Fort-Whiteman was determined not to give his detractors any fuel to attack the Congress. When *Courier* columnist Floyd Calvin charged that the ANLC "was not taken seriously" by black workers, Fort-Whiteman simply ignored him.[14]

In Baltimore, he continued to keep a low profile. He told a mostly black audience at the YMCA that the ANLC would battle against school segregation and job discrimination. Fort-Whiteman seemed to score points as long as he stuck to the racial uplift theme. "If this is red propaganda," Jones exulted," then for God's sake, let all our readers supply themselves with a pot and brush and give twelve million colored people a generous coating."

Within two years, the ANLC had more than forty-five "functioning locals." New York, Pittsburgh, Chester, Pennsylvania, Kansas City, and

Chicago had the biggest and most active chapters. There were "provisional committees" in a dozen other cities strung out across the country from Buffalo to Seattle. But the numbers remained small. The Chicago local, with seventy members, was nearly twice the size of the next largest local. Fort-Whiteman was confident that as more black workers heard about the ANLC they would join.

There was another problem that could not be so easily sidestepped. Rank-and-file black workers were ignoring the Congress. In Chicago, the ANLC produced an impressive roster of black trade locals that purportedly endorsed the ANLC. After the Congress, they seemed to vanish. The reason for their disappearance was that they had not existed in the first place. "A hard boiled organizer," Robert Minor confessed, "will have to say that there were only a very few thousand of organized Negro workers behind the delegates."[15]

Fort-Whiteman's racial moderation did not bring any black workers into the organization. Even before the year was out, it was painfully clear that the ANLC was in trouble. It did not schedule any conferences for the next three years. It was fast being reduced to a small group of labor militants.

The Congress even managed to get into hot water with the friends it made. A few black churchmen in New York and Pittsburgh had shown some receptivity to the Congress initially. But Party leaders viewed this as a little too un-Marxist. The edict came down. ANLC organizers should cease breaking bread with Christians and start attacking them. "The power, influence, and reactionary policies of the Negro churches become a great obstacle," Party leader Clarence Hathaway warned.

Communists, in effect, had put black churches on equal footing with the capitalists. They could always, Hathaway asserted, be "depended on to support the bourgeoisie against the workers." In a report to the Sixth Party Convention in 1929, Huiswood made it clear where Communists should stand: "Our recent experiences with meetings in the churches ought to be adequate proof that we must intensify our agitation against the church."[16]

The beleaguered Fort-Whiteman could not reverse the skid so the Party decided to give him some help. They assigned Richard Moore, who had gained valuable experience as a street organizer in Harlem, the task of helping him shore up the sagging organization. In a speech at the Interracial Forum in Pittsburgh in 1927, Moore skipped the polite talk about equal rights and building coalitions with moderate blacks. He fervently appealed to his Pittsburgh audience to believe it

35

was "inevitable" that whites would see blacks as "working champions" and come to their defense.[17]

Moore also took some heavy flak from Marcus Garvey, who had come to regard the Communists as a threat to his nationalist movement. His *Negro World* was livid when the Associated Press incorrectly reported that Moore represented the UNIA at an international conference on colonial problems in Brussels. The *Negro World* called him an "impostor" and assured *Associated Press* that "there is a great gulf between communism and Garveyism." In July 1927 the paper cautioned that blacks "would suffer more if they should fall in with the ANLC." To prove the point, the *Negro World* reprinted an alleged government "white paper" that showed that Fort-Whiteman and Moore were ordered by Moscow to form the ANLC as "a clearinghouse for Bolshevik propaganda."[18]

The Congress may have been an ailing body, but it was still alive. In 1928, Party leaders decided to try and breathe new life into it. Party national committeeman John Pepper got the ball rolling. "The American Negro Labor Congress," he noted, "must be reorganized and activized." Pepper wanted the ANLC to target farmers and agricultural workers with a "carefully worked out program." As part of his revival scheme, Pepper proposed that the ANLC hold another convention. Party leaders were engaged in wishful thinking.

By reducing the ANLC to little more than a Communist cell, the Party had virtually eliminated any chance to salvage it. Pepper did not even bother to hide this. He instructed Briggs, Fort-Whiteman, and Moore to turn the ANLC into "a medium through which the Party can extend its work among the Negro masses and mobilize the Negro workers under its leadership."[19]

The following year the ANLC made a stab at an alliance with the Marine Workers Progressive League, a leftist-influenced organization of ship stewards, attendants, and kitchen workers. The most that came out of the alliance was a "mass meeting" the Congress sponsored in Harlem to pay tribute to the black crew members from the transport ship, the Vestris. The crewmen were honored for their courage in testifying against the "brutal treatment" by the ship's officers.

During the fall of 1929, the ANLC got another break. Black projectionists, angered at the theater owners for their low pay and long hours, began picketing Harlem's Lafayette theater. The theater owners played hardball. They slapped a court injunction on the Motion Picture Operator's Union to halt the picketing.

The strike gave the ANLC a wedge to work with other labor and community groups. Briggs and Moore persuaded the UNIA, the Sleeping Car Porters Union, and the ACLU to sponsor a mass rally in front of the Lafayette. During the rally, Moore was hauled by the police from the speaker's stand and arrested for being on theater property in violation of the injunction. Moore was quickly bailed out. Later, the ACLU agreed to defend him on the grounds that the arrest violated his right to free speech. Although the case was quietly dropped, Moore's arrest gave the ANLC momentary visibility. Later in the year, Moore marched in front of the Manhattan office of the Upholsterers and Linoleum Layers Union. The ANLC demanded that the union admit black workers.[20]

When President Herbert Hoover refused to withdraw American Marines from Haiti, the ANLC had yet one more issue. Following the assassination of Haitian President Jean Vilbrun Guillaume Sam in 1915, President Woodrow Wilson had ordered in the Marines. Wilson claimed he took the action to restore order and to stave off the wartime threat of a German takeover of the island.

Critics charged that Wilson had sent in the Marines to prevent a revolutionary movement of peasants from overthrowing the wealthy landowners and sugar cane operators. Whatever the true cause, fourteen years later the Marines were still there and black leaders, outraged over Hoover's stubbornness, held protest demonstrations nationwide. Cyril Briggs, who was now the National Secretary of the ANLC, wrote an angry editorial in his *Crusader News Service* urging blacks and "class conscious white workers" to support "the heroic workers and peasants of Haiti." Briggs, DuBois, and other black leaders demanded that Hoover remove the troops. The ANLC sponsored its own "mass" demonstration in New York. Hoover finally agreed to appoint a special commission to determine whether the island had achieved political stability. The Commission reported it had. By then Hoover was out of office. Roosevelt withdrew the troops in 1934.[21]

The Final Days

Briggs tried to keep up the pretense that the ANLC was still a vibrant political organization. Overshadowed by Ford, Huiswood, and Fort-Whiteman, he had kept a relatively low profile within the Party. In 1929, his fortunes changed. In addition to his leadership role in the ANLC, he was also appointed as temporary head of the Party's newly created National Negro Department.

In his first report on the Party's "Negro Work," Briggs claimed that during the Party-designated National Negro Week in May 1929, the ANLC held successful memorial meetings in Boston, Chicago, Detroit, and Cleveland. He also extended the fiction of ANLC gains to the South. He cited Hall's address at meetings in Virginia and North Carolina as proof that the ANLC was "drawing in proletarian elements from both races."

By the middle of 1929, Party leaders made the decision to close the ANLC down. The *Negro Champion* was even being sold to its dwindling subscribers as part of a package deal with *The Communist*. Briggs half-heartedly criticized Party leaders for not providing funds to issue an edition of the paper during National Negro Week. He took Party leaders to task for not putting out a special ANLC leaflet to commemorate black achievements.[22]

In January 1930 the ANLC took its last breath. Along with the Young Communist League and the National Textile Workers Union, it co-sponsored a bring-the-troops-home rally in Charlotte, North Carolina. The rally was held in Charlotte's black section. The keynote speaker was not black nor was he a member of the ANLC. Si Gerson, the YCL district organizer, told the crowd that occupation and lynching could only be ended through "the united efforts of black and white workers." No mention was made in the *Daily Worker* of an ANLC speaker.

Party leaders held the last ANLC convention in St. Louis in July 1930, not to revive the organization but to give it a new name and a new cast of characters. It resurfaced as the League of Revolutionary Struggle.[23]

For four years the ANLC weathered the assaults of the AFL, the white press, and black critics It even survived despite the near total indifference of black workers. However, there was one enemy it could not escape—itself. Huiswood got it right when he called it a "propaganda sect" with no connection to the industrial workers.

But Huiswood deliberately downplayed the Party's role in the organization's failure, implying that the fault lay with the ANLC organizers: "discipline was little enforced, and the work of the comrades in charge was not checked, with the result many grave blunders were committed." He conveniently left out the Party's own narrow sectarianism as a cause for the break-up.

Although he had played only a peripheral part in the Congress, mostly distinguishing himself by getting arrested at the ANLC's anti-Haitian occupation rally in New York City, Ford still ticked off several reasons for the ANLC's failure. They included "rigid local councils," "bad methods of work," and failure to work "co-operatively" with other black organizations. Some years later, Ford would add to his list the ANLC's rejection of the black church as a cause for its collapse.

Haywood got a little more personal than Ford or Huiswood. He blamed Fort-Whiteman. Haywood considered him too much the dilettante and showman, with an egregious ego that prevented him from working harmoniously with others. He told how Fort-Whiteman discouraged Industrial Workers of the World leader Ben Fletcher from attending the convention for fear that he would upstage him.

While the Party sharpened its knife and carved up the ANLC, a good word came from a surprising source. In his weekly "Views and Reviews" column in the *Courier*, George Schuyler praised the Communists for bringing "white and colored Americans together at dances, socials and meetings." Schuyler believed they were among the few whites in America who were trying to practice the social equality other radicals only preached. He gave them "credit for meeting the racial issue squarely."[24]

While the criticisms of Huiswood, Briggs, Ford, and Haywood were all accurate, they still left out one other significant cause for the ANLC collapse. It simply looked too much like other black protest organizations.

In 1930, DuBois did a point-by-point comparison of the ANLC's program and the NAACP's: "The interesting result, however, of most of these criticisms is that when it comes to practical programs they are all in essential agreement with ours." DuBois did not say it directly, but the message was obvious. Why should blacks join the ANLC when there was an NAACP?

A final reason the ANLC failed was because it could not sustain the early enthusiasm it aroused among many blacks. On paper, it had a sound labor program and could put experienced organizers in the field. It had the resources of the Workers Party behind it.

Yet if blacks had joined the ANLC *en masse* and agreed to join trades and work with white labor, what guarantee could the Communists give that white labor would welcome them? In his assessment of the ANLC, Abram Harris asked a pointed question: If whites would not unite with blacks to promote common economic interests, then how "could they unite to promote the social revolution?"[25]

Fort-Whiteman and Moore left the question dangling. But Workers Party leaders had slowly begun to figure out that black workers gave their answer when they flocked by the thousands to join the Universal

Negro Improvement Association headed by the squat Jamaican nationalist Marcus Garvey. His appeals for race pride and self-sufficiency made more sense to black workers than the Communist call for alliances with hostile white trade unionists.

Communists would never publicly admit it, but the ANLC in part was an effort to capitalize on the black nationalist sentiments aroused by the Garvey movement. While it fell flat, Party leaders did not miss the lesson. Their next move would shock many.

Notes

1. Harry Haywood, *Black Bolshevik* (Chicago: Liberator Press, 1978) 144-45; Robert Minor, "The First Negro Workers Congress," *Workers Monthly* 5 (December 1925): 71-72. See Howard Bell, *A Survey of the Negro Convention Movement, 1830-1861* (New York: Arno Press, 1969).
2. Herbert Aptheker, *A Documentary History of the Negro People in the United States, 1910-1932* (Seacaucus, New Jersey: Citadel Press, 1973), 479-80. Time and again Garvey stated his hatred of Communists in editorials and articles in his newspapers and books, see *The Negro World, The Black Man, The New Jamaican* and *Philosophy and Opinions*, which are frequently cited throughout this study.
3. *Chicago Defender*, 7 November 1925, *Pittsburgh Courier*, 31 October 1925; Haywood, *Black Bolshevik*, 145; *Daily Worker*, 30 October 1925.
4. *Daily Worker*, 28 October 1925; *Defender*, 7 November 1925.
5. *Time*, 9 November 1925; *Afro-American*, 31 October 1925.
6. *Amsterdam News*, 20 May 1925. For a brief account of the Sweet case see: John Hope Franklin, *From Slavery to Freedom* (New York: Vintage Books, 1969), 484. *Afro-American*, 18 April 1925.
7. Brown fends off attacks on his off-beat mix of Communism and Christianity in his pamphlet *Why I Am A Communist Lecture No. 12* (Gallion, Ohio: Brown Educational Co., 1932). There are a total of thirteen lectures in the series. In all of them Brown comes back to his theme that "it was Karl Marx who finally brought me to Jesus" (19); *The Crusader* 3 (June, 1921) 29-31; *Defender*, 7 November 1925.
8. *Afro-American*, 12 August 1925; *Afro-American*, 3 October 1925; Ira DeReid, *Negro Membership in American Labor Unions* (New York: Alexander Press, 1930), 127-28; *New York Times*, 13 August 1925; *Daily Worker*, 29 October 1925.
9. *Pittsburgh Courier*, 9 May 1925; *Pittsburgh Courier*, 31 May 1925; *Manifesto, Resolution, Constitution*, First National Conference, Chicago, June 28, 1925 (Chicago, International Labor Defense, 1925), 4.
10. *Amsterdam News*, 20 May 1925; *Afro-American*, 25 April 1925; *Daily Worker*, 30 October 1925.

11. *Daily Worker*, 27 October 1925; *Daily Worker*, 28 October 1925; *Daily Worker*, 30 October 1925; *Defender*, 7 November 1925; *Independent* 115 (5 December 1925): 631; quoted in Ira DeReid, *Negro Membership in American Labor Unions*, 128.

12. *New York Times*, 17 January 1926; *The Crisis* 30 (December 1925): 60.

13. *The Messenger* 7 (September 1925): 324-25; *Pittsburgh Courier*, 7 November 1925; *Defender*, 7 November 1925; *Daily Worker*, 14 November 1925.

14. Abram L. Harris "Lenin Casts His Shadow upon Africa," *The Crisis* 31 (April 1926): 272-75. For a summary of the attitudes of the black press toward the Communists during this period see Henry Williams, *Black Response to the American Left, 1917-1929* (Princeton, New Jersey: Princeton University Press, 1973), 49-70; *Opportunity* 4 (December 1925): 29; *Afro-American*, 7 November 1925; *Pittsburgh Courier*, 23 January 1926.

15. *Afro-American*, 13 March 1926; *Daily Worker*, 9 and 11 March 1929; Minor, "The First Negro Workers Congress," 74.

16. Clarence Hathaway, "The American Negro and the Churches," unpublished manuscript, ca. 1927, copy at Southern California Research Library; *Daily Worker*, 9 and 11 March 1929.

17. *Pittsburgh Courier*, 29 October 1927. Roi Ottley gives a first person view of the impact Powell's Abyssinian church had on Harlem blacks in the 1920s in *New World A-Coming* (Boston: Houghton Mifflin Co., 1943), 220-35.

18. *Negro World*, 19 February 1927; *Negro World*, 2 July 1927; *Negro World*, 14 July 1927; *Negro World*, 13 August 1927.

19. John Pepper, *American Negro Problems* (New York: Workers Library Publishers, 1928), 14-16.

20. *Labor Defender* 6 (January 1929): 7; *Pittsburgh Courier*, 12 July 1929; *Pittsburgh Courier*, 9 October 1929.

21. See "Haiti: History and Government," in *The Encyclopedia Americana International Edition* (Danbury, Connecticut: Grolier Inc., 1988) 703; *Crusader News Service*, 12 December 1929; *Pittsburgh Courier*, 4 January 1930.

22. *Daily Worker*, 9 June 1929; Haywood, *Black Bolshevik*, 145-46; The advertisement appeared in *The Communist* 8 (May 1929).

23. *Pittsburgh Courier*, 25 January 1930; James Ford "Build the National Negro Congress Movement," *The Communist* 15 (June 1936): 559.

24. *Daily Worker*, 9 March 1929; *International Press Correspondence*, 16 (29 March 1916); Ben Davis Jr., *James W. Ford* (New York: Workers Library Publishers, 1936), 21; Ford, "Build the National Negro Congress," 558-59; Haywood, *Black Bolshevik*, 146; *Pittsburgh Courier*, 14 December 1929.

25. *The Crisis* 37 (April 1930): 137; Abram L. Harris, "Negro Labor's Quarrel with White Workingmen," *Current History* 21 (September 1926): 907.

3 "The Negro Nation"

The first real sign of a racial shift among Workers Party leaders surfaced at the Fifth World Congress of the Communist International in Moscow in 1924. John Pepper told the delegates that the Party was "not in a position to separate the various nationalities or races." Pepper insisted the Comintern should stick with the slogan "Equal rights for all nationalities and races." Fort-Whiteman did not agree.

At the time, he was in Moscow attending classes at the Toilers of the East, the Party training school. Although he was not an official delegate at the Congress, Pepper's remarks bothered him and he had to speak. He took the floor and lashed out at the Comintern delegates: "The ideas of Marx have spread slowly among Negroes because Communists have not realized that the problem must be dealt with in a specialized way."

Fort-Whiteman implored the Comintern to devise a program "carrying a special appeal" to blacks. He did not say it but he probably had Garvey in mind as he spoke. Fort-Whiteman watched the massive Garvey parades in Harlem and he knew the large influence that the nationalist leader held over black workers. As he saw it, Communists had no choice but to change their racial strategy. His warning carried weight, mainly because Comintern officials also saw the huge Garvey parades and knew that the black nationalist leader was having a strong impact on the black masses. Workers Party leaders were also not oblivious to Garvey. In fact, three years before the Moscow meeting, they had made a friendly overture to him.[1]

When Rose Pastor Stokes asked to speak at the 1921 UNIA convention, Garvey immediately reserved a spot for her on the program. He knew that Stokes was a Communist and that she would appear at the

43

convention on behalf of the Friends of the Soviet Union. But he invited her because he wanted to show that his movement had broad appeal to all political factions.

At the convention, he was an exceedingly gracious host, complimenting her in his introductory remarks. He cheered with the rest of the UNIA throng when Stokes said that the Bolsheviks would help the Haitians and Africans in their struggle to kick the imperialists out of the "black and brown man's territory."

Garvey did not seem to be offended when Stokes told the crowd, "I am a Communist; I am a Bolshevik." The audience gave her a loud ovation when she saluted blacks for defending their communities during the "Red Summer" of 1919, when race riots rocked Northern cities: "We Bolsheviki were proud and glad that there were black workers who had the courage and the manhood to stand up against their oppressors."

Party leaders were ecstatic at Stokes' reception. But they were listening with only half an ear to Garvey. At the same time Garvey was praising her, he was also disclaiming her views. With a careful eye on the press, he stressed that the Stokes speech should not "misinterpret us as being Soviets." He added, "We are not adopting the methods of any government." To be sure no one would mistake his views, he announced that a Republican, Democrat, and even an Irish representative would also address the convention. Garvey thanked Stokes for appearing and the convention moved on.[2]

Still, Stokes had given the Party an opening with Garvey. Later in the year, Minor requested a meeting with Harlem's Communists to explore ways to approach him. Moore, Domingo, Grace Campbell, McKay, Huiswood, and Briggs showed up at the *Liberator* offices for the meeting. When McKay later recounted the meeting in his autobiography, he gave no indication that anything ever came out of it.[3]

Matters rested there until the Comintern decided after the Moscow Congress that the Workers Party should try again to work out a relationship with Garvey. When the UNIA held its fourth international convention in August 1924, Foster, now the Party's national chairman, sent a long letter of greeting to Garvey. Foster diplomatically touched on all of Garvey's concerns—African independence, anti-imperialism, racism, lynchings, and disfranchisement. Foster praised the UNIA proposal for a Negro Political Union, and offered support for their campaign to promote black educational materials, black history, and black pride. He appealed to Garvey to reject the League of Nations and to send UNIA delegates to the Communist International: "Your representatives would find themselves honored guests at its deliberations." He reminded Garvey that there was a "class struggle going on within the imperialist countries." Then he made his pitch: "We suggest that it is not your enemies that you should direct your appeals to, but to the enemies of your enemies." Foster implied that Garvey and the Communists shared the same capitalist foe.[4]

With the exception of the offer to join the Communist International, which Garvey had no intention of taking up, Foster left him with little to quibble about. He gingerly skirted the subject of trade union racism, a continuing sore point for black labor organizations. He also did not challenge Garvey's apologetic remarks on the Klan. Foster simply dismissed the Klan as "a class instrument for the oppression of the working class, of whatever race."

Foster's opinion was certainly news to the thousands of blacks who felt the rope, torch, and bullets of night riders. The Klan was an instrument of racial terror aimed not just at "whatever race" but at blacks. If he had been completely honest he would have admitted that lynch mobs were not just made up of capitalists but workers, too. But that would have opened a door that the Workers Party still preferred to keep firmly shut.

The Workers Party leader was playing for big stakes with Garvey. At the convention, several black Communists, including Fort-Whiteman and his wife Olivia, were delegates. Assigned by the Party to speak to the convention, Olivia gave two brief talks that steered close to the Party line.

She attacked the capitalists and urged that blacks "train for their rights in America" before going to Africa. Fort-Whiteman, however, did make two significant departures from the Party position. Both Garvey and the Communists had virtually ignored black women and downplayed the issue of social equality. She intended to correct the record. She called on the UNIA to "take a definite and independent stand" against the "special mistreatment" of black women. She finished by making a strong demand for social equality for blacks: "I for one intend to fight for the equality of my people, any kind of equality, every kind of equality, everywhere—including social equality."[5]

Despite her impressive speech, Garvey had not changed his opinion about the Communists. He would listen to them, but he did not trust them. The UNIA passed resolutions praising the League of Nations, African emigration, and capitalist business development. The UNIA said nothing about trade unions, economic reorganization, or support of the Soviet Union.

The love affair between the Workers Party and Garvey lasted less than a week, and the divorce was swift and brutal. Disturbed by Garvey's refusal to denounce capitalism and put forth a militant program for black labor, Foster and C. E. Ruthenberg, Party National Executive Secretary, wrote the nationalist leader: "The UNIA offers the Negro people no program for meeting the atrocities of the Klan." They now demanded that the UNIA pass a stronger resolution denouncing the Klan. Garvey refused.

The two men picked the weakest spot in Garvey's armor to attack. Nearly every black leader had roundly criticized Garvey for failing to speak out on the brutality of the Klan. Garvey's thinking was oddly skewed on the issue. He believed that white violence would force blacks to retreat into greater racial isolation and that this would be a benefit: "Lynchings and race riots all work to our advantage by teaching the Negro that he must build a civilization of his own or forever remain the white man's victim." Such an indefensible position gave Foster and Ruthenberg the chance to take the moral high ground.[6]

Some months later, Robert Minor tore the whole UNIA program to shreds. He called it "primitive and unclear." Garvey was anti-working class, pro-imperialist, and a black chauvinist who believed in the "supreme authority of our race." The Workers Party, Minor asserted, was happy that it could expose him as a charlatan masquerading as the black savior, "By a process of elimination, all demands which were offensive to the ruling class were dropped one by one, and the organization settled down to a policy of disclaiming any idea whatever of demanding any rights for the Negro people."

He also claimed to have inside information that Garvey had sent a pamphlet on the UNIA's "Aims and Objects" to rich whites to get money and gifts for his various schemes. With Minor's broadside, the Party slammed the door shut on any future cooperation with the UNIA's supreme leader.[7]

But it was not as easy to ignore Garvey's influence. Briggs, Fort-Whiteman, Domingo, and Moore still could not walk the streets of Harlem without hearing blacks talk about Garvey. Writing under the Party alias of James Jackson, Fort-Whiteman argued that the Garvey movement embodied the "pent up hatred and rebellious discontent" blacks felt toward American institutions. Like it or not, Fort-Whiteman said, the Party could not dismiss a movement with such enormous

46

impact: "No organization in the history of the American Negro has stirred the masses as has the Garvey movement." Party leaders did not dispute Fort-Whiteman.

A Party-sanctioned editorial in *The Communist* that accompanied Fort-Whiteman's article was self-critical: "By ignoring the question of racial antagonism our Party has allowed the Negro liberation movement to take a wrong path and get into the hands of the Negro petty bourgeoisie which has launched the nationalist slogan—'Back to Africa.'"[8]

The ANLC was, in part, the Party's first attempt to use race to pry blacks away from the NAACP and the Garveyites. When that failed, Communists shifted gears and tried to give themselves an edge by endorsing the black demand for social equality. This was fairly easy to do since Briggs, Fort-Whiteman and Haywood had been pushing for this from the moment they entered the Party. In 1926, the Workers Party finally came out for social equality in its congressional platform: "The workers and farmers fight for repeal of all laws that discriminate against the Negro and for complete political, industrial, educational—in a word, complete social equality for the Negro." For the next half-century, social equality became the obligatory watchwords of the Communists whenever the "Negro Question" was raised.[9]

The Workers Party now had to convince blacks that they would fight for their platform. After years of racist abuse, many blacks distrusted whites and wanted to develop their own programs and organizations. Garvey and the nationalists understood this and were able to channel this into constructive programs that promised to renew black self-identity and awareness. Marxists, on the other hand, had repeatedly argued that blacks were workers and were victims only of economic exploitation.

But racial self-realization in blacks had deep roots in the black experience that transcended class. In America, blacks had two souls. DuBois called this "twoness" a consciousness of being American and black. Whites poked fun at Garvey's followers for their outlandish regalia, their flamboyant parades, and their impossible rhetoric about going "back to Africa." For blacks, however, these were important symbols of their identity and power. Few blacks really believed that Garvey could build ships and take them back to Africa. That was not the point. He gave them something they could call their own. Black self-assertion represented freedom from white control. Haywood recognized that Garvey did not invent nationalism but swam in a tradition that was age-old in black America. "The Garvey movement crystallized in itself the powerful nationalist sentiment of the Negroes."[10]

If nothing else, Garvey taught the Communists, Haywood said, "that separatist tendencies are present among the Negro masses which become stronger in periods of crisis." This was the secret to his appeal among blacks. Could the Communists replicate that? They had to keep trying if, as Party leader Jay Lovestone wrote, they ever expected to see "the Negro proletariat assume the hegemony in the entire Negro movement."[11]

Moscow Intervenes

In 1928 Workers Party leaders again turned to Moscow for help. For nearly a month and a half during the hot, dry Russian summer, endless rounds of private meetings, conferences, and debates took place behind the Kremlin walls. Hundreds of delegates from the world's Communist parties had gathered at the Comintern's Sixth World Congress to revamp Communist policy on the colonial struggles. The special focus was on the United States and South Africa.

For days, papers, memos, and directives flew wildly back and forth. Finally, the Comintern's Executive Committee formed a Negro Commission. Haywood, Otto Hall, Ford, and two other blacks sat on the thirty-two-member Commission. While the Executive Committee welcomed input from the four black Americans, the CI considered whites to be equally knowledgeable and sensitive to the problems of non-whites. So, when the final appointments were made, Japanese, Hungarian, English, and Finnish "race experts" also sat on the Negro Commission.[12]

Everybody got a chance to speak. The wrangling went on for days. The Commission wisely cleared the air and agreed that racial oppression of blacks was far more severe than the economic exploitation of white workers. They conceded that white Communists had failed to organize effectively among black workers.

But what to do about it? Some participants insisted that the demand for social equality adequately addressed the problems. Racism was a class question and would be eliminated when capitalism was destroyed. Ford and William Patterson—who wrote under the pseudonym William Wilson—disagreed. They blistered this idea as a "parody of Marxism." A brilliant young attorney, Patterson had joined the Party in 1927. The Party had big plans for his future. Patterson was then in Moscow studying at the Toilers of the East.

48

Patterson and Ford submitted their own "discussion article" to the Commission. They argued that the Party should discard its outdated view that class struggle alone would solve the race problem. While they agreed that blacks were exploited as workers, they still felt that racial discrimination was more damaging. Ford and Patterson contended that "class demands alone are not enough to weld together" blacks.

They called on Party leaders to create new types of organizations among blacks that did not put the entire emphasis on class aims: "The non-party Negro mass organization must be a race organization. It is not possible in one blow to make Communists out of unorganized, backward black workers." The pair also had some choice words for their white Party comrades who refused to examine racism "not only in political life but in their private life as well." Racism, they said, was eating the Party up from within and alienating blacks. Patterson and Ford then wandered into a lengthy discourse on the nature of race prejudice.

They ended by reprimanding the whites for not including blacks in their social activities. From here on, Patterson and Ford would impose a draconian penalty on the white Communists for the "slightest expression of race prejudice." They would be warned first and, if they did not change, expelled from the Workers Party.[13]

Patterson, Ford, Haywood, and the Commission members all had their say. However, as the days wore on the Commission was still up in the air on whether the "Negro question "was a class or a race issue. Commission members studied the Marxist classics for guidance. They combed the writings of Marx and Engels, neither of whom were much help. Their philosophy of social struggle had been totally shaped by European geopolitics and could not sufficiently explain colonial oppression.

During the height of European imperial expansion in the nineteenth century, Asia and Africa were the backwaters of the world. Colonial peoples were mainly peasants in loosely structured rural agrarian economies. There was no industrial working class. European traders and explorers generally disdained the culture, art, religion, and social institutions of the colonials. They cared only about markets, trade, minerals, raw materials, and profits.[14]

Marx and Engels wrote sparingly on colonial people and then mostly in letters to newspapers and correspondence to each other. Their views were fragmentary, often contradictory, and sometimes tinged with racism. To Marx, the Indians were "oriental despots" and the Chinese were endowed with "hereditary stupidity." The Russians did not fare much better. Russian society, he wrote, was "base and slavonic dirt." Engels' opinion of colonial people was not much better either. The Mexicans, he wrote, were "lazy," and the Algerians were "dirty fellahs."

Neither Marx nor Engels believed that colonials could contribute much to the "proletarian struggle." Engels scotched the idea that once these peasant people learned "from experience" they were oppressed they would rebel. Only the proletariat within a colonial nation, he insisted, could lead the struggle for independence.

Marx and Engels also saw benefit in French and English colonial rule. They brought order, stability, efficient government and, most importantly, capitalist economy to the "backward" peoples. Marx opposed slavery as an archaic system that impeded the growth of capitalist industry. But so did many British industrialists for almost the same reason. In none of his writings did he say anything about the status of blacks in post-Civil War America, or urge American Marxists to fight for racial equality. Marx did give future Communists a slender branch to hang their theories of self-determination on. He viewed the Irish as a colonial people crushed by the British crown. He likened their oppression to that of non-whites and supported them in their bid for independence and self-determination. With the Irish, however, Marx did not have to face the thorny issue of color.[15]

Lenin labored to bring Marxist theory in line with modern realities. However, his writings about self-determination and independence were confined mostly to non-Soviet European minorities—Finns, Poles, Czechs, and Slovaks. He argued that when minorities were oppressed by a nation's majority, Marxists should defend their right to use whatever political means they chose to end the domination. This included the right to secede: "Self determination means the political separation of these nations from alien national bodies, and the formation of an independent state." Lenin did not consider the oppressed minorities simply subject peoples but captive nations.[16]

Stalin, piggy-backing on Lenin, tried to give this concept more body. He defined a nation as a "stable community of language, territory, economic life, and psychological make-up." Neither Lenin nor Stalin ever intended that self-determination inside the Bolshevik state would lead to actual independence for any of the country's nationalities. They had in mind a sort of federation of peoples, with power resting in the hands of a strong central government.

While Lenin and Stalin advocated working-class support of nationalist movements, there was a hitch. Self-determination to Lenin did not mean support of nationalism. The working class, he stressed, should resist "the nationalist policy of every nationality." Stalin noted that the leaders of nationalist movements were always small capitalists, landowners, business people, and professionals. Once independence was gained they would exploit the workers as viciously as the capitalists. So, while Marxists should aid the nationalist movements against outside oppression, they should also undermine them and clear the way for the workers to take over. "Power," Stalin said, must pass "into the hands of the toiling masses of the nationalities." In other words, he advocated temporarily supporting the nationalists and then dumping them as quickly as possible for the proletarians.[17]

But that created problems even within the new Soviet state. Several nationalities that were persecuted under czarist rule also stiffly resisted Lenin and the Bolsheviks' policy of federation. The Muslims in southern Russia were prepared to wage war against the Bolsheviks to safeguard their religious and cultural traditions. To head off trouble, the Bolsheviks established a Commissariat of Internal Muslim Affairs in January 1918. The Commissariat promised the Muslims religious freedom, cultural autonomy, and limited self-government through their own local councils. Lenin even pledged that the Muslims could organize their own Communist Party and elect their own Central Committee.

The promises were broken as soon as the Bolsheviks consolidated their power throughout the country. Within two years, the Soviets took charge of all party and government affairs in every region. They severely restricted Muslim decision-making to minor local affairs. All major policy decisions had to carry Moscow's stamp of approval.[18]

Despite the fateful ending to the Bolsheviks' self-determination policy, these were the precedents that the Negro Commission in 1928 drew on to devise a plan for non-whites. Now all that was needed to weave this ill-shaped cloth into a smooth-fitting new garment was to find a word or two from Lenin or Stalin specifically on blacks.

Stalin was a dead-end. He had not published a single line on blacks. They scoured Lenin's treatises, speeches, letters, and pamphlets. They finally found what they were looking for in an isolated passage that Lenin seemed to have thrown in as an afterthought. Reporting to the Second Congress of the Communist International in 1920, he urged Communist parties to assist "revolutionary movements among the dependent and under-privileged nations (for example, Ireland, The American Negroes, etc.)."

It was not much, but the sought-after words were there, and blacks instantly were transformed into a subject nation like the Irish. Haywood gave it a little more polish. He called blacks an "internal colony" of American imperialism and insisted that blacks suffered the same brutalities as other colonials: "It is clear that the character of their exploitation as well as their oppression does not differ from that of the Negroes in Africa or the West Indies."

Most of the Commission members agreed with Haywood and bestowed on blacks Stalin's characteristics for a nation. They had the same language (English), culture (their religion and music), psychology (racial homogeneity), and economy (farmers and workers). Now all that was left was to pinpoint their territory. They immediately fastened on the American South.

Blacks were the majority of the population in a handful of counties in Mississippi, Georgia, and Alabama called the Black Belt region because of its dark, rich soil. Despite the northern migrations, blacks still had a claim on the land and economy of the area. As slaves and sharecroppers, Haywood stated, blacks had paid for the right to control the land with their sweat, toil, and blood.[19]

Next, the Commission set out to concoct a program for the new "Negro Nation." The fight for racial equality would hardly do. As a nation blacks must have the same right to independence and self-determination as any other majority people. The twin slogans became "full equality" and "self-determination."

In October the Comintern released a preliminary draft of the resolution. Party members in America did not learn of the policy change until the *Daily Worker* published the resolution in February 1929. It took another year for the Comintern to smooth out the crude language, make political revisions and put the final touches on it. The "Resolution on the U.S. Negro Question," released to the public in October 1930, was a stunner.

Blacks could "exercise governmental authority in the entire territory of the Black Belt" as well as negotiate their own treaties with the U.S. government. Whites that lived there would have to support the new "Negro Nation" or leave. Under the Comintern resolution, the "Negro Nation" also could secede from the U.S. if blacks so decided. "Self-determination," Pepper wrote, "means the right to establish their own state, to erect their own government, if they choose to do so."[20]

It was audacious, brash, and ridiculous, but not entirely unique. Thirty years earlier an obscure liberal reform group in Boston—the

Nationalist Education Association—came up with something remarkably similar. Since whites would never accept blacks as equals, they said "Our answer establish THE NATION." Rather than make forced removals or depend on migrations, the group would simply establish the black nation "in the far South" where the black man could be "left to govern himself." Briggs later boasted that as early as 1917 he had called for self-determination and a black nation to be carved out of several western states.[21]

Resistance Back Home

The Negro Commission may have drawn up the resolution, but most American Communists knew that it was Moscow's doing. While Party leaders were searching for a new racial policy, most did not expect Moscow to go that far. With a stroke of the pen, the Soviets proposed solving America's racial problems the way it looked to the world they had solved their own. Benjamin Gitlow, a high-ranking party official until his dethronement in 1929, swore that when Pepper returned from Moscow he confided that "had we not fallen in line we would have been severely condemned as deviators who neglect work among the Negro masses."[22]

While Pepper and the Americans may have had their arms twisted by the Soviets, it did not dampen their enthusiasm. Pepper told the comrades back home that the battle now was to establish "a Negro Soviet Republic." The Party disavowed Pepper on that one. A year later he also was expelled.

Haywood liked the resolution so much that he was ready to take on all challengers. And there were challengers. Huiswood could not stretch his imagination far enough to conceive of southern blacks as a nation. He thought it was absurd to compare the condition of blacks in America to that of blacks in Africa and the West Indies. In those countries, blacks were a majority. They had defined national boundaries and were ruled by an outside European power. Huiswood agreed that American blacks were "racially persecuted," but they were not "colonially exploited."

After dutifully citing Lenin's writings to refute Huiswood, Haywood went for the kill: "All this merely shows that comrade Huiswood's 'world aspects of the Negro question' are different from those of the Comintern." How could Huiswood dare argue with the divine Marxist word?[23]

Huiswood was not ready to quit. In August 1929 he traveled to Kingston, Jamaica to attend the UNIA convention as a representative of the ANLC. Following his deportation from the U.S. in 1927 after serving a sentence in federal prison for mail fraud, Garvey had tried to reestablish his organization in Jamaica. At the convention, Huiswood engaged Garvey in a debate on capitalism and the working class. Although he clung tightly to the Party's line, his Communist days were numbered. After 1930, Huiswood's name was no longer mentioned by the Party. He soon departed for his native Dutch Guiana for good.

Fort-Whiteman took a different route away from American communism. In October 1929 a group of Americans touring the Soviet Union at the invitation of the Society of Cultural Relations were shocked to find a black American teaching a political science class at the Cercerin Institute near Moscow. Fort-Whiteman had decided that the Soviet Union was a good place to study and lecture. It was his last stop. Fort-Whiteman did not return to America. A few years later, rumors surfaced that Fort-Whiteman was a broken man, living a penniless existence after having fallen out of favor with the Soviet government. He died just before World War II.[24]

Meanwhile, Garvey in his exile years had not mellowed toward the Communists. "We never had any confidence in the offers of Communism," he warned his followers. "We still have none." Communists were still wolves in sheeps' clothing to him. "It is true that the communistic whites pretend a kind of sympathy for and fellowship with the Negro, but that is only a means to an end." Whether whites called themselves Communists or capitalists, Garvey believed, "The Negro will always suffer from the prejudice of the dominant whites."[25]

Still, the Comintern resolution did open the racial dike. Workers Party leaders floated proposals for every conceivable kind of black organization. They demanded separate unions, farmers and tenants groups, and race congresses.

In July 1929 Ford took a break from the deliberations at the Second World Congress of the League Against Imperialism and called the black delegates together in the corridor. He was unhappy with the lack of attention black workers were getting. What was needed, he said, was a black trade organization. The blacks agreed and eventually so did the Comintern.

The result was the First International Conference of Negro Workers in Hamburg, Germany in July 1930. In his keynote speech, Ford blasted DuBois, Pickens, and Garvey for "betraying the Negro workers to the big white bourgeoisie." The Conference elected an all-black Provisional Executive Committee. Ford probably got his "Negro Workers Committee" because of the Comintern resolution—and Garvey.[26]

Back home, the Workers Party had big plans for blacks in the "Negro Nation." From here out, they would take the lead in the revolutionary struggle against capitalism. During the 1930s, James Allen, who became the Party's resident expert on the "Negro Nation," would trot out a battery of charts, statistics, and government reports to give the "Negro Nation" an aura of scholarly legitimacy. Haywood would continue to toss his "Negro nation" postulations into Allen's theoretical stew. Long after Communists had stopped talking about black separation, Haywood would still write: "Negro self-government is conceivable in the frame of our present federal system of government."[27]

Looking back, it all seems pretty strange. But the resolution did move race from the backroom of Marxist politics to center stage. Ultimately, it did more for white Communists than blacks. It forced them to shed their stereotypes and see blacks as important players in American society. White Communists realized they would have to confront head on not only the racism of white workers but their own, too. This would require nothing short of a revolution in their own thinking.

Long-time Party members were shocked to hear Party leaders say they would fight hard against "tendencies to 'soft pedal' the Negro question, and to compromise with Jim Crowism." If white members were not ready to fight, Party leaders put the word out that they were no longer welcome.[28]

The new political shift spilled over to the 1928 presidential campaign. The 1928 Workers Party platform contained sweeping demands for the abolition of all segregation, the enactment of federal lynching laws, integration of the armed services, equal employment opportunities, public accommodations, and voting rights. The platform even supported the "abolition of laws forbidding intermarriage." Foster, who was the Party's presidential candidate, showed some courage when he told southern whites during his campaign tour through Dixie that the Workers Party was going to be the "champion of the oppressed Negro race."[29]

The Communists had taken Garvey's nationalism and then reshaped and filtered it through a red sieve until it became their preposterous

"Negro Nation" scheme. Still, the resolution in a curious way came at an opportune time for American Marxists. America's racial consciousness was changing, and in the waning days of 1929 an event would shake the country that would elevate Marxists to the pinnacle of glory and bring their cherished dream of winning the black masses closer to reality.

Notes

1. *Report, Fifth Congress of the Communist International*, Moscow 17 June-8 July 1924 (London: Communist Party of Great Britain), 207, 200-1; Amy Jacques Garvey, *Garvey & Garveyism* (New York: Collier Books, 1963), 136.
2. *Negro World*, 27 August 1921; Robert Hill, ed., *Marcus Garvey and the UNIA Papers* (Berkeley: University of California Press, 1983), 4: 675-81.
3. McKay, *A Long Way from Home*, 108-9. Foster sheds some light on why the Party began to gradually see the importance of the black struggle beginning in 1921, in *History of the Communist Party of the United States* (233).
4. *Daily Worker*, 5 August 1924; Foster, *History*, 228.
5. As late as 1932, Communists persisted in placing the blame for lynchings exclusively on the capitalists. Harry Haywood wrote: "And the greatest victory for the capitalist rulers is to get white workers to be the agents of their campaign of terrorism. Lynchings defend profits!"; *Daily Worker*, 15 August 1924; *Daily Worker*, 19 August 1924.
6. Rollin Hartt, "The Negro Moses and His Campaign to Lead the Black Millions into their Promised Land," *Independent* 110 (26 February 1921): 219; *Negro World*, 16 August 1924; *Daily Worker*, 23 August 1924; Foster, *History*, 226-27; Amy Garvey, *Garvey & Garveyism*, 145.
7. *Workers Monthly* 5 (April 1926): 268-71. Minor continued the attack on Garvey in his article "After Garvey—What?" *Workers Monthly* 5 (June 1926).
8. David Cronin's *Black Moses* captures the power and dynamism the Garvey movement had among blacks. *The Communist* 4 (February 1925): 51-54.
9. *American Labor Year Book* (New York: Rand School), 130.
10. DuBois, *The Souls of Black Folk* (New York: Fawcett, 1961 [1903]); Harry Haywood, "The Negro Problem and the Tasks of the Communist Party of the United States," *The Communist International*, 5 September 1928.
11. Haywood, "The Negro Problem,"; Haywood, *Black Bolshevik*, 227-35, 246-68; Benjamin Gitlow, *I Confess*, (New York: E.P. Dutton, 1940), 452-56.

12. Gitlow and Lovestone describe the political and social scene in Moscow during the days surrounding the Congress; Jay Lovestone, "The Sixth World Congress," *The Communist* 7 (September 1928): 673-74; *Communist International*, 5 September 1928; Interview with Don Wheeldin, 2 December 1989.

13. Mike Gold, "William L. Patterson: Militant Leader," *Masses & Mainstream* 3 (February 1951): 36-43; *The Communist International*, 28 August 1928.

14. *International Press Correspondence*, 30 October 1928; Draper, *American Communism and Soviet Russia*, 345-47. Of the many books that have discussed nineteenth-century European Imperial expansion in the Third World, I have found Paul Kennedy, *The Rise and Fall of the Great Powers* (New York: Random House, 1987); David Horowitz, *Empire and Revolution* (New York: Random House, 1969); J. A. Hobson, *Imperialism* (New York: Monthly Review Press, 1967 [1938]); and Walter Rodney, *How Europe Underdeveloped Africa* (Dar es Salaam, Tanzania: Tanzania Publishing House, 1972) to be the most useful.

15. *New York Tribune*, 14 June 1853; *New York Tribune*, 12 April 1853; *New York Daily Tribune*, 8 February 1860. Horace B. Davis presents a summary of the newspaper articles of Marx and Engels on colonial problems in *Nationalism and Socialism* (New York: Monthly Review Press, 1967), 59-71. For a collection of their correspondence on the Third World see Shlomo Avineri, *Karl Marx on Colonialism and Modernization* (New York: Doubleday, 1969). Marx's lengthy writings on Ireland were collected in Karl Marx, *Ireland and the Irish Question* (New York: International Publishers, 1969).

16. V. I. Lenin, "The Right of Nations to Self-Determination," in *The Lenin Anthology*, edited by Robert C. Tucker (New York: Norton, 1975), 154; Wilson Record, "The Communist Position on the National Question," *Phylon* 19 (Fall 1958): 312-16.

17. J. V. Stalin, *Marxism and the National Question* (New York: International Publishers, 1942), 12 and 23; Lenin, "The Right of Nations to Self Determination," 166.

18. N. N. Agarwal, *Soviet Nationalities Policy* (Agra, India: Sri Ram Mehra and Co., 1969), 225-27; Joseph S. Roucek, "The Soviet Treatment of Minorities," *Phylon* 22 (Spring 1961): 15-23; Nahaylo and Swoboda, *Soviet Disunion*, 32-59.

19. V. I. Lenin, *Selected Works,* vol. 10 (New York: International Publishers, 1967), 235; Harry Haywood, "Against Bourgeois-Liberal Distortions of Leninism on the Negro Question in the United States," *The Communist* 9 (August 1930): 704; Draper, *American Communism and Soviet Russia*, 346-47.

20. *Daily Worker,* 12 February 1929; "Resolution on the Negro Question in the United States," *The Communist* 9 (January 1930) 48-55; Pepper, *American Negro Problems,* 10-12.

21. *The Nationalist* (Boston: The Nationalist Education Association, 1890), 96-97; Briggs to Pat Alexander, 8 May 1957, Briggs Papers, Southern California Research Library; Interview with Don Wheeldin, December 2, 1989.

22. Gitlow, *I Confess,* 481.

23. *International Press Correspondence,* 8 August 1928, 811-12; Otto Huiswood, "World Aspects of the Negro Problem," *The Communist* 9 (February 1930): 132-47; Pepper, *American Negro Problems,* 11; Haywood, "The Negro Question," 704-5.

24. *Kingston Gleaner,* 15 August 1929; Cronon, *Black Moses,* 152-53; Draper, *American Communism and Soviet Russia,* 353; *Chicago Whip,* 6 August 1929.

25. *The Black Man* 11, no. 1 (May-June 1936): 2-3; *The Black Man,* 11, no. 3 (September-October 1936): 8-9.

26. *Daily Worker,* 9 March 1929; *Daily Worker,* 11 March 1929; *Daily Worker,* 16 May 1929; *Proceedings and Decisions of the First International Conference of Negro Workers Hamburg, Germany* (International Trade Union Committee of Negro Workers, 1930), 30-35.

27. James Allen, *The Negro Question in the United States* (New York: International Publishers, 1936); Allen, "The Black Belt: Area of Negro Majority," *The Communist* 13 (June 1934): 581-84; Haywood, *Negro Liberation* (New York: International Publishers, 1948), 166.

28. Foster, "The Workers Party in the South," *The Communist* 7 (September 1928): 681; "Resolution on the Negro Question," *The Communist* 9 (January 1930): 51-53.

4 The Hey Day

As the decade of the Great Depression began, the Workers Party, now renamed the Communist Party, was still politically distant from most blacks. The ANLC had failed. The Party had struck out with Garvey, the NAACP, and black labor groups. But time and events were on their side.

By 1932, one out of two blacks were out of work in New York, Chicago, Philadelphia, and Detroit. Thirty-two percent of black families were on relief. "Last hired, first fired" became the practice in major industry toward blacks. White men and women no longer sneered at restaurant, hotel, and porter jobs as "Negro jobs." They elbowed blacks aside and gladly snapped them up.

In Atlanta, unemployed whites formed "Black Shirt" vigilante groups to prevent blacks from working. Their slogan was "No Jobs for Niggers Until Every White Man Has a Job." Blacks fared little better in the nation's soup kitchens. Many religious and charitable organizations drew a color line around their pots and storehouses and refused to ladle out any food or clothing to blacks.[1]

Franklin Delano Roosevelt would be well into his second term as president before blacks saw any appreciable change in their plight. Only then would some of the benefits of his New Deal programs begin to trickle down to the black poor. In the meantime, what could poverty-stricken blacks do?

Many turned to the Reds. Sociologists St. Clair Drake and Horace Cayton, who chronicled life on Chicago's southside during the 1930s, pointed out that even middle-class blacks had something good to say about the Communists. "Some preachers," they wrote, "opposed the Reds publicly, but remarked privately, 'If the Reds can feed the people let them.'" The *Chicago Defender* said of the Party, "We do whole-heartedly agree with the zealousness with which it guards the rights of the race."[2]

Changing Its Racial Face

Party leaders were determined that past failures would not hamper them in their drive to give blacks a new place in Communist ranks. After much internal political debate, they conceded that few white Communists actually practiced the idealistic resolutions on civil, political, and social equality that the Party passed. Communists idealized the black worker in their Party literature, but few really accepted blacks as the social equal of whites. Communists might agree that blacks should have their rights, but fighting with them for those rights was something else. Marxist dogma simply had not prepared whites for that experience.

To help his white comrades overcome their racial blinders, black Communist Cyril Briggs announced that the moment had come for the Party "to push the Negro comrades to the front in Party work." As early as 1929, he revealed that the Party had established a National Negro Department to formulate policies and direct all future work among blacks. Blacks were expected to take the lead in all future party activities.

Party leaders moved feverishly to create new programs for miners, tenants, laundry workers, and fig and date workers. Blacks were elected to the National Executive Committee, the Party's supreme policy-making body. Ford's criticism of the Communist failure to organize black workers rang loudly in the ears of Party leaders.

They agreed with him that Communists had spent too much time courting the NAACP and the Garveyites when they should have been organizing black workers. "The creation of working class organizations and the extension of our influence in the existing working class Negro organizations," Browder observed, "are of much greater importance than the work in bourgeois and petty bourgeois organizations."[3]

Party leaders no longer shied away when detractors mockingly labeled them "the Negro party." Not only did they now take the accusation as a compliment, they were proud to show what Briggs called their "Negro face." Briggs got the ball rolling. He cited a number of cases where blacks were discriminated against by whites. He announced that the Party would begin to enforce the Comintern policy which called for expelling whites guilty of racist acts. "The time is ripe to begin with the Party a courageous campaign of self-criticism concerning the work among Negroes."

The first wave of expulsions shook the Party in the fall of 1929. In Seattle, St. Louis, Chicago, and Norfolk, Virginia, whites were summarily given the boot for acts of "white chauvinism" against blacks. As Briggs saw it, blacks would not join the Party unless the racists were purged.

And he was right. In Chicago and St. Louis, black members had dropped out of the Party in protest against the racist acts by whites. In Philadelphia, he said that white racism had split the branch so badly that more than forty-five blacks and whites quit the Party. Unless Party leaders "rooted" white chauvinism out, he warned, Communists would continue to lose the few black supporters they had. Briggs said that he had heard blacks denounce the Party as being "just like the Republican, Democratic and Socialist parties."

Communists looked anxiously for some sign that their anti-racist campaign was succeeding. Otto Hall happily reported that a group of striking white textile workers in Gastonia, North Carolina had saved him from a near lynching during an organizing expedition in the region. "The Southern white workers soon learned that all this talk of race superiority did not mean anything to the exploited workers."[4]

Party leaders recognized that disciplining white members was a volatile issue that had to be approached carefully. If the Party expelled every white that committed a racist act, it ran the risk of alienating white workers from the Party. Many of these whites had proven themselves to be dedicated and loyal Party workers. To simply dump them would create ill feelings that could permanently cripple a small, politically weak organization.

Yet another problem existed. If the Party got rid of the "white chauvinists," who would replace them? There was no guarantee that a vigorous campaign against white racism would draw more blacks into the Party. Still, the National Committee had to send a message to blacks that they were wanted and to whites to do their part to make them feel wanted. Briggs called on "the Negro comrades" to take the lead in "exposing" and "cleansing our Party" of the white racists.[5] Throughout 1930, whites in the Party were on guard. Even the slightest racial indiscretion, they knew, could bring a reprimand. But it still did not solve the problem. Many Communists continued to commit flagrant racial acts that embarrassed the leadership.

In November, 1930, the Party received a protest letter from a black mother who sent her two sons to a scout camp in Beacon, New York, run by the Workers International Relief. She charged that the camp's white manager called the boys "niggers" and sent them home before the camp ended.

When her letter was not answered, the boys' father sent letters to black newspapers denouncing the Party for not expelling the manager. He threatened to launch a nationwide protest to "expose those who preach one doctrine and practice another." Ever alert for any opportunity to slam their adversaries, Marcus Garvey's anti-Communist *Negro World* made the incident a feature story, under the heading "Communist Jim Crow." Party leaders promised to investigate the incident.

Still the Communist Party continued to have an image problem. Most blacks paid little attention to what the Party was doing. For the few who did, the Beacon incident only heightened their suspicions about the Communists. It still looked to them as if the racial etiquette of white Communists was no better than that of other whites. Even more damaging, they could not see where blacks were being given any significant decision-making authority in the Party: "We have no objection to any Negro flirting with Communism," the *Negro World* cautioned, "but as we have often pointed out they become YES MEN to the Communist leaders."

A young recruit to the Party in Alabama had his own jaundiced view of how the Party operated at the top. Hosea Hudson called it a "two class" system, with a few whites making policy and the blacks at the bottom carrying out the marching orders. Party leaders knew they were being watched. "The Negro masses," Browder told a group of students at the Party's training school, "know everything that goes on in our Party that relates to the Negro question."[6]

In January 1931, Party leaders decided to get tougher. They would make racism within the Party a crime. Their new-hard line policy required a test case, someone who would serve as both example and warning to other whites.

Stalin had provided a brutal model for the Americans with his first round of show trials in the late 1920s. At Stalin's behest, the Soviet Central Committee would convene a "people's court" where the luckless victims would be put on trial and forced to confess their "crimes" against the people. The accused were usually old Bolsheviks who had challenged Stalin's rule. A guilty verdict was a foregone conclusion.

62

Other potential deviates from the Party's edicts quickly fell in line. American Communists prepared to follow Moscow's example. Now all the Party needed was its own sacrificial lamb to lower the ax on.[7]

Show Trials—American Style

The January evening in 1931 began like any other for the stocky, pleasant-faced janitor at the Finnish Workers Club in Harlem. August Yokinen usually came to the hall straight from work to socialize with his friends, most of whom were Communists like him. The club was a popular meeting place for the small Finnish community in New York.

On weekends the club sponsored socials and dances that he frequently attended. The Finn was grateful to the Party. When he arrived in America, Yokinen, like many newly arrived immigrants, was penniless and without friends or relatives to depend on. With the Depression grinding on, the prospects for a man like Yokinen with little education were not particularly bright, but the Communists had come to his rescue and secured him his janitor's job.

Apparently he did not completely understand the ways of America. Nor did he know much about blacks, since he had had little contact with them. So, on that January evening when he noticed three black men enter the club, he was apprehensive. The three men had come to the club for the dance. Almost immediately, they noticed they were getting frowns and icy stares from the others in the room. The room got quieter and quieter. Soon the music stopped, and couples scurried from the dance floor. The three blacks heard the men cursing and muttering threats. They did not know it then, but some of the whites actually wanted to throw them out of the hall. The men took the hint and left.

What Yokinen did not know was that the three men were also CP members. They promptly reported the incident to Party headquarters. A few days later the Harlem Section was asked to investigate. They wasted no time. The investigators wanted to know who the Communists at the hall had been and what they had done to defend the three blacks.

They called in three Party members for questioning. Two of them immediately caved in and "admitted their mistake." They apologized for not coming to the aid of the three blacks. They agreed that they should have "thrown out" the racists. The investigators, satisfied with their confession and their contrition, sent them on their way with a warning to behave.[8]

Yokinen did not fare as well. He was a proud man. He could not see where he had done anything wrong. He liked things at the club just the way they were. If blacks started coming, he said, they might monopolize the pool tables and try to take baths at the club. Yokinen, for one, did not relish the idea of having to bathe with them. Under questioning, he stubbornly insisted that he had not done anything wrong.

The investigators had heard enough. They had their scapegoat. A recommendation was made to the District Committee that he be disciplined. A few days later he got his "summons" to appear March 1 at the Worker's Court to be convened at the Harlem Casino. Yokinen was going to stand trial for "views and practices" that bring "disunity among the Negro and white workers." He was also accused of violating the "fundamental laws of the Communist Party."

The Party appointed a judge to try the "case." Clarence Hathaway, head of the New York District Committee, was to conduct the prosecution. Yokinen's fate would be decided by a racially balanced jury of seven blacks and seven whites. The jurors were Communist Party members.

More than 1,500 Party members and sympathizers from 113 "fraternal organizations" packed the Harlem Casino on trial day. It had almost a carnival air. Many black women held babies in their arms. Party members strolled through the aisles hawking Communist literature and buttons. The walls were draped with signs reading "Smash All Jim Crow Laws," "Race Inferiority is White Ruling Class Lie," and so on. The Party even provided black reporters with their own press table. Four police officers stood stiffly at the door, alert for any disturbance. The star attraction sat on stage, his eyes cast down. A button with the hammer and sickle dangled loosely from his shirt lapel.

Richard Moore was chosen to handle the Finn's "defense." Since the collapse of the Communist-run American Negro Labor Congress the previous year, he had served as director of the Negro Department of the International Labor Defense. To insure a speedy trial and quick verdict, Party leaders decided not to call any defense or prosecution witnesses.

Hathaway did not have to establish his guilt; the Finn defiantly admitted it. All he had to do was present the "facts' of the case, and let the jury decide the guilty man's fate. Hathaway approached his job with delight. The "prosecutor" contended that Yokinen had imbibed all the racist myths and stereotypes about blacks. In a rambling

64

discourse, Hathaway indicted Wall Street, the Hearst press, and the Republican and Democratic parties along with Yokinen for their oppression of blacks. He demanded that Yokinen be found guilty to show black workers "that our promises about equality are not just words."[9]

The defense was brief. Moore argued that Yokinen should not be blamed for his crimes. He was only an innocent dupe taken in by the "capitalist chauvinist propaganda through church, press, and school." He pleaded for mercy and recommended "a period of probation." If he carried out all the conditions that Hathaway set, he would be reinstated to Party membership.

Hathaway had the last word, and he was not buying the plea for leniency. The man was guilty. His tough line was not difficult to understand. Yokinen was not on trial, the Party was. Communists had their eyes focused squarely on blacks outside the Party and whites inside the Party.

Hathaway bellowed to the crowd: "Our Party must prove in action that we are ready to fight unflinchingly on behalf of Negro rights." As for the whites, he noted that some white Party members thought the trial "was specially staged, that it did not mean a thing." This was precisely the reason, Hathaway insisted, that Yokinen be severely punished to show "the determination of the Communist Party to burn white chauvinism out of its ranks." The vote was unanimous: Yokinen was found guilty. As punishment, he was assigned to work on "definite tasks" to "fight for Negro rights."[10]

The Yokinen trial was a hit in the press. The *New York Times* featured it on page one. Newspapers across the nation picked up the story. Communist leaders patted themselves on the back. Browder boasted that the Party had declared "war on white chauvinism." But many Communists remained skeptical. They doubted that a stacked-deck "trial" would polish the Party's image among blacks. A white Harlem Communist leader came close to the truth. Nothing looked worse, Vera Sanders said, than a black worker telling the world "that the Communists tried to push him out of their hall."

To Party leaders, this was sour grapes. They had their victory over racism and for the next year and a half the mass trial became the rage among Communists. They searched everywhere for the next Yokinen. Communists agreed that each trial must be given intense publicity to "educate the masses." In the wake of the Yokinen trial, many white Party members walked on eggshells. They knew that one wrong word or a furtive glance at a black might send them to the defendant's docket, and no one wanted to be another Yokinen.[11]

As always, there were slow learners. Joe Burns, a lowly Party worker in Brooklyn, had to sit for five hours at the Harlem Casino and listen to the Communist "prosecutor" accuse him of every act of racism imaginable. Burns was on trial for getting into a shoving match with Maude White, a black Party member. During the heated exchange between the two, Burns allegedly shouted that "Negro workers do not show any appreciation for all we have done for them." Burns was found guilty and placed on probation for six months.

In May 1932 three whites who were members of the Young Communist League found themselves on "trial." They belonged to the Amil Athletic Club in Detroit and the club barred blacks. The Party chose a judge, prosecutor, and a mixed jury of black and white workers. The trio were quickly found guilty of "acts against the working class" and expelled.

A leading Communist organizer in New Jersey thought "it was purely a personal matter" when his daughter declined to dance with a black man at an International Labor Defense dance in July 1932. After he was called on the carpet by Party investigators, he pleaded that he was in "the habit of talking with Negroes." The next month he had a chance to do more talking when he was brought before a "people's court." He was accused of being in "agreement with the Southern landlords and bosses" and drummed out of the Party.

After a Bronx furniture worker and Party stalwart foolishly called a Party demonstration against a swimming pool that excluded blacks "a waste of time," he was put on trial. The jury decided he should have known that "it was his duty to educate the working class." He, too, was expelled.

In Buffalo, local Communist officials found themselves in hot water when they moved a little too slowly against a guilty member. The secretary of the Workers International Relief Center in Buffalo excluded black children from a Party picnic. When asked the reason, he said all the seats at the picnic tables were filled. The local Party Secretariat did not buy his excuse. He was charged with "abuse, discrimination, and concealed white chauvinism." A "mass trial" was ordered. However, this time the victim would not cooperate. Calling the charges "a frame up," he refused to attend his trial. The Secretariat waffled. Instead of putting him on trial, the members of the Secretariat decided to "discuss the issue further with him." The *Daily Worker* found their actions inexcusable. "It is no accident," wrote *Daily Worker* columnist Ethel Stevens, "that Negroes will not join the Workers International Relief when such individuals are around."[12]

Young Communists who were being trained at the Party's school apparently were learning lessons not among the course curricula. In early 1932, Browder received a disturbing report that white and black students at the Party's cadre training school were "dividing into groups against each other." Browder warned that any students who did not fight white racism would find themselves "outside the Party."[13]

Whether the Party ran out of steam, lost too many members, or the mass trials had simply outlived their usefulness, in 1933 Party leaders decided to put a stop to the show trials. Browder compared the trials to an outdated auto: "We have begun to develop a certain 'Model T' white chauvinist trial, the quality of which is very bad." In the future, he said, the Party would scrap the "mass production" trials and correct the "bad workmanship." In effect, he was conceding that the mass trials were ineffectual and that racism was still alive and well in the Party. Browder further concluded that the trials had done little to "educate" whites about the importance of "Negro work." He demanded that National Committee members step up their efforts to train blacks for Party leadership positions.

Even though the campaign was shelved, whites were on notice that they would still be held accountable for any racial misbehavior. "One cannot be a Communist and a white chauvinist at the same time," the Committee cautioned, "White chauvinists are not allowed to remain in the Party."

The Party's "war against white chauvinism" may have ended in a stalemate but it was not a total loss. Party leaders believed they had shaken the white rank and file out of their inertia toward blacks. Whites calling other whites racist and blacks sitting in judgment on whites were obviously novel departures that had to have some impact. Also, by 1932 the Party had brought thousands of whites into the streets, marching against mob violence and Jim Crow employment and living conditions. It all added up to a changing political climate.

Dorothy Healey, who at the time was a recent convert to the Communist cause, agrees that the "war against white chauvinism" was a turning point for the whites in the Party: "Despite some of the silliness that went on, it shook many whites out of their complacency that they were somehow immune to racism." Party stalwart Louise

Thompson Patterson also thought that it was good therapy for many whites: "Too many whites felt that they had all the answers, and that blacks were there to learn from them. Well, they got a rude jolt." There would be many more.[14]

New Campaigns

With Depression bread lines lengthening, Communists prepared to fan out on as many fronts as their meager troops and resources would allow. One of them was the South. On street corners in Birmingham, Atlanta, Memphis, and in many backwater rural hamlets in Dixie, blacks and whites did double takes at the sight of whites actually marching for civil rights and not leading lynch mobs. When William Z. Foster took his Communist presidential campaign south in 1928, he promised that the Party would build an integrated organization throughout the South and they did.[15]

By 1932 there were functioning Party chapters in North Carolina, Virginia, Georgia, Alabama, and Florida. Communists in Virginia boldly declared that "there was no truth whatever to white superiority." While many southern whites were not particularly thrilled to hear this, blacks were.

Despite massive hostility from police and public officials, Communists actually were able to make some gains in the South. More than five thousand blacks in Talooposa, Alabama joined the Communist-run Sharecroppers Union in 1932. Hundreds of blacks signed up in the Party's unemployed councils in Atlanta and Birmingham. The councils fought pitched street battles with police in both cities for unemployment relief.

Communists were rewarded in Alabama and Georgia when they found two young black men who emerged as daring leaders. Hosea Hudson in Alabama and Angelo Herndon in Georgia would give the Party greater visibility and stature among blacks.[16]

A pipe fitter and foundry worker, Hudson joined the Party in 1931 and was assigned to unemployment organizing in Birmingham. Since blacks and whites were strictly forbidden by state law from mingling, he used every conceivable ploy to stay a step ahead of the authorities. He did his work well. By 1933, Communists were leading job and relief marches on city halls in Birmingham and Atlanta that sometimes drew thousands of poor blacks and whites. As Hudson later recalled, blacks were at the center of the action. "Up in the top years, in '33,

68

'34, '35, the Party in Birmingham and Alabama was dominated by Negroes. We had only a few white, and I mean a few white."[17]

Herndon was a different story. He spent his early years laboring in coal mines in Kentucky and Alabama until the Depression caught up with him. Drifting about the streets of Birmingham in 1929, the jobless Herndon happened to pick up a leaflet printed by the newly formed Birmingham Unemployed Council. The leaflet, addressed to the "workers of Birmingham," contained seventeen demands that ranged from abolition of child labor to outlawing segregation. He was thunderstruck. "All my life I'd been sweated and stepped on and Jim-Crowed." He immediately joined the Party. Communists were eager to find a place for a young energetic black like Herndon. In 1930, he was elected a delegate to the National Unemployment Convention in Chicago.

Following the convention, he returned to Atlanta to organize the unemployed. Under his leadership, the Unemployed Committee of Atlanta increased its activities in the city. For weeks, during the spring of 1932, the Committee flooded the city with leaflets appealing to the jobless: "Organize and fight for unemployment insurance at the expense of the government and the bosses! Demand immediate payment of the bonus to the ex-servicemen."

After a demonstrations and clashe with police in July 1932, he became a marked man. The following January he was indicted for insurrection, found guilty, and sentenced to 18 to 20 years on a Georgia chain gang. Georgia had given the Communists another martyr.

For the next five years, the Party had two prime cases that it held up as symbols of oppression. Herndon was one. But Herndon paled in importance to the Scottsboro Boys case, the famous case in which nine young black men were charged with the rape of two white prostitutes in Alabama in 1931. The Party raised money, staged marches and demonstrations, and rallied national and international support in defense of the young blacks. The case boosted the prestige of the Party enormously among blacks nationally.[18]

As more whites protested racial injustice and demanded relief, the Party was ready to take credit. In a report to the Alabama District Committee, Party organizer Robert Hall bragged: "A trade union worker who, after years of prejudice, learns that he must organize together with the Negro worker and struggle shoulder to shoulder with him remembers that it was the Communist Party who first told him that great truth."[19]

While the South was a major battleground, Party leaders had not forgotten the North. Scarcely a day passed without the Communist-run Harlem or Chicago Tenants League putting some furniture back into the home or apartment of a poor black evicted for non-payment of rent. A picket line thrown up by the Communist unemployed councils in front of relief offices became such a common sight passerbys barely gave the demonstrators a second look.

On more than one occasion, Communists put several thousand marchers in the streets of Harlem heading for City Hall to demand the end to discrimination in relief payments. If overzealous police attacked marchers, city officials knew that the Communists would quickly muster their forces for even bigger protest marches. When police fired on a crowd of blacks in Chicago in 1932, the Party led a funeral procession of several thousand blacks through southside streets with placards that read "death penalty to the murderers."

Jazz musician Duke Ellington was so impressed with the spirit the Reds aroused in Harlem that he agreed to provide entertainment for a Party sponsored-dance at Harlem's Rockland Palace in March 1931. More than one thousand black and white activists showed up for the affair. In between dancing to Ellington, they sang the Internationale, watched an interracial dance troupe, and listened to speeches by Party leaders. Foster, basking in the glow of the evening's revelry, promised to "organize Negro workers side by side with white workers" and that the Communists would be in the street shouting "death penalty to the murderers."[20]

Briggs and Party activist Eugene Gordon also thought the Party should pay more attention to black women. With the Depression tossing thousands of men out of work, black women often were the only ones able to find work in the black community. They considered black women the most exploited part of the work force: "The dirty deal that falls to all working women in capitalist society falls heaviest on the Negro woman worker." But Party leaders let the ball drop here. This was the 1930s, and when Communists thought of the proletarian struggle they generally thought of men first. Party leaders never came up with any systematic plan to organize or recruit women into the Party.

Communists always tried to spot young blacks with leadership ability. If they spotted talent they felt could be useful to the Party, they would provide the recruit with a "scholarship" to their Workers School in Harlem to take courses on the "Problems of Negro Liberation

70

Movement," "Traditions of the Negro People," and "Principles of Organization." If they could not read or write, as many could not, the Party offered a basic English class.[21]

For the dreamers, who looked beyond the mundane grind of daily life in Harlem or Chicago's southside, the Party provided a fantastic vision of utopia. Foster promised that, under a "United Soviet States of America," racism "will be punished as a serious crime of society." Foster would also confiscate land from "the great landowners" and redistribute it free to blacks.

Ford and Party racial theoretician James Allen outdid Foster. In 1935 they published a rhapsodic scenario of black life in the United States under Bolshevik rule. Jim Crow signs would be thrown on bonfires, thousands of school buildings would be built, free medical and health care would be provided for all, old plantations would be confiscated and turned over to local Soviets or land committees composed of poor farmers and sharecroppers who would run them as state farms, and dozens of blacks would be elected Senators and Congressmen. Ford and Allen then tossed in the obligatory Comintern line: "One of the first steps of the central Soviet government will be to grant the right of self-determination to the Negro people in the Black belt." The new nation would include the area that extended from Atlanta to Little Rock, with New Orleans and Savannah thrown in.[22]

Despite their best efforts, Communists were well aware it was one thing to attract blacks to the party but quite another to keep them in the ranks. "Very few Negroes," Party General Secretary William Weinstone complained in a report on black party membership, "have been organized into revolutionary trade unions and unemployed councils." A Party head count in 1934 claimed that blacks comprised thirteen percent of the nineteen thousand Party members.

That figure was probably high. Skeptical Party watchers always subtracted numbers from whatever totals the Communists released. They charged that the Party commonly carried blacks on the membership rolls long after they had dropped out or were inactive.

Still, by 1934 many diverse Harlem organizations had begun to open their doors to the Party. Ford claimed that there were "Red factions" in the Elks, Phi Beta and Alpha Phi fraternities, women's auxiliary groups, and black churches. At one service at Abyssinian Baptist Church, Adam Clayton Powell Sr. listened as Ford delivered the "sermon" for the day to hundreds of worshippers at his church.[23] Through 1934 and 1935, hundreds of blacks walked in from Harlem and

Chicago's mean streets to sign Party membership cards and attend meetings. The Party seemed to offer an instant panacea to their crushing burdens. When the Communists could not deliver fast enough, it cost them.

Louis Sass, organizational Secretary of the Harlem Section, pointed to the dilemma: "We have lost many sincere revolutionary Negroes who have joined the party expecting a solution to their problem." That was not the only problem. The members that did stay were not the ones the Party wanted. "We have built the League of Struggle for Negro Rights from the unemployed and the petty bourgeoisie," Sass observed.

Even the most dedicated Communist could not build a proletarian movement without the proletarians. Party leaders tried to find some way to stop the revolving door. In 1935 they ordered all sections to organize more marches, demonstrations, and recruitment drives. Individual letters were sent over Ford's signature to all Negro "comrades" and "sympathizers" imploring them to join the Party. Laggard members were urged to get more involved in Party work.[24]

Harlem's eleven branches were always the flagship branches for the Party. For five years the Party steadily worked to create a Communist presence in the area. It was slow going at the start. In 1929 a Lenin Memorial Drive netted only two recruits. Two years later, the picture had not improved much.

Weinstone reported to the Eleventh Party Plenum in 1931 that "very few members have been brought into the Party as a result of the Scottsboro campaign, very few Negroes have been organized into the revolutionary trade unions and the unemployed councils." As late as 1933, Browder was still convinced that Party leaders were not giving their all to black organizing: "I am quite sure that the pamphlet, 'The Communist Position on the Negro Question,' has not been taken seriously as the basis of political education of every leader in our Party."[25]

Never one to understate figures, Ford estimated in 1935 that the Harlem branches had "an active core of about 200 members." Sass was not as generous. He guessed that only about 12 to 60 members bothered to show up regularly at the meetings. The task of reporting on the progress of black recruiting in 1935 fell on the shoulders of New York District Committee member, Jack Stachel. He told the National Committee that there were 2,227 blacks, less than 10 percent of the membership. Stachel tried to put a cheery note in his report by pointing out that the current year's recruiting drive netted 792 blacks.

At the Ninth Party convention in 1936, Party leaders mercifully relieved him of his reporting duties. This time F. Brown delivered the count. The messenger may have changed but the news was still the same. Said Brown, "the percentage of Negro workers in our Party is practically the same as two years ago." Party leaders chafed at Brown's charge that they had failed "to connect such struggles" around Scottsboro, Herndon, the Negro Congress, and Ethiopia "with mass recruiting of Negro workers."

Harlem organizer George Charney gave Party leaders something to smile about in 1938. In a report to a convention of the Harlem Division in May, he said that the number of new members doubled between 1936 and 1938, yet only thirty percent were black. They were less pleased to hear him say that "several thousand members were lost in the course of five years." The Party was also plagued by members who failed to pay their dues and avoided doing any organizing work.[26]

Black Communists frequently complained that not only were the training and education they received superficial, but the Party failed to provide adequate meeting facilities. Ford, who usually brushed off most gripes about the Party's actions, had to side with the critics on this one. He observed that Party training "dwarfed the training of Negro Communists." With the hindsight of passing years, Charney commented that "we never quite knew to what degree, if any, the idea of Socialism penetrated the minds of the party members."[27] Even though the Communists appeared to be sincere in their battles against segregation, and for relief for the black poor, they could not overcome all of the old doubts and suspicions. Any racial incident within Party ranks was enough to open the Pandora's box of criticism and lead to renewed charges that the Communists were insensitive to blacks.[28]

The bold headline in the *Amsterdam News* in September 1936, "Communists Expel Ex-Candidate," did just that. The man expelled was Charles White. Many Harlem blacks could not believe that the Party would unceremoniously dump White after all the valued work he had done for the Reds. White had been the Party's candidate for New York state senator in 1934. The Party sent him on important missions to Moscow. He was a section organizer for the Young Communist League. When the *Amsterdam News* asked for an explanation, Theodore Bassett, the Party's educational director in Harlem, complied. White was dropped, Bassett said, because of "petty bourgeois nationalist tendencies, factional indiscipline, inactivity, and negligence of his tasks and general irresponsibility."

As broad as Bassett's catchall list of reasons was, the charge of nationalism was the most serious. By this, Communists meant that blacks had rejected the Marxist international class-organizing approach for an exclusively black-organizing approach. To Communist leaders, this was tantamount to racism-in-reverse and would further split white workers from black workers. For a black Party member to be called a nationalist ranked only a shade under a white member being tagged a chauvinist. Both were high crimes in the Party. Blacks who questioned the Party's racial practices too vigorously were nearly always hit with the charge.

And White did level a damaging array of racial accusations against the Party. He accused white Communists of removing blacks from the posts of district and state organizers, refusing to hire blacks in apartment buildings and businesses they owned, and firing all the blacks who worked for the Amtorg Soviet Trading Corp. This was a Party-run business to promote trade and economic ties with the Soviet Union. White said the Party kicked him out to cover its "lily whiteism."

After Bassett called him a liar, White snapped "let them show one Negro working there." Bassett did not feel it was necessary to "answer the allegations" of an "enemy of the working class, and all progressive forces." He did offer to reinstate White within six months if he "corrected his errors." Neither Bassett nor White really believed that a reconciliation would happen.[29]

Four years later, an embittered White told the House Appropriations Committee that the Communists were "capitalizing on the hunger of the unemployed." His career as a Communist was over. But the odor of the scandal lingered in the air.[30]

Taking Care of Their Own

The bread and butter issues that directly hit blacks in their pocketbooks were the issues that won over the community and brought fresh recruits to the Party. So in 1930 Communists decided to put themselves directly in the business of relief. They formed the International Workers Order Mutual Benefit Society.

The IWO was a hybrid organization that combined political agitation, social welfarism, and insurance benefits. Initially, the IWO confined its assistance to sick and aged Party members. Needy members could receive groceries and occasionally a few dollars to tide them over. An ailing dues-paying member could receive as much as $10.00 a week. If the member had tuberculosis, the IWO would shell out a "consumptive benefit" payment of up to $20.00 per week. If the member died, the Society covered funeral costs, bought a cemetery plot, and paid survivors benefits up to $2,000. For $9 yearly, the IWO would write a policy guaranteeing payments up to $1,000. The plan caught on. By 1936, the IWO had more than thirty-one thousand members in seven hundred branches nationwide.[31]

It was even more popular than the Party because it provided help and it tried to bring some fun into the grim business of political organizing. In November 1936, IWO branch leaders on Chicago's southside challenged the Harlem branches to a recruitment contest. They made the recruitment drive a football game. The branch who could score "more touchdowns" (new members) won. The victorious "coach" of the southside team "proved that she knew IWO football as well as the best of them." As head of the winning team she got a gold engraved gavel for a prize.

The members enjoyed coming to the meetings because they knew they would not have to sit through lengthy lectures on Marxism or be regaled by Party leaders about their proletarian responsibilities. Instead, they could relax and watch movies, skits, or dances. For months, Langston Hughes' IWO-sponsored proletarian mixed-media play "Don't You Want to Be Free" was staged before packed houses in Harlem. Throughout 1937, the IWO sent Hughes on a twelve-city tour with the play.[32]

In 1936 Samuel Patterson, the IWO's New York Field Organizer, spent four months on the road trying to build up black support. Patterson reported that there were "healthy branches in Negro neighborhoods" in Newark, Detroit, Chicago, Harlem, Cleveland, and Philadelphia. He told IWO leaders that blacks would support the organization only if they saw whites fighting for black rights. Patterson singled out the branches in Harlem, Philadelphia, and Norfolk as good examples of interracial unity. In Philadelphia, he said, blacks joined the branch "because there the white members began to join in the campaigns for Negro rights not only in Negro communities but in the white neighborhoods as well." In Harlem, Patterson reported that white members visited sick black members in their homes, and in Norfolk he found that whites willingly served as pall-bearers at funerals for black members.

The IWO continued to make headway with blacks throughout 1937. Dozens of local black organizations in Los Angeles participated in an

IWO-sponsored conference for Constitutional Rights For Negroes in April. The Kappa and Alpha Fraternity, Central Baptist Church, and the United American Democratic Club sent representatives. The principal speakers were either blacks or prominent white liberals such as noted author Carey McWilliams. Mrs. Jessie Terry, President of the Negro Democratic Group, was elected conference chairperson.

The IWO always kept its targets a little softer than the Party's. In Homestead, Pennsylvania, the Order picketed a theater that segregated blacks to the balcony. It passed indignant resolutions demanding that the baseball owners open the American and National Leagues to black baseball players, and called on Roosevelt to strengthen the Social Security and the Old Age Pension Acts.[33]

Black members took full advantage of the informal political atmosphere in the branches. They had more freedom to be themselves or even not to be themselves. A black recruit in Jersey City was assigned to a branch of mostly Ukrainian workers. He liked the Ukrainians so much that he began to learn their language. There were no reports on whether the four blacks in the Italian branch in Youngstown actually took up Italian, or whether the blacks in the Jewish branch in New Jersey took up Yiddish.

Louise Thompson Patterson, who served as an IWO national officer from 1933 to 1948, believes that the organization did far more than the Party to break down racial and cultural barriers: "Even though we had sixteen separate ethnic divisions, it was nothing to have blacks in a Jewish or Italian lodge. It was probably the only real chance that people had to really learn something about each other."

Despite the IWO's less rigorous organizational structure and sound welfare network, racism still existed within the group. It was no secret that outside New York, blacks were invisible as leaders in the Order. IWO officials were caught red-faced when it was revealed that no blacks were employed in the IWO offices or businesses and that many branches refused to let blacks use their facilities. Fiery resolutions were passed at their conventions, and impassioned speeches were made by the leaders promising to make changes.

But at the IWO's Fourth National Convention in 1938, the Secretariat admitted there were still some leaders "who feel that to show the face of Negro participation will keep away a lot of white people who are not yet won over to our ideas." The Secretariat warned that the "cancer" of white chauvinism was "eating in the very vitals of the organization."

76

But the organization showed resiliency. For the next decade, IWO advertisements could be seen in the *Daily Worker* soliciting members for its insurance plan. It continued to provide benefits for members during the immediate post World War II years. The demise of the organization finally came during the McCarthy anti-Communist purges of the 1950s.[34]

Communists Rethink Black Culture

The Party's political and social activism among blacks also changed the cultural tastes of many whites. They began to appreciate black art and culture. They started listening to black music, patronized plays that starred black actors and actresses, and made a special effort to induce black performers to entertain at Party events. None of this came easy. It was the rare white American in 1930 who could cut through the thicket of Sambo, Uncle Remus, and assorted "darky myths" about blacks and emerge with insight into the rich diversity of black culture.

One of those who did was V. F. Calverton. Born George Goetz to German-American parents in 1900, he became Calverton in 1923, the same year he founded his literary magazine, the *Modern Quarterly*. During the 1920s, he contributed articles to the *Daily Worker, New Leader,* and *The Communist.* In 1927, he visited the Soviet Union. Calverton was a maverick Marxist who refused to be pigeon-holed into a narrow political corner. He never joined the Party.

He demanded the freedom to criticize wrongs no matter if they were committed by capitalists or Communists. He called the Party's notion of a black republic in the South "absurd," and believed American Communists should develop their own initiatives toward blacks and not blindly follow Soviet dictates.[35]

Calverton seemed to have two basic requirements that writers had to meet to get published in the *Modern Quarterly:* They had to write well and write from a radical viewpoint. From the moment he began publishing, Calverton was fascinated by blacks. When one inquisitive admirer asked why he liked them he simply replied, "I am interested in the Negro people because they represent such remarkable qualities."

During the 1920s, his admiration for those "remarkable qualities" continued to grow. He came to regard black culture as spawning the only truly original American art form: "In song, the Negro spirituals and to a less extent the blues; in tradition, Negro folklore; and in music, Negro Jazz—these three constitute the Negro contribution to

American culture." Calverton was determined to introduce the art and literature of black America to whites.

Between 1925 and 1929, *Modern Quarterly* became a forum for the views of black writers. In its pages, W.E.B. DuBois explored "American Negro Art," Alain Locke surveyed "American Literary Tradition and the Negro," and E. Franklin Frazier gave readers a glimpse into the world of the black middle class in "La Bourgeoisie Noire." Charles C. White revealed "labor Motif in Negro Music." And George Schuyler, who Calverton grew particularly close to, discussed "Emancipated Women and the Negro."

By 1929 he had accorded black artists a royal position in American culture: "The Negro is more important in the growth of an American culture than the white man." The same year, he convinced Random House to publish a collection of fiction, poetry, and essays from major black writers in his *Anthology of American Negro Literature*. Locke's Anthology, *The New Negro*, published two years earlier, was the only other collection of black writings published by a white publishing house.

Abram Harris, Langston Hughes, Alain Locke, and other black writers often turned up at Calverton's Baltimore home for weekly lectures on politics and art. It was said that Calverton's home was the place where many white radicals met their first black socially.[36]

Although she never was quite as blunt in her views on blacks as Calverton, Nancy Cunard certainly believed that black culture had to be freed from the shadows. The daughter of a wealthy British aristocrat and shipping magnate, she was a free-spirited woman, as well known for her romantic trysts as her embrace of radical causes.

In 1928 Cunard found a new love affair—blacks. During the 1930s she used her wealth and contacts to raise funds for the Scottsboro Boys and the International Labor Defense. She was hungry to discover everything about the language, intrigues, and social life of this new black world. She traveled to Harlem in 1932, where she spent days visiting cabarets, attending poetry readings, and talking to black Harlemites. She was obsessed with publishing her new-found literary jewels.

Two years later she dug into her purse and published *The Negro Anthology*. Cunard set the tone in her introduction: "Every Negro worker is the potential victim of lynching, murder and legal lynching by the white ruling class, simply because he is a worker and black." The book was an odd mix of the writings of Communists and black poets and essayists. She had one more bit of scandal left to shock the public. At her own expense, she published a pamphlet "Black Man and White Ladyship." The tantalizing title told the story.[37]

For every Calverton and Cunard, there were still hundreds of Mike Golds—individuals who called themselves Communists but who knew nothing about black culture and who were just as quick as many other whites to debase it. As editor of the *New Masses,* Gold usually had the final word among Communists on what was proper art and culture for the working class.

Gold took his job seriously as supreme arbiter of mass culture. He clashed repeatedly with black radical writer Claude McKay when both served as executive editors at *Liberator.* Gold simply could not abide his style, which he deemed not proletarian enough. McKay lashed back, charging that Gold was only interested in "printing doggerels from lumberjacks and stevedores." Soon after, McKay resigned his position in disgust.[38]

In 1926, Gold chastised Langston Hughes in the *Nation* magazine for not writing correct "Negro themes" in his poems. He suggested that Hughes could take lessons from poet Vachel Lindsay and play-wright Eugene O'Neill. He thought they "handled" Negro themes "more effectively than the Negroes themselves." Gold had a last piece of proletarian advice for Hughes: "The Negro intellectuals can do a fine thing for their race. They can leave the cabarets of the jaded dilet-tantes and the colleges of the idle class strivers, and help the mass of their brothers in the economic fight."

With the stroke of his pen, he reduced black culture, history, and social aspirations to worthless debauchery. Three years after attacking him, Gold was still not satisfied that black writers were listening to him. In a *New Masses* editorial, he lectured blacks to stop their "saxo-phone clowning" and "cabaret obsession." He then dangled what he undoubtedly considered a tempting prospect before black artists. If they could "stop wasting their time on the gutter side of Harlem," the self-assured editor wrote, they might in some future millennium pro-duce works worthy of a Tolstoy, Gorky, Walt Whitman, or Beethoven. Gold and other Communist writers were adamant that black writers should exorcise all "pie in the sky illusions" from their works.[39]

By 1934, Party leaders, probably spurred by pressure from black Communists, had done some reevaluation of black culture. Suddenly, the poems and music the Party had once labeled 'gutter' became acceptable. Many Party members became staunch defenders of black cultural traditions. Communists were ordered to "fight against the suppression of Negro culture by the white ruling class." Ads for Party-sponsored "All Negro Recitals" and spirituals and African dance shows occasionally ran in the *New Masses* and *Daily Worker*. The poetry and plays of Langston Hughes, Countee Cullen, and other Harlem Renaissance writers were hailed by the Party.

Even Gold changed his tune. "It is the Negro writers," Gold crowed, "who must write the plays." Gold looked to Harlem to provide the "friendly soil" out of which a Negro national theater would grow. By now, Hughes could do no wrong with Gold. He was "a voice crying for justice for all humanity." The proletarian critic deemed it an honor to write the introduction to Hughes' collection of poems, *A New Song*.[40]

The records of Billie Holiday, Duke Ellington, and W. C. Handy were on the must-listen-to list of white Communists. The Party encouraged black members with musical talent to join the Liberator Chorus, which performed a repertoire of spirituals, classical, and blues-oriented songs at Party-sponsored socials and community events.

At Party forums and lectures, Communists lionized Frederick Douglass, Nat Turner, Harriet Tubman, and African history. At Party gatherings in Harlem and on Chicago's Southside, black Communists were more likely to discourse on Duke Ellington or Joe Louis than on Marx or the *Communist Manifesto*.

Black writers like Countee Cullen and Alain Locke liked the Party's new attitude. In 1936 Cullen endorsed Party electoral and anti-lynching campaigns. Locke proclaimed the triumph of "social realism" and "proletarian expression" in art. Locke suggested that America should emulate the cultural program for minorities "brilliantly developed" in the Soviet Union.[41]

But there were still limits to how far they could pursue this logic. The Party leaders had not changed their basic Marxian view that black culture was only valid if it depicted the struggles of the masses. Hughes, now a strong Party sympathizer, spelled out his proletarian blueprint for "good Negro writing." In a speech to the American Writers Congress in 1935, he said that the black writer was obliged to "unite blacks and whites" on "the solid ground of the daily working class struggle to wipe out now and forever, all the old inequalities of the past."

Eugene Gordon, whose short stories were held up by Party leaders as stellar examples of true working-class art, was even less compromising than Hughes. He told the Congress that black writers were pushing "dangerous" and "divisive" anti-white themes in their writings. He accused black novelists, presumably Hughes and himself excepted, of "writing for the Genteel upper class." They did not care a whiff about the working class, he said, but were "chiefly interested in getting special rights for themselves." The cultural debate would continue to stir inner Party fights throughout the remainder of the decade.[42]

Despite misgivings about black recruiting, white chauvinism, and Moscow-directed policy shifts, Communists were generally satisfied that they had made more friends than enemies among blacks in the Depression's early years. Now it was time to raise the stakes.

Nineteen-thiry-two was an election year. Depression discontent among blacks and whites was so great that it was practically a sure bet that Americans would pick a new president. The big migrations from the South had swelled the ranks of black voters in northern cities. For the first time since Reconstruction, the political arena might offer fresh opportunities for the redress of black grievances. Shrewdly casting their eyes across the American political landscape, Communists recognized that since the Democrats and Republicans had virtually written blacks out of American politics, it would be to their advantage to write them back in.

Notes

1. Historians have told the story of the Great Depression countless times and ways. The works that I have found most useful are Harvey Sitkoff, *A New Deal for Blacks* (New York: Oxford University Press, 1978); Raymond Wolters, *Negroes and the Great Depression: The Problem of Economic Recovery* (Westport, Connecticut: Greenwood Press, 1970); Ralph Bunche, *The Political Status of the Negro in the Age of FDR* (Chicago University of Chicago Press, 1973 [1940]); Arthur M. Schlessinger Jr., *The Politics of Upheaval* (Boston: Houghton Mifflin Co., 1960); E. Franklin Frazier, "Some Effects of the Depression on the Negro in Northern Cities," *Science and Society* 2 (Fall 1938): 491-92; "Negroes Out of Work," *Nation* 132 (22 April 1931): 441-42.
2. St. Clair Drake and Horace Cayton, *Black Metropolis* (New York: Harper and Row, 1962 [1945]), 2:734. Frazier explained the leftward shift of blacks during the Depression this way: "Perhaps one of the chief effects of the depression has been the spread of radical ideas among working class negroes through cooperation with white workers" ("Some Effects of the Depression," 498). *Defender*, 14 January 1933.
3. Interview with Carlton Moss, 12 December 1989; Interview with Charles Morgan, 6 December 1989; Briggs, "Our Negro Work," 494;

"The Communist International Resolution on the Negro Question in the United States," *The Communist International* 9 (January 1930): 51.

4. F. Markosch, *The Negroes in the United States of North America*, (Berlin: MOPR-Verlag, 1930), 45; Briggs, "Our Negro Work," 497 and 499-500; Otto Hall, "Gastonia and the Negro," *Labor Defender* 4 (August 1929): 153.

5. Interview with Charles Morgan, 6 December 1989; Briggs, "Our Negro Work," 500.

6. Interview with Lester Rodney, 5 December 1989; *Afro-American*, 22 November 1930; *Negro World*, 22 November 1930; *Negro World*, 8 August 1931; Nell Painter and Hosea Hudson, "Hosea Hudson," *Radical America* 11 (July-August 1977), 4; Earl Browder, *Communism in the United States* (New York: International Publishers, 1935), 293.

7. For two widely contrasting views on the meaning and intent of the Stalin show trials and Party purges of the 1920s and 1930s see *The History of the Communist Party of the Soviet Union*, Central Committee of the CPSU (New York: International Publishers, 1939), 346-51; and Isaac Deutscher, *Ironies of History* (Berkeley: Ramparts Press, 1971), 3-17.

8. The official proceedings of the "trial" are presented in *Race Hatred on Trial* (New York: CPUSA), 7-9. Howe and Coser provide a summary in *The American Communist Party*, 208-11. Naison also briefly touches on the trial in *Communists in Harlem*, 47-49. The *New York Times* devoted two issues to trial coverage (1 March 1931, 2 March 1931).

9. *Race Hatred on Trial*, 5, 9-24 and 25; Interview with Louise Thompson Patterson, 10 December 1989; *New York Times*, 2 March 1931.

10. *Race Hatred on Trial*, 24, 25 and 40-41; *New York Times*, 2 March 1931; Harry Haywood, "The Leninist Position on the Negro Question," *The Communist* 12 (September 1933): 892-93; Howe and Coser, *The American Communist Party*, 211.

11. *New York Times*, 1 March 1931; Browder, *Communism in the United States*, 291; *Daily World*, 26 February 1931; Interview with Carlton Moss, 12 December 1989; W. G. B. "On fighting White Chauvinism," *Party Organizer* 5 (May 1931): 15.

12. *New York Herald Tribune*, 8 March 1932; *Defender*, 28 May 1932; *Defender*, 27 August 1932; *Defender*, 30 October 1932; *Daily Worker*, 11 October 1932.

13. *Harlem Liberator*, 16 September 1933; Browder, *Communism in the United States*, 297.

14. Browder, "Tasks of Our Party," *The Communist* 12 (March 1933): 241-42; W. G. B., "On Fighting White Chauvinism," 15; "The Communist Position on the Negro Problem," *Internal Discussion Bulletin*, ca. 1934, 2, CP-File, undated, Southern California Research Library; Interview with Dorothy Healey, 16 December 1989; Interview with Louise Thompson Patterson, 10 December 1989.

15. Tom Johnson, *Reds in Dixie* (New York: Workers Library Publishers, 1935), 29; *The Road to Liberation for the Negro People* (New York: Workers Library Publishers, 1937), 12, 13; *American Labor Year Book* (New York: Rand School, 1929), 163; Foster "The Workers Party in the South," 679-81; *Daily Worker,* 23 June 1928

16. Anthony Bimba, *A History of the American Working Class* (New York: International Publishers, 1927), 368; Various leaflets issued by the Trade Union Unity League announcing unemployed marches in 1931 and 1932 are in the Communist Party File-1931 and 1932, Southern California Research Library. See Robin Kelly, "Hammer N' Hoe: Black Communists in Alabama," Ph.D. diss., UCLA, 1987.

17. Nell Painter and Hosea Hudson, "Hosea Hudson," 18; Nell Irvin Painter, *The Narrative of Hosea Hudson* (Cambridge: Harvard University Press, 1979). In what must rank as one of the South's great ironies, Birmingham declared 26 February 1979 "Hosea Hudson Day." The official proclamation was signed by Birmingham's black mayor, Richard Arrington. Even more interesting, city officials did not try to hide Hudson's work with the reds. It read: "Not limiting his commitment to blacks Hudson gave leadership to the Worker's Alliance" (*Party Organizer* 14 [July 1980], 32).

18. Angelo Herndon, *Let Me Live* (New York: Arno Press, 1969 [1937]), 3-95 and 355-402; Herndon, *You Cannot Kill the Working Class* (New York: International Labor Defense, 1935), 22; Leaflet in CP File—1931, Southern California Research Library. The Randolph resolution on Herndon is reprinted in the preface to *Let Me Live* (vi); Charles H. Martin, "The International Labor Defense and Black America, *Labor History* 26 (Spring 1985): 174-75. The two works that present the issues in the Scottsboro case and capture the spirit of organizing engaged in by the NAACP and the Communists are: Dan T. Carter, *Scottsboro: A Tragedy of the American South* (New York: Oxford University Press, 1971) and Haywood Patterson and Earl Conrad, *Scottsboro Boy* (New York: Doubleday, 1950).

19. *The Road to Liberation for the Negro People*, 12; *Negro Worker* 2 (15 August 1932): 29-30; *Negro Worker* 1 (October-November 1931): 10-12.

20. Roy Rosenzweig, "Organizing the Unemployed," 1929-1933, *Radical America* 10 (July-August 1976): 44-46. *Harlem Liberator*, 15 July 1933; Horace Cayton, *Long Old Road* (New York: Trident Press, 1965), 178-83; Naison, "Harlem Communists and the Politics of Black Protest," 73.

21. Eugene Gordon and Cyril Briggs, *The Position of Negro Women* (New York: Workers Library Publishers, 1935), 2; Interview with Dorothy Healey, 16 December 1989; Interview with Don Wheeldin, 2 December 1989; *Harlem Liberator*, 5 August 1933; *Harlem Liberator*, 22 September 1933; *Negro Liberator*, 7 September 1935.

22. James Ford and James S. Allen, *The Negroes in a Soviet America* (New York: Workers Library Publishers, 1935), 31 and 39-47; William Z. Foster, *Toward Soviet America* (New York: International Publishers, 1932), 303.

23. William Weinstone, "Report on the XI Plenum," *The Communist* 10 (October 1931): 793; *Communist International* 11 (20 June 1934): 393; James W. Ford, "Development of the United Front Work in Harlem," *The Communist* 14 (February 1935): 167-70; Interview with Don Wheeldin, 2 December 1989; Roi Ottley, *New World A-Coming*, 224.

24. *Party Organizer* 7 (March 1934): 20-21; *Party Organizer* 9 (February 1936): 7.

25. Naison "Harlem Communists and the Politics of Black Protest," 71; *Daily Worker*, 25 April 1929; Earl Browder, "Tasks of Our Party," 241.

26. Jack Stachel, "Organizational Problems of the Party," *The Communist* 14 (May 1935): 627; *Party Organizer* 9 (July-August 1936): 7; George Blake (Charney) "The Party in Harlem," *Party Organizer* 11 (June 1938): 14-15, 16 and 18; *Daily Worker*, 30 March 1936; *Daily Worker*, 10 July 1936. Charney did pay special tribute to the Milton Herndon branch in Harlem as an exemplary model for Communist organizing among blacks. Herndon was part of a small group of black volunteers that went to Spain and fought on the side of the leftist Republican Government (Arthur H. Landis, *The Abraham Lincoln Brigade* [New York: The Citadel Press, 1967], 319-20). Vaugn Love commanded two international brigades at the battlefront. There is some dispute over how many blacks actually did go to Spain. Communist leaders said there were "hundreds." Robert A. Rosenstone puts the number at one hundred (*The Crusade of the Left* [New York: Pegasus, 1969], 109-10). Arthur H. Landis claims only about "60 to 80" blacks actually fought (*The Abraham Lincoln Brigade*, 73).

27. George Charney, *A Long Journey* (New York: Quadrangle, 1968), 105.

28. *Daily Worker*, 10 July 1936; Interview with Carlton Moss, 10 December 1989; Interview with Marian Sherman, 7 December 1989.

29. *Amsterdam News*, 5 September 1936

30. *Lanett Times*, 21 July 1939.

31. International Workers Order (advertisement brochure), International Workers Order File, Southern California Research Library; *Harlem Liberator*, 24 March 1934 (advertisement); *Proceedings of the Fourth National Convention of the International Workers Order* (Pittsburgh: IWO, 1938), 125-26; Interview with Louise Thompson Patterson, 10 December 1989.

32. *New Order* 3 (November 1936): 9; *Harlem Liberator*, 7 April 1934; Interview with Louise Thompson Patterson, 10 December 1989; Rampersad, *The Life of Langston Hughes* (New York: Oxford University

Press, 1988), 1: 357-59; Langston Hughes, *A New Song* (New York: IWO, 1938), 7-8.

33. Samuel Patterson, "Recruiting Negroes," *New Order* 3 (September 1936): 7; Patterson, "My Tour for the Order," *New Order* 4 (February 1937): 10; *New Order* 4 (May 1937): 10; *Proceedings*, 126-27, 248.

34. *Proceedings*, IWO Fourth National Convention, 128; IWO insurance advertisements appeared in various issues of the *Daily Worker* in 1945 and 1946; Interview with Louise Thompson Patterson, 10 December 1989.

35. For background on Calverton's early years see Haim Genizi, "V.F. Calverton: A Radical Magazine for Black Intellectuals, 1920-1940," *Journal of Negro History* 57 (July 1972): 241-42; Walter C. Daniel, "Calverton and the Black American Writers," *Negro History Bulletin* 41 (July-August 1978): 868; *Daily Worker*, 23 April 1927; *New Leader*, 23 October 1926; Genizi, "V.F. Calverton," 246.

36. Genizi, "V.F. Calverton," 241-42. Each of these writers appeared in the *Modern Quarterly* between 1925 and 1929. George Schuyler appeared to have an even more lasting affectionate relationship with Calverton. Schuyler, in fact, wrote his last paean to Socialism in the *Modern Quarterly* in 1940: "Everywhere the old unrestricted capitalist individualism ins under serious attack or has given way to self-regulation inherent in monopolistic control" ("The Negro in the New Order," *Modern Quarterly* 11 [Fall 1940]: 84). Alain Locke, ed., *The New Negro: An Interpretation* (New York: Albert and Charles Boni, 1925); V. F. Calverton, ed., *Anthology of American Negro Literature* (New York: The Modern Library, 1929), 4; Genizi, "V.F. Calverton," 249.

37. James R. Hooker, *Black Revolutionary*, 26-31; Nancy Cunard, *Negro Anthology* (London: Lawrence and Wishart, 1934), 6. Maybe it was her family name or her father's wealth, whatever the reason, Cunard was the one white Communist that Garvey had a soft spot for: "When Miss Cunard is gone (as she must go) the way of physical beings, her kindly thoughts, her gentle mental sympathies for a race downtrodden and oppressed shall live forever" (*The New Jamaican*, 28 July 1932). Cunard, *Negro Anthology*, 15.

38. Samuel Sillen gives a short sketch of Gold's early Party career in *The Mike Gold Reader* (New York: International Publishers, 1954), 7-13; McKay, *A Long Way From Home*, 141-42.

39. *The Nation* 123 (14 July 1926): 37; *New Masses* 5 (February 1930): 3.

40. Interview with Carlton Moss, 12 December 1989; *New Masses* 9 (October 1930) (advertisement); Mike Gold, *A New Song*; Michael Gold, "At Last, a Negro Theater?" *New Masses* 18 (10 March 1936): 18-19.

41. Naison, *Communists in Harlem*, 298-304; Interview with Carlton Moss, 12 December 1989. For Cullen's involvement with the Communists see

chapter on Ford; *Proceedings of the Second National Negro Congress* (Philadelphia: NNC, 1938). Locke made his remarks in the "Cultural Session" workshop.

42. Langston Hughes, "To Negro Writers," *Proceedings of the American Writers Congress* (New York: International Publishers, 1935), 139; Eugene Gordon, "Social and Political Problems of the Negro Writer," *Proceedings of the American Writers Congress* (New York: International Publishers, 1935), 144.

5 The Red Special

Almost everyone on the Erie special was in high spirits. Their singing and shouting could be heard throughout the train as it pulled out of New York's Grand Central Station on the afternoon of May 27, 1932. The Erie was bound for Chicago. Few would have guessed that the happy travelers were delegates to the National Nominating Convention of the Communist Party. They were riding on what the Party dubbed "The Red Special."

The Party's National Campaign Committee had worked out a deal, including reduced rates to all delegates and special priority was given to ex-servicemen, trade unionists, party members, and blacks, with the Erie Rail Road to carry delegates and visitors from throughout the East to the two-day Communist convention in Chicago.[1]

The Campaign Committee was especially anxious that a huge black contingent attend the convention, wanting them in Chicago to witness and participate in one of the Party's greatest moments, the nomination of a black man for Vice President of the United States. It was no secret to whom the honor would go.

At a pre-convention campaign rally at Detroit's Arena Garden in April 1932, 6,000 Communist partisans had shouted out James Ford's name for the vice presidential nomination. Ford for Vice President clubs popped up in several cities. The truth was, he had been chosen weeks before by the Party's nominating committee, and the *Daily Worker* announced the selection in several editions that appeared prior to the convention.

Communists were careful to get the right racial balance at the convention. Twelve blacks were appointed to the convention advisory council, and fourteen blacks were elected to the fifty-member executive committee. Half the speeches at the convention would be given by black delegates. The Campaign Committee, with surgical precision, parceled out slots to blacks on every convention committee. Of the actual delegates, twenty-five percent would be black.

Before the first delegate arrived, the nominating committee had ranked the convention along with slavery and emancipation as one of three "epoch-making" landmarks for blacks in America. Mike Gold, who covered the convention for the *New Masses,* boasted that it was the first time in American history that a political party had so honored a black. But Gold read history wrong. The Paris Edition of the *Chicago Tribune* reminded Gold that the International Workingmen's Association nominated Frederick Douglass for vice president in 1872.[2]

For the 39-year-old Ford, the nomination was the crowning reward for his years of dutiful party service. If there was anyone who could truly be called a Red careerist among blacks it was Ford. By 1932 he had served stints with the International Trade Union Committee of Negro Workers, the *Negro Worker,* and the Party's Negro Commission. Currently, he was vice president of the League of Struggle for Negro Rights. During the winter of 1932, Ford had traveled to Germany, Czechoslovakia, and the Soviet Union, drumming up support for the Scottsboro Boys. Party leaders had supreme confidence in his abilities.[3]

The 1932 Communist Convention

Ford stood before 1,200 delegates ready to claim his place in history. In his nominating speech, Clarence Hathaway called Ford a "leader in this struggle for the emancipation of the toilers." When Ford finished his brief remarks the delegates went wild. They gave him an eighteen-minute standing ovation.

Banners and placards were tossed in the air, as Ford was hoisted on the shoulders of four husky white delegates and paraded around the floor of the Chicago Coliseum. A brigade of black and white Young Pioneers, their arms locked together, trailed behind waving red handkerchiefs. Delegates stomped and shouted.

Many stood transfixed in the aisles, tears streaming down their faces as the band played the music of the "Red Flag." All joined in with one voice and sang the worker's solidarity hymn to the tune of "John Brown's Body." Foster, Ford's presidential running mate, was nominated by a black delegate, B. D. Amis of the League of Struggle for Negro Rights. Following his speech, Foster was hoisted on the shoulders of four black delegates and paraded around the Coliseum.

The venerable Mother Ella Reeve Bloor, a veteran of dozens of labor battles since the turn of the century, placed the Party's official imprimatur on the choices when she seconded the nomination of both men. Langston Hughes, who was at the convention as an observer, was so moved by the spirit of the delegates he not only endorsed Ford on the spot but also volunteered to help prepare campaign literature.[4]

Ford considered his nomination more than just a personal triumph. He believed that it was a blow against racism and for democracy. The line of black and white speakers that trooped to the podium confirmed his feeling that racial cooperation could be achieved in America. He glanced around the Coliseum and beamed at the giant posters that read "Down With the Boss's War," "Equal Rights For Negroes," and "Stop Scottsboro Murder."

Ford listened as Mary Osbee, a Chicago stockyard worker, told the crowd that "the Communist fight is for equal human rights and social equality." He perhaps glowed with pride as Henry Story, a black farmer from Georgia, shouted, "We black and white workers realize the party is our only refuge."

Ford cheered with the other delegates when Foster said that "the Communist Party is the party of the Negro." The convention also nominated blacks for congressional offices in some states as well as for the office of governor in Illinois, senator in Indiana and Wisconsin, and lieutenant governor in New York.[5]

The only sour note at the convention came during a minor wrangle over the wording in the platform. Some black delegates thought that the words "equal rights" were not strong enough. An eighteen-year-old black woman from Newark, New Jersey settled the debate. She angrily asked the other delegates what equal rights meant. Her answer: "equal rights to the kitchen, equal rights to the worst jobs." The platform committee saw her point and promptly inserted the words "full and unconditional" before "equal rights."

Communists tried to cover all bases in their platform, from self-determination for the Black Belt to a vast array of proposals to end segregation. Foster brought the delegates out of their seats when he defiantly declared "death to lynchers." Communists felt they had to outdo the other parties. The Republicans "pledged to preserve equal rights." The Socialists called for "political, economic, and legal equality," but not social equality for blacks. The Democratic platform said nothing at all about civil rights.

For those who still questioned the Party's sincerity in nominating Ford, Hathaway assured that it was "not a cheap vote-catching motive." The political reality, Hathaway said, was that the Party's program "flew in the face of the strong anti-Negro sentiment" and would probably cost them white votes.[6]

The delegates and supporters were primed for the fall election fight. Their mission was to convince as many Americans as possible that the Communist Party was worth their vote. Campaign officials returned to New York and waited to see what the reaction would be. The press, especially the black newspapers, would give them the first clue of whether their "epoch-making" convention registered any impact on the public.

The first returns were disappointing. The mainstream press largely ignored the convention. The *New York Times* sent no correspondent to the convention, and none of the local Chicago papers mentioned it. Communists chalked up the black-out to the hostility of the "capitalist press."

They probably were not unduly alarmed at the negative reaction they got from Garvey's *Negro World* and the *Pittsburgh Courier*. The *Negro World* was at its insulting best when it editorialized, "The Communist party is known in the South as a 'Nigger Party'. Hence what else could they do but use Comrade Ford as bait?" The *Courier* did have a reporter at the convention, and his account was no less flattering. He called the delegates "a motley looking crew" who represented a "Party of a scant minority." He dismissed Ford's nomination with "1200 ragged reds, wildly, fanatically chose James Ford."

The *Afro-American* reporter saw a different convention than the *Courier* correspondent. The *Afro-American* covered all the sessions and provided a thorough and fair account of the proceedings. Carl Murphy, publisher of the *Afro-American*, was dazzled by the event. He agreed with Gold that the Communists had made history. Murphy wrote an accompanying editorial urging white and black workers "to give the Communists a hand in November." During the campaign Murphy released his managing editor, William N. Jones, from his editorial duties to take over as chairman of the "Ford-Foster Committee for Equal Negro Rights." He organized support meetings and spoke at campaign rallies in New York and Chicago.

At a get-out-the-vote rally at Harlem's Renaissance Casino in October, Jones greeted the cheering crowd with "I bring you the greetings of fourteen million colored Communists." He told the mixed group of blacks and whites that "where the struggles of white workers end, there the struggles of blacks begin."[7]

The *Daily Worker* continued to keep close tabs on the black press. It treated any favorable comment as an important news item. The *St. Louis Argus* called the campaign a "pretty good start for the new order of things." The *Cincinnati Bulletin* saw the Communists bringing about "a big change in the votes in November." The *Daily Worker* praised both papers and took their words as an indication that "the Communist candidate for Vice President rouses workers; enthusiasm."

Party leaders, however, recognized that a positive word in the *Commercial Bulletin* was not the same as one in *The Crisis,* the *Defender*, or the Urban League's *Opportunity* magazine. A good word in these publications could have tremendous influence on black voters. Neither of these publications gave Party leaders cause to cheer. Except for an expressionless picture of Ford at the bottom of the front page, the Communist campaign was pretty much a non-entity in the pages of the *Defender*. Not even Ford's visit to the *Defender's* offices during the campaign could get the paper's testy publisher Robert Abbott to devote more space to his campaign.[8]

Party leaders hoped for more from *Opportunity*. In March the magazine stated in an editorial, "There is support for the Communist Party." The Urban League's research department took the Reds seriously enough to include them in their April poll on "How Should the Negro Vote." The results, published in May, showed modest support for the Communists. *Opportunity* was impressed by their showing. Ira De Reid, League Research Director, made special mention of the fact that Communist candidates "showed a marked increase" in the number of reader votes they got since the League's first poll taken at the beginning of the year. That was about as far as the Urban League was prepared to go.

Other than a picture and a blurb describing him as "an effective campaigner," Ford was shut out of the pages of *Opportunity*. Foster fared a little better. He got a full page to answer *Opportunity's* query to each candidate on how many public works jobs blacks would get if they won. Foster was emphatic that once the Communists captured the White House, "segregation or differentiation of any sort would be punished as a crime against the welfare of the state."[9]

The Crisis was even stingier in its coverage of the campaign. It ran a picture of Ford and a short quote from Hathaway's nomination speech.

In September *The Crisis* did publish a short article on the convention by Mabel Byrd.[10]

If the leading black publications failed to acknowledge the significance of the Communist feat, campaign officials comforted themselves with the belief that they were winning the people. A voter opinion survey by the *Afro-American* appeared to justify their optimism. Although most blacks said they would vote for either Roosevelt or Hoover, they made no disparaging comments about the Communist ticket. A reader from Brooklyn wrote to the editor of the *Afro-American*, "Foster should win. Ford his running mate is a Negro. Let every Negro give him his vote."

In Atlanta, Herndon reported that Foster and Ford campaign clubs "buzzed like bee hives" in black and working-class neighborhoods. Even though city officials forced the campaign "underground," he claimed that the spirits of blacks and whites were "feverishly" high. Herndon said that Atlanta blacks were "proud to see a Negro sharing honors with a white man—the highest honors a political party could bestow."

The Communist Campaign Committee worked round the clock to get Ford and Foster maximum exposure. The committee distributed seven million political leaflets and a million pamphlets. Thousands of postcards with pictures of Ford and Foster transposed over a hammer and sickle were mailed to supporters nationally. Foster-Ford clubs were active in most major cities, registering voters and soliciting campaign workers. Blacks, trade unionists, and veterans were targeted.[11]

The Party also made a big push for support from artists and writers. Communist leaders recognized they could serve a valued role as attractive attention-getters. John Dos Passos, Theodore Dreiser, and many of the country's leading writers were either Party members or sympathizers. To coordinate its cultural work, the Campaign Committee pressed the Party-run John Reed clubs into service for Ford and Foster. The clubs, which gave young writers an outlet to discuss their works, operated in twenty cities and produced a steady volume of pamphlets and literature for the campaign.

The Party formed the League of Professional Groups for Foster and Ford in twenty cities to get more big-name writers to endorse the ticket. The League did not do much other than produce a pamphlet, "Culture and Crisis," that called for "workers in the professions and arts" to produce "integrated creative personalities" under the Communist leadership.[12] Put simply, Communists wanted writers and artists to reflect the party line in their "creative" works.

That summer many blacks found letters in their mailboxes with a New York return address. The letters bearing the signature of Foster and Ford asked for their endorsement. Countee Cullen was the recipient of one such letter. The popular Harlem Renaissance poet had no problem with the request. He endorsed Ford and Foster.

The Party also had not forgotten Hughes' offer at the convention to help the campaign. But in the weeks that had passed since the convention, he had taken on other commitments. He was making preparations that fall to go to Russia to work on a film project with a group of other black artists. In between, he agreed to a month-long lecture and poetry-reading tour at black colleges in the South. But Hughes had not completely forgotten his promise. During a stop in Los Angeles, he told radical newspaper columnist Loren Miller that blacks could help themselves by building "the largest possible vote for Foster and Ford." Hughes took a slap at black leaders who were afraid to speak out for the Communists because "it might cost them their $5,000 a year incomes."[13]

The 1932 Campaign

Early on, campaign officials decided that Ford was not going to be simply "the black candidate" who spoke only to black audiences. Despite Hathaway's allusion to the Party losing white votes because of Ford, they had not written whites off. The Party gambled that there were many whites who were like the white man from Tennessee who wrote a short article for the *Daily Worker* on the Ford nomination.

Walter Wilson described himself as a man whose "forefathers settled in the South many generations ago." Ford's color did not matter to him; he "would vote the Communist ticket even if two Negroes were the candidates." He complimented the Party for having the courage of "being the first party in the history of the country to take a stand" for equal rights. Wilson perhaps revealed more than he realized about his feelings: "I do not consider the Communist Party is doing more for the Negro worker than for the white worker."[14]

Ford got a tumultuous send-off from 10,000 black and white supporters who turned out for a party campaign picnic in Chicago on July 1. The next three months he was on the go from coast to coast. He spoke to miners in Montana, farmers in Des Moines and longshoremen in Tacoma, and led demonstrations in Seattle and Madison, Wisconsin. In Brooklyn, he worked a crowd of five thousand supporters at an

Ex-Servicemen's League rally into such a frenzy that some audience members lifted him onto their shoulders. Ford seemed to have a cure for every problem that ailed Depression-ridden America. If elected, he promised to end Prohibition, eliminate speakeasies, and free more than 500,000 inmates locked up in insane asylums.[15]

Not everything went smoothly. Ford had to cancel a speaking engagement in Albany, New York when the police chief denied the Campaign Committee an outdoor permit to hold a rally. In Washington, D.C., Ford found himself packed in the rear of an army truck with forty-one other supporters. Mounted troops and police drove them to a small town in rural Maryland. His candidate status did not impress the chief of detectives, who shouted at Ford at the detention center, "You may be vice presidential candidate to the United States but don't you put your black ass in that chair." After his release, Ford had to make his way back to the city as best he could. A month later, he got into more trouble in Los Angeles. Police crashed into a Ford campaign banquet and beat up several diners. Ford, along with the Party's local assembly candidate and the Party's California campaign manager, wound up in jail. He was released and warned to get out of town. Earlier in the summer, Foster was thrown into jail in the city when he tried to speak.

Ford's western swing was not a complete waste. A columnist for the *California Eagle* predicted, "thousands of blacks are going over to the Reds each year." He claimed to have it on good authority that the Hoover administration was "alarmed by the Communist drift."[16]

Ford presented a confident face to the public, and the Campaign Committee brimmed with enthusiasm, but away from the hoopla and noise there were problems. Party insiders grumbled about the way the campaign was going. An unsigned article in the *Party Organizer* brought the criticisms to the fore. Local issues and demands were being neglected, no support committees were being developed, and few new workers were joining the Party. According to the writer, the campaign also was spending to much energy "name calling" and "shouting" against "fascist misleaders." Instead of educating workers, the mystery writer charged that the campaign was turning them off.

Some Communists also noticed that most of the faces in the crowds at the Ford and Foster rallies were white. Frank Rogers of Youngstown wanted to know where the blacks were and what the Party was doing to get more blacks involved in the campaign. A campaign organizer, Rogers wondered if there were not some "hints of white chauvinism circulating" in the Party. He cited the example of white party leaders in Cleveland. They unanimously rejected a proposal by black members to hold their own special conference to plan a strategy to get more black endorsements for Communist candidates. The blacks demanded the right to hold their own conference because "of the deep mistrust the Negro workers have for conferences organized and led by whites." The whites dismissed their request as a" distortion of the party line." When the national office demanded that the locals "explain their basis of disagreement," the locals backed off and the blacks held their conference. But the damage had been done.

In July the Campaign Committee made plans to hold its own special conference in Washington to explain the Communist platform to blacks. About a hundred mostly Party members and sympathizers showed up. Ford appealed for black organizations to endorse and do more work for the campaign. Very little changed. For the rest of the campaign most of the faces at the rallies continued to be white.[17]

On election night there was more excitement as friends and supporters of the two candidates gathered at campaign headquarters in New York to wait for the returns. They were keeping especially close tabs on the vote in Chicago and New York. Toward the end of the campaign, Ford had spent most of his time shuttling between Harlem and the Southside of Chicago, prepping the troops, walking the streets, and speaking at campaign rallies. The Party banked on a good return in both places. A big turnout here meant that blacks would vote for Communists. Campaign officials also hoped for a good showing in working-class areas. This would prove that whites could pull the lever for a black man.

In 1932 votes were counted by hand, and it often took days before complete returns were in. However, as sketchy as the early returns were, they did show that the Democrats were doing well. In the big cities and in the South, they were rolling up huge margins. It quickly became apparent that the country would have a new president.

This was no great surprise. With the Depression in its third year and no end in sight, few political experts had given Hoover much chance against Roosevelt. Voters blamed the man in the White House for their troubles. Hoover stubbornly clung to outdated free-market palliatives and refused to prime the government spending pump to provide badly needed jobs and relief. Roosevelt might not be any better, but to the majority of Americans in 1932, he could not be any worse than Hoover.[18]

When the numbers were finally in, Campaign Committee members wore restrained smiles. Communists received nearly 12,000 votes in Chicago's Cook County. In the predominantly black wards of Chicago they got five to six percent of the vote. The totals in New York looked even better. Foster more than tripled the number of votes he got when he ran in 1928.

Campaign officials rejoiced at the rest of the national figures. The two candidates got votes in every state where they had campaigned. In Arizona, where Ford spoke, the Party got 128 votes. The final tabulation showed that 102,991 Americans had voted for Foster and Ford. Their bold experiment with a black man on the ticket seemed to have paid modest dividends.[19]

Sociologists St. Clair Drake and Horace Cayton, after talking with hundreds of blacks on Chicago's Southside, found that while most blacks might not have voted for the Communists, many complimented them for boosting Ford and other blacks as Party leaders: "And who had ever put Negroes in a position where they led white men as well as black? Every time a black Communist appeared on the platform, or his picture appeared in a newspaper, Negroes were proud."[20]

Don Wheeldin, a Party campaign worker, believes that Ford appealed to many blacks because he was a novelty: "Here was a black guy who was talking about voting rights, integrated schools, and job discrimination at a time when hardly any other politician was. So it was hardly surprising that blacks would love to hear him."[21]

Despite the meager Communist vote total, the 1932 national elections put the Party, albeit tenuously, on the political map in America. Communists believed they had a solid program for militant change and an effective organization to unite blacks and whites. Party leaders now prepared to capitalize on the mass discontent of Americans and their hunger for change.

During off-year elections in New York City in 1933 and 1934, Communists fielded a full slate of candidates in races for assembly, senate, controller, and mayor. The versatile Ford did double duty as a candidate for two separate assembly districts both years. During the 1934 campaign, the Party made the first real effort to involve black women in Communist politics.

The Communist press took every opportunity to let Harlemites know that Williana Burroughs, a prominent community activist, was the Party's candidate for lieutenant governor. The *Harlem Liberator* and the *Daily Worker* carried photos, interviews, and background features on Burroughs, and she made certain to praise the Party for showering blacks with such high political honors.

Party leaders had no illusions about winning offices, but they expected that their candidates would "more than double the number of votes from 1932." Echoing the feeling of Party officials, Ford said that Communists would achieve political success because the "Negro masses were discontented with the New Deal." But were they discontented enough to vote for the Communist Party candidates in 1936? The Party bet that enough blacks were.[22]

1936: Bigger and Better?

There were no "Red Specials" this time. They were not needed. Communists were going to turn their 1936 convention into a public spectacle. The nominating committee rented Madison Square Garden for five days during the last week of June. When the doors opened, 25,000 wildly cheering men and women poured into the Garden. Three thousand more stood on the street outside listening to the proceedings on loudspeakers. The press and the general public were warmly welcomed.

Massive banners festooned the Garden with political slogans that demanded "Death penalty for Lynchers," "No Intervention in Imperialist Wars," and "Freedom for Angelo Herndon." Behind the podium hung two gigantic pictures of John Brown and Frederick Douglass.

Spaced throughout the Garden were enlarged photos of lynchings and pitiful-looking men and women in bread lines, contrasted with heroic caricatures of well-fed Russians. The theme was decidedly Americana. The stars and stripes fluttered throughout the Garden, while the hammer and sickle was nowhere to be seen.

This reflected the new policy shift by Moscow. Because of the threat from German and Italian fascism, Stalin and the Communist International had called for the Communist Parties in Europe and the United States to form "Popular Front" alliances with the middle class, small capitalists, and farmers in their countries. The idea was to build as broad a support base as possible to combat fascism. Since the Party had dutifully agreed to drop its anti-capitalist rhetoric and opt for conciliation, the convention would serve as their showpiece for Popular Front politics in America.[23]

Almost immediately on taking their seats, the delegates and supporters began chanting "We Want Ford." There was little doubt who the

Vice Presidential candidate for 1936 would be. As Ford mounted the podium to give his acceptance speech, the bright lights from the rafters seemed to wash his face with a near angelic glow.

Ford hit all the familiar themes in his acceptance speech: the defense of Angelo Herndon, the Scottsboro Boys, the political corruption of the Democratic and Republican parties, segregation, and working-class unity. He had a special word for whites: "I appeal to the white workers to remember that the colored people must not be left to fight alone."[24]

The vice presidential candidate sprinkled his speech with references to John Brown, Frederick Douglass, and Abraham Lincoln. Communists, he said were the real keepers of the flame of American traditions. He promised, "We Communists, Negro and white, will carry out what they dreamed of." The *Daily World* took its own historical license and called Ford the "Frederick Douglass of 1936."

Ford's presidential running mate, Earl Browder, said that "the issue of the 1936 election is not a choice between socialism or capitalism. It is a choice between progress and reaction, between democracy and the path toward fascism. "The presidential candidate got off what had by now become the standard Party line when he proclaimed: "The Communist Party is proud to be known as the Party of the Negro people."

Ford and Browder had an immense audience this time. Their speeches were broadcast live to the nation by NBC and CBS. Millions of Americans nationwide had never heard a Communist or a black man before. It was another Party first. Ford would make eight radio broadcasts during the campaign.

The candidates made hard pledges to make discrimination a crime, ensure the death penalty for lynchers, and bring blacks full equality. The Party's equal rights platform was such a model of interracial progress that the *Afro-American* headlined its report, "Communists do not mince words in platform pledges."[25]

Despite the glowing words, there were fewer blacks at this convention than in 1932. A small article tucked away at the end of the Campaign Committee's report on the delegate make-up admitted that "the slow recruiting of Negro workers found its reflection in the comparatively small number of Negroes among the delegates." Of the convention delegates, only forty-eight were black, less than fifteen percent of the total. Party leaders were hardly unaware of the problem. No sooner had the convention closed than Ford called a meeting of the

Party's Negro Commission to figure out ways to get more blacks into the campaign. The meeting was attended by the top black Communists and white Party leaders from the South.

The opinions were as varied as the participants. Hall wanted the campaign to focus on voting rights in the South. He said that the Party was preparing literature on the poll tax. Haywood was thinking of the South too, but in a different way. He argued that the Party should further "popularize the black belt nation demand." He was putting together his own pamphlet on the subject.

Ford thought along more conventional Party lines. He believed that the campaign should stress the Party's Popular Front program of building a Farmer-Labor Party. He styled the Party "the people's movement" that would "advance the rights of the Negro people and other oppressed sections of the population." The meeting ended with no conclusive agreement on a unified plan of attack. Ford took his cue from campaign officials who would determine what issues the campaign would stress.[26]

There was one man that the Communists prudently decided to handle with great care: Roosevelt. During the election, Ford and Browder made little mention of him. The most that Ford would say about the President came in a radio address in which he made an oblique reference to the Democrats as "the party of the South."

They could, however, let fly against the Republican standard-bearer Alf Landon, the "rabid anti-Negro" Hearst press, and the right-wing Liberty League. Ford made it plain that he thought any black who backed Landon "was helping to put a lynch rope around the neck of his people." So, when Olympic hero Jesse Owens endorsed Landon, he blasted him as a man who "is not serving the cause of the colored people."

Party insiders knew that they were being disingenuous with their campaign: "The Party could not say that we should be for Roosevelt," Lester Rodney remembers, "so they said 'defeat Landon at all costs,' but we were sophisticated people so we knew what 'defeat Landon' meant."[27]

Roosevelt was off limits simply because he was so popular. The New Deal not only had provided jobs and relief for millions of Americans, but also had restored their hope. Despite racism in the administration and the glaring inequities in Roosevelt's relief and farm programs, blacks viewed the New Deal as a godsend. Loren Miller wrote that blacks "feel somewhat like the starving woman who accepted stolen goods because she felt that 'God sent this blessing even if the devil did bring it.'" When it came to the President, however, Miller could leave the devil bit out. Most blacks merely stopped at the divinity.[28]

On election day the *Amsterdam News* reported that Roosevelt rode down Harlem's Seventh Avenue in the back seat of a Cadillac Sedan and watched as "Fathers held their youngsters high on their shoulders to give them a glance at the 'second great Roosevelt,' and aged women muttered kindly wishes and prayers that FDR would be returned to the white House."

Not since Lincoln had blacks spoken of a white man with such reverence. An *Afro-American* reporter took his pad to the streets and asked blacks at random, "Has the New Deal been a benefit to the colored people?" All but one respondent said yes. One man best summed it up. He simply remarked, "It put me to work."

Even the black conservatives jumped on the Roosevelt train. Kelly Miller got so excited about the New Deal that he wrote a pamphlet, "Why Colored Americans Should Vote For Roosevelt." The *Nation* gave a state-by-state pre-election political tally and found him handily winning the black vote. The Republicans, the *Nation* observed, had no chance with blacks because "the Negro masses have never got anything in return for their allegiance to the G.O.P."[29]

On The Road Again

The 1936 campaign was a virtual repeat of 1932, only with less bombast and more sophistication. In June Party members received notices from the Illinois State Committee, urging them to come to Chicago for the annual Fourth of July picnic. The committee reminded the members that the "picnic is not just a 'picnic' but an event of the greatest political importance."

Party members did not need to be prompted, they came in droves. More than 20, 000 Party members and supporters filled Birutis Grove Park on Chicago's Southside for the two-day picnic. Browder and Ford pledged to make the campaign the biggest and best yet for Communists. The Illinois campaign committee issued its own release promising "to mobilize the broadest possible people's front to defeat the menace of reaction and fascism."

The National Campaign Committee distributed millions of leaflets and flyers. A lengthy pamphlet chronicling Ford's life and detailing the Party's position on "Negro rights" was authored by Benjamin Davis Jr.

The Atlanta-born black attorney had fought successful battles in the Georgia courts in 1932 and 1933 on behalf of Angelo Herndon. Davis was so impressed by the Communist's support of equality that he joined the Party and relocated to New York to work in the national office.[30]

The Campaign Committee sent letters to prominent blacks requesting endorsements and "communications" of support to be read at political rallies. Often, the letters were sent under the auspices of a local "Ford Reception Committee." In September the Oakland Ford Committee asked Ralph Bunche to send his "greeting" to a mass rally planned at the Oakland Municipal Auditorium. The committee appealed to him to recognize Ford's position as "an outstanding leader of the Negro race." There is no indication that he responded.

Browder and Ford clubs were formed in dozens of cities. In black neighborhoods Browder's name was discreetly omitted and the campaign clubs became "Ford" clubs. The California campaign committee planned to run paid ads in all local black newspapers.

Ford was back on the campaign trail again. He crisscrossed thirty-eight states, from Washington to New York, always careful to tailor his pitch to the particular audience he was addressing. In Los Angeles he went after Hollywood. He accused the film industry of "forcing colored people to take parts that degrade their people and encourage the disgusting ideas of fascism."

His next stop was Berkeley, where he told an overflow crowd of 2,000 students to get involved in campus actions for labor and peace. In Montana Ford attacked Landon's farm policy before 400 white farmers. In Denver he worked up a crowd of 1,500 with a call for a Farmer-Labor Party.

Ford also appeared to be gaining broader support among blacks. Hundreds of blacks in Springfield, Ohio showed up to hear him demand that the government enforce the thirteenth, fourteenth, and fifteenth amendments. Black ministers in Cleveland gave him a reception at the Phyllis Wheatley Center, and the American Negro Congress hosted a Ford dinner tribute in Buffalo. Observers were struck by the increased number of blacks at his campaign stops in Philadelphia, Indianapolis, and Columbus, Ohio.

For a brief moment, Ford's campaign enthusiasm was infectious. Lester Rodney recalls standing on a street corner in Harlem as hundreds of blacks gathered for an impromptu Browder-Ford rally: "Ford would get up on a box and the crowd would whistle and cheer as he rapped Landon and the Southern racists. They loved to hear that kind of talk."[31]

101

The Communist campaign would not have been complete without controversy. When it occurred, the Party quickly tried to turn it to their advantage. When Ford was denied a room at the YMCA hotel in Scranton, he promptly instructed his attorneys to sue the manager. Ford told the press that this was only "one of the many instances of Jim-Crowism" that he encountered while campaigning. In Springfield, Ohio Ford took to the radio airwaves and complained about the racial indignities he suffered during his tour. In Richmond, Virginia he got a chance to turn the tables on the American Legion. The Legion pressured the school board to cancel a permit for him to speak at a local school auditorium. The Virginia campaign committee condemned the board for infringing on his freedom of speech. It worked. Local papers wrote editorials supporting Ford's right to speak. "What James Ford believes is of little moment to this community," the *Richmond Dispatch* solemnly declared, "but free speech is a cherished right." The board caved in and rescinded the ban.

But the American Legion was not finished with him. Local legionnaires in Durham, North Carolina threatened to assault Ford if he spoke in their city. He was not intimidated. He mounted the stage bedecked in his army ribbons and devoted most of his speech to describing his experiences in a segregated army unit in France during the war. After his talk, he was surrounded by what an *Afro-American* reporter called "a flying wedge of white college students" and escorted safely to the train station. The students were from Duke University.[32]

When Browder was forbidden to speak in Terre Haute, William Pickens wrote an angry letter to the mayor of Terre Haute defending his right to speak. The *Afro-American* and other black papers wrote editorials blasting the city fathers for denying Communists their free speech rights.

Browder also came off looking like a hero to many blacks when he refused to stay at a hotel in Philadelphia. He started his one-man protest when the hotel manager ordered a reporter from the *Afro-American* to ride on the freight elevator. Browder did not let the matter drop. He called a press conference and promised, if elected, to "pay special attention to the colored victims of discrimination."

He pressed the advantage. As president, he said, he would appoint several blacks to his cabinet. That evening, with a huge electric sign flashing "Vote Communist" at the back of the stage and a black choir belting out gospel songs, Browder and Ford spoke to 11,000 cheering supporters at the Market Street Arena. B. D. Amis, a black Communist candidate for Pennsylvania state auditor, read a telegram Browder sent to Pennsylvania's governor "condemning this violation of the civil rights law." That was all many Howard University students needed to hear. In a student poll conducted by the student newspaper the *Hilltop,* eleven percent said they would vote for Browder.[33]

But students were not old enough to vote, and if they were, they were not likely to influence their elders to vote for Browder and Ford. When the *Afro-American* polled nearly one hundred black voters in Baltimore, New York, and Philadelphia, only one person said he planned to vote for the Communist candidates.

On the other hand, the black press was not unsympathetic to Ford. Columnists for the *Pittsburgh Courier* took no unkind cuts at the Reds, and the *Defender* called Ford "an outstanding labor leader and radical" and ran a large front-page picture of him. The *Amsterdam News* reported on Ford speeches in several cities.

Sympathy, however, did not translate into endorsements. The *Courier's* Floyd Calvin, in a survey of more than one hundred black papers, could not find one backing Ford (or Landon either). Even the usually sympathetic *Afro-American* did not plan to march the final mile with Ford. Murphy wrote, "The road to continual prosperity is clear under the leadership of 'General' Franklin Delano Roosevelt."

Whether Party leaders regarded *Afro-American* columnist Ralph Matthews' remark that the Communists and Roosevelt "want the same things" as a compliment or an insult did not matter. The point was that blacks did not see any reason to desert Roosevelt. Communists only *promised* more jobs, relief, and a brighter future. Roosevelt delivered.[34]

The election was almost a foregone conclusion. The Roosevelt deluge washed away not only Landon but Ford and Browder too. The national vote total for the Communists was so dismal—Browder got 31,900 votes in New York City—that the Party fell short of the minimum number needed to keep its name on the ballot in the next election.

Nationally, the two Communist candidates received officially 80,195 votes. The *Amsterdam News* pointed out the obvious: "If it had not been for the New Deal, Ford would have polled thousands of votes which went to Roosevelt." But the paper's generosity to the Communist candidates stopped there. Brutally frank about the Communist electoral fate, the *News* declared, "the Communist Party is now dead at the ballot."

A Party worker who looked back on the campaign did not dispute that view: "Most people saw the candidates as too sectarian, too way off to the left, to give them any measurable support. The campaign just didn't really have any lasting effect on people's thinking."[35]

Still, the naked political fact was that Roosevelt had indeed done in the Communists at the ballot box. Indeed, many Communists were not terribly disappointed at their candidate's electoral failure. FDR was clearly the lesser of two evils in the eyes of most Party members. Even more, a Roosevelt victory was pretty much in line with the Party's "Popular Front" strategy of seeking allies among the "progressive capitalists." His administration had passed no legislation nor instituted any programs specifically aimed at blacks. He did not even speak out against lynching until well into his second year in the White House. Yet the president still came off as a man who cared about blacks. The thirty-six black delegates at the Democratic National Convention in June were the largest number of blacks ever at a major party's national convention. This time they were not penned behind chicken wire as they had been at the 1928 Democratic convention.

Roosevelt regularly invited black leaders to White House functions and consulted them on social and racial policy matters. He also had the best ambassador to the nation's downtrodden beside him in the White House. The popular Eleanor Roosevelt lent her name and prestige to a wide range of social reform organizations.

He was the consummate politician, who masterfully melded blacks into a coalition of labor, farmers, Southerners, big-city machine Democrats, and blue-collar ethnics that would hold political sway for the next three decades. The Communist Party had nothing to match the Roosevelt aura.[36]

Ford would run again in 1940. While his name would be on the ballot in twenty-one states, the campaign was only a half-hearted gesture. There were no "Red Specials," no gala celebrations in Madison Square Garden, no CBS and NBC radio broadcasts, and no ringing declarations of death to lynchers. He tried as best as he could to keep up appearances. At a campaign rally in Denver in August, Ford was at his rousing best. This election, he shouted, "will be a grave lesson and warning to the labor-haters, Negro-baiters, and war mongers everywhere."[37]

Denver was the first stop on a sixty-city tour that would carry him into the Deep South. Holding a stack of letters, he played his man-of-the-people part to the hilt: "These people who write in are telling us of their needs and struggles and fears."

104

It made for good theater. But with war clouds gathering in Europe, the Party was more anxious about the peril to the Soviet Union than the danger to blacks in Harlem and on Chicago's Southside. Few political observers were surprised when the Browder-Ford ticket garnered only 46,251 votes. More than a quarter century would pass before the names of Communist candidates would again appear on a presidential ballot.[38]

The Communist political campaigns of the Depression years did not result in a massive black voter shift to the Party. Roosevelt and the Democrats proved too formidable a barrier. However, thousands of blacks did praise the Party for forcefully making equal rights an issue on the national agenda. And that was enough to force moderate black leaders to take a step they never dreamed they would take—a step toward the Reds.

Notes

1. Interview with Don Wheeldin, 2 December 1989; *Daily Worker*, 18 May 1932.

2. *Daily Worker*, 16 May 1932; Interview with Don Wheeldin, 2 December 1989; *Daily Worker*, 31 May 1932; Nominating Speech of James Hathaway in Nancy Cunard, ed., *Negro Anthology* (London: Lawrence and Wishart, 1934), 277-78; *Afro-American*, 27 May 1932; *Daily Worker*, 6 May 1932; *Daily Worker*, 18 May 1932; *Afro-American*, 9 July 1932; *Chicago Tribune* (Paris edition) quoted in *Afro-American*, 9 July 1932. Phillip Foner gives a brief background on the Douglass Vice Presidential nomination in *Frederick Douglass* (New York: Citadel, 1964), 300-1.

3. "Sketch of the Life of James W. Ford," *Negro Anthology*, 279; Ben Davis Jr., *James W. Ford*, 21-23.

4. *Daily Worker*, 31 May 1932; *Afro-American*, 27 May 1932; *New York Herald Tribune*, 29 May 1932; *New York Herald Tribune*, 29 July 1932; *Daily Worker*, 28 May 1932.

5. *Afro-American*, 27 May 1932; *Daily Worker*, 16 July 1932; Interview with Don Wheeldin, 2 December 1989.

6. *Afro-American*, 27 May 1932; *The New Republic* 71 (27 July 1932); *Daily Worker*, 28 May 1932; *Daily Worker*, 31 May 1932.

7. Interview with Don Wheeldin, 2 December 1989; *Negro World*, 11 June 1932; *Pittsburgh Courier*, 4 June 1932; *Afro-American*, 27 May 1932; *The Liberator*, 19 November 1932.

8. *Daily Worker*, 17 June 1932; *Defender*, 28 May 1932; *Defender*, 10 September 1932.

9. *Opportunity* 10 (March 1932): 71; *Opportunity* 10 (April 1932): 141; *Opportunity* 10 (November 1932): 353, 71.

10. *The Crisis* 39 (July 1932): 222; *The Crisis* 39 (September 1932): 279-80; *The Crisis* 39 (November 1932): 343; *The Crisis* 39 (November 1932): 353; *The Crisis* 39 (December 1932): 366.

11. *Afro-American*, 8 August 1932; Angelo Herndon, *Let Me Live* (New York: Arno Press, 1969 [1937]), 186-89; Interview with Louise Thompson Patterson, 10 December 1989; James Ford, "The Fifteenth Anniversary of the C.P.U.S.A.," *The Communist* 14 (September 1934): 842-43; Foster-Ford Postcard, Foster-Ford flyers, Ford-Foster-Ford campaign booklet, copies are in, Communist Party Presidential Campaign File-1932, Southern California Research Library.

12. "Every Vote a Blow," (editorial), *New Masses* 7 (November 1932): 4; Daniel Aron, *Writers on the Left* (New York: Harcourt, Brace and World, 1961), 196-97.

13. Copy of Foster-Ford letter in Communist Party Presidential Campaign File, 10 August 1932, Southern California Research Library; *Defender*, 1 October 1932; *Defender*, 25 June 1932; *Afro-American*, 25 June 1932. Hughes gives a personal account of the fiasco that the film project ultimately turned into in his autobiography *I Wonder as I Wander* (New York: Hill and Wang, 1964), 69-99.

14. *Daily Worker*, 31 May 1932; *Daily Worker*, 29 June 1932.

15. Copy of Foster-Ford picnic announcement, 10 June 1932, Communist Party residential Campaign File-1932, Southern California Research Library; *Daily Worker*, 6 July 1932; *Daily Worker*, 30 July 1932; *Daily Worker*, 15 September 1932; *Daily Worker*, 22 September 1932; *Afro-American*, 9 July 1932; *Defender*, 23 July 1932.

16. *Daily Worker*, 8 June 1932; *Daily Worker*, 2 August 1932; *California Eagle*, 12 August 1932; *Time*, 11 June 1932; *Daily Worker*, 22 September 1932; *California Eagle*, 23 September 1932.

17. *Party Organizer* 5 (August 1932): 1-3, 8-9; *Afro-American*, 16 July 1932.

18. Harold F. Gosnell, *Negro Politicians: The Rise of Negro Politics in Chicago* (Chicago: University of Chicago Press, 1935), 352. In delivering his view of economic history, Hoover was blunt: "I am opposed to any direct or indirect government dole. The breakdown and increased unemployment in Europe is due in part to such practices" (Richard Hofstader, *The American Political Tradition* [New York: Random House, 1973], 400). On the other hand, in "The Hoover Myth," Murray N. Rothbard, argues passionately that liberal historians have butchered the Hoover record. Rothbard insists that Hoover was a man of public conviction who stood for public works, moderate government spending, and minimal controls on corporate industry. (Reprinted in James Weinsten and David W. Eakins, eds., *For A New America* [New York: Random House, 1970], 162-79).

19. David Caute, *The Great Fear* (New York: Simon and Schuster, 1978), 186; Gosnell, *Negro Politicians*, 352-53; Gunnar Myrdal, *An American Dilemma* (New York: Harper and Bros., 1944), 495; *Afro-American*, 4 November 1932.

20. St. Clair Drake and Horace Cayton, *Black Metropolis,* 736

21. Interview with Don Wheeldin, 2 December 1989.

22. *Harlem Liberator,* 14 October 1933; *Harlem Liberator,* 13 November 1933; *Harlem Liberator,* 27 November 1934.

23. *Daily Worker,* 1 July 1936; *Afro-American,* 4 July 1936; *Amsterdam News,* 4 July 1936; Interview with Don Wheeldin, 2 December 1989.

24. *Afro-American*, 4 July 1936; Ella Reeve Bloor, *We Are Many* (New York: International Publishers, 1940), 280.

25. *Daily Worker*, 1 July 1936; Bloor, *We Are Many*, 285; *Amsterdam News,* 4 July 1936; James Ford, *The Negro and the Democratic Front* (New York: International Publishers, 1938), 211-12; *Afro-American*, 4 July 1936; *Daily Worker*, 23 June 1936; *Afro-American,* 12 September 1936; Communist Party National Campaign Committee Release, 5 September 1936, Communist Party Presidential Campaign File-1936, Southern California Research Library.

26. *Daily World*, 1 July 1936; Interview with Mariam Sherman, 6 December 1989.

27. *Afro-American*, 12 September 1936; *Crusader News Agency*, 24 September 1936; Interview with Lester Rodney, 5 December 1989.

28. Loren Miller, "The Negro and the Parties," *New Masses* 11 (13 November 1936): 7-8; John B. Kirby, *Black Americans in the Roosevelt Era* (Knoxville: University of Tennessee Press, 1980), 13-35.

29. *Amsterdam News,* 7 November 1936. Excerpts of the Kelly Miller pamphlet were published in the *Amsterdam News,* 24 October 1936; Paul Ward, "Wooing the Negro Vote," *The Nation* 143 (1 August 1936): 119-20.

30. Morris Childs to Party Members, 6 June 1936, Communist Party presidential Campaign File, 1936, Southern California Research Library; Ben Davis, *James Ford* (New York: Workers Library Publishers, 1936). The best sources on the legal battle of Angelo Herndon and Ben Davis, and their subsequent journey to Communism are found in Herndon's autobiography *Let me Live* and Gerald F. Horne's *Ben Davis Black Liberation/Red Scare* (unpublished manuscript). Horne is the chairman of the Afro-American Studies Department at University of California Santa Barbara.

31. William Wilkerson to Ralph Bunche, 21 September 1936, Communist Party Presidential Campaign File-1936, Southern California Research Library; Communist Election Campaign Handbook, Los Angeles, California Election Campaign Committee, 1936, Southern California Research Library, 1, 7, 11 and 13; James Ford, "The Negro People and

the Elections," *The Communist* 16 (January 1937): 72; *Daily World,* 12 October 1936; *Amsterdam News,* 17 October 1936; *Afro-American,* 5 September 1936; Interview with Don Wheeldin, 2 December 1989; Interview with Lester Rodney, 5 December 1989.

32. *Afro-American,* 5 September 1936; *Afro-American,* 1 August 1936; *Norfolk Journal and Guide,* 1 August 1936; *Crusader News Agency,* 3 August 1936; *Richmond Dispatch,* 23 July 1936; *Richmond Dispatch,* 25 July 1936; *Afro-American,* 31 October 1936; *Afro-American,* 7 November 1936; *Crusader News Agency,* 2 November 1936.

33. *Afro-American,* 19 September 1936; *Afro-American,* 24 October 1936; *Crusader News Agency,* 28 October 1936; *Afro-American,* 7 November 1936.

34. *Defender,* 4 July 1936; *Afro-American,* 10 October 1936; *Afro-American,* 17 October 1936; *Afro-American,* 24 October 1936. The results of Calvin's survey was published in the *Amsterdam News,* 24 October 1936. Interview with Miriam Sherman, 7 December 1989.

35. Caute, *The Great Scare,* 186; *Amsterdam News,* 7 November 1936.

36. Ralph J. Bunche, *The Political Status of the Negro in the Age of FDR* (Chicago: University of Chicago Press, 1973 [1940]), 80 and 82; Sitkoff, *A New Deal for Blacks,* 93-97; Harold F. Gosnell, "The Negro Vote in Northern Cities, " *National Municipal Review* 30 (May 1941): 267. In analyzing the black political shift to Roosevelt, *Time* displays the casual bigotry of much of the mainstream press of the day. It described the black delegates to the 1936 Democratic convention as "black-amoors," and claimed that blacks voted Democratic because they allowed "numbers games and other rackets to flourish under protection in Negro quarters." Finally, *Time* asserted that many whites were leery of Roosevelt because they feared he "would have to smile graciously while his daughter danced with Negro Congressmen and Senators" ("The Black Game," *Time* 28 [17 August 1936]: 10-11).

37. *American Free Press,* 1 November 1940.

38. Press Release, National Election Campaign Committee, CPUSA, 9 August 1940, 1, 3, Communist Party Presidential Campaign File-1940, Southern California Research Library, 1, 3; *Election Platform of the Communist Party, 1940* (New York: New Age Publishers, 1940), 10-11; Caute, *The Great Fear,* 186.

6 Should Blacks Be Red, Too?

The Communists in 1934 regarded Harlem as their stronghold. The Party's unemployment, tenant, and relief organizations had organized angry Harlemites in dozens of street demonstrations and mass rallies. The Party now had supporters in Harlem churches and civic and social organizations. Lately, they had moved hard into trade union work. Communists had either created or exerted strong influence over the leadership of such unions as the Tobacco Workers Union, Needle Trades Union, Metal Workers Union, and the Food and the Laundry Workers Union. The Party had even penetrated the National Urban League's Harlem Workers Council.[1]

Howard University Dean Kelly Miller felt that the appeals that he and other black leaders had made for moderation and patience were falling on deaf ears. Blacks were tired, hungry, and desperate. They wanted radical solutions and the Communists seemed to offer them.[2]

It was hard for a man like Miller to admit that the Communists could get any blacks to accept their line. He was a genuine man of culture who firmly believed in American ideals and values. He had an unshakable faith that the only "ism" that could end racial oppression and exploitation was Americanism. His fond hope was that white Americans would observe the Constitution and protect black rights. The day that happened, blacks would have no need to turn to the Communists—so he believed. But that day had not yet come.

White society seemed to make little distinction between Miller and poor blacks. His prestige as an educator, his comfortable salary, and the respect of presidents still could not get him a room in many hotels or restaurants in New York City. Many whites would call him a "nigger" as quickly as they would a destitute black vagrant or menial laborer. It

109

was not his dilemma alone. It was the dilemma of even those blacks relatively secure economically in Depression-era America.[3]

Most blacks were aware that Communists did not erect the racial barriers. Miller's coworker, Howard University Professor Alain Locke, observed that hard times were making the masses "regard the race question as likely to resolve itself into the issues of the economic class struggle and proletarian radicalism." While many prominent blacks like Miller would not relent in their hostility to the Communists, more black leaders had begun to react to the desperation of the black masses and seek a détente with the Communists. One of them was a young Harlem minister.[4]

Adam's Gospel

In 1934 Adam Clayton Powell Jr. was a busy man. Most days he could be found in his small office at the rear of the Harlem Abyssinian Baptist Church, the largest black Baptist church in America. He would greet the flocks of visitors and needy that daily streamed into the church from Harlem's streets seeking food, clothes, or a place to stay for the night.

Tall, handsome, and with skin so fair he could easily pass as a white man, Powell had assumed the assistant pastorship of the church in 1930. The elder Powell, who still kept a tight rein on the pastorship, gave his son the task of directing the church's relief bureau. The program was set up in the early days of the Depression when it became obvious to Powell Sr. that government programs were not adequate to meet the needs of the Harlem poor. Working with the church relief bureau gave him a firsthand view of the suffering of the black poor. He was angry and wanted to do more. He spent many Depression days walking Harlem streets, battling rent-gouging landlords and picketing relief offices. Many of the people Powell Jr. found himself on the lines with were Communists. He would sometimes let them use his name on committees like the Scottsboro Defense Committee to get wider black support.[5]

The elder Powell had his own soft spot for the Reds. He left NAACP Executive Secretary Walter White sputtering for words at the 1932 NAACP annual conference when he told the delegates, "We are likely to have the Communists in control of this country in 2, 3, or 5 years." White recovered fast and corrected his "friend," as he called him, telling the delegates that the Communists would not take over. In

110

later years, Powell Sr. would offer a prayer for the Communist-influenced Labor Party because "it is nearest to Communism in its liberal attitude toward colored people."[6]

Powell Jr. supported the Communist call for black-white working-class unity. In an *Amsterdam News* column, he defended their right to speak, and would correct anyone's "political etiquette" for dragging "the red herring across the scene." However, while he appreciated the Communists because they fought for black rights, that did not mean he thought blacks should become Communists. He probably spoke for many blacks when he wrote: "He appreciates the Communists for their unceasing efforts on his behalf. He will support common causes, join willingly in united fronts, fight side by side in every crusade, but he does not join the Party."

And neither would Powell. He was the middle-class son of a black minister. Like most upward-bound blacks, he kept his eye firmly fastened on the future. He was sure that communism was not the final answer. When the Communists went astray, he was quick to take them to task: "Sometimes the infallible followers of Marx ,or rather Stalin, can be wrong. On such occasions they should take the criticism and not smear it with bait for reds."

Historian John Henrik Clarke, who knew Powell well, marveled at his ability "to turn the Communist Party on and off at will." He noted that Powell permitted the Communists "to use his church for rallies if he agreed with their viewpoint, otherwise he denied them use of his church." Powell would often be harshly criticized in later years for double-dealing and opportunism in using Communists or anyone else who would boost his career. But in the early 1930s, he was not saying anything different than other black leaders.[7]

Caught in the Middle: The Black Press

The black masses in the Depression era searched for leaders who were not afraid to demand radical reforms. Black leaders, if they expected to stay leaders, had to do what Powell did and stay a step ahead of the masses. Howard University professor Abram Harris was not sure whether black middle-class leaders could be fast enough on their feet to realize that black workers were in a desperate battle to survive.

He lobbied for a labor party that would "connect the Negro's special racial demands with its broader economic and social demands." He was convinced that established black leaders would never approve such

a program. He regarded them as "too opportunistic and petty bourgeois" to identify with the masses and radical politics. A labor party,
Harris added, would only give "economic reality to our contemporary
Negro bourgeoisie which is temperamentally detached from the realities of working class life."[8]

His public questioning of black leaders was yet one more sign that
they had to speak out. And in the black press they had a ready-made
forum available to articulate their views. When Roosevelt took office in
1933, there were 150 black newspapers in the country with a paid circulation of 600,000. However, the influence of the black press
extended far beyond the numbers. Blacks depended on their newspapers for hard news, updates on current events, and society gossip.

The editorials in the *Amsterdam News, Defender, Afro-American,*
and *Courier* shaped and influenced the thinking of many blacks. The
views of columnists like George Schuyler, Floyd Calvin, Miller, Powell,
and Roi Ottley triggered hot debates among blacks. Briggs, an experienced journalist, knew how influential black editors were. As early as
1929 he warned Party leaders not to cross swords with them. While he
considered most black editors "hopelessly reactionary," their one sav-
ing grace was that they "retained a large measure of militancy on racial
demands."[9] Many of the editors were first-class newsmen who recognized they had both a duty and an obligation to present news and
information of importance to their community. The Depression confronted them with a crisis that devastated blacks and that had to be
reckoned with in their pages.

So when DuBois presented the editors of seventeen of the leading
black newspapers in America with a remarkable request, fourteen readily accepted. He proposed that they hold a symposium in *The Crisis*
and tell black America what they thought about communism. The
Crisis editor thought it vital that blacks hear what the editors had to
say about the Reds, since they were obviously gaining in influence.
DuBois had certainly made his own views about the Communists
known, and they were not favorable. He accused them of treachery in
their handling of the Scottsboro Boys case. DuBois was convinced that
the Communists used the case "to appeal to the American Negro to
join the Communist movement."

The Scottsboro experience had made him even more pessimistic
about the future of black-labor alliances: "Whatever ideals white labor
today strives for in America, it would surrender nearly every one before
it would recognize a Negro as a man." At the same time he blistered

112

the Communist Party, he also wrote with no sense of contradiction, "I believe in Karl Marx."[10]

With his views a matter of public record, DuBois stood on the sidelines and let the editors have their say. He chose the editors whom he believed would present a good cross section of black opinion. On one side there was Fred Moore of the *New York Age,* an outspoken conservative. Moore noted: "Whatever the American Negro has gained has been through loyalty to his government, respect for law and order and by appealing to the better nature and hearts of the dominant race." The problems of blacks, he assured, "are going to be solved in the United States—not in Russia; and not by Russia."

The editor most likely to present the case for the Reds was Carl Murphy. Under Murphy's editorship, the *Afro-American* had moved steadily leftward. If black readers wanted to know what the Reds were doing among blacks without subscribing to the *Daily Worker,* they could often find out in Murphy's paper. Briggs, in his survey of the black press called the *Afro-American* "the least reactionary." With a nod toward the heavens, Murphy anointed the Communists with an "Allah be praised" salutation for being the only whites since the abolitionists to "openly advocate the economic, political and social equality of black folks." Murphy closed with a thanks and a reminder that "the Communists are going our way."

While no other editor stooped to the red-baiting of Moore, no others defended them with the uncritical adulation of Murphy. They gave credit to the Communists for supporting black rights, but they were wary of the Party's intentions particularly, in their unabashed defense of the white worker. The editors simply did not trust white labor to be the exemplary proletarian comrades that the Communists promised. *Amsterdam News* editor William Kelley advised blacks to wait and see "how Communism in America would be practiced by those poor whites upon whose shoulders would ultimately fall the responsibilities of government."

In a "postscript" to the symposium, DuBois tried to appear as the impartial arbiter, taking no position but summarizing the views of the editors. Even though they had not "made any study of classic Marxian socialism," DuBois praised the editors for their candor and political erudition.

"On the other hand," he assured, "every one of these writers knows the particular difficulties of the Negro problem and the labor situation in America much better than either Russian or American

Communists." With that said, DuBois would let *Crisis* readers make up their own minds on communism by "thought, study, and experiment." To help them reflect, he recommended several books. There were no Communist authors on his list.[11]

Communist leader Eugene Gordon closely followed the debate among the black editors and concluded, "Most of these editors of the Negro press discuss the black Red weightily and fearfully, but it is patent that few of them have learned from an original source what Communism is." Predictably, the only editor that he considered a "far-seeing" man was the *Afro-American*'s Murphy.[12]

Perceptive *Crisis* readers may have noticed that *Chicago Defender* editor Robert Abbott did not take part in the symposium. For a quarter century, he had run the paper with a tight fist. The *Defender* was as close to being the national newspaper of black America as any. Political and religious leaders, socialites, and businessmen all vied for space in the paper. Abbott enjoyed all the adulation. He was the prototypical self-made man who symbolized to blacks the strong-willed "race man" who would not compromise on civil rights. He was also the man perhaps most instrumental in prompting thousands of blacks to abandon the farms and plantations of the South and migrate to the North after World War I. His sensationalist articles depicted a North where jobs were plentiful and blacks did not have to fear terror and violence.

When Lenin died in 1924, Abbott treated him as a fallen hero: "A man of gigantic intellect, deep feeling and undaunted courage, the civilized world recognized and feared his diplomatic skill." At a time when A. Phillip Randolph had nothing good to say about any black moderate leader, he called Abbott "a man of vision and character."

In 1925, Abbott treated the meeting in Chicago of the Communist-run American Negro Labor Congress like a major event and editorially praised the Congress' manifesto. When the Young Communist League asked to march in the annual Bud Billiken parade that the *Defender* sponsored, Abbott's nephew John was horrified. So was Bud Billiken organizer, David Kellum. He regarded the parade which drew wide support from church and civic groups on Chicago's Southside as a tribute to black pride and achievement. Kellum threatened to resign if the Communists were allowed in.

Abbott listened patiently to both men and then said, "If there is a Bud Billiken parade, these young white people will march." He told the American Legion they could withdraw if they chose; his decision was final. The Legion withdrew and the Communists marched.[13]

A man like Abbott—and indeed, the other black moderate editors—perplexed the Communists. They did not know whether he stood with them or against them. They were not sure whether to take seriously or ignore Briggs' admonition to treat the black press gingerly. In truth, Communists really had little to complain about. They were getting more favorable coverage of their activities from the black press then they could ever hope to get from the mainstream "capitalist press." The *Defender, Courier,* and *Amsterdam News* diligently covered Communist marches, demonstrations, and political campaigns. The *California Eagle* even gave a gentle plug to Foster's book, "Toward A Soviet America." The *Eagle* was especially impressed that Foster promised to punish "white chauvinism and ostracism of blacks as a serious crime."[14]

Black Leaders Turn Left

Lukewarm sympathy from the black press was not enough, however, Party leaders wanted nothing less than recognition and respect from mainstream black organizations. And in that era that could mean only two—The NAACP and the Urban League. Both presented special challenges to the Communists.

Unlike the NAACP, the Urban League had never been an activist organization. While the League occasionally worked with the NAACP on labor issues, the two groups pretty much went their separate ways. The Urban League's suave, dapper director, T. Arnold Hill, was more comfortable talking with such men of wealth as Rockefeller, Carnegie, and Rosenwald about training programs and job assistance than talking to ordinary people about social reform.

Now the Depression forced Hill to come to grips with the dire economic needs of the black masses. Much as he hated to admit it, he could not deny that the Communists had a program for organizing black workers. They were fighting for jobs for unemployed blacks, pressuring the unions to drop their color barriers, and recruiting blacks into their Trade Union Education League.

When Hill testified before a congressional committee in 1930 probing Communist infiltration, he came off as a thoughtful man trying to understand them. Later, in *Opportunity*, he tactfully wrote, "The Communists have made the Negro's discontent with the prevailing system their point of approach to Negro membership in their ranks."[15] But Hill had to be cautious. If the League's wealthy backers perceived any hint of a swing to the left, the funds could dry up immediately. League officials had to lace their words with a little venom toward the Communists. In his review of the 1932 edition of the Communist-published *Labor Fact Book*, Ira De Reid, the league's director of research, laid it on thick: "The volume should aid many of the Communist front-running orators in inserting some teeth in their gummy babblings."

Not everyone in the Urban League drew the same conclusion as Reid. Asbury Smith, as a member of the League's Baltimore Executive Board, took care to disclaim any Communist sympathies, but then said that he was "in complete agreement with the Communist desire to use economic and political power for the benefit of the common man."

Even this mild endorsement was too much for Kelly Miller. He tore through the pages of *Opportunity* in November 1933, rehashing every argument he ever used against the Communists. He ended with the somber warning that "a Communistic state in America would put the Negro outside the pale." The following month *Opportunity* gave Loren Miller, a columnist for the Party-published *Harlem Liberator*, the chance to tell the Howard University professor that blacks should "quit kidding themselves;" there was only "One Way Out—Communism." Miller enjoyed pointing out the foibles of the black middle class. "The more clever Negro leaders do their part by advising Negroes to remain aloof from the class struggle." But, he warned, "there is no neutrality in modern society."

For the next year or so, *Opportunity* ran ads for V. F. Calverton's *Modern Quarterly*, and regularly featured poems by Langston Hughes. *Opportunity* editors apparently found sufficient literary merit in Eugene Gordon's short story "The Agenda" to award it honorable mention in the magazine's annual fiction contest. Gordon's tale dramatized the experiences of a black Communist organizer in Georgia.[16]

The remarks of A. L. Foster, executive secretary of Chicago's Urban League, also raised more than a few eyebrows. Following the International Conference of Social Workers in London, Foster spent the next few weeks traveling through Europe and the Soviet Union. A reporter who cornered him in Kiev asked what he most enjoyed about his trip. Foster did not hesitate. He effusively praised his Soviet hosts for their courtesy and attention. Foster had more to say: "I came here with an open mind and have thus been able to fully appreciate what is being done in the Socialist society." Foster, apparently feeling expansive, said that all blacks were bound to be "Communists at heart."

Urban League officials were both awed and alarmed by the Communist program for black workers. Following a regional conference in September 1933, the national office sent a memo to local league secretaries advising them not to choose between the AFL and the Communist-led left-wing unions. While the national office preferred that black workers affiliate with the AFL, the memo made it clear that black workers "may expect the development of bargaining power" in the Communist unions.[17]

The League then paid the Communists the sincerest form of flattery. It stole a big page out of their play book. In 1934, the League formulated a labor program and organized a nationwide network of Workers Councils to carry it out. League executive secretary Lester Granger felt that black leaders had failed miserably to confront the economic crisis.

It was "utterly hopeless," he argued, "to expect the intellectuals and professionals of the race to plan the way for Negro labor." Hill felt that the councils should be as tough as the Communists and "plan a program of action suitable for Negro labor, and integrate them into similar movements seeking the advancement of all workers." Hill pledged that the workers would run the councils and Urban League officials would keep hands off. He came close to attacking capitalism without naming it: "The Negro worker has been brought to his present plight through a steady grind of economic forces over decades and even centuries."[18]

Under Granger's lead, the councils mounted a free-wheeling program in various cities to press action on black workers' demands. A delegation went to see the local Works Project Administration director in Baltimore and demanded more professional jobs for blacks in the WPA.

A telegram was sent to Pennsylvania's governor urging him to reject Georgia's request for extradition of a black sharecropper charged with theft. In Cincinnati, the council took on the local Building Trades Federation. The council vowed to wage a vigorous fight to get the federation to admit blacks to building trade unions. The councils went to bat for sharecroppers in Mississippi, farmworkers in New Jersey, and ferryboatmen in Seattle.

Granger did not shy away from the leftists. He worked closely with the CIO's Steel Workers Organizing Committee in its drive to unionize blacks in the steel industry. He also supported the organizing drive of the International Ladies Garment Workers Union in Baltimore. Hill and Granger were not averse to throwing around big numbers like the

Communists. Hill claimed that the league had established fifty councils in sixteen states, and that more than thirty thousand blacks were members. He promised to add fifty more councils by 1937.

Granger boasted that the workers councils would organize black workers by the thousands. The councils caught the attention of Ford. Impressed by Hill's and Granger's efforts, he noted that the councils had taken "certain progressive steps."[19]

Granger, however, did not want anyone to get the wrong idea and think that the Urban League was getting too cozy with the Reds. He never envisioned the workers councils cooperating with the Communists. He even boasted that he had foiled attempts by the Communists to infiltrate the councils and Urban League locals.[20]

Communists versus the NAACP

In truth, the Urban League was never more than only a minor consideration to the Communists. Their real target was the NAACP. Throughout the 1920s, the organization had maintained a tough hands-off policy toward the Communists. During the early 1930s, Communists and NAACP leaders frequently traded hostile jibes on a range of social and economic issues. But the biggest source of friction was the Scottsboro case. In the initial stages of the defense campaign, the Communist-affiliated International Labor Defense and the NAACP joined in an uneasy alliance to try to save the boys. NAACP officials even gave indications that they appreciated the defense work of the ILD.

NAACP national secretary William Pickens sent a letter to the *Daily Worker* in April 1931, praising the ILD for moving "more speedily and effectively than all other agencies" on the case. He urged blacks to send funds to the ILD.

In 1934, the fragile alliance broke apart. On May 1, NAACP executive director Walter White announced that the NAACP "had no connection whatsoever with the efforts of Communist groups or the ILD in the case." White not only spurned all offers of reconciliation, he leveled the fresh charge that the Communists sought to use Scottsboro "for propaganda purposes." He accused the Communists of disrupting defense meetings and haranguing NAACP leaders as "plotters to murder the Scottsboro boys." Warming to the attack, White seemed to lose his handle on the facts. Without citing any proof, he said that the Party tried to bribe black editors to plug Communist meetings.

He claimed the Party was so unscrupulous that it produced fake Scottsboro mothers at rallies when they ran out of the real ones. White said that the phony Scottsboro mothers would pump the audience up with tear-jerking stories of their "sons'" plight and then depart after fleecing the audience of hefty donations. He was certain that the money went straight into the Party's coffers.[21]

Party leaders, of course, told a different story. They proudly declared that it was the Communists who marched, rallied, and raised the funds for the Scottsboro defense. Patterson explained the Party's position and the root of conflict with the NAACP: "We felt that the case was not primarily a legal matter; it was a political struggle of national and international import."

Browder maintained that it would have been "impossible to stir the entire world" if Scottsboro " had been taken up from the liberal-humanitarian view." Stung by White's accusations, Ford noted that the Party sought coalitions with a broad range of groups. He cited an ILD-sponsored conference in Harlem in October 1934 that brought together unionists, church groups, black editors, and liberal activists.

To refute White's charge that the Party misused defense funds, Ford produced a letter from ACLU Secretary Roger Baldwin, urging organizations to "contribute to the legal defense fund to be used solely for retaining lawyers and for the heavy incidental expenses. " Ford gave an itemized account of the money the ILD had raised and how it had been spent.[22]

As for the "fake" mothers charge, the *Harlem Liberator* pointed out that the NAACP denied Mrs. Heywood Patterson, the mother of one Scottsboro defendant, the right to speak at its Pittsburgh convention in 1932.

The *Liberator* pointed out that when Ada Wright, a "real" Scottsboro mother, finally was allowed to speak at the NAACP's 1934 convention, she thanked the International Labor Defense, not the NAACP, for defending the boys. Mrs. Wright spent much of her hour-long talk describing the "warm reception" she had received during her recent tour of the Soviet Union. The tour was sponsored by the ILD.

Back in America, there was nothing fake about the hardships that Wright had to put up with while touring the country on behalf of her son. Marion Sherman, an ILD organizer who traveled with Wright, remembered those days: "We never slept in hotels because we couldn't afford them. We were put up in various people's homes. We never had any spending money, and whatever food we ate had to come from the people that put us up. Ada was thankful to the ILD because she could see the sacrifices people were making."

Patterson also called on Mary Church Terrell, President of the National Council of Negro Women, to vouch for the ILD. Few women were held in higher esteem at the time. In May, Patterson asked Terrell to accompany five Scottsboro mothers to the White House for a Mother's Day meeting with President Roosevelt. The mothers planned to petition the president to "speak out against the murderous prosecution" of their sons. Although Roosevelt declined to meet with them, Terrell accompanied the group as they protested in front of the White House.[23]

Robert Minor and Angelo Herndon ground their axes with NAACP officials. They claimed that NAACP field secretary William Pickens made a hasty exit through the back door of a Chattanooga, Tennessee church in 1931 rather than appear with Communists at a Scottsboro rally. Pickens fired back. The only reason Communists were there in the first place, he said, was because he insisted they be allowed to speak.[24]

While Party leaders continued to apply the heat, they were also hoping that the NAACP would crack from within. The Depression was not going away. Party leaders knew that dissension was mounting within the organization.

The Depression had radicalized a growing number of militant activists within the organization who were not happy with the NAACP's conservative approach to social reform. They wanted the NAACP to launch a frontal attack against racism and poverty. Some even pressed for more direct involvement in workers' struggles. The courts were too slow and ineffectual for their tastes. The NAACP board of directors was having an increasingly difficult time holding these activists in line. A clash was imminent.

The Battle Within

The political conflict within the NAACP first surfaced at its annual conference in 1932. By majority vote, the organization passed a resolution that sounded decidedly out of character for the NAACP: "The Negro as a worker has interests identical to those of white workers." The resolution called for the "redistribution of present wealth," "systematic taxation of large incomes," and "industry for public wealth, and not for private profit."

120

The wording on another resolution had DuBois' unmistakable imprint, which was not too surprising since he chaired the resolutions committee. "We favor world peace and international comity and disarmament; and the withdrawal of our military forces from Haiti and Nicaragua, and let Liberia regulate her own internal affairs."[25]

Whether NAACP officials were trying to out-flank the Communists, hold the shaky allegiance of the black masses, or appease its young activists, the NAACP was inching leftward.[26] Meanwhile, NAACP officials were finding it more difficult to ignore the Communists. With the NAACP's annual conference rapidly approaching, they grudgingly invited the Party to send a speaker. On 1 July 1934, Harlem Party leader Herbert Newton took the stage to deafening applause at the NAACP's twenty-fifth annual conference in Oklahoma City.

The Board of Directors invited Newton as the official representative of the ILD to address the more than one thousand delegates and observers. Newton gave a near textbook recitation of the Party's "Negro work." Newton ticked off the Communist campaigns around Scottsboro, voting rights, job discrimination, and anti-lynching legislation. He announced that the Communist-initiated League of Struggle for Negro Rights and the ILD had drawn up a "Civil Rights Bill of the Negro People." The bill would make lynching a federal crime and rally "the masses of toilers against the whole system of national oppression."

Newton, at the time running for the Southside Chicago congressional seat held by black Republican Oscar DePriest, promised that, if elected, his first act would be to introduce the LSNR bill in Congress. Newton was in no mood to spare the feelings of NAACP officials: "Our methods are revolutionary class struggle methods as opposed to class collaboration, reformist, legalistic methods."

Newton knew that there was bitter infighting in the NAACP between the activists and the old guard. At an earlier convention session, the radicals had nearly forced through a rule change that would have dramatically changed the structure of the organization. The change would have amended a clause in the NAACP constitution that gave the board of directors exclusive authority to hire officers and set official policy. The new rules would have liberalized— "democratized," as the *Negro Liberator* termed it—the organization by expanding the number of board members. This would have effectively crippled the power of the old guard. Ultimately, decision-making

121

would have passed to the local branches, where the radicals were growing in strength. The rule change was defeated by only four votes.

Newton closed his address with an appeal "to those delegates who are closest to the masses to carry through joint action with us." He was clearly trying to deepen the fissure between the radicals and moderates within the NAACP.[27] And it was deepening. Immediately following the convention, the board appointed Abram Harris to head a Committee on the Future Plan and Program of the NAACP. He tossed his hat completely into the camp of the left radicals. He was determined that the organization do an about-face and join in the economic struggle of black and white workers.

There was bitter in-fighting within the committee. The conservatives were opposed to any changes, but the tide was rolling against them. In September the committee presented its report. It was a radical document that called for "the building of a labor movement, industrial in character, which will unite all labor, white and black." The committee directed the NAACP to form producers and consumers cooperatives, conduct classes in workers education, and print literature geared to "the needs of workers." The board made a few minor word changes and approved the report. The majority of delegates at the NAACP's 1935 annual conference followed suit.[28]

A casualty of the organization's internal squabbles was DuBois. Unhappy with what he viewed as White and the board's timidity on political and economic issues, the *Crisis* editor offered to resign in June 1934. The board accepted.

While many were saddened by his departure, the Communists shed no tears. The *Harlem Liberator* got in its licks at the magazine: "Most of the articles appearing in it dealt with the 'nice white people' the 'nice colored people' had met along their way." The paper assured its readers that even with Dubois out, there would be no change in NAACP and that *The Crisis* "would continue to betray the Negro people." Party leaders took the Dubois ouster as proof that the NAACP was in deep trouble.

The *Liberator* claimed that thousands of blacks were quitting the organization. "Naturally the Negro people who were being forced into the bread lines in ever increasing numbers withdrew their support." Privately, the Communists knew better. As Loren Miller knowingly observed, the NAACP was "a very vital factor in Negro life."[29]

Détente

Nineteen thirty-five promised to be a big year for the Party. In August, at the Seventh World Congress of the Communist International, Bulgarian Communist Party leader Gerogi Dimitrov announced that Communists would "strive for short-term and long-term agreements" with "Social-Democratic Parties, reformist trade unions, and other organizations of the working people" to oppose the fascists. The "Popular Front" was now official Communist policy.

The Comintern gave American Communists the specific objective of organizing a "united front" to "fight for the equal status for Negroes." Communists were told they must embrace black ministers, black editors, black businessmen and professionals. It was now more urgent than ever that Party leaders cement ties with the NAACP.[30]

Ford was ready to do just that. Several months before the Comintern made public its new position, he had asked the NAACP board if he could speak at their annual conference in June. While the Board brusquely informed him that the "program was already prepared," he did not come away completely empty handed. The board made a concession. They granted Herndon ten minutes to discuss his case before the Board's business session at the annual conference. The Board would listen to Herndon only because of "interest in the fundamental principle involved in the case."

It was a no-risk concession to the Communists, since the NAACP had already filed an Amicus Curiae brief with the Supreme Court on behalf of Herndon. NAACP chief counsel Charles Houston viewed the brief as a bow "to agitation for social reform." His assistant, whose name also appeared on the Herndon brief, was a young attorney who already was handling the NAACP's toughest desegregation cases. In the years to come, Thurgood Marshall would prove more than able in the battle against segregation.[31]

The twenty-sixth annual conference in St. Louis in June 1935 did not turn into the raucous affair of the previous year's convention. Most of the controversial issues had already been settled. White and the board, now firmly in charge, appeared more self-assured. White would show the radicals that the Communists were not the only ones who could turn a sharp phrase. White thundered to the delegates, "Unless justice is given the Negro he may be driven by desperation to the use of force."

The delegates also heard from John P. Davis. His specialty was the National Recovery Act. A Harvard graduate, Davis had joined the Labor Department in the early days of the Depression to study New Deal programs and their impact on blacks. He was given the post of Secretary of the Joint Committee on Recovery. He did not like what he saw.

He spent much of his time battling bureaucrats and racist administrators who continually shortchanged blacks in their NRA benefits. Convinced that the New Deal "worsened" the conditions of blacks and that reformism was passe, Davis was tired of trying to make the system work: "Now we should be willing to challenge the old order with all the force we can command."

The final resolutions stretched the NAACP beyond its usual bounds of moderation. They backed the Scottsboro and Herndon cases, and demanded major economic restructuring of the system to bring justice to sharecroppers, farmers, the unemployed, and workers. The NAACP pledged to lobby for laws on old-age pensions, unemployment insurance, child and female labor, and trade union reform. Party leaders felt vindicated by the NAACP's turn. It was "grudging endorsement," Loren Miller crowed, "that the Negro question can only be solved through cooperation with the working class."

Miller thought that white liberals held too much power in the organization. He specifically singled out Ovington and NAACP president Joel Spingarn. To Miller, White and the other black officers were mere hirelings who played no real role in shaping policy. But this was nitpicking. The radicals had forced the black middle class to learn, Miller insisted, "that the lot of the Negro worker will not be improved until the lot of the entire working class is bettered."[32]

While the Communists seemed to be winning the test of political wills with the NAACP, the path was still fraught with hidden dangers. Party leaders decided to tread lightly and not make any blunders that would shatter the fragile peace. The Party had to make some adjustments.

The first casualty was the "Negro Nation" idea. It was relatively easy to put this on hold since it had never really caught on with rank and file Communists and was universally condemned by black leaders as "segregationist." A leading proponent of the "Negro Nation" concept set out to clear away any misunderstanding that the NAACP had about the Party's position on the "Negro Question."

James Allen explained to *Crisis* readers in May 1935 that "the right of self-determination means nothing more nor less than the most complete realization of democracy and equal rights." The following year,

Allen took up the issue again in his book *The Negro Question in the United States*. This time Allen backtracked. He told critics that "the principle of self-determination is diametrically opposed to the undemocratic practice of segregation."

Sociologist Sterling Spero, reviewing the book in the *Nation*, immediately spotted the Communist shift. Spero asked if Allen planned to redefine self-determination "as a name for the movement for Negro democratic rights?" He did. And for the next two years, the political honeymoon between the Communists and the black moderates was in full bloom.[33]

The first pleasant by-product of the détente was the new editor of *The Crisis*. When DuBois was ousted from *The Crisis*, the Communists fully expected the magazine to become more reactionary. They knew nothing about the new editor, Roy Wilkins. In 1931 Wilkins gave up a promising career with the *Kansas City Call* to become White's assistant.

White found Wilkin's penchant for accurate reporting particularly valuable. He sent him on forays into trouble spots in Mississippi and Arkansas to investigate abuses against sharecroppers. When DuBois resigned, White asked Wilkins to take over the magazine. He was reluctant, but White was persuasive. He resolved that for the time being he would not tinker with DuBois' editorial policies.

By 1936, Wilkins had also begun to lean slightly leftward. He agreed with the radicals that blacks and the poor had not gotten very much out of the Democrats or the Republicans. If it were not for the Communist program, he told a *Defender* interviewer, "the plight of the race and the underprivileged" would not have been brought "to the attention of those parties." By keeping the pressure on both political parties, he insisted that the Communists contributed "the chief most useful function at the present time."[34]

The ILD's *Labor Defender*, pleased with Wilkins' apparent warmth, invited him to share his views with their readers. He obliged and traced the history of NAACP legal cases and legislative activities. He closed with a call for "all forces" to join "with others in behalf of all persons who are oppressed, intimidated, and robbed." The *Labor Defender* returned the compliment and praised him as a leader "who has done outstanding service to his people and to the cause of liberty and justice." A few months later, Wilkins seemed pleased that a number of blacks were chosen as delegates to the convention of the leftist Congress for Peace and Democracy. He took it as a healthy sign that "the trend today is toward radical alliances."[35]

125

If Communists thought that Wilkins had come around, they were mistaken. A key Party organizer in Harlem, Abner Berry, evidently labored under that delusion. Berry wrote to him as one would to a cordial associate. He gently rebuked him for hitting too hard on racism in the labor movement, and reminded Wilkins that the CP "supported wholehearted the NAACP's anti-lynching campaign." Wilkins ignored Berry and continued to attack the lily-white unions.

Before the decade closed, Wilkins and White were severely attacking their leftist critics. When Ralph Bunche committed the unpardonable sin of criticizing the NAACP for being "too legislative," White complained that his accusation sounded like "a hangover from the theoretical approach of the American Communists in the middle thirties concerning the Negro problem." To Wilkins, Bunche was just "returning to the wars with this old argument as a weapon."

If Bunche had a better understanding of the Communists, Wilkins felt, he would know that "the identification of the Negroes with a political and economic revolutionary program would be suicidal. " Wilkins and White were in reality protecting their turf against the Communists, as Pickens and Johnson before them had done. Wilkins and White saw the NAACP as a sacred trust to safeguard civil rights within, not without, the democratic framework of American society. Any violation of it would spell peril for blacks.[36]

Following the Roosevelt landslide in 1936, Wilkins and White rudely yanked the frayed welcome mat from under the Communists. The New Deal was firmly in place. Blacks were receiving more WPA jobs, relief, and farm payments, and had substantially increased their political leverage within the Democratic party. Blacks were elected to a record number of state and local offices, including several positions in the South, and Roosevelt made more black appointments than any previous president.

After 1937, no Communist would ever officially appear again at an NAACP annual conference or business meeting. The NAACP board would instantly reject every Communist offer of joint action on civil rights. A decade later, the organization would pass a resolution barring Communists from membership.[37]

The Political Mood of Black Moderates

If the NAACP was momentarily softened by the Party's "Popular Front" tactics, other blacks completely lost their bearings. By 1935, the black press was filled with accounts of blacks who had traveled to Russia. They came home raving about the "color-free" society they found there.[38]

Black professionals and educators, impressed by the Communists' stance on civil rights in America, wanted to see how socialism worked in the Soviet state. *Afro-American* managing editor William Jones could barely contain himself during a week-long visit to the Soviet Union: "I feel that I have dropped onto a new planet." He was awed to find that a place on earth existed where "there is absolutely no color problem." Jones wanted more blacks, especially black leaders, to go to the Soviet Union and discover for themselves how "better human relations" had been achieved "under the leadership of the Bolsheviks."

Even a hard-bitten journalist like Henry Lee Moon went to Moscow and came away a believer. Moon found a government that made the cause of blacks "dear to the hearts of millions of Soviet citizens who have never seen a Negro." Moon admitted that blacks in America were materially better off than the Russians, but the journalist was convinced that blacks would "willingly exchange comparative comfort" for "the freedom from persecution" that the Soviet Union seemed to promise.[39]

Delegations of film actors, writers, and artists regularly trooped to Moscow to work as guests of the government. A few stayed on to work on film projects or to serve as engineers and technicians. DuBois, Paul Robeson, and Langston Hughes made their pilgrimages and came away convinced they had found utopia. Moscow was so popular that even a well-known black scientist told friends that there was "something good" in Marx. The scientist briefly contemplated taking his test tubes to Moscow and working on agricultural projects there. Fortunately for Tuskeegee, George Washington Carver decided to stay home.[40]

But if a staid and respected academic like Carver could toy with the Communists, it was obvious that the radical fervor of the Depression years could not long bypass the campus. Many black students and professors got their first grounding in politics through radical protest. And Howard University, perhaps the best known of the black universities, quickly became a testground for radical ideas.

In December 1933 the National Student League chose Howard University as the site for its first national conference. The League was created by the Communists in 1931. It was a racially mixed unit that had begun to take some interest in the issue of campus discrimination.

About four hundred students showed up for the conference and about fifty of them were black. The first day of the conference was uneventful. Adam Lapin, editor of the *Student Review*, tried to stir the delegates by appealing to white students "to take the initiative in fighting against every trace of racial discrimination in the colleges." The next evening the fireworks began.

Even though Dean Kelly Miller was opposed to the Marxist students coming to Howard, he reluctantly agreed to speak at a symposium on lynching. He was confident that he could influence the other side. Mindful of who he was speaking to, Miller struck a note of militancy: "Lynching is a moral malady and reflects a bad conscience. We must shame Americans out of this practice by appealing to their conscience."

The Dean had barely taken his seat when Richard Moore, recently promoted to the post of general secretary of the Communist-run League of Struggle for Negro Rights, grabbed the stage. Moore shouted that Miller had a "pacifist attitude" toward lynchers. He reminded Miller that blacks had delivered "sermons against lynching for the past 157 years" and had gotten nowhere. Militant action, not appeals to conscience, Moore argued, would stop lynching. A furious Miller beat a hasty retreat from the hall. He blamed Howard dean Dr. Mordechai Johnson for bringing the Reds to Howard. Miller was going to go all out to oust him from his post at the school.[41]

At the time of the League meeting, Johnson was nearing the finish of his tenth year at Howard. He was the school's first black president. The years at the school were satisfying ones for him. He was proud of the part he played in the growth of the campus. Under his administration, Howard had expanded its faculty and student body and the federal government had increased its funding. The school had become a national symbol of educational progress for blacks. He was also delighted that new opportunities were opening up for talented, trained, and educated young blacks in government and some professions.

But Johnson was not content to rest on his laurels. He was a political activist who had to walk a careful line. Howard was dependent on the federal government for nearly every penny it needed to operate. This presented a huge problem for him because he believed in speaking his mind. At commencement ceremonies in 1922, he had told graduating seniors that there was more to the world than fine homes, prestigious careers, and pursuing wealth. He urged them to appreciate radical movements for change because they "are home grown fruits, with roots deep sprung in a world of black American suffering." He continued to strike radical themes whenever he ventured from Howard.

At the World Conference on International Justice in 1928, observers thought he was championing communism when he called for economic reform. In 1933 at Harlem's Mt. Olivet Baptist Church in New York, they were sure of it. The *Amsterdam News* christened his Mt. Olivet speech with the headline, "Dr. Johnson defends Communism Before Large Harlem Audience."

The paper was close. Johnson told the audience that not only did he not mind being called a Communist but that "the day will come when being called a Communist will be the highest honor." *New York Age* editor Fred Moore was so scared that his candor would prompt Roosevelt to cut off the school's federal appropriation that he advised him to "spend more time making friends close to Congress and the White House." For some congressmen it was already too late.

In February 1934 Mississippi Democrat Robert Hall introduced House Resolution 160, calling for a federal probe to end "the continuous tumultuous conditions" at the college. Congressman Oscar DePriest, who had known Johnson for years felt the heat in Congress. He told angry Southerners, who wanted to do just what Moore feared, that he did not think Johnson, a Baptist minister, could be a Communist. However, to quiet them down, DePriest said that he would introduce a resolution that "colleges should be scrutinized more closely for Red influences."[42]

When Johnson permitted James Ford, Socialist Party chairman Norman Thomas, W.E.B. DuBois, and A. Phillip Randolph to attack the New Deal and the Roosevelt administration at a Howard economic planning conference in May 1935, Miller was livid. He claimed that he sat through all the sessions and not once did he hear Johnson challenge anything that the radicals said. He intensified his effort to get rid of him. He told his story of how the Reds had captured Howard to the U.S .Solicitor, Department of Interior officials, and finally to the House Un-American Activities Committee. Miller was encouraged by Perry Howard, a Republican national committeeman from Mississippi. The Republican told House investigators that Howard University was such a hot bed of radicalism that his own son had been polluted by "Communist views" when he attended the school.

Black Illinois Democrat Arthur Mitchell jumped into the fray and announced that he was introducing his own resolution demanding that

Congress investigate whether "Communism is being taught openly at Howard." Mitchell also wanted to see for himself what was going on at the school. Mitchell accompanied a House Appropriations Committee to Howard to determine if Johnson was abusing academic freedom by courting the Reds.

At the campus, he spoke to a faculty assemblage and threatened more investigations similar to those then in process at the University of Chicago if academic freedom continued to be abused. As soon as he finished, Johnson rushed to the podium and told the audience that if he had to choose between an appropriation and the right to speak, he would rather see the students and faculty "go back to the cornfield." Johnson did not have to put on overalls. Howard not only got its appropriation but an increase for 1934-1935 to $665,005.[43]

The Howard president did not break stride. In February 1937 he gave the keynote address at the Communist-organized Southern Negro Youth Congress convention in Richmond. He called fascism, not communism, "the greatest danger to democracy." Miller did not get Johnson removed.[44]

What irked Miller as much as Johnson's apparent Red taint was that he appeared to be "shielding radical professors." Students came and went, so did Red speakers, but radical professors with tenure did not. To Miller, they used their cloak of academic respectability to spread their inflammatory ideas to legions of naive and unsuspecting black students. He probably had Ralph Bunche in mind. After a brilliant academic career at UCLA and Harvard, where Bunche earned his doctorate, he joined the Howard faculty in 1932. Shortly afterward, he took over as chair of Howard's political science department.

Appalled by the destitution of black workers, Bunche blamed capitalism for creating the huge disparities in wealth. While he never called himself a Marxist, he did believe that "Race issues tend to merge into class issues." He saw a coming world struggle between rich and poor: "Throughout the world the issue between the working and owning classes is sharpening." He made it clear where he stood: "The Negro must develop a consciousness of class interest and purpose, and must strive for an alliance with the white working class in the common struggle for economic and political equality and justice."[45]

He reserved his harshest words for the black middle class. To him, they labored under too many illusions that they could make it in the system. The black elite, Bunche insisted, must snap out of their slumber and recognize that "American capitalistic society simply does not offer the economic basis for the perpetuation of a significant black bourgeoisie."[46] He ripped apart the tactics and programs of all the established black organizations. They were too politically cautious to suit him. "Neither prayer, nor logic, nor emotional or legal appeal," he counseled, had gotten blacks very much. Until black leaders understood that class, not race antagonism, defined oppression in America, Bunche believed they would fail to win any tangible rewards for blacks. Communist Party leader Abner Berry, always appreciative of radical words from black intellectuals, called him "an active friend and supporter" of the working class.[47]

While Bunche's and Miller's political views were polar opposites, they were not the only blacks who voiced opinions about the Communists. Black nationalists also rejected the Communist appeal for racial harmony. They regarded Marxism as just another white man's "ism" that could not solve the problems of the black poor. The nationalists argued that white Communists would betray blacks the first chance they got. They countered the Communist call for class solidarity with their own pitch for race solidarity. They insisted that blacks must develop their own organizations and programs free of all white influences, and that included the Communists. Party leaders had bumped heads in the 1920s with Marcus Garvey, and now it was time for a return bout.

Still, the mid-1930s were fruitful years for the Communists. They changed their policies in line with Moscow's directives and made new friends among the black moderates, but the storm clouds had not completely cleared. This time they would find the enemy both without and within.

Notes

1. *Amsterdam News,* 24 January 1934; Interview with Don Wheeldin, 2 December 1989; James Ford, "Development of Work in the Harlem Section," *The Communist,* 14 (April 1935): 312-25.

2. *Amsterdam News,* 24 January 1934. Miller's views on communism and labor unions were detailed in the chapter, "On with the Dance." Also see Miller's *Radicals and Conservatives; Springfield Republican,* 19 September 1933 and Ottley, *New World A-Coming,* 242-44.

3. Miller, "Should Black Turn Red?" *Opportunity* 11 (November 1933): 329; Kelly Miller, *An Open Letter to Woodrow Wilson,* (Washington, D.C., 1917).

4. John Hope Franklin, *From Slavery to Freedom,* 477-96; Miller, "Should Black Turn Red?" 329; Alain Locke, *The Negro in America* (Chicago:

American Library Association, 1933), 35; *Afro-American,* 16 May 1932; Drake and Cayton, *Black Metropolis,* 2:734-35.

5. There are many works on the controversial Harlem Congressman, however, two authors who knew him well and observed his political machinations give the best glimpse of Powell in his early left leaning years: John Henrik Clarke, "The Early Years of Adam Clayton Powell, *Freedomways* 7 (Summer 1967): 199-211 and Ottley, *New World A-Coming,* 220-21 and 226-35. Also, the FBI conducted an intense surveillance campaign of Powell's political activities during the 1940s and the 1950s. They were particularly interested in uncovering Powell's alleged Communist ties (see Charles V. Hamilton, *Adam Clayton Powell Jr.* [New York: Atheneum, 1991], 175-78).

6. *Afro-American,* 9 January 1932; Quote from Adam Clayton Powell Sr.'s book, *Riots and Ruins* is in Clarke, "The Early Years of Adam Clayton Powell," 208.

7. *Amsterdam News,* 25 January 1936; *Amsterdam News,* 15 February 1936; *Amsterdam News,* 19 September 1936; Adam Clayton Powell Jr., *Marching Blacks* (New York: Dial Press, 1945), 68; John Henrik Clarke to Earl Ofari Hutchinson, 24 January 1990.

8. Abram L. Harris, "The Negro Worker: A Problem of Progressive Labor Action," *The Crisis* 37 (March 1930): 84-85. Harris hinted at the same need for independent black labor organizing in *The Black Worker* (468-69).

9. See John H. Burma, "An Analysis of the Present Negro Press," *Social Forces* 26 (December 1947): 170-72; Ted Poston, "The Negro Press," *Reporter* 1 (6 December 1947): 14-15; Lee Finkle, "The Conservative Aims of Militant Rhetoric: Black Protest during World War II," *Journal of American History* 40 (December 1973): 693-94; P. B. Young, "The Extent and Quality of the Negro Press," *The Southern Workman* 62 (August 1933): 324; Cyril Briggs, "The Negro Press as a Class Weapon," *The Communist* 8 (August 1929): 454. By 1940 the paid circulation of black newspapers had grown to 1,276,000. Lee Finkle, *Forum for Protest: The Black Press During World War II,* 55-60 Ph.D. diss., New York University, 1971

10. *The Crisis* 39 (April 1932): 117; *The Crisis* 38 (September 1931): 314 and 318; DuBois to George Streater, 24 April 1935, DuBois Papers, University of Massachusetts.

11. *The Crisis* 39 (May 1932): 155, 170 and 191; *The Crisis* 39 (April 1932): 117.

12. Eugene Gordon, "Blacks Turn Red," in Nancy Cunard's *Negro Anthology,* 239-40.

13. *Messenger* 5 (July 1922): 446; *Chicago Defender,* 3 February 1924; Carol Marks, "Black Workers and the Great Migration North," *Phylon* 46 (June 1985): 155; *Chicago Defender,* 7 November 1925; Roi Ottley, *The Lonely Warrior* (Chicago: Henry Regnery Co., 1955), 350-51.

14. *California Eagle*, 11 June 1932.

15. *Opportunity* 11 (August 1933): 250; Guichard P. Parris and Lester Brooks, *Blacks in the City: A History of the National Urban League* (Boston: Little, Brown & Co., 1971); T. Arnold Hill, "Communism," *Opportunity* 8 (September 1930): 278.

16. *Opportunity* 10 (August 1932): 258; Asbury Smith, "What Can the Negro Expect from Communism?" *Opportunity* 11 (July 1933): 212; Miller, "Should Black Turn Red?" 350; Loren Miller, "One Way Out—Communism," *Opportunity* 12 (July 1934): 214 and 216; *Opportunity* 11 (December 1933): 429.

17. *Afro-American*, 12 September 1936; A Regional Conference Memorandum for Local Secretaries, 28 September 1933, Urban League Papers, Library of Congress, 2; Horace Cayton and George S. Mitchell, *Black Workers and the New Unions* (Chapel Hill: University of North Carolina, 1939), 401-2.

18. *Chicago Defender*, 19 May 1934; Lester Granger, "What Objectives Shall the League Set for the Next Five Year Period in the Field of Organization in Industry," 27 November 1935, NUL Papers, Library of Congress; Lester Granger, "The Negro—Friend or Foe of Organized Labor?" *Opportunity* 13 (May 1935): 144; Arnold Hill, "Building New Roads," *Opportunity* 12 (December 1934): 376; T. Arnold Hill, "The Plight of the Industrial Workers," *Journal of Negro Education* 5 (January 1936): 46.

19. *Amsterdam News*, 17 September 1936; Workers Council Bulletin, nos. 1-10, NUL Papers, Library of Congress; Hill, "The Plight of the Industrial Workers," 46; Ford, *The Negro and the Democratic Front*, 80.

20. *Hearings, Communist Infiltration of Minority Groups, House Un-American Activities Committee*, 14 July (Washington, D.C.: Government Printing Office, 1949), 467; Parris and Brooks, *Blacks in the City*, 225-26 and 256.

21. *Daily Worker*, 24 April 1931; *New York Times*, 1 May 1934; Walter White, "The Negro and the Communists," *Harpers* 64 (December 1931): 68.

22. Hugh T. Murray, "The NAACP versus the Communist Party: The Scottsboro Rape Cases, 1931-1932," *Phylon* 28 (Third Quarter 1967): 276-87. Murray makes a convincing case that the Communists were sincere in their actions and that there were no financial irregularities involved in their defense work. Miriam Sherman who toured with Scottsboro mother Ada Wright and worked closely with the ILD throughout the campaign noted: "The Defense Committee was always strapped for money. To my personal knowledge, every penny that we raised went to pay for legal fees, and expenses" (Interview, 7 December 1989). Ford, "The United Front in the Field of Negro Work," *The Communist* 14 (February 1935): 163-65 and 167. Elizabeth Dilling

reprints a list of the members of the Scottsboro Committee of Action as of May 1933. Although many of the names on her list are well-known Communist leaders and activists, there is also a generous sprinkling of non-Communist liberals and moderates such as Roger Baldwin, Channing Tobias, Adam Clayton Powell, and W. C. Handy (*The Red Network*, 227).

23. *Negro Liberator*, 7 July 1934; Interview with Miriam Sherman, 7 December 1989; William Patterson to Mary Church Terrell, 10 May 1934; William Patterson to Mary Church Terrell, 13 May 1934; William Patterson to Mary Church Terrell, 18 May 1934, Mary Church Terrell Papers, Library of Congress.

24. Angelo Herndon, *Let Me Live*, 124-25; *Afro-American*, 25 May 1940. *Pittsburgh Courier* editor Robert L. Vann tried to rally the forces behind the NAACP: "Negroes should stand firm for the NAACP against the blandishments of the Reds" (*Pittsburgh Courier*, 4 July 1931).

25. *Amsterdam News*, 1 June 1932; Record, *Race and Radicalism*, 76-78.

26. *Amsterdam News*, 17 August 1932; *Harlem Liberator*, 16 December 1933.

27. Interview with Don Wheeldin, 2 December 1989; *Negro Liberator*, 7 July 1934; *Afro-American*, 8 July 1934.

28. *Preliminary Draft of the Report of the Committee on the Future Plan and Program*, NAACP Papers, Library of Congress, 6-8; Mary White Ovington to Joel Spingarn, 23 September 1934, Charles Edward Russell to Walter White, 14 June 1934, NAACP Papers, Library of Congress; Raymond Wolters, *Negroes and the Great Depression: The Problem of Economic Recovery*, 314-320. Perhaps more than any other New Deal era black intellectual, including DuBois, Harris developed the deepest sympathy for Marxian theory. By 1950, however, Harris had changed his tune. He now considered Marxism "anarchistic in character" (Abram L. Harris, "Utopian Elements in Marx's Thought," *Ethics* 60 [January 1950]: 96).

29. In his letter of resignation to the Board of Directors, DuBois hints that the conflict stemmed from the NAACP's refusal to take a strong position on wealth redistribution: "My program for economic readjustment has been totally ignored." *The Crisis* 41 (August 1934): 245; *Harlem Liberator*, 2 March 1934; Loren Miller, "How 'Left' Is the NAACP?" *New Masses* 18 (16 July 1935).

30. The twists and turns of Russian foreign policy during the "Popular Front" period of 1934-1939 are traced in Fernando Claudin's, *The Communist Movement, From Comintern to Cominform*, (New York: Monthly Review, 1976), 166-242; Georgi Dimitrov, *For Unity of the Working Class Against Fascism* (Sofia Press, 1969 [1935]), 32 and 37-38; James W. Ford, "Build the National Negro Congress," *The Communist* 15 (June 1936): 555.

31. *Minutes of the meeting of the NAACP Board of Directors*, 10 June 1935, NAACP Papers, Library of Congress; Charles H. Martin, "Communists and Blacks: The ILD and the Angelo Herndon Case," *Journal of Negro History* 64 (Spring 1979): 137-38: Herndon, *Let Me Live*, 318-19.

32. *Chicago Defender*, 6 July 1935; *California Eagle*, 5 July 1935; Miller, "How 'Left' is the N.A.A.C.P.?" 12-13; Miller, "The Negro Middle Class," *New Masses* 18 (7 April 1936): 21.

33. James Allen, "The Communist Way Out," *The Crisis* 42 (May 1935): 146; Allen, *The Negro Question in the United States* (New York: International Publishers, 1936), 189 and 202; Sterling Spero, "The Negro Question," *Nation* 143 (27 June 1936): 845.

34. *Harlem Liberator*, 2 March 1934; Roy Wilkins, *Standing Fast* (New York: Viking Press, 1982); *Chicago Defender*, 27 June 1936; *Amsterdam News*, 31 October 1936.

35. Roy Wilkins, "Sweet Land of Liberty!" *Labor Defender* 12 (April 1937); *Amsterdam News*, 4 December 1937.

36. Abner Berry to Roy Wilkins, 24 April 1937, NAACP Papers, Library of Congress; Memo to Mr. White, From Roy Wilkins, In Re: Myrdal Report on the NAACP, 12 March 1941, Bunche Papers, UCLA Special Collections; Walter White to Guy B. Johnson, 15 March 1941, Bunche Papers, UCLA Special Collections.

37. *Washington D.C. Tribune*, 9 February 1935; *Boston Chronicle*, 6 April 1935; James Weldon Johnson, *Along This Way*, 411. While Johnson pulled no punches with his anti-communism, he was not blind to the growing threat of fascism during this period: "I have said that there is no apparent possibility that the United States will go over to communism, but the same cannot be said about Fascism. We should oppose with our utmost strength any encroachment of Fascism" (Johnson, *Negro Americans What Now?* [New York: Viking Press, 1936], 10-11).

38. Sitkoff, *A New Deal for Blacks*, 93-101; Record, *Race and Radicalism*, 141-46; Herbert Hill, "The Communist Party—Enemy of Negro Equality," *The Crisis* 58 (June-July 1951): 424.

39. *Afro-American*, 7 September 1935; Henry Lee Moon, "A Negro Looks at Soviet Russia," *The Nation* 138 (28 February 1934): 244.

40. Allison Blakely, *Russia and the Negro: Blacks in Russian History and Thought* (Washington, D.C.: Howard University Press, 1986), 160-85; Interview with Miriam Sherman, 7 December 1989; Linda O. Hines, "White Mythology and Black Duality," *Journal of Negro History* 62 (April 1977): 177.

41. George Streater, "Negro College Radicals," *The Crisis* 41 (February 1934): 47; Preston Valien, "I attended the N.S.L. Conference" (March 1934): 67-68; St. Clair Drake, "Communism and Peace Movements," *The Crisis* 43 (February 1936): 44-45.

42. Rayford Logan, *Howard University: The First Hundred Years, 1867-1967* (New York: New York University Press, 1969), 292-304; *The Nation* 115 (19 July 1922), 65; *New York Age,* 3 June 1933; *Afro-American,* 25 July 1936; *Portland Advocate,* 24 June 1933.

43. *Report of the Hearings, House Un-American Activities Committee,* vol. 1, no. 3, 2148 (Washington, D.C.: Government Printing Office, 1938) October-November, 1938; *Afro-American,* 3 August 1935; *Afro-American,* 1 June 1935; Logan, *Howard University,* 277-78

44. *Richmond Planet,* 20 February 1937; C. Alvin Hughes, "We Demand Our rights: The Southern Negro Youth Congress, 1937-1949," *Phylon* 48 (March 1987): 40.

45. "Ralph Johnson Bunche," *Current Biography* 1948 (New York: H.W. Wilson, 1948), 77-78. For more on Bunche's early family history and Howard University career see Peggy Mann, *Ralph Bunche: U. N. Peacemaker* (New York: Coward, McCann and Geoghegan, Inc., 1975); Mrs. A. J. Peterson to Ralph Bunche, 11 December 1933, Bunche Papers, UCLA Special Collections; Ralph J. Bunche, *A World View of Race* (Washington, D.C., 1936), 98.

46. Bunche, "Black Capitalists," *New Masses* 17 (10 November 1936): 24.

47. Ralph Bunche, "A Critical Analysis of the Tactics and Programs of Minority Groups," *Journal of Negro Education* 4 (July 1935): 313; Bunche, *Programs, Ideologies, Tactics,* 147-48; Abner Berry, "A Step toward Negro liberation," *The Communist* 16 (October 1937): 965.

7 Reds Stay Away

The black nationalists had adopted the slogan, "Don't Buy Where You Can't Work." Throughout 1933 they picketed white merchants in Harlem who refused to hire black sales personnel. They were led by former Garveyites from the African Patriotic League and Sufi Abdul Hamid, an off-beat street agitator. They repeatedly warned the Reds to stay away from the picket line.

The nationalists rejected the Communist appeal for racial harmony and working-class alliances. Marxism, to them, was just another white man's "ism"—like capitalism—that could not solve the problems of the black poor. They insisted that blacks develop their own organizations, leadership, and philosophy free of all "white influences."

But the Communists could not ignore them because their campaign was gaining ground and seemed to be getting results. A few stores had already caved in and agreed to hire blacks. Also, Party leaders felt it was crucial to show Harlemites that Communists could wage a fierce campaign against racist store owners, too.[1]

Prelude to Conflict

The problem was that the Communists believed the nationalists were going at it the wrong way. Party leaders charged that picketing small shopkeepers would only get "a limited number of jobs for Negroes, and would not bring real relief to the suffering unemployed masses." Party leaders ridiculed the jobs campaign, saying that the store owners would hire only the scrubbed, well-spoken college students they considered "acceptable," not the neediest black workers.

137

Ford, who now directed most of the Party's operations in Harlem, opposed the campaign because it would "antagonize white workers already employed in Harlem stores." He feared that the storekeepers would replace wage-earning whites with blacks. The whites would hate the blacks more for taking their jobs.

Richard Moore was increasingly uneasy with the Party's hard line of opposition to the boycotters. He wondered if the whites were not "occupying jobs that rightfully belong to Negroes?" Party leaders said no, and told him not to ask the question again. Moore obliged and dutifully sent a cheerful greeting to the 1934 Communist convention hailing the Communist International for leading "the exploited toilers along the path of united, militant, revolutionary struggle."

To further silence critics like Moore, and to establish their credentials as Harlem activists, Communists launched a rival boycott campaign. In July 1933 Communists demanded that Harlem shopkeepers hire black clerks until they comprised fifty percent of their personnel.[2]

Moore was not the only Communist who questioned the Party's wisdom in opposing the boycott. Grace Campbell, the elegant and sophisticated first lady of Harlem Communists, was also puzzled about what the Party was doing. She began her career as a radical activist when she joined the Socialist Party in 1916. During the early 1920s, Campbell, convinced that the Communist Party would deliver on its promise of equal rights, shifted her allegiance.

She was an educated and erudite lady who held a doctorate in social science. Campbell had seen much in her years in Harlem. She felt the same anger that Harlemites felt toward the white merchants, and argued that the Party should support the boycott and help the community set up businesses to provide employment for blacks. Campbell thought that English and Scandinavian co-ops provided the ideal model for black business.

Campbell might possess a doctorate, but to Ford she still had much to learn about the working class. He noted: "It is dangerous to the real interest of the Negro masses for the leaders to advocate the replacement of white workers employed in Negro neighborhoods." Since Moore and Campbell were Party insiders they could take their protest only so far without completely breaking ranks. Other blacks were not hampered by the same political shackles. Newspaperwoman Charlotta Bass, whose *California Eagle* usually spoke well of the Communists, skipped the niceties. She bluntly asked, "Do they build an institution that can give employment to unwanted Negro labor?" She answered her own question: "No, they beat their head against the stone wall, instead of digging a tunnel through it."[3]

But Party leaders were not about to compromise proletarian ideology for Moore or Campbell, let alone their nationalist opponents. Party leader Tom Johnson called the jobs campaign counter-productive, since it only "sabotages the real struggle of the Negro toilers for real unemployment, relief and insurance, against job discrimination, and by confining this struggle to the Negro ghettoes."

Johnson accused the nationalists of using the jobs movement to foment riots between black and white workers. Party leaders insisted that the jobs campaign could only succeed if black and white workers fought together against the government and the corporations.

Communists cited their own Harlem Unemployed Council as the best example of what an interracial, mass movement with the right target and tactics could accomplish. The sit-ins, marches on city hall, and demonstrations conducted by the councils at relief and employment offices had gotten blacks increased benefits and focused national attention on the plight of the jobless.[4]

Shift to Blackness

The jobs campaign in effect revived the frightening apparition of "Negro Nationalism" which Party leaders thought had disappeared with Garvey's deportation and the break-up of his movement in the latter 1920s. Their experience with the Jamaican had taught them they could neither trust nor work with nationalists.

In the Party's eyes, black nationalists taught blacks to hate white workers and not the capitalists. Communists took great care to steer black workers toward class alliances and away from nationalist movements. As Haywood maintained, "Only the leadership of the Negro proletariat can give a revolutionary direction to such movements." Party leaders deliberately blurred the racial lines in their battle against nationalism to the point where they hurled shrill epithets at white racists and race-conscious blacks with equal abandon. Ford reminded the delegates at the Sixth Congress of the Communist International in 1928 "that any nationalist movement on the part of the Negroes does nothing but play into the hands of the bourgeoisie by widening the gulf between the white and Negro workers."[5]

Party leaders were not naive. They did recognize that "the question of color," as black Communist Vaugn Mise wrote, "is a factor which plays an important role in the economic exploitation" of black people. They could not defeat race sentiments by simply lecturing blacks on the virtues of the class struggle. Their experiences in Harlem organizing during the first years of the Depression made Ford and Briggs more sensitive to the anti-white, nationalist feelings among many blacks. Ford soon warned Party leaders that they would have to "comprehend the necessity for special work among Negroes." Ford intended that the Party should fight fire with fire and try to undercut the nationalists with race appeals of their own. The difference, as he saw it, was that the race approach was simply a tactical weapon to strengthen class resolve.[6]

By 1933, Party leaders recognized that the nationalists, with their appeals to boycott white stores that refused to hire blacks, were gaining adherents not only in Harlem but Chicago, Los Angeles, and other major cities, too. To blunt the nationalist drive, Party leaders countered with the League of Struggle for Negro Rights.

Although in existence since 1930, the League had floated around in a state of limbo. Its only distinction was that Langston Hughes was its president. He did little but carry the title. He made no speeches on behalf of the League and took part in no League-connected activities. Party leaders took his presidency so lightly he was seldom listed on the masthead of the scattered League handouts. This was not too surprising since the Party itself did not think much of the League. Browder chastised Party leaders for not "convincing the leading cadres of the Party that we meant what we said when we outlined the organizational structure of the L.S.N.R." Until the summer of 1933, the League had the grand total of one branch with 35 members. But times had changed. As Browder now put it, "We will not be afraid to make organizations composed entirely of Negroes."[7]

At an "Extraordinary Conference" in New York in July 1933, Communists decided to take the LSNR out of mothballs. The League's Manifesto called on blacks to join a "militant central organization" that would "strike out for Negro freedom, and for Negro rights." The Manifesto put the burden on whites to "convince the Negro masses that you are worthy of an alliance, and entrust their battle to you."

Party leaders authorized publication of the *Negro Liberator* and appointed their savviest newspaper professional, Cyril Briggs, as editor. They also decided that black Communists would direct the newspaper and the League. The Party wanted the *Liberator* and the League to have their own special black slant. Moore was appointed general secretary, Ford vice president, and Haywood sat on the National Council. Patterson would be available on legal call to the League, along with his other duties as chairman of the International Labor Defense.

The Communists had fertile ground to work with in Harlem. Ford set up control units, assigned organizers territories, and instructed them to canvass the neighborhoods to find issues around "which neighborhood struggles could be developed."

During the next few months League members stayed busy. They picketed the Harlem Hospital over its poor medical services, and marched on government offices to protest discriminatory hiring practices. The *Daily Worker* castigated New York prison authorities for the death of a black prisoner under suspicious circumstances.[8]

In late 1933 the League prepared to launch a major campaign against the practice that DuBois sardonically labeled "America's national pastime"— lynching. When a lynching occurred anywhere in the nation, a collective tremor convulsed the hearts of blacks. Over the years, blacks had nearly exhausted themselves with countless campaigns demanding that the federal government take action against mob violence. Between 1892 and 1933, sixty-one bills were introduced in Congress to make lynching a federal crime. The Dyer anti-lynching bill that passed the House in 1922 was the closest blacks came to enacting an anti-lynching law.

Roosevelt had given blacks hope that the White House would finally take a firm stand for new laws. They were bitterly disappointed. At first, Roosevelt was silent. Eventually, he did condemn lynching, but he did not introduce legislation to make it a crime. He could count his Southern votes, and most of the key congressional committees were controlled by southern Democrats. He feared that if he pushed too hard for an anti-lynching law, the Southerners might retaliate and bottle up his New Deal programs.

While blacks could take comfort in the 1930s that the number of lynchings had declined, they had not stopped. In 1933, twenty-eight blacks were lynched. In November 1933, the NAACP's legal council drafted a new anti-lynching bill that prescribed fines and jail terms for local officials who failed to prosecute lynchers. New York Senator Robert Wagner and Colorado Senator Edward Costigan agreed to co-sponsor the bill in the Senate.[9]

But the LSNR was not going to wait on Congress to act. That same month it issued a call for a two-day national anti-lynching conference in Baltimore. The Party planned to put on a show in the city. The League's executive board announced that it would hear testimony from blacks who had barely escaped lynchings. A "tribunal of workers and intellectuals" would then convene and "pass judgement on the lynchers." Brimming with confidence, Moore declared, "we'll put a stop to lynching." Although Robert Minor made a pitch for white workers to support the anti-lynching campaign, the conference was designed as a black-run affair. The League invited dozens of black groups to send representatives to Baltimore. Countee Cullen was the first—and only—"big name" endorsement they got.

He was fascinated by the Harlem Communists. In 1932 he had seriously considered joining the leftist National Committee for the Defense of Political Prisoners. Cullen helped the LSNR along by sending a $12.00 donation from a friend to National Council member J. Adler. When the League asked him to support the anti-lynching conference, he wrote a personal letter to the *Liberator* praising Patterson and Hughes for their "effort to awaken the country at large to a realization of the deadliness of this terror."

The Pen and Hammer Society also sent a letter to the *Liberator* supporting the conference. The Society was a national organization of black professionals, scientists, and technicians.

For two days, two hundred delegates at the Anti-Lynching Conference listened to black farmers, sharecroppers, and laborers tell woeful stories about southern violence and poverty. The conference ended with Moore promising to "publish the findings to expose the brutal practice to the world." The League announced that it would hold a second conference the following spring.[10]

The next year the League unveiled its "Bill for Negro Rights." The National Council of the League announced that it would "wage a mass struggle for the passage and enforcement of the bill" by Congress. The bill largely repeated the Party's demand that lynchers be tried for murder and given the death penalty. The one new wrinkle was a section that specified the length of jail sentences for discrimination. The first offense would be a misdemeanor and the violator would land in jail for six months. A second violation would be treated as a felony, and the defendant would be sentenced to two or more years in prison and also pay punitive damages to the victim of discrimination.[11]

The League was making some progress. In less than a year, they added fifteen new branches with more than 625 members. Communists believed they had turned the tide against the black militants. By the fall of 1935, the jobs campaign had fizzled out and the Garveyite leaders of the boycott were gone from the political scene. The Party had even taken back the reins of the boycott movement with their own integrated picket lines in front of a Harlem cafeteria that refused to hire blacks. The cafeteria quickly capitulated and agreed to hire black countermen. Party leaders bragged that no white employees lost their jobs.[12]

Triumph and Failure

When the League held a May Day rally that year, blacks from Harlem's women's councils, political clubs, and churches fell in line behind the LSNR marching division. One distinguished gentleman told Ben Davis, now editor of the *Liberator,* that he considered it an honor to march in the May Day parade. And Davis certainly considered it an honor to have Father Divine in the parade.

By 1935, the flamboyant Harlem minister had already become a household name among blacks. Father Divine made news with his lavish life-style and integrated coterie of white-gowned "angels" and other assorted devotees. The public watched in awe as Divine's "Peace Mission" provided free clothes and overnight shelter to the destitute and his soup kitchens ladled out free food to three thousand poor blacks and whites daily. Divine pumped his worshipers with the grand delusion that he was sent by heaven to free the planet from war, poverty, and racial conflict. He told his followers: "Just what the Communists have been trying to get you to see and do and be, I have accomplished."

He promised Davis that his followers would carry their own signs for the Scottsboro Boys, against war and fascism, and in support of workers unemployment and social insurance. He was as good as his word. The Divine motorcade was conspicuous in the Communist march. Their cars were draped with stuffed artificial white doves, flags, and pennants declaring Father Divine as God. Divine said he was pleased to be "participating with my Comrades, the Communists." To God's messenger, the Communists were "fulfilling the Scriptures more than many of the preachers and those that are called religious."[13]

The Communists gloated over the coup they scored in getting a man like Divine to side with them. Party leaders were ready even to forgive the black church leaders for their pro-capitalist "reactionary" sins. Ford applauded Father Divine for "reacting to the pressure of the masses on Scottsboro" and other issues. A few Party members whose

143

memories were better than Ford's questioned the leadership's new love affair with Father Divine. Browder silenced them by explaining that the Party was using Divine to "reach the backward Masses" and to further the revolutionary struggles. Davis went a little further. He professed to see Communist tenets in Divine's "Righteous Government Platform" and his economic program. He praised Divine for supporting the death penalty for lynching, the abolition of war, and government reform, and for opposing corporate exploitation. Davis also noted that Divine branded trade union bureaucracy as "unjust and autocratic" and demanded that they stop "extracting hard-earned money from the members in the form of heavy membership fees while giving them nothing in return."

Benjamin Stolberg, a liberal Party critic, charged that Communists were so "anxious for a 'mass base' in the black" world that they were "catering to this very chauvinism." Two years earlier, Party leaders might have agreed with Stolberg. Now it was merely a case of practical politics. Still, the Party had not completely dropped its guard against nationalism. When a few Chicago blacks led by Oscar C. Brown proposed a 49th state for blacks only, James Allen took exception and called the idea a "fantasy."[14]

Party leaders were confident that 1936 would be the year that they would finally become a major force in the urban ghettoes. The future looked bright until a small news item appeared in the *New York Times* on September 8, 1935. The report claimed that the Soviet Union was selling coal tar, wheat, and oil to Italy at below-market prices. Even though it was only a small column item, it might as well have been plastered on billboards throughout Harlem and other black communities. Blacks were in an uproar and Communists had some explaining to do.

In December 1933, Mussolini used the pretext of a border clash between Ethiopians and Italians in Somalia to invade Ethiopia. At the time, Ethiopia and Liberia were the only independent nations in black Africa. It was a savage war in which thousands of Ethiopian civilians were killed by Italian bombs. Impoverished Ethiopian peasants fought valiantly but their spears and shields were hardly a match against tanks, airplanes, and heavy artillery.

Blacks in America were enraged at the slaughter. They held marches and mass protest rallies against the invasion. William N. Jones, *Afro-American* managing editor, carried a petition signed by thousands of blacks to Geneva and presented it to the League of

Nations. The petitioners implored the League to intervene and impose sanctions against the Italians. Although the League did nothing to stop the carnage, blacks felt that at least they could count on the "friendly" Soviets to support the Ethiopians. And now the *Times* was reporting that the Soviets were helping the Fascists.

Party leaders at first attempted to deny the reports. The *Daily Worker* accused the *Times* of "questionable judgment" in excepting as fact "the vicious bias and Soviet-hating imagination of the writer of the story." When the Soviets later admitted that they did sell the Italians oil, Party leaders downplayed it, but the damage had been done. For DuBois and Randolph it was simply a case of "See, I told you so." Both men cited the oil deal as a perfect example of how the Communists would sell out blacks to further their own objectives.[15]

Before the *Times* revelation, Communists had led the pack in denouncing Mussolini's "dirty war." At the Seventh Comintern Congress in 1935, Ford had called on Communists to organize "Hands Off Ethiopia" committees to stop the shipment of troops, munitions, and military supplies to the battlefront. In Party reports, Ford made it seem like the Communists were the only ones protesting Italian aggression in Ethiopia: "Many of the followers of the Garvey movement have learned to like us because of our work and initiative on the Ethiopian issue."

The *Liberator* blazoned with headlines denouncing the Italian fascists. The paper featured pictures of Haile Selassie and Ethiopian troops in battle. Sandwiched in between were battlefront reports, maps of the country, and accounts of Italian troop mutinies. Every victory was hailed as a triumph "against the fascist butchers." Party leaders even shared the stage with Randolph, Garveyites, and black ministers in massive "Hands Off Ethiopia" rallies at Abyssinian Baptist Church and Madison Square Garden. In Chicago, Haywood worked with the *Defender* and local leaders in a "Hands Off Ethiopia" parade in August that drew 25,000 blacks.[16]

Now, in one stroke, the *Times* report seemed to wipe out much of the goodwill Communists thought they had built up with black leaders. Herman Mackawain resigned from his post as the assistant general secretary of the LSNR. It was not just Soviet duplicity on Ethiopia that bothered him. He had a litany of complaints against the Party. He accused Party leaders of discouraging independent black organizing, failing to promote black leadership, and ruthlessly suppressing all internal dissent.

While Mackawain did not mention them by name, he perhaps had Moore and Briggs in mind when he accused the Party of clamping down on dissenters. Party leaders never fully trusted either man. Briggs and Moore often criticized the Party's single-minded pursuit of working-class unity at the expense of local black organizing. At times, the two men sounded more like nationalists than Communists to the Party leaders. Their dissent cost them. Moore was dumped from his position as League general secretary in 1934. Briggs was replaced by Davis as editor of the *Liberator* in October 1933 and reassigned to a staff position on the *Daily Worker*. (In 1942, both were expelled from the Party for what Schuyler called "their Negro nationalist way of thinking").[17]

Ford and the other Communist loyalists gamely tried to keep up appearances. However, by January 1936 the League was practically defunct. Ford attributed the failure to "sectarianism." He lamented the fact that "no effort was made in any part of the country to build the LSNR as a united front" with other black organizations.

B. D. Amis probably came closer to the truth. He thought that the *Liberator* and the League had fallen apart because they were "too much patterned after the Party and the *Daily Worker*." The League was a dead issue to Ford. He urged Party leaders to "liquidate" it. In early 1936 the League was shut down.[18]

Black Defections

More blacks were becoming disillusioned with the Party. These were not just the small fry who had joined the Party for a quick look-see and then drifted away. Men like Mackawain knew Party secrets and were ready to tell the world. The charges the defectors made were nearly always the same: whites made the major decisions and blacks carried them out; organizing white workers was always the highest priority, black issues were given short shrift.

They had once believed the Communists offered them the opportunity to think and act as black men and women. To them the Party had reneged on its promise. They felt betrayed. Party leaders called the black defectors disgruntled malcontents, or worse, "petty bourgeois nationalists." Given the Party's relatively good track record in the fight against segregation, the criticisms were not totally fair. But the black Party defectors believed they were right and that was enough for them.

The first prominent "name" black leader to go was a young pipe-smoking, Trinidad-born Communist leader, Malcolm Nurse, better known as George Padmore. When he joined the Party in 1927, Communist leaders had high hopes for him. He was bright, articulate, and he believed fervently in the Communist program. Padmore had a knack for turning a sharp phrase, especially when it came to denouncing the British and French colonialists.

In 1930, the Party installed him in Hamburg, Germany as the secretary of the International Trade Unions Congress of Negro Workers. The next year he took over as editor of the organization's publication, the *Negro Worker*. Briggs and Ford were contributing editors. He went at his job like a man possessed.

The imperialists to him were "lackeys," "parasites," and "thieves" who brought nothing but death and misery to the world's workers. Only revolution could remove them. "Down with the capitalist governments of starvation and war," Padmore railed at the capitalists in his monthly "World" column in the *Negro Worker*. He told Africans and Asians that "what the Russian workers have done they can also do."[19]

Padmore was pitiless on established black leaders. All of them were "Negro Misleaders" who sold out the black masses. In Africa the greedy chiefs were the "black stooges of British imperialism." In America, DuBois, White, and the NAACP were corrupt Negro intellectuals. Garvey had a special place in Padmore's hierarchy of villains. The Jamaican nationalist was "chief among this array of international betrayers of the revolutionary struggles of the Negro masses." He dutifully recited the Party line when he charged Garvey with "exploiting the racial consciousness and nationalistic tendencies" of blacks.

Even while he fumed at Garvey and the black "misleaders," Padmore was having some second thoughts of his own about the Party's racial policies. Talks with African and West Indian nationalists had convinced Padmore that the African freedom movements must be black-led and that blacks must organize for political and economic control.

At the same time, Party leaders were having their misgivings about him. In February 1934 the smoldering hostility came to a head when Padmore was removed as secretary of the Negro Workers Congress. The expulsion order was signed by Charles Woodson, who replaced Padmore as Secretary. Woodson said that he had violated Party doctrine when he tried to raise five million dollars for Liberian independence. His far greater offense, Woodson said, was "advocating the necessity for the unity of all Negroes on a racial basis." By taking up the Garvey call of "Africa for the Africans," Padmore had become a renegade to the cause of "working class unity."

Woodson's order was stiff. He forbade all Communists to "give aid and support to his anti-working-class activities." Helen Davis escalated the attack. She called him an agent of the capitalists: "In reality he is concerned about the coffee and cocoa growers, the small estate owners, not the poor tenant farmers."[20]

Padmore did not deny that his political sentiments had changed. He believed that the struggle against colonialism should take precedence over the class struggle. He supported the nationalist goal of "Africa for the Africans" and saw nothing wrong with black-led independence movements. He did not quibble with the charge that he believed in racial solidarity and not class alliances with white workers. He accused the Party of fabricating lies about his activities. He claimed that he had spelled out his differences with the Communists in a political statement submitted to the Comintern Executive Committee.

Padmore's close friend, West Indian Marxist C. L. R. James, remembers Padmore coming to his London flat a few months after his break with the Party. When James asked him what was wrong, he said, "I have left these people. You know they are changing their policy." The "change," Padmore said, was that Moscow had ordered Communist parties to attack the Germans and the Japanese, rather than the British and the French who had African colonies. After Padmore protested that "Germany and Japan have no colonies in Africa," he was told, "Well, that is the line." He told the Comintern that he could not abide the Soviets' "sacrifice of the young national liberation movements in Africa and Asia."[21]

He soon got his revenge. Shortly before the *Times'* story on Soviet oil sales to Italy, Padmore wrote a lengthy piece in *The Crisis* attacking the Party for betraying the black movement. Patterson was infuriated that these articles received wide publicity in the black press: "We cannot finish this fine fellow for all time, but we can expose his hypocrisy, his degeneracy, and his renegecy from the Negro liberation movement."

The Party had made an enemy for life. Padmore would attack the Communists at every turn. In the 1950s, when he became friend and advisor to Ghanaian Prime Minister Kwame Nkrumah and other future African statesmen, he warned them all to stay away from the Communists. Padmore argued that the only philosophy suitable for Africans was Pan Africanism. In 1955 he explained his thinking: "Pan Africanism rejects the Communist intolerance of those who do not subscribe to its ever-changing party line." Padmore was convinced that

Pan-Africanists were democrats and Communists were not: "Democracy and brotherhood cannot be built upon intolerance and violence."[22]

The Communists could easily brush Padmore off. He was a West Indian who had spent most of his Party days abroad. Few black Americans had heard of him. The same could not be said of a soft-spoken young man from Mississippi.

In 1940 Richard Wright shocked the nation with his best seller, *Native Son*. The novel told the searing tale of a young black man driven by racist degradation to commit murder. While *Native Son* firmly established Wright's credentials as one of America's leading literary figures, it did not improve his standing in the Party to which he had devoted seven years of his life.

Before joining the Party, Wright's early days in Mississippi had been a hard struggle against grinding poverty and racist violence. The first chance he got, Wright, like thousands of other southern blacks seeking a better life, packed up and headed for Chicago. After a series of odd jobs, he landed a position at the post office. The Depression was in its first years, and Wright was restless. He listened to Communist speakers in Chicago's Washington Park and was impressed by their fiery denunciations of Jim Crow and the "capitalist exploiters." Soon he began attending meetings of the John Reed Club. Organized in the fall of 1929, the clubs were the Party's outlet for its most promising writers.

Carlton Moss, himself a budding playwright then, recalls that the clubs had special meaning for black writers: "They were like a breath of fresh air to us. It was a place where blacks could get serious criticism and real encouragement from white writers for their works."[23] By 1932 there were thirteen clubs throughout the country. Wright was overjoyed to find that a key plank in the Club's six-point program called for "the fight against white chauvinism (against all forms of Negro discrimination or persecution)." Wright took this to heart. "But it seemed to me that here at last in the realm of revolutionary expression was where the Negro experience could find a home, a functioning value and role." The next year he joined the Club and the Party. He served as the Club's executive secretary until the Party disbanded the clubs in 1934.

Life in the Party was a mixture of storm and euphoria for him. Party leaders were never quite sure what to make of their budding young talent. At the tenth Party convention in 1938, Ford publicly singled Wright out as a writer who was "keenly aware of the Negro's past and present position in American history."

He moved to New York in 1937 and joined the *Daily Worker's* Harlem Bureau. For the moment, Wright was happy. He wrote features on Joe Louis, black theater, the National Negro Congress, James Ford's 44th birthday party, and a wide range of other subjects. To outward appearances, the Party gave him the security he needed. In a report on a branch meeting in Harlem, Wright was ecstatic. "They love this Communist Party which is the only organization caring enough for them."[24] A Party organizer was hardly surprised that Wright would say those words then: "You have to remember in those days few major white magazines or newspapers would publish blacks. Now along comes the *Daily Worker* and gives them a forum. So they were bound to be grateful."

While Wright piled on the Party platitudes, Communist leaders were not as enthusiastic about him. They repeatedly warned him to confine his writings to appropriate proletarian themes. To them, he was veering ominously close to "petty bourgeois nationalism." Moss, who was a close friend of his during those days, says that Ford and Davis would tell Wright that he should write about "the true courage and heroism of union organizers, or people like Frederick Douglass, and not about people who just go out and commit destructive acts." None of this set well with Wright: "He would tell them that they were interfering."[25]

Still, in his "Blueprint for Negro Writing," Wright tried hard to sound like the proletarian loyalist Ford and Davis wanted him to be. But he also said, "One of the great tasks of Negro writers of the future will be to show the Negro himself, to forge in the smithy of our souls the uncreated conscience of our race." When the Party continued to criticize him, he was perplexed: "Why was it that I was a suspected man because I wanted to reveal the vast physical and spiritual ravages of Negro life, the profundity latent in these rejected people?"

Langston Hughes had an answer. The duty of black writers was to "unite blacks and whites in our country on the solid ground of the daily working class struggle." Wright could not understand why Party leaders were so offended when blacks wanted to establish a "purely Negro committee" within the Party.

He did not quit. Whatever private doubts he may have had, he continued to heap praise on the Party: "I owe my literary development to the Communist Party and its influence, which has shaped my thought and creative growth."[26] Subtle differences, however, could still be detected between the Party's and Wright's vision of the working-class struggle: "I have found the Negro worker the real symbol of the

150

working class in America." By 1941 nearly everyone in the Party leadership had written him off as a "petty bourgeoisie" deviationist. Yet Wright still had enough red sentiment in his heart to send a cable to the "Red Army's great commander" extending the comradely hand of blacks to Stalin and the Russians: "Proletarian factory workers, collective farmers, Soviet intellectuals, writers, and artists, we want you to know that we American Negroes clasp your hand in enduring solidarity."[27]

But his Party tenure was nearly up, and in 1942 the Party expelled him. Wright, insisting that he had quit before the expulsion, preferred to put his Communist experience behind him and get on with the business of writing. Other than a celebrated article, "I Tried To Be A Communist," that appeared in the *Atlantic Monthly* in 1944, and an interview with the *New York Herald*, Wright did not take shots at the Party.

But *New Masses* writer Samuel Sillen was not as generous with him. Sillen denounced Wright as a "defeatist" and "isolationist." Wright had become, in his view, a writer who had "betrayed" his vision of the progressive struggle.[28] Sillen, like Party leaders, could not really understand Wright's complexities. He broke with the Communists not because he felt betrayed or harbored ill feelings. He was a black writer who simply wanted the freedom to interpret the black experience the way he saw it.

In later years, Wright was still ambiguous in his feelings toward communism. In a 1956 foreword to Padmore's book *Pan Africanism or Communism*, he was harsh: "Today nobody is more immune to the call of Communism than black men who found, to their bitter sorrow, that they were being used for ends that were not theirs." But a year earlier, he wrote to a friend, "I was a Communist because I was a Negro. Indeed the Communist Party had been the only road out of the Black Belt for me."[29]

The loss of Padmore, the recalcitrance of Wright, the flap over Ethiopia, and the demise of the LSNR were seen by Party leaders as only temporary setbacks. The era was filled with too much promise to dwell on these problems.

While the Depression was on and millions remained in bread lines, Communists calculated they could generate enough backing among blacks to make up for these losses. Party leaders remained on the alert for fresh opportunities to tap that sympathy. It did not take long for the ever-inventive Ford to spot one.

Notes

1. Mark Naison, "Harlem Communists and the Politics of Black Protest," *Marxist Perspectives* 1 (Fall 1978): 29-30. McKay gives a detailed account from the nationalist point of view of the battle between the Communists, Sufi Abdul Hamid, and the Garveyites during the years 1933-1935 in *Harlem: Negro Metropolis* (New York: Harcourt, Brace and Jovanovich, 1968 [1940]), 181-206. Louise Thompson Patterson who witnessed the nationalist demonstrations was a sharp critic of the violence in the campaign. Interview 10 December 1989. Naison attempts to make sense of the positions of both sides in *Communists in Harlem during the Depression* (New York: Grove Press, 1984). Gary Jerome Hunter details the impact this little-known black protest campaign had on opening clerical and professional jobs to blacks at major department stores in *Don't Buy Where You Can't Work: Black Urban Boycotts During the Depression, 1929-1941,* Ph.D. diss., University of Michigan, 1977.

2. Tom Johnson, *The Reds in Dixie* (New York: Workers Library Publishers, 1935), 27; *Daily Worker*, 23 August 1935; Naison, *Communists in Harlem*, 101; *Negro Liberator*, 7 April 1934; Naison, "Harlem Communists and the Politics of Black Protest," 29.

3. *The Worker*, 12 March 1950; McKay, *Harlem Negro Metropolis*, 223-24; Charlotta Bass, unpublished editorial, ca. 1935, Charlotta Bass Papers, Southern California Research Library. During the late 1940s Bass published numerous editorials in her *California Eagle* attacking the government trials of Communist leaders. In 1952 she claimed a small piece of history by becoming the first woman chosen as a Vice Presidential candidate in a national election. She ran on the Progressive Party ticket (see Charlotta Bass, *Forty Years* [Los Angeles: Charlotta Bass, 1960] and "Biographical Notes on Mrs Bass," Progressive Party [flyer], Bass Papers, Southern California Research Library).

4. Johnson, *The Reds in Dixie*, 27-28; Roy Rosenzweig, "The Early Years of the Great Depression: Organizing the Unemployed," *Radical America* 10 (July-August 1976): 44-45; *The Harlem Liberator* and the *Daily Worker* filled their pages with stories of Party-led fights over relief, evictions, and unemployment between 1932 and 1935 (Interview with Lester Rodney, 5 December 1989; Interview with O'Neil Cannon, 4 December 1989). Roi Ottley, *New World A-Coming*, 113-21. The *Los Angeles Sentinel* newspaper organized a successful and long running campaign to open jobs for blacks in Woolworths and other department stores on Central Avenue in the mid- and late-1930s (Interview with Dorothy Healey, 16 December 1989). At first, Police and city officials tried to blame the two-day riot that broke out in Harlem on 19 March 1935 on the Communist boycott campaign. However, black community leaders

later told a different tale. In testimony before the Mayor's Commission on Conditions in Harlem established by Mayor Fiorella LaGuardia most agreed that the riot stemmed from severe unemployment and deprivation in Harlem. The final report concluded: "While one, in view of the available facts, would hesitate to give the Communists full credit for preventing the outbreak from becoming a race riot, they deserve more credit than any other element in Harlem for preventing a physical conflict between whites and blacks" (11). The complete report was published in the *Amsterdam News*, 18 July 1936; also, Naison, *Communists in Harlem*, 140-45; *New York Herald*, 26 March 1935; *New York Times*, 21 March 1935; *New York Times*, 22 March 1935.

5. Harry Haywood and Robert Minor attacked black nationalism in *The Road to Negro Liberation* (New York: Workers Library Publishers, 1935) and "The Negro and His Judases," *The Communist* 10 (July 1931): 625-34, respectively. *International Press Correspondence*, 74 (25 October 1928): 1346.

6. *Party Organizer* 8 (May-June 1934): 62; *International Press Correspondence*, 21 (3 May 1929): 460 and 465; *International Press Correspondence* 61 (25 October 1929): 1323. Before World War II, four Pan-African Congresses were held in 1900, 1919, 1923, and 1927. The Congresses brought together leading black American and African professionals to hammer out an anti-colonial program for economic and political control of African land and resources. For the history and politics behind the Pan-African Congress movement see: W. E. B. DuBois, *The World and Africa* (New York: International Publishers, 1965 [1946]), 7-12 and 235-45; George Padmore, *A History of the Pan-African Congress* (London: Hammersmith Bookshop, 1963); Padmore, *Pan-Africanism or Communism* (Garden City: Doubleday, 1971 [1956]), 95-114; *The Crisis* 18 (April 1919): 7-9.

7. *Party Organizer* 8 (May-June 1934): 61; Dilling, *The Red Network*, 188; Earl Browder, "The Tasks of our Party," *The Communist* 13 (March 1933): 241.

8. *Party Organizer*, 8 (May-June 1934): 62; *Harlem Liberator*, 4 November 1933; Dilling, *The Red Network*, 188-89. Briggs is listed on the *Liberator's* editorial masthead until October 1933; *Harlem Liberator*, 20 December 1933; (editorial), *Daily Worker*, cited in *Party Organizer* 8 (May-June 1934): 61-62.

9. Jesse W. Reeder, *Federal Efforts to Control Lynching*, Ph.D. diss., Cornell University, 1952, 231-36; Robert Zangrando, "The NAACP and a Federal Anti-Lynching Bill, 1934-1940," *Journal of Negro History* 50 (April 1965): 106-17; *New York Times*, 30 November 1933; *The Crisis* 41 (January 1934): 66; Sitkoff, *A New Deal for Blacks*, 46. John Peter Kellogg presents a convincing case that not only was President Roosevelt slow to grasp the devastating impact that lynching had on blacks, but

many prominent liberals as well, see *Northern Liberals and Black America: A History of White Attitudes 1936-1952*, Ph.D. diss., Northwestern University, 1971, 9-12.

10. *Harlem Liberator*, 18 November 1933; *Harlem Liberator*, 25 November 1933; J. Adler to Countee Cullen, 13 September 1932; Elliot Cohen to Countee Cullen, 23 September 1932, Countee Cullen Papers, Amistad Research Center, Dillard University.

11. *Negro Worker* 4 (August 1934): 8-9; Ford, *The Negro and the Democratic Front*, 83.

12. *Party Organizer*, 8 (May-June 1934): 61-62; Naison, *Communists in Harlem*, 120-23; *Negro Liberator*, 15 September 1934.

13. For a revealing look at the Messianic world of Father Divine, see Hadley Cantril and Muzafer Sherif, "The Kingdom of Father Divine," *Journal of Abnormal and Social Psychology* 33 (Spring 1938): 147-67; McKay, *Harlem: Negro Metropolis*, 48; *Negro Liberator*, 15 April 1935.

14. James Ford, "The United Front in Negro Work," *The Communist* 15 (February 1935): 171; *Daily Worker*, 25 April 1935; *Daily Worker*, 23 February 1936; Benjamin Stolberg, "Black Chauvinism," *Nation* 140 (15 May 1935): 571; James Allen, "The Communist Way Out," *The Crisis* 42 (May 1935): 154.

15. *New York Times*, 8 September 1935; *Afro-American*, 7 September 1935; *Daily Worker*, 29 June 1935; *Daily Worker*, 23 February 1936; *The Crisis* 42 (October 1935): 305. With the lone exception of Dennis Mack Smith, most political analysts have paid too little attention to the Italian-Ethiopian war as a springboard for Italian military aggression during World War II (see *Mussolini's Roman Empire* [New York: Viking Press, 1976], 59-81 and *Mussolini* [New York: Alfred A. Knopf, 1982],188-202). Even during the 1940s, Randolph continued to cite the Soviet oil sales as the prime example of Communist "duplicity" (*Black Worker* 11 [November 1945]: 4).

16. Ford, *The Negro and the Democratic Front*, 164; Ford, *The Communists and the Struggle for Negro Liberation* (New York: Harlem Division of the Communist Party, 1935), 63; *Negro Liberator*, 15 March 1935; *Negro Liberator*, 16 September 1935; *Amsterdam News*, 5 October 1935.

17. *Amsterdam News*, 17 August 1935; Naison, *Communists in Harlem*, 173-74; *Harlem Liberator*, 11 November 1933; Naison, *Communists in Harlem*, 103; *Pittsburgh Courier*, 7 November 1942.

18. W. Burghardt Turner, "The Richard B. Moore Collection and its Collector," *Caribbean Studies* 15 (April 1975): 135-45; Ford, *The Negro and the Democratic Front*, 83, 88; B. D. Amis, "The Negro Question in the United States," *The Communist International* 12 (May 1935): 508.

19. Interview with Louise Thompson Patterson, 10 December 1989; James R. Hooker, *Black Revolutionary* (London: Praeger, 1967); 1-38; *Negro Worker* 2 (15 August 1932): 1-3.

20. Padmore, "Bankruptcy of Negro Leadership," *Negro Worker* 1 (December 1931): 5; *Negro Worker* 4 (June 1934): 14-15; *Negro Worker* 4 (August 1934): 16-17.

21. Hooker, *Black Revolutionary*, 30-31; C. L. R. James, "George Padmore," *Radical America* 2 (July-August 1968): 24-25.

22. Padmore, "Ethiopia and World Politics," *The Crisis* 42 (May 1935): 138-39; William L. Patterson, "World Politics and Ethiopia," *The Communist* 14 (August 1935): 730; Padmore, *Pan-Africanism or Communism*, xvi.

23. Richard Wright, *Native Son* (New York: Harper and Bros., 1940). Of the many works on Wright, the two most comprehensive biographies are Constance Webb, *Richard Wright* (New York: G.P. Putnam's Sons, 1968) and Michael Fabre, *The Unfinished Quest of Richard Wright* (New York: William Morrow, 1973). Interview with Carlton Moss, 12 December 1989.

24. *New Masses* 7 (June 1932): 1-2; Ford, *The Negro and the Democratic Front*, 192; *Daily Worker*, 16 August 1937; *Daily Worker*, October 14, 1937; *Daily Worker*, October 27, 1937; *Daily Worker*, December 23, 1937; *Daily Worker*, July 5, 1938.

25. Interview with Carlton Moss, 12 December 1989.

26. Richard Wright, "Blueprint for Negro Writing," *New Challenge* 2 (Fall 1937): 58-59; Quote in *The God That Failed*, edited by Arthur Koestler (New York: Harper & Bros., 1950),132; Richard Wright, *American Hunger* (New York: Harper and Row, 1977 [1944]), 82; Mark Naison, "Communism and Harlem Intellectuals in the Popular Front: Anti-Fascism and the Politics of Black Culture," *Journal of Ethnic Studies* 9 (Spring 1981): 13

27. Eugene Gordon, *Social and Political Problems of the Negro Writer*, *American Writer's Congress*, edited by Henry Hart (New York: International Publishers, 1935), 144; *Daily Worker*, 1 September 1941.

28. Wright, "I Tried to be a Communist," *Atlantic Monthly* 159 (August 1944); *New York Herald Tribune*, 28 July 1944; Samuel Sillen, "Richard Wright in Retreat," *New Masses* 71 (29 August 1944): 25.

29. Padmore, *Pan-Africanism or Communism*, (Wright, introduction), xxiv; Richard Wright to Edward Aswell, reprinted in Fabre, *The Unfinished Quest of Richard Wright*, 230. According to Wright's close friend and collaborator, Ollie Harrington, Wright flatly refused to contribute another piece attacking the Communists to a planned tenth anniversary reissue of *The God that Failed*. Harrington, however, says Wright told him, "If they were ever thinking of publishing an anti-racist book, which was highly unlikely, he would definitely be interested" (Ollie Harrington, "Ordeal of a Native Son," *Political Affairs* 40 [June 1981]: 21).

8 New Friends, Old Enemies

Party leaders were never reluctant to take credit for originating the idea of a National Negro Congress. Their idea was to unite black professionals, workers, and Communists in a joint program to combat segregation and economic injustice. Ford frequently reminded audiences that he had made the first call for the Congress during a debate with Socialist Party moderate Frank Crosswaith and Illinois Congressman Oscar DePriest in New York in January 1934.

It was highly unlikely that DePriest and Crosswaith would lend their names to such an undertaking. At that time, the idea sounded too much like an entangling alliance with the Communists, and caution was still the watchword of the black moderates when it came to dealing with the Party. For the remainder of 1934, Ford did not mention the idea again. He had floated his trial balloon and it came fluttering down unnoticed.[1]

By the fall of 1935, things had changed. Moscow's Popular Front strategy dictated that Communists push for the broadest cooperation possible with the black moderates, so it was time to refloat the Congress trial balloon. Party leaders hoped that blacks would be sufficiently fed up with the slow pace of New Deal reform and disillusioned with Roosevelt to break with the Democrats and turn to the Communists.

In February 1935 the Party started dropping hints. News items appeared in the *Negro Liberator* that created the impression "the Scottsboros are rising everywhere." Communists were working hard to energize blacks to take even more radical action. A *Liberator* editorial called for a "National Congress for Negro Rights." The paper cited the mass anti-war demonstrations around the Italian-Ethiopian war as evidence that "the Negro masses have shown their willingness to unite on a common ground of struggle."

Harlem Communists solemnly pledged that the National Negro Congress would not be strictly a Communist affair but a broad movement extending "beyond the narrow confines of the LSNR." The program would be strictly limited to fighting for "the basic rights of the Negro people." A timetable was set for the Congress to be held in Washington within four or five months. Party members were urged to begin immediately discussing the Congress "inside the existing Negro organizations." At a meeting in March 1935, Communists formalized plans to push the Congress. They intended to follow to the letter the guidelines they spelled out in the *Negro Liberator* and promote the Congress in black civic and church groups. District officials recognized that the success of the Congress hinged on getting moderate black leaders to cooperate.

But it would be a hollow success if the Congress, as Browder said, did not have "a firm working-class core." Ford was equally determined that the Party not be "deterred by the charges of Communist domination." Party leaders gambled that the timing was right and that they could attain their ends with minimum conflict: "We were guided," Ford commented, "by what we knew of the desire of the Negro masses for united action."[2]

Armed with a timetable and a strategy, the next step was implementation. The Party's first task was to convince the moderate black leaders that the Congress was not another Communist ploy to ensnare blacks. Although Ford had become a credible figure among many blacks with his vice presidential campaign, black leaders generally remained frosty toward him. During the 1932 election campaign not one black newspaper had endorsed the Foster-Ford ticket. Ford clearly was not the right man to smooth the easily ruffled feathers of the black moderate leaders. Party leaders needed someone whom they could work with who would not alienate the conservatives. Such a leader had to be sensitive to the diverse and often competing political interests among blacks, yet be a tough, patient, and skilled negotiator. It had to be someone who was sufficiently well known and admired for speaking out on black rights, yet someone who could not be identified in any way with the Party.[3]

John Davis fit the specifications perfectly. Although there was no evidence that Davis was a Party member, he agreed with the Communist economic positions and was not afraid to work with them.

Equally important, he had respectable credentials. He had a keen sense of business and politics. He possessed a degree from Harvard, and had taught for a brief time at Howard University. In Washington circles, he was regarded as a comer.

In 1933, he took over as director of the Joint Committee on National Recovery. The committee, sponsored by more than twenty black and liberal organizations, was set up to lobby against discrimination in New Deal agencies. Davis battled hard against insensitive bureaucrats at the Tennessee Valley Authority, the Civilian Conservation Corps, and the Agricultural Adjustment Administration, who refused to provide blacks with equal benefits, subsidies, and job opportunities.

Davis waged his biggest fight against the National Recovery Administration. The NRA was the centerpiece of Roosevelt's New Deal program. NRA codes required that employers pay blacks and whites the same wages. Many employers ignored the codes and either fired the blacks or replaced them with machines. In the South, employers used loopholes that allowed wage differentials in certain occupations and reclassified black workers as domestics and non-union workers, thereby removing them from NRA protection. To thousands of blacks, the NRA was virtually worthless.

By 1934 he had had it with the NRA. He mockingly called it the "Negroes Ruined Again" agency. He said that the NRA's emblem, Blue Eagle, may as well have been a "predatory black hawk" for blacks. That same year Davis attacked the NRA before a Congressional committee.

Davis was not the only black outraged over the practices of the NRA. Black leaders repeatedly complained to Roosevelt and Labor Department officials about the abuses. Even highly placed blacks within the administration had their gripes. Robert Weaver, fresh out of Harvard with a degree in economics, was commissioned by the Interior Department to prepare a study on the economic status of the Negroes. Though careful to disassociate himself from Davis, Weaver documented a pattern of discrimination within New Deal agencies.

The anger of Davis and other black leaders over the New Deal gave the Party the wedge it sought. When the Party's Central Committee met in November 1935, Ford angrily charged: "The present Democratic Party with its New Deal policies has many shortcomings. Practices of discrimination and other limitations have prevented Negroes from receiving the full benefits of New Deal measures." Party

159

leaders were working hard to take advantage of black impatience with New Deal programs. By then many black leaders were willing to listen.[4]

A few months earlier, when Ford and Davis put out feelers to other black leaders for a planning conference to examine New Deal programs, many eagerly responded. Mordecai Johnson offered a conference hall on the Howard University campus to Davis. In May 1935, 250 participants, representing more than twenty black groups, took part in Davis's National Conference on the Economic Crisis and the Negro." The speakers were an odd mix of government bureaucrats, social planners, political activists, and black moderate leaders who in the past had waged intense political warfare against each other. During the three-day conference, Norman Thomas, James Ford, T. Arnold Hill, Randolph, and DuBois took the podium. Despite their serious differences, the speakers agreed that the New Deal was failing blacks and something drastic had to be done.

Davis did not waste words: "Capitalism is only a few hundred years old; as feudalism is dead, so may it die." He designated black and white workers as the gravediggers for the capitalists: "The problem of achieving a solidarity of Negro and white workers becomes one which principally concerns us."

George Edmund Haynes had a different concern than Davis. Haynes, who served as race relations director of the Federal Council of Churches, was worried that blacks might be swayed into mouthing "foreign or other groups' economic philosophies." He preferred that blacks avoid extremes and develop solutions that "will meet our needs under existing American conditions." Most of the participants probably knew that Haynes was talking about the Communists without mentioning them by name.

Since his resignation, DuBois, no longer constrained by the dictates of the NAACP's Board, was free to say what he pleased. He proposed a curious blend of nationalist, black capitalist, and Socialist economic solutions to attack the crisis. DuBois had not changed his opinion about white workers. The prospect of them aligning with blacks was still just as "discouraging" to him. He cautioned the participants that "there is no automatic power in socialism to override and suppress race prejudice." He remained as unforgiving of the Reds as ever: "One of the worst things that Negroes could do today would be to join the American Communist Party or any of its branches." Following the conference, DuBois would quietly withdraw his support. He would

160

take no part in any future activities associated with the Congress movement.

When the first NNC met, DuBois was in Washington, D.C delivering a talk at the Lincoln Temple Congregational Church. Afterwards, when asked what he thought of the National Negro Congress, his terse reply was, "It was an interesting idea" but he did not "think much of its practical possibilities."

Thomas and Ford mostly recited the Socialist and Communist criticisms of capitalism. Ford closed with another pitch for "a broad National Negro Congress." By now, most of the participants were with him. The conference hammered out a six-point program on civil rights, war, racism, and economic reform.[5]

Chasing the Black Moderates

The participants expected the Congress to be an historic event, so they felt it had to have a symbolic meeting date. They decided to hold the NNC in Chicago on February 14, the birthday of Frederick Douglass. Davis wanted Randolph to serve as president of the Congress. Randolph agreed to take the post after Davis assured him that the NNC would not be a Communist show that would "usurp the work of any organization."

Randolph had to have that assurance, since he had long suspected that the Communists wanted to control black organizations for their own self-serving political ends. There was also more than a little ego involved in Randolph's decision to come aboard. As president of a potentially influential national black organization, he could realize his cherished dream of taking a high place in the pantheon of civil rights leaders. When Davis issued his call to "Let Us Build a NNC" as a pamphlet, Randolph wrote the introduction. He gave his personal pledge to the moderates that "this Congress will not be disposed to supplant or take over the work of any existing organization."[6]

In June Davis appeared at the NAACP convention and tried to sell the NNC idea to the organization's reluctant officials. Davis enjoyed relatively good relations with the NAACP Board of Directors. For a time they had supported his Joint Committee, but the board was not ready to endorse the NNC. They took a wait-and-see attitude.

He was patient. He knew how to play the political game as well as anyone. Time, he believed, was on his side. Everywhere he traveled he found blacks overwhelmingly in favor of the NNC. The NNC's

161

National Planning Committee distributed fifty thousand copies of Davis's pamphlet nationwide.

In December 1935 Davis made another pitch to the NAACP board for support. They did not turn him down outright but instead coyly replied that the board "does not know the objective of the proposed NNC." He took this as a sign that the board was keeping the door open. Whatever momentary hope he may have had vanished the next month when the board informed him that the organization would no longer continue to contribute to the Joint Committee. In an effort to salvage something out of the board's rejection, Davis pleaded with them to give the NNC its "moral support." The board voted to send an observer to Chicago.

It was not information or lack of it that prompted NAACP officials to keep hands off the NNC. The board just did not buy his promise that the NNC would be the "independent" organization that he swore it would. There were just too many doubts "in the minds of many," Wilkins said, "as to how they can carry out their plans if they stuck to their promise not to form a new organization." What Wilkins did not say was that the NAACP did not trust Davis to keep the Reds out. Wilkins, along with White and NAACP Legal Counsel Charles Houston, privately were convinced that the Communists not only would dominate the proceedings but also the NNC leadership. It was just too risky for them to lend their name and the prestige of the NAACP to the NNC. But Wilkins, White, and Houston realized that they did not speak for everyone in the organization. There were many local chapters who were excited by the NNC. Regardless of what the board decided, they were going to work with the NNC.

Ever alert for internal cracks in the organization, Party leaders moved fast. Browder told delegates at a party convention at Madison Square Garden that the NAACP "has itself been forced by the new mood among the masses to reorientate itself towards the Left." He was not far off. While NAACP officials would not endorse the NNC, they decided to yield to the growing enthusiasm and "not to object to the branches affiliating with the NNC."[7]

Party leaders also geared up for Chicago. The National Research League, a Party-affiliated think tank, published a special issue on the National Negro Congress. The magazine gave a detailed report on the dire economic plight of Illinois blacks. In a foreword to the report, Richard Wright called the brutal statistics on black misery "dry symbols of a desperate and blood-smeared reality." He hoped that the Congress would spark "a new comradeship in the Negroes' struggle for freedom and progress." Wright later would give a detailed report on the NNC for the Party's monthly, *New Masses*.

Communists were none too modest about their role as initiators of the Congress. *The Communist* threw modesty out the window and trumpeted that the Congress was due to "the pioneering and trail-blazing work of the Communists."[8]

The First National Negro Congress Convenes

The Headline in the *Defender*, "Universal Unrest Among Black People Revealed At National Congress Here," was the best testament that Davis had done his work well. Lifting the gavel crafted by Hampton University students from the wood of the last slave ship to America, Davis opened the first NNC. Above his head was a giant banner that read BLACK AMERICA DEMANDS AN END TO MOB VIOLENCE AND LYNCHING.

More than four thousand delegates and observers crowded into Chicago's Eighth Regiment Armory. Their voices blended into a swelling cacophony of sound as they sang the words of the Negro National Anthem written by James Weldon Johnson as a tribute to black pride. They came from twenty-six states and represented 551 organizations. In all, 817 delegates were officially accredited. Preachers, farmers, laborers, professors, business persons, students, politicians, artists, and social gadflies all rubbed shoulders. Dozens of NAACP and Urban League chapters sent representatives.

Official greetings came from all over the world. One telegram urged blacks to "strengthen your ranks in a united fighting front" behind the "militant Negro leadership" of the NNC. It was signed by Mao Tse Tung, Provisional Chairman of the Chinese Soviet Republic. The "special envoy" of the London Legation of Ethiopia was loudly cheered when he compared the Ethiopian fight to the "American War of Independence's pursuit of life, liberty, and happiness." When the Cuban delegation ran out of money and was stranded on the dock in Havana, the crowd missed a chance to jeer Yankee imperialism with them.[9]

For three days, the Chicago Armory was filled with some of the hottest rhetoric ever heard by black audiences. It seemed everyone had an opinion on how to solve the problems of blacks. Every issue was up for debate, and the delegates were not bashful about letting their fury show. Speakers would shout, wave their arms, spew out volleys of angry words. Hecklers from the upper balconies interrupted with catcalls and boos if they did not like what was said. Frequent cries were heard, such as, "What about the Scottsboro Boys?" "What about the racist unions?" "Enforce the Constitution!" and "We want the right to vote!" Enraged over the "pro-fascist" stance of the Hearst press on Ethiopia, the delegates tore up copies of Hearst newspapers and threw the pieces into the air, shouting "Boycott Hearst!" Some of the observers got so carried away by the debates that they had to be ejected from the armory.

Both the Communists and Socialists sent large contingents to Chicago. Norman Thomas and Ford were prominently featured as speakers. Thomas' kept his remarks purposely low key. He merely praised the NNC for fighting discrimination. Ford was even more circumspect. He did not want to give Wilkins and the other conservative critics any ammunition to attack the NNC as a Communist front. He stayed close to the standard NNC themes of anti-lynching legislation, debt relief for farmers and sharecroppers, and civil rights.

Ford did not even make an issue of Armory officials barring Browder from speaking. He continued to strike the right chords when he gave his impressions of the NNC in *The Communist*. The old enemies of the Party had suddenly become friends. The small businessman was progressive, Ford contended, "as he hates big capital. " He praised the black fraternities, sororities, lodges, social clubs, and student groups for their actions. He praised the church for its "solid contacts with the Negro masses." Whether Ford discussed his new-found respect for religion with the Rev. Archibald Carey is not known, but the Communist and the well-known black Methodist churchman did have a convivial lunch at the Southway Hotel the last day of the NNC.[10]

Several hundred whites came to the NNC, nearly all of whom were Communists or Socialists. While they remained discreet, some of the more vigilant blacks were irritated that they were there at all. The *Defender* overheard one delegate quip that the Congress was "a black gathering with red and white trimmings."

The *Defender* also got in its dig: "Would Hitler permit membership of Jews in a Nazi Congress?" Dr. Harold Kingsley, a delegate from Chicago, had a similar thought which he expressed in better taste than the *Defender*. "If the whites were to be present, why not representatives from the American Missionary Society, the Rosenwald Fund, or the Educational Board of the AME church?"

A flap in the press room did not endear the whites to some blacks. Wilkins, who came to Chicago as an NAACP observer, bitterly complained to Davis that a "bossy white woman with a New York accent" denied black reporters access to the press room facilities. Wilkins claimed that she told the black reporters that they would get only prepared statements. Her arrogance persuaded Frank Marshall Davis of the Associated Negro Press that whites controlled all the key positions at the NNC, "including direction of the all-important press headquarters." An embarrassed Davis quickly stepped in and ordered the press room open to everyone.[11]

But most blacks were satisfied that no faction dominated the proceedings and democracy prevailed. Wilkins also got into the convivial spirit and spoke at one of the sessions on the NAACP's campaign to make lynching a federal crime. Later he claimed that when the Congress closed, Davis took him aside and whispered that the NNC would give him a job when it replaced the NAACP as the leading civil rights group. The Urban League's Lester Granger had not completely dropped his guard. He agreed that the NNC was not "a Communist gathering." However, Granger said he would rest easier if assured that the Congress "will deal not with political parties but with economic and civil issues." This was his diplomatic way of telling them to keep the Communists out.[12]

The speaker that everyone wanted to hear was not present in the Armory. A. Phillip Randolph did not attend the Congress because of illness. However, in a prepared speech read to the audience, he pulled out all stops. He evoked the name of every major historical figure dear to black Americans, including Frederick Douglass, Nat Turner, Denmark Vessey, and Harriet Tubman, and somewhat immodestly, he put himself in their company.

Randolph's speech also touched on war, racism, fascism, the bankruptcy of capitalism, the Depression, and the alleged failure of the New Deal. He boldly stated: "The next instrumentality which the workers must build and employ for their protection against economic exploitation, war and fascism, is an independent working-class party." Ford was probably elated when he heard those words. It might mean that Randolph was moving toward the Communists. Wright said that his speech "demonstrates that the rapid march of imperialism and the trustification of monopoly capitalism require the immediate united effort of the broadest masses of the people."

More than one hundred resolutions were passed with virtually no dissent. The Congress had something for nearly everybody. The major resolutions called for aid to farmers and sharecroppers, women's equality, anti-lynching laws, voting rights, educational opportunities for black youth, social and unemployment insurance, labor equality, and opposition to war and fascism.[13]

Davis could now breathe easier. He had done what a few months ago seemed impossible. He had brought Communists and black moderates together under the same roof to fashion a progressive program for blacks. The worst fears of Wilkins and the established black leaders—that the NNC would be a rubber stamp for the Communists—vanished for the moment.

They were further consoled that only ten Communists were given seats on the seventy-five member NNC National Council. In the words of one delegate, the "'Red scare' was a joke." Historian Carter G. Woodson was personally satisfied that the Reds had played a positive role at the Congress. He said that he had talked with a lot of the black Communists at the Congress and did not hear any of them "express a desire to destroy anyone or anything but oppression." Frank Marshall Davis went further. Not only should blacks not fear the Communists, Davis said, but they should welcome them "as the salvation of the proposed permanent organization."

Not everyone, however, was pleased over the way the NNC was run. A group of black bishops claimed that NNC officials deliberately excluded them from Congress activities. In a letter to the *Defender*, the churchmen reminded the NNC officials that the church "had the largest following of any organized group." A delegate who described himself as a "dyed -in-the-wool churchman" accused the bishops of sour grapes. He said that the presiding committee, of which he was a member, was chaired by Powell. He added: "The ministers seemed to be very much in the forefront throughout and their opinions were freely sought."[14]

T. L. Evans of the Associated Negro Press also covered the NNC and he agreed with Miller that there were some shady goings-on behind the Congress. Evans remarked: "The burning question was when the Communists would take the Congress over." The *California Eagle* was more subtle. The paper found it odd that so "many of the leaders were at least extremely liberal."

Randolph resented the criticisms. He lashed back that the Congress was "a Negro movement" pure and simple. While he conceded that Communists participated in the Congress, he reminded the critics that "Democrats, Republicans, and Socialists as well as Negroes of various religious creeds and denominations" also were at the NNC. Besides,

Randolph argued, "Communists are not criminals." If blacks wanted to become Communists, "they need make no apology for it." He even vouched for the political purity of John Davis, claiming that he was not a Communist. For the moment, anyway, Randolph had made a shaky peace with the Party.[15]

Not all the criticisms of the NNC came from the conservatives. Some believed that the NNC was not radical enough. Bunche could not reconcile himself to the resolution on Negro business. He argued that the NNC was spreading too many illusions that catered to "the traditional reactionary philosophy" of black capitalism. He wanted the NNC to unite "solidly behind the American labor movement." But he remained loyal to the cause. He was appointed to the NNC's Executive Council and was frequently asked to uphold the NNC position at political symposia. At one event in Philadelphia, he was even invited to give the Communist view on the Farmer-Labor Party. Bunche politely declined.

There were too many "petty capitalists" and "big shots" in Chicago to suit George Streater, as well. He asked, "Where were the Negro workers?" Streater thought that the NNC officials had deliberately discouraged trade unionists from coming to Chicago. But he was off target. The NNC had invited all the unions to send delegates. Many simply did not show up. Ford was so perturbed by the failure of many unions to attend that he publicly ripped the leaders of the Harlem Labor Council. The irony was that the council was a loose alliance of 100 affiliated unions, all of whom were closely linked to the Communists.[16]

National Negro Congress Organizes

Ford and Davis left Chicago buoyed by their triumph. Ford was appointed to the Committee on International Relations. Moore, Ben Davis, and Party newcomers B. D. Amis and Ed Strong also got important committee assignments. The Communists had an ambitious program and had made many new friends. The real question was how long they could keep the momentum going.

In April T. Arnold Hill appeared with other prominent blacks at an open membership meeting of the Party's Harlem Section. Although Hill claimed that he did "not officially represent the Urban League" and that he was not a Communist, he felt compelled to praise Ford as an outstanding leader. Hill's words only deepened Ford's conviction

167

that the Party had hit pay dirt. The NNC gave the Communists the chance they had waited for to work "in cooperation with the NAACP, the Urban League, and other organizations." If all went well, Ford hoped that it could even lead to the "possibility for Communists to work in local branches" of the NAACP.

The Party's Herb Newton believed that Communists had successfully split what he called the "progressive" moderate black leaders from the conservatives, and that in time Communists could educate them to "make considerable contributions to the immediate struggles of the Negro people." Browder was more reserved. He said merely that the Party had done "substantial work among the NNC."[17] Browder had good reason to be cautious. If the Party truly desired to take over the NNC, as some blacks charged, they would have to figure out how to work around the NNC's structure. The NNC was not an organization with an ideologically unified core of loyalists and a central command. It was an unwieldy and fragile coalition of dozens of black organizations with diverse interests and views. The delegates were united in Chicago only by their color and the desperate economic conditions of the times.

At the first meeting of the National Executive Council in March, Ben Davis, Richard Moore, and Manning Johnson, a prominent union activist and recent Party convert, showed up prepared to help develop strategy. Lester Granger also came. The council decided to send a delegation to Washington to present its demands for anti-lynching legislation to Roosevelt and Congress. The plan fizzled when the council failed to assign someone to follow-up on the request for an appointment with the President.

In June, the Executive Council held its second meeting in Cleveland. Johnson, Davis, Moore, Herndon, and Edward Strong attended. Randolph did not come because of illness. The meeting was called to "review past work and map a militant program for civil liberty, unionism, and employment." Strong and Davis spoke. Later, Herndon was the principal speaker at an NNC "mass meeting" at the Mt. Zion Congregational Temple. While no details were made public of the three-day meeting, the council pledged to escalate the "fight against inequality, intolerance and oppression."[18]

It was too vague. The council as yet showed no evidence it had a central plan for the NNC. Council leaders were mainly titular spokesmen from their respective organizations. They had no real authority to commit their members to a specific plan of action. In part this was by

168

design. Davis, always mindful that the Congress was being closely scrutinized by black moderates, deliberately kept the Congress's structure loose. "Decisions must be made by the council and not by small groups within the council." He still hoped to get the endorsement of the NAACP. He knew he would not get it by trying to jam the entire NNC program past them. "There may be some organizations who will not wish to affiliate with the local councils." So he compromised. "I urge that we join with these programs on a specific program of action."

As a result, each of the twenty-six NNC councils operated autonomously. All decisions on planning and tactics were left to the local leaders. To plant a stronger toehold within the NNC, Ford ordered Communists to "merge" their activities with the local NNCs. With the exception of New York, Philadelphia, and the East Bay Oakland councils, there is no evidence at that point that the Communists exercised any more influence than local businessmen, ministers, and local politicians did in any of the local councils.[19]

Out of the dozens of scattershot protests the locals undertook nationally in 1937, Davis got personally involved in only one—the campaign against the steel owners. More than 85,000 blacks worked in the steel plants. They held the dirtiest, most dangerous jobs, and were paid about $3.60 a day. When the AFL refused to organize them, the fledgling CIO saw a golden opportunity to eliminate its rival in a major industry.

In 1935, the CIO targeted the steel industry for its first major organizing push. The CIO differed from the AFL in three fundamental ways. It rejected craft unionism, it pledged a militant anti-discrimination policy, and it did not bar Communists. The CIO organizing approach mixed idealism with a heavy dose of pragmatism: "The wages and working conditions of both Negro and white workers suffered—until the CIO started to organize on the new, democratic policy."

The skirmish lines were drawn when the CIO formed the Steel Workers Organizing Committee. Davis was ready to help. He called a conference in February 1937 in Pittsburgh. Dozens of black steel workers from across the country, their expenses paid by SWOC locals, attended. A broad coalition of community leaders, including Randolph and the Urban League's Hill, participated in the conference. Ford also came and gave the conference the Party's blessing: "The Communist Party sees in these Negro steel workers fine, militant forces."

169

The SWOC and the NNC announced plans to call strikes at the smaller steel plants in the East and Midwest. After a few plants were shut down, the steel barons gave in and signed pacts that improved wages and working conditions for the black and white workers.[20]

To mount successful drives against discrimination took money, and the NNC had almost none. To survive, the local councils had to rely exclusively on nickel and dime member contributions. Local organizers spent much of their time trying to bring in a few dollars.

Occasionally, a lucky council might get Duke Ellington, Langston Hughes, or stage actors Rex Ingram and Canada Lee to do a benefit performance, but for most locals it was a hand-to-mouth existence. Whatever private suspicions Wilkins had about Communist influence in the NNC, he regarded the rumors that Davis depended on them for money as "wholly without foundation."[21]

The Second National Negro Congress

By the summer of 1937, Davis had begun making plans for the second National Negro Congress. Mindful of the criticism of black ministers the year before, he decided to win their favor by dedicating the next Congress to the black church. In press statements, he hailed "the great leaders of the Negro church" and announced that the Congress would salute the church that "has been in the vanguard of liberty in America." The *National Negro Congress News* ran a feature on Richard Allen, a founder of the African Methodist Episcopal church, and praised the long list of historic black religious leaders.

Davis then set his sights on winning the full support of the NAACP. Roy Wilkins seemed favorably impressed in Chicago. Davis was optimistic that this would work to his advantage. He knew that many NAACP board members still had doubts about the NNC, but he wanted their endorsement.

It was a touchy matter. The board had to be approached gingerly. This time he let Randolph run interference. Randolph asked to meet with the board at the NAACP's annual conference in June in Detroit. The board turned him down, but did agree to "discuss specific issues" with NNC representatives.[22]

Davis was non-plussed by the seeming rebuff. The fact that the board had invited him to speak on labor issues at their conference indicated to him that he was still in their good graces. He decided to try an end around. Rather than go over the board's head and ask the conference to endorse the NNC, he made a pitch for them to support the CIO's organizing drives. He was already thinking about a future alliance with the labor organization, and it was a good opportunity to test the water.

The NAACP was caught off guard. The CIO had a good reputation and few delegates would question its strong track record on civil rights, but there was also a heavy Communist presence within the CIO. Board members were nervous about any entangling alliances. Following heated debate, the conference narrowly voted against a resolution endorsing the CIO. A *Crisis* editorial, which generally reflected the board's views, applauded the decision and advised blacks to "go into no labor organization blindly."

Davis did not come away empty handed. As a gesture of good will, Walter White agreed to address the next Congress. The presence of White was almost as good to him as a formal endorsement by the NAACP board. With White on the podium, Davis at last had removed the final obstacle from the NNC's path.[23]

In Philadelphia, he made good on his promise to the ministers. The 4,000 delegates and observers who poured into the Metropolitan Opera House on October 15, 1937 saw a giant picture of Richard Allen hanging above the speaker's stage. Davis designated the closing session "Richard Allen Night" and the delegates were provided buttons with Allen's picture to sport on their lapels.

More than one-thousand delegates, from twenty-seven states and several foreign countries, came to Philadelphia. They all broke into shouts and prolonged applause when Davis read the following message: "I am glad to extend greetings to the Second National Negro Congress." The greeter was President Roosevelt.

Dignitaries vied with each other for attention. On the stage, looking somber and businesslike sitting less than an arms-length apart, were Pennsylvania Lieutenant Governor Thomas Kennedy, Randolph, White and Houston of the NAACP, Granger from the Urban League, and Ford. An original copy of the Thirteenth Amendment was on display under guard in the lobby.

This time there was no heckling, outbursts, or disruptions. The applause for the speakers was loud but measured. To make sure the convention was orderly, the Executive Committee issued to all delegates a detailed checklist of procedures the Congress would follow from registration to resolution selection.[24] The speakers were careful not to offend anyone or disturb the harmony. No one disparaged the

171

New Deal or vilified Roosevelt. Herndon came closest to attacking government policies when he called the Supreme Court "reactionary" for releasing only four of the Scottsboro Boys.

Communist speakers had the easiest job. They had two safe themes to play on: democracy and civil rights. Ford came on as the true patriot, building his speech around Browder's line, "Communism is Twentieth Century Americanism." Shouting the names of American heroes from Lincoln to Douglass, Ford exhorted the crowd to "march forward with the support of our sympathizers among white workers, intellectuals, and middle classes." Henry Winston, president of the Young Communist League, praised Roosevelt for "coming forward with real progressive legislation." Patterson and Moore wanted NNC delegates to know that the International Labor Defense stood behind them in "the vital American task of stopping lynchings and winning civil, democratic and economic rights for the Negro people."

At a symposium on war and fascism, *Daily Worker* editor Clarence Hathaway reminded the delegates that Japan, Germany, and Italy threatened world peace. "There is war and there is fascism," he declared. "Our tasks are how to stop them from spreading throughout the world." He called for a worldwide boycott of all goods produced by the three nations.[25]

White took the podium and gave a grim account of several recent lynchings. He traced the NAACP's campaign to secure congressional approval of anti-lynching legislation. He ended with a rousing call for the NNC congress to get behind the NAACP's current push to get the Senate to pass a federal anti-lynching bill. Mutual admiration flowed through Davis's speech. He urged the delegates "to rally behind the National Association for the Advancement of Colored People to fight the reactionary forces which aim to prohibit the passage of the bill." Arthur Huff Fauset, the NNC's first vice president, was equally expansive in assuring the delegates that the NNC deeply appreciated "the valiant work of the NAACP, the Urban League, and the churches."

This time nothing would keep Randolph away from Philadelphia. As he strode to the podium the entire hall rose as one to give the NNC president a standing ovation. He was in top form as he sounded the alarm against the fascists. He recited the familiar list of abuses against blacks and workers, and he demanded that the nation stop "trampling on Negroes' rights." Randolph struck the "Popular Front" high note: "Let us build a united front in cooperation with the progressive and liberal agencies of the nation whose interests are common with Black America."

Ben Davis, who covered the NNC for the *Daily Worker*, quoted Randolph extensively and approvingly. He praised Randolph for assailing "the reactionary industrialists and the turpentine and cotton magnates who would seek to smash the labor movement." When Randolph uttered the Party's sacred words "united front," Davis was ecstatic. To the Communists, their old adversary had finally seen the light.[26]

The final resolutions were mostly a repeat of those passed at Chicago. The NNC pledged to fight for an anti-lynching bill, more jobs, relief, civil rights laws, open unions, and against fascism. The one exception was labor. Davis pooh-poohed the Urban League and NAACP's labor program and instead threw his full support to the CIO. It did not happen by chance. Since Chicago, Davis had worked feverishly behind the scenes to get CIO locals to endorse the NNC. In May CIO director John Brophy agreed to beat the drums to get the locals to send delegates to the next Congress. Randolph could see what was happening and he did not like it. He mildly protested against "tying up the Congress too closely with the CIO."

More than a few delegates shared his unease. Some delegates were plainly scared of the CIO and its "Red ties." Others felt that an alignment with the CIO would compromise the NNC's independence and black orientation. But the CIO was riding a strong crest of black favor. It fought the steel barons, gave blacks leadership roles, and provided thousands of blacks with decent wages. Equally important, the CIO opened union doors to more than 150,000 unorganized black workers. Many blacks also were favorably impressed with CIO chief John L. Lewis. He appeared to be a tough fighter who would go to the wall for black workers. Although Lewis did not attend the Congress, he sent a personal message extending "warm greetings" to the delegates and the promise of a "great future for the American Negro in our labor movement."

The delegates also vigorously applauded when Phillip Murray, SWOC chairman, said that blacks were "entitled by all the laws of nature itself to the same opportunity in the game of life as any white man." Murray seemed genuinely sincere when he beseeched the NNC officers to support CIO struggles. The presence of nearly 400 trade unionists as official delegates also may have stifled dissent. They formed the single largest bloc of delegates at the NNC.[27]

Granger was in an especially conciliatory mood toward the CIO. He called the organization's labor campaign in the South "a happy development." For the time being, partisan politics would take a back seat to the good feelings that flowed in Philadelphia. White, Houston, and

Granger left Philadelphia with Max Yergan's guarantee that the NNC would remain "non-partisan." An African affairs expert, Yergan, was Davis's assistant. He was also a Party member. In his speech, Yergan sounded convincing when he promised that the NNC would "not interfere with or weaken" any other black organization.[28]

The NNC had survived a second year. No crisis had emerged to split the ranks of radicals and moderates. Ford, Abner Berry, Johnson, and Herndon were appointed to the NNC's fifteen-member National Executive Council. Davis was riding higher than ever on the crest of popular favor. The black press was nearly unanimous in hailing the Congress. The *Defender* said, "It is destined to re-create hope for greater freedom and liberty." The *Afro-American* delivered a tongue-in-cheek rebuff to NNC critics, noting that the Communist Party "skillfully" fooled the NAACP, Urban League, Republicans and Democrats into attending the "Red Congress." The only grumbling came from Claude McKay, who had become even more embittered with the Communists with each passing year. McKay went to Philadelphia as an observer and left convinced that the Communists were "cleverly controlling" the NNC.[29]

Davis planned bigger things for the NNC when it met in Detroit in September 1938, but they never came off. The NNC did not meet in 1938 or 1939. Critics maintained that the third NNC was canceled because of internal ideological feuds, lack of interest, and the war in Europe. The real reason was less dramatic. The NNC simply had too many administrative problems and too little funding. The two years the NNC did not meet, many local councils continued to protest discrimination, unemployment, and relief. Davis stayed on the move, trying to raise money and rally the troops. But despite his cheery front, the fragile bond that he had worked so hard to build between the Communists and moderate black leaders was already coming apart. As events would soon show, Davis would do his part to finish it off.

Notes

1. *Negro Liberator*, 15 February 1935; Naison, *Communists in Harlem*, 178; Ford, *The Negro and the Democratic Front*, 163-85; James Ford, "The National Negro Congress," *The Communist* 15 (April 1936): 322; *Daily Worker*, 10 July 1936.
2. Harvard Sitkoff, *A New Deal for Blacks*, 47-57; *Negro Liberator*, 15 March 1935; *Daily Worker*, 23 May 1935; *Party Organizer* 8 (March

1935): 21; Earl Browder, *The People's Front* (New York: International Publishers, 1938), 47; Ford, "Build the National Negro Congress Movement," 555.

3. Interview with Miriam Sherman, 7 December 1989; Interview with Don Wheeldin, 2 December 1989.

4. Sitkoff, *A New Deal for Blacks*, 50-51 and 258-59; John P. Davis, "Blue Eagles and Black Workers," *The New Republic* 81 (14 November 1934): 8-9; Davis, "A Black Inventory of the New Deal," *The Crisis* 42 (May 1935): 141-42; Robert C. Weaver to W. E. B. DuBois, 1 May 1935, DuBois Papers, University of Massachusetts, Amherst, Massachusetts. Weaver later went on to become the first black cabinet member when Lyndon Johnson appointed him Secretary of Housing and Urban Development. For a biographical sketch of Weaver see *Current Biography Yearbook, 1961* (New York: H.W. Wilson, 1961), 474-76. Ford, *The Negro and the Democratic Front*, 30.

5. *Daily Worker*, 23 May 1935; *New York Age*, 1 June 1935; Raymond Wolter, *Negroes and the Great Depression* (Westport Connecticut: Greenwood Publishers, 1970), 354; Davis, "A Survey of the Problems of the Negro Under the New Deal," *Journal of Negro Education* 5 (January 1936): 12; George Edmund Haynes, "The American Negro in the Changing Economic Order," *Journal of Negro Education* 18; DuBois, "Social Planning for the Negro: Past, Present," *Journal of Negro Education*, 123; *Afro-American*, 14 March 1936; W. E. B. DuBois to Harrison S. Jackson, 22 August 1934, DuBois Papers, University of Massachusetts, Amherst, Massachusetts; Norman Thomas, "The Socialist's Way Out for the Negro," *Journal of Negro Education*, 104; James Ford, "The Communist's Way Out for the Negro," *Journal of Negro Education*, 95. Eleanor Ryan gave the Party's "official" view of the Howard conference in "Toward a National Negro Congress," *New Masses* 4 (4 June 1935): 14-15.

6. "The National Conference on the Economic Crisis and the Negro" (editorial comment), *Journal of Negro Education*, 1-2; Anderson, *A. Phillip Randolph*, 231; John P. Davis, *Let Us Build a National Negro Congress*, (Washington, D.C.: National Negro Congress Papers, 1935), 4 and 30; Kelly Miller, *Affidavit*, 27 June 1935, submitted to House Un-American Activities Committee, vol. 3, no. 3, 2148, October-November 1938, Washington D.C., 1938; Ibid. 5 November 1938, 2142-2144, 2150; U.S. Congress, Senate, *Senate Miscellaneous Documents*, 74th Congress, 2nd sess., Document 217, 54.

7. James Ford, "The National Negro Congress," 323; Walter White to Randolph, 3 February 1936, NAACP Papers, Library of Congress, Washington, D.C.; Randolph to Walter White, February 4, 1936, NAACP Papers, Library of Congress, Washington, D.C.; Minutes of the NAACP Board of Directors Meeting, 9 December 1935, NAACP

Papers, Library of Congress, Washington, D.C.; Board Minutes, 6 January 1936, NAACP Papers, Library of Congress, Washington, D.C.; Roy Wilkins to Charles O. Houston, 15 February 1936, NAACP Papers, Library of Congress, Washington, D.C. Browder's speech is quoted in Ford and Berry, "The Coming National Negro Congress," 140.

8. "National Negro Congress," *Illinois Labor Notes* 4 (March 1936): 2; "Review of the Month," *The Communist* 15 (March 1936): 202.

9. *Chicago Defender*, 22 February 1936; *The Official Proceedings of the National Negro Congress, 1936* (Washington, D.C.: National Negro Congress Papers, 1936), 41; James Ford, "Political Highlights of the National Negro Congress," *The Communist* 15 (May 1936): 458 and 461; *Daily Worker*, 17 February 1936; *Daily Worker*, 23 February 1936.

10. *Chicago Defender*, 22 February 1936; Ford, "Political Highlights of the National Negro Congress," 463-64.

11. *Chicago Defender*, 22 February 1936; *Amsterdam News*, 14 May 1936.

12. Roy Wilkins, *Standing Fast*, 161; Lester Granger, "The National Negro Congress," *Opportunity* 14 (May 1936): 153.

13. Anderson, *A. Phillip Randolph*, 230; *Official Proceedings of the National Negro Congress, 1936*, 7, 10, 11, 19-37; *Chicago Defender*, 22 February 1936; Steve Kingston, *Frederick Douglass* (New York: National Negro Congress Papers), 3-4; Richard Wright, "Two Million Black Voices," *New Masses* 4 (25 February 1936): 15.

14. Party leader Herbert Newton saw the Davis triumph as "proof of the rapidly growing cleavage in Negro leadership." Herbert Newton, "The National Negro Congress," *The Negro Worker* 6 (April 1936): 25; *New York Age*, 14 March 1936; *Afro-American*, 29 March 1936; *Defender*, 28 February 1936; *Defender*, 7 March 1936.

15. *Afro-American*, 7 March 1936; *California Eagle*, 28 February 1936; *Amsterdam News*, 2 March 1936.

16. Ralph Bunche, "Triumph? or Fiasco?" *Race* 1 (Summer 1936): 95; P. J. Frye to Ralph Bunche, 17 September 1936, Bunche Papers, UCLA Special Collections; George Streator, "A Criticism," *Race* 1 (Summer 1936): 96; Ford, "The National Negro Congress," 325.

17. *Official Proceedings of the National Negro Congress, 1936*, 40-41; *Defender*, 11 April 1936; Ford, "Uniting the Negro People," *The Communist* 16 (August 1937): 728; Earl Browder, *Build The United People's Front* (New York: Workers Library Publishers, 1936), 59.

18. *Louisville Leader*, 14 March 1936; *Defender*, 27 June 1936.

19. Gunnar Myrdal, *An American Dilemma* (New York: Harper and Brothers, 1944), 818; *Report of National Secretary*, Cleveland, Ohio, 19-20 June 1936, 20, 21; National Negro Congress Papers, Schomberg Research Library, New York; *New Order* 4 (December 1936): 20.

20. The local National Negro Congress Papers Councils undertook a number of nationwide protest actions from 1936 through 1939 (see Ralph

Bunche, *Program, Ideologies, Tactics*, 340-45, Bunche Papers, UCLA Special Collections). *California Eagle*, 6 March 1936; Lawrence Witmer, "The National Negro Congress: A Reassessment," *American Quarterly* 22 (Winter 1970): 887-89; *Official Proceedings of the National Negro Congress, 1937* (Washington D.C.: National Negro Congress Papers, 1937); National Negro Congress Papers, SL; "Report of Business Sessions of the National Negro Congress," National Negro Congress Papers; Cayton and Mitchell, *Black Workers and the New Unions*, 190-224; *The CIO and the Negro Worker* (Washington D.C.: CIO), 5; *Official Proceedings of the National Negro Congress, 1937*, "Report, Business Sessions"; Ford, *The Negro and the Democratic Front*, 113. Phillip Murray details the political activities in Pennsylvania that stemmed from the CIO steel strike in his address to the 1937 National Negro Congress Papers, *Official Proceedings of the National Negro Congress, 1937*.

21. *Amsterdam News*, 22 August 1936.

22. (Advertisement), *New Masses* 6 (24 May 1938); Bunche, *Program, Ideologies, Tactics*, 339; "Composite Financial Report of the National Negro Congress," *Official Proceedings of the National Negro Congress, 1937*; Roy Wilkins to the Board of Directors, memorandum, 9 March 1936, NAACP Papers, Library of Congress, Washington, D.C.; *National Negro Congress News*, 26 September 1937; *NAACP Board Minutes*, 1 July 1937, NAACP Papers, Library of Congress, Washington, D.C.

23. James S. Olson, "Organized Black leadership and Industrial Unionism: The Racial Response, 1936-1945," *Labor History* 10 (Summer 1969): 475-86; *National Negro Congress News*, 20 September 1937; *The Crisis* 44 (July 1937): 212; *The Crisis* 44 (August 1937): 241.

24. *Official Proceedings of the National Negro Congress, 1937*; *Afro-American*, 23 October 1937; *Daily Worker*, 14 October 1937; *Daily Worker*, 18 October 1937; *Daily Worker*, 20 October 1937.

25. *Daily Worker*, 19 October 1937; Ford, *The Negro and the Democratic Front*, 133-35.

26. *Afro-American*, 23 October 1937; *Official Proceedings of the National Negro Congress, 1937*; *Daily Worker*, 19 October 1937.

27. *Official Proceedings of the National Negro Congress, 1937*; Cayton and Mitchell, Sumner Rosen, "The CIO Era, 1935-1955, " in Julius Jacobson, *The Negro and the American Labor Movement* (New York: Anchor Books, 1968), 188-208; John Brophy to John P. Davis, 13 May 1937, National Negro Congress Papers; John L. Lewis to National Negro Congress, 22 September 1937, National Negro Congress Papers; *Daily Worker*, 20 October 1937.

28. *Defender*, 4 November 1937; *Defender*, 23 October 1937; *Official Proceedings of the National Negro Congress, 1937*.

29. *Defender*, 4 November 1937; *Afro-American*, 30 October 1937; *Amsterdam News*, 17 September 1938.

9 Resignations

During the fall of 1939, Davis criss-crossed the country giving pep talks to the local councils and firming up his contacts with black leaders and union officials. At the same time, he even managed to make news when he ran afoul of the Dies Committee.

The House Committee headed by Texas Congressman Martin Dies was then in the early stages of its investigation of Communists' activities. In September 1939 Dies considered subpoenaing Davis to testify. For some unexplained reason, Dies changed his mind and he never appeared.

Davis did not break stride as he turned his attention to the third NNC scheduled for April 1940 in Washington, D.C. He was determined to make it the biggest and best yet. He was optimistic that his tenuous truce with the NAACP would hold. Since White's appearance in Philadelphia, NAACP officials had been civil, if not friendly, toward him. Pickens even explored the possibility of attempting to get a formal agreement with the NNC for "conference and consultation" when actions by either organization were being planned.

Immediately before the Congress convened, Patterson and Charles Houston made a joint call on Assistant Attorney General O. John Rogge at the Justice Department. They demanded that the department clamp down on Klan violence in South Carolina.[1]

Davis had good reason to feel pleased as he stood under the gilded chandeliers of the newly built auditorium of the Labor Department and gazed at the crowd of more than two thousand delegates and observers seated at the third NNC. Before the first delegate was seated, Davis had already won one fight. He forced the previously segregated Washington Tourist Camp to accommodate 200 black delegates. The

179

camp was located on federal land, under the jurisdiction of Harold Ickes' Interior Department.

New York actress Laura Duncan opened the Congress with a stirring rendition of Billie Holiday's "Strange Fruit." More organizations sent official delegates, more foreign countries sent their greetings, and more union delegates were present than at the Philadelphia gathering. There were also more Communists—which immediately touched off whispers that the Communists were packing the NNC.—and there were 370 white delegates. While Randolph sensed that trouble was brewing, he remained optimistic. He told a reporter, "I am very fond of John P. Davis and consider him a capable person."

For his part, Davis would not allow innuendoes or rumors to detract from the NNC. He read a message from President Roosevelt: "It is more than ever important that the place of a minority group in society not be obscured by ignorance and prejudice." Beneath the calm surface, however, there were differences that anyone who had attended the two previous NNCs could spot. John L. Lewis and his daughter sat on the podium instead of Walter White and Lester Granger.

The speakers hit on all the familiar problems of discrimination, jobs, and violence. But the delegates seemed to be steering the NNC toward endorsement of the CIO and a pacifist, non-intervention policy in Europe. One observer who roamed between various NNC workshops found it almost uncanny that "this was one of the few times in history when a group of 1,285 people agreed in toto on everything." All, that is, he wryly added, "with the exception of Randolph."[2]

Davis aggressively took center stage during all the proceedings. He left nothing to chance. The CIO and non-intervention were almost his sole concerns. In his address he did call for an anti-lynching law and blast abuses in federal job and relief agencies, but then he came quickly to his main point: "This administration is taking sides in this imperialist conflict. Its actions menace our neutrality and our peace."

Stalin and Hitler had signed their infamous non-aggression pact in August 1939 and American Communists were dutifully beating the drums against American intervention in Europe. By calling for neutrality Davis, in effect, was voicing the same line. He added: "We must join with labor to insist upon an end to this disastrous policy." When he said labor, he meant the CIO and John L. Lewis.

Davis accorded Lewis the kind of welcome traditionally reserved for a visiting potentate. Two black miners presented him with a bronze plaque "for distinguished service to the Negro people." His speech, broadcast via a coast-to-coast radio hookup, was largely a recitation of CIO labor accomplishments. He told the audience, "It was a great mistake for any class of laborers to isolate itself and weaken the bond of brotherhood." With that said, he put his proposition straight to the NNC—"To affiliate or to reach a working agreement with Labor's Non-Partisan Political League so that our common purposes may be better attained." It was a bold offer. Davis was asking the NNC to surrender its independence and become an appendage of the CIO's political organization.[3]

The next day Davis answered Lewis: "I have no doubt that the delegates to this great Congress will unanimously and enthusiastically accept the invitation of Mr. Lewis." He had the majority of the crowd with him. Many delegates climbed on seats, slapped backs, waved hats and handkerchiefs, and shouted that they wanted to approve the alliance. After Davis sat down, Randolph took the floor. Someone shouted at him, "What about approval?" Randolph grimly answered, "There is no doubt about approval."

When Davis spoke of neutrality, he did not speak as a man who personally abhorred the horror of all wars. He had something else in mind: "The American people will refuse to follow American imperialism in an attack upon the Soviet Union." This was not the Davis that many blacks had heard before. The words were his, but they sounded like he was reading from a script prepared by the Party. The Communists were so put out with Roosevelt that when Davis was asked whether Mrs. Roosevelt would address the NNC as she had in 1937, he brusquely replied, "No, we're tired of Mrs. Roosevelt."

Davis tied the NNC not only to the coattails of the CIO but to the Communist Party as well. By accepting Lewis's offer of partnership, he violated the sacred principle that the NNC was founded on—its independence. That principle was spelled out in its charter and had been reiterated over and over by Randolph and Davis himself.[4]

It was a painful moment for Randolph. He looked tired as he walked slowly to the podium to deliver his speech. He had tried his best to make the NNC a symbol of black political independence. He had never wavered in his conviction that blacks could only attain their freedom through their own united efforts.

For three days he sat politely through the proceedings and listened as Davis and other speakers betrayed the principles of the NNC. Randolph knew what he had to do. He spoke in the sonorous, deliberate voice that audiences had become so familiar with: "Russia, like Japan, is a dictatorship which takes no cognizance people's rights." He took on the CIO and the Communists next: "Neither the AFL nor the CIO can save the Negro. The Communist Party cannot save the Negro." His words reflected the bitterness and disgust he felt toward the Communists. "Personally, I would not be a member of the Negro Congress or any other organization which was a Communist front." Randolph's warning rang throughout the hall. The day the NNC lost its independence, he said, was the day it "lost its soul."

The catcalls and boos rained down on Randolph from the audience. Half of the delegates were making for the exits before he finished speaking. Boos and shouts of "traitor" and "red-baiter" continued as he turned the gavel over to Max Yergan. Returning to his seat he stared straight ahead with the same placid look so characteristic of him. He watched the delegates dance and shout in jubilation as Yergan was chosen to replace him as president.

Novelist Ralph Ellison, attending his first NNC, left the auditorium disgusted with Randolph and said, "I felt I had witnessed a leader in the act of killing his leadership." Randolph stayed for the rest of the proceedings. Perhaps he still had a flicker of hope that he could salvage something from the crumbling organization. He told an interviewer that "the Congress must remain a Negro organization."

It was a forlorn hope. Randolph was now a stranger in the house he had helped to build. In a prepared statement, he predicted that blacks would reject a Communist-controlled NNC: "I am convinced that until the stigma of the Communist Front is wiped from the Congress, it will never rally the masses of the Negro people."[5] By then, few delegates were listening to anything he had to say. As one observer remarked, "Of the progressive Randolph of 1936 only a hollow mockery remains." In a veiled reference to him, Ben Davis wrote, "There are those who would have us turn our back on the friendly offer of John L. Lewis in the name of labor."

The National Council, now firmly dominated by the left, ratified Yergan as president without dissent. In Max Yergan they had the perfect candidate for NNC president. He was scholarly, sophisticated, and erudite, some even said arrogant. A loyal Party man since 1936, he got his radical baptism in South Africa, where he worked as a YMCA director for fifteen years.

The NNC also struck the non-partisan clause from the preamble to its constitution. The most significant part now read, "The Congress is a federated organization which seeks to unite the Negro people and all friends of Negro freedom."

Meanwhile, Randolph took out some of his anger and frustration on Lucious Harper. In a letter to the *Defender* a week after the NNC, Harper had dared suggest that "every Negro is a potential communist." Randolph erupted. He called Harper "inept and childish" for praising the Soviet Union and believing that "the American Communists were without race prejudice." He assured Harper that the Communist Party had roped in "only a handful" of blacks in Harlem and on Chicago's Southside.[6]

A week later, Lewis, Yergan, and Davis met to formalize their pact. They agreed to work together on the Wagner Anti-Lynching Bill before Congress, and to prevent any changes in the National Labor Relations Act. Davis and Lewis also announced that the league and the NNC Executive Council would hold a conference to "collaborate on a legislative program." According to their agreement, most of the work would be done through joint local and state committees.

The *CIO News* spread the word quickly through labor ranks that the NNC "enthusiastically accepted" the Lewis concordat. In June Lewis repeated his performance at the NAACP's annual conference. He blamed Roosevelt for high unemployment and demanded that the U.S. remain neutral in Europe. He then offered the NAACP the same deal as the NNC: affiliation with his Non-Partisan Political League. The board turned him down flat.[7]

The Decline of the NNC

The fall-out from the Davis-Lewis pact was immediate. Democrats and Republicans in Congress were livid. New York Democrat Hamilton Fish was the first through the door. "Communists have done everything to exploit" black injustices. Fish's attack was mild stuff compared to that of Pennsylvania Democrat Robert G. Allen. Parodying the NNC's name as the "Negro Communist Conference," Allen labeled the NNC resolution on non-intervention "treasonable."

Mississippi Democrat William Colmer warned the NNC to stay out of the South. "White people will not tolerate the communistic agitation of the Southern Negro." The Congressmen demanded an immediate investigation of NNC activities. Black Democrat Arthur Mitchell, not to be outdone by his colleagues, went "on record thoroughly disapproving of the appeal made to the Negro by John L. Lewis."[8]

Wilkins was not surprised by the events in Washington. Before the first delegate took a seat, he gleefully noted that "everyone was taking

183

potshots at the Communists." When the dust settled, Wilkins lined up to take his best shot. He was blunt: "Negroes have been taken for a ride." Later, he told a Bronx audience that the Party's program for blacks in the South was "little short of violent."

Bunche, who had already begun to politically mellow, saw a gloomy future for the NNC: "My prediction is that the Congress membership will soon be reduced to devout party members, fellow travelers, and representatives of the CIO." The *Afro-American's* "inquiring reporter" asked blacks on the street. "Do you think we ought to join Lewis's third party?" Nearly all of the respondents said no. A female clerk who replied it "smacks of communism" was typical of the general sentiment.[9]

At the same time, many blacks remained hopeful that the organization would not completely abandon the civil rights fight. The worst ravages of the Depression were past, but blacks still faced monumental social and economic problems. After years of political lobbying, the NAACP was no closer to getting anti-lynching legislation on the books than it was in 1922. Between 1941 and 1945, eighteen blacks would be lynched. Segregation was just as rigid for blacks in housing, education, and public accommodations. In the Deep South, Jim Crow voting laws kept nearly all blacks from the polls. New Deal laws had only marginally improved the wages and working conditions of black labor. A black labor survey in 1940 revealed that industry still relegated blacks to positions as "mainly common laborers or miners." The majority of AFL unions still barred blacks from membership.[10]

Given the harsh conditions that still confronted black America at the start of 1940, the *Defender* lost patience with the "promoters of undemocratic practices" who "attack every progressive stand by labeling it 'Red'." The paper had faith that the NNC would continue to provide blacks with a "program of struggle." One irate letter-writer reminded Randolph that in the Soviet Union "they don't have to pass any anti-lynching bill." Before the year ended, more than one hundred prominent blacks signed their names on the NNC's "Statement To The Negro People," which called for an end to all Jim Crow laws. Most were not Party members or "fellow travelers" but a respectable amalgam of college presidents, church leaders, local politicians, and fraternal groups.[11]

Bunche was only partially correct in his forecast that the NNC would collapse under the heavy hand of the Communists. As much as some Party leaders may have wanted to take full control of the NNC, they could not. Hitler's attack on the Soviet Union in June 1941 changed everything.

Stalin and Hitler's non-aggression pact had turned Communists into rabid pacifists. It was absolute sacrilege for blacks, as Davis told the NNC, to even think of anything other than non-intervention. As late as October 1940, Yergan, speaking on behalf of the NNC, told a gathering of the Church League for Industrial Democracy, "We desire to see our country kept out of the war. Such involvement can solve no problems for the people of America."

After the attack, Communists were instantly transformed into impassioned militarists. In September 1942 Yergan could not contain his patriotism: "This is the Negro people's war because it is the nation's war." The flip-flop was amazing to behold.[12]

But there were also casualties of the Party's about-face. With the possible exception of Ben Davis, who continued to attack Jim Crow from his seat on the New York City Council, Party leaders virtually closed the book on their fight for civil rights during the war years. Party theoretician Doxey Wilkerson made it official when he said that blacks had no choice but "to declare their full support of the win-the-war policies of President Roosevelt."

Black leaders, black organizations, and the black press were fair game for Communist abuse when they did not toe the line. Defense of the Soviet Union became the Party's first and, most observers felt, only priority. Although many local Communists waged private battles against segregation, they did it without the leadership's blessing. Black leaders were outraged. Randolph repeatedly pointed the finger at the Communists as "proof of their treachery." During the coming years, black leaders would not let the Communists forget what they had done.[13]

Surprisingly, many blacks still wanted to think the best of the Party. Blacks remembered the courage Communists had shown during the 1930s in opposing segregation. They could not easily write off men and women who had fought valiantly for the Scottsboro Boys, jobs, and relief. When *Negro Digest* asked its readers, "Have the Communists quit fighting for Negro Rights?" Seventy percent answered "no."

Part of the reason for their continued faith in the Party may have been the work carried on by the NNC itself. Indeed, in some of its literature the NNC did keep very close to the Party line on the war: "The single and compelling task which faces us now is the total destruction of Hitler." But contrary to what critics said, it did not completely abandon the civil rights fight.[14]

185

The National Council distributed flyers urging members to support Randolph's proposed march on Washington in 1941 for fair employment. The NNC also sent a statement over the signature of Powell and the prominent educator Mary McLeod Bethune to black leaders urging them to increase the pressure on Roosevelt to end segregation in the armed forces. The NNC continued to go after "home front" targets like the defense industry.

Airplane manufacturers had steadfastly refused to employ blacks and other minorities in their plants. When a Douglas Aircraft official was asked in 1934 about his company's hiring practices, he replied, "No, it is not our policy to hire colored employees, or Mexican employees either." Six years later, Robert S. Robinson, the Executive Secretary of the NNC's L.A. Council, asked another aircraft company about its policies. "I regret to say," Vultee Aircraft's Industrial Relations Manager responded, "that it is not the policy of this company to employ people other than of the Caucasian race."

In 1940, the U.S. Employment Service sent its own inquiry to selected defense manufacturers asking whether they would hire blacks. More than half of them said they would not. Ten New York defense plants employed 29, 215 workers, only 142 of whom were black.

A *Defender* editorial stated: "On the West Coast the action of the plane manufacturer pushes black Americans deeper into despair." The *Courier* asked Washington, "What are you going to do about it?" The paper prodded the government to take direct action against the defense industry. The aircraft manufacturers were especially vulnerable to pressure, since much of their business came from federal contracts. Throughout 1941 the L.A. Council continued to push the issue.

At first, Robinson's letters to personnel managers at Lockheed and Douglas were ignored or brought evasive responses. Robinson would not be put off. With backing from the UAW, the Los Angeles CIO Industrial Union Council, the NAACP, and dozens of church, civic, and community groups, Robinson urged government officials to refuse contracts to defense companies that discriminated. The L.A. County Board of Supervisors passed a resolution condemning discrimination in the industry and requested Congress "to take immediate steps to end it." By October 1941 aircraft companies began taking applications, and the following year blacks began to trickle into L.A. plants.

When Sperry Gyroscope Company in Brooklyn brushed aside NNC queries about its hiring practices, more than fifty pickets braved a March snowstorm to demonstrate outside its plant, but Sperry refused to bend. The NNC got the NAACP, the Urban League, local YMCAs, and church groups to form a Joint Committee on Employment. The Committee flooded the company with calls and letters demanding that it hire blacks. Sperry finally gave in and hired four blacks. In 1945 the NNC sent an investigator to the Sperry plant at Great Neck, Long Island. In his report he said that Sperry had substantially increased "the percentage of Negroes" in its factories.[15]

In Detroit, the issue for the NNC was not bigotry but union busting. Henry Ford hated unions with a passion. Since 1937, Ford had kept the United Auto Workers local out of his auto plants with guns, clubs, police, hired thugs, goons, scabs, and the courts. But the UAW, then a part of the CIO, was persistent. It picketed outside Ford plants, secretly organized workers inside, and bombarded the National Labor Relations Board with lawsuits against Ford for unfair labor practices.

The irony was that, by the standards of his day, Ford was considered mildly progressive in his willingness to employ large numbers of blacks. The *Courier* called him "one of America's most broadminded men." Now Ford was calling in his cards. In one last-ditch effort to break the UAW, Ford officials tried to pit blacks against the union. Black Ford officials played on company loyalties, issuing dire warnings to blacks against mixing with the union.

The Michigan NNC Council supported the UAW organizing campaign. Davis denounced Ford for trying "to create bad racial feelings among the citizens of Detroit." The National Office deluged black auto workers with pamphlets and flyers pleading the UAW cause. "The record which they have made in these unions," he reminded blacks, "has brought credit to the Negro people as a whole." After a few months of skirmishing, Ford capitulated and in June 1941 signed a closed-shop bargaining agreement with the UAW.[16]

With the close of the war, Communists could now give their full attention to domestic issues. Bunche's prediction that the NNC would go Red was about to become a reality. Henry Winston gave the first signal that the Party was ready to take full control. "The present situation makes it urgently necessary," he wrote, "to have a fighting National Negro Congress that reacts militantly to the problems of the Negro people."

From the time Winston joined the Young Communist League in 1932, his star had continued to rise in the Party. He served a long stint as the Party's National Youth Director in the 1930s. He also was a key organizer in the Party-controlled Southern Negro Youth Congress.

Winston wanted to return the NNC to the glory days of 1936. He envisioned thousands of blacks uniting in action campaigns "on the burning issues of civil rights." The difference was that this time Communists would direct the campaigns.

As part of their rejuvenation plan, Party leaders planned a tenth anniversary NNC celebration for Detroit in June 1946. Winston rallied the rank-and-file: "Our Party must assist in helping to assure the broadest participation in this celebration." Party leaders drew up an optimistic plan for the convention. They sent out more than 25,000 calls to various groups throughout the nation. They expected more than a thousand delegates to show up. It was wishful thinking. The handwriting was on the wall when the Greater New York CIO Council, under one-time NNC friend Phillip Murray, refused to send even one delegate.[17]

On May 11, 1946, only seven hundred black and white delegates trekked to Detroit from twenty-four states to give a "Death Blow to Jim Crow." Gone were the support greetings from Roosevelt and prominent officials. Instead, the delegates had to settle for a message from the assistant prosecuting attorney of Wayne County. Unlike 1937, no prominent political leaders, NAACP, Urban League, or government officials graced the podium. Only a few local politicians were seen. NBC turned down a request from the NNC to carry the speeches. The best media coverage they could get was a local Detroit radio station, and even then the station agreed only to carry Paul Robeson's keynote address.

The NNC had a new secretary. Revels Cayton, the ex-seaman, California CIO official, and Party loyalist had replaced Davis as Secretary. The Party gamely tried to revive the spirit of the past. A few local NAACP and Urban League chapters sent representatives. So did a handful of churches and fraternal organizations. This was just enough for Party leader Claudia Jones to call it "a great demonstration of the vitality of the Negro peoples-labor alliance."

The tenth celebration was almost an exclusive Party affair. Roughly eighty-five percent of the delegates were from Communist-run or influenced unions. With Cayton and Yergan in control, there would be no disagreement or debate over items that did not fit the Party's political agenda. There was no need to appease any black moderate leaders. Yergan made it clear where the power would rest: "Labor must be the dominant force in the National Negro Congress." Paul Robeson hammered hard on the need for unity with labor: "An

188

attack upon organized labor is an attack upon the Negro people."
Robeson also gave a preview of the pro-Soviet remarks that would
plunge him into a firestorm of controversy three years later: "We will
join in the fight for peaceful collaboration with the Soviet Union as
our own."[18]

The NNC meeting took care of one piece of business that would
eventually have an impact. Cayton announced that he had sent a letter
to Trygve Lie, United Nations General Secretary, and President
Truman on behalf of the NNC. It read, "The Negro citizens find the
recent conditions intolerable and are therefore presenting their appeal
to the highest court of mankind —the United Nations." This was part
of a daring plan by Cayton and Yergan to present black grievances
directly to the U.N. Before the Congress closed, they drafted a petition
to the United Nations "on behalf of the thirteen million oppressed
Negro citizens of the United States of America." Attached to the petition was a fact statement on "The Oppression of the American Negro,"
compiled by Party historian Herbert Aptheker.

The delegates perked up at this new development. Cayton called
Edward Strong to the podium to read the entire text of the petition.
Party leaders expected the petition to attract press attention to the
NNC. At least that is what Davis hoped. In a *Daily Worker* column, he
noted that the "one slight exception" to the "blanket of silence" the
press threw over the Congress was the petition.[19]

Three days after the NNC ended, Yergan presented the petition to
three U.N. officials at Hunter College. The officials promised to send
the petition to Eleanor Roosevelt, who chaired the U.N.'s Human
Rights Commission. Yergan offered to personally deliver copies of the
petition to the Economic and Social Council of the U.N. The Council
had the authority under Article 71 of the U.N. Charter to consult with
"non-governmental" organizations on social problems. The NNC
Petition called on the U.N. to immediately enact an "international bill
of rights" for the "protection of minorities." Critics charged that the
petition was a desperate stunt by the Reds to embarrass the U.S. and
grab a few headlines.

While the NNC's petition remained at the head of Cayton and
Yergen's agenda, they also endorsed demonstrations held in New York
and Washington over mob violence in Georgia and Mississippi. Yergan
spoke at an open air rally in Washington, demanding that the government "prosecute the lynchers and their instigators Bilbo and Talmadge."
Cayton invited black leaders to attend an emergency conference in New

York "to counteract the vicious attacks on the labor movement and the Negro people."

Meanwhile, the petition campaign sputtered along. In February 1947 Yergan tried to pump new life into it by bringing in fresh players and a new plan. At a day-long conference in New York, he announced that the NNC was forming a Continuations Committee to "enlarge" the petition campaign. The committee would be responsible for soliciting support from national organizations. He also floated the idea of drawing up an entirely new petition. After some debate, the participants decided to submit a "supplementary" petition containing "additional documentary evidence" on black oppression. The conference was an exercise in self-delusion. Yergan may have guessed that neither a new nor a supplementary petition was likely to gain any more support than the original one. The members of the Continuations Committee charged with drumming up broad support were from the National Lawyers Guild, the Council for Pan African Democracy, and the International Workers Order. All were either closely aligned with the Party or were outright Communist-front groups.

In May, eight members of the NNC's Finance Committee announced yet another series of "sweeping" campaigns. The NNC would support striking tobacco workers by boycotting Camel cigarettes, push for a presidential Executive Order banning discrimination in federal government employment, and demand the rehiring of anyone fired for failing to take a loyalty oath.

The committee members fully expected to be around for the fall. They planned to have mass rallies in Detroit and Chicago in September to celebrate the signing of the Emancipation Proclamation. However, there was a more telling sign of the NNC's real future. If Edward Strong had not been present, all the Committee members who sat in the room would have been white.[20]

The NNC leaders made one more effort to make friends with the NAACP. They directed all members in Los Angeles to join the NAACP in picketing a Sears store for refusing to hire black sales clerks. It was the last directive that NNC leaders would make.

In December Wilkerson and National Committee member Ernest Thompson released a "Statement on the Merger of the National Negro Congress with the Civil Rights Congress." Under the agreement, the CRC would take over the NNC's national headquarters in Harlem, local councils would become CRC affiliates, and members of the NNC National Board would serve on the CRC Board.[21]

190

Davis wrote the obituary: "When the National Negro Congress existed it was called a 'Communist front.' When it goes out of existence, it is called a 'Communist plot'." Carlton Moss, an NNC official in Los Angeles during the war, feels that the Davis view does not completely tell the story: "Even in its best days, the Congress was never a mass organization. It was mostly intellectuals that put out propaganda. You can't sustain any organization like that."

In December 1947 it was a moot point. Attorney General Tom Clark made it official. He presented letters to the U.S. Civil Service Commission and the loyalty board citing the NNC as a "communist" and "subversive" organization.[22]

What began more than a decade before as the Communist Party's grand design to win the hearts of black America ended in quiet failure. For a fleeting moment, the National Negro Congress united Communists and black moderates in a shaky alliance for jobs and rights. But in the end Communist hopes for a permanent alliance with black leaders crashed against the hard bedrock of fear and distrust between blacks and Reds. The Party would never again come so close. Still, a short, bespectacled attorney found that he could not forget the NNC's U.N. petition. As an alternate member of Yergan's ill-fated Continuations Committee, William Patterson knew exactly what went wrong. He would figure prominently in yet another plan by the Party to win black sympathies by once more championing civil rights.

Notes

1. *Daily Worker*, 2 February 1940; Raymond A. Ogden, *The Dies Committee: A Study of the Special House Committee for the Investigation of Un-American Activities, 1938-1944* (Washington, D.C.: Catholic University of America Press, 1945); William Pickens to Thurgood Marshall, 2 May 1939, NAACP Papers, Library of Congress, Washington, D.C.; *Defender*, 27 April 1940.

2. *Afro-American*, 4 May 1940; *Daily Worker*, 24 April 1940; *Daily Worker*, 27 April 1940; *Daily Worker*, 28 April 1940; Theodore R. Bassett, "The Third National Negro Congress," *The Communist* 19 (June 1940): 544-45; Bunche, *Programs, Ideologies, Tactics*, 359-60; *Defender*, 4 May 1940; William B. Bryant, "Notes on the 3rd National Negro Congress," 26, 27 and 28 April 1940, Miscellaneous Memorandum, Bunche Papers.

3. *Afro-American*, 4 May 1940; Interview with Don Wheeldin, 2 December 1989; *Pittsburgh Courier*, 18 May 1940.

4. *Daily Worker*, 28 April 1940; Interview with Carlton Moss, 12 December 1989; *Afro-American*, 27 April 1940; Bassett, "The Third National Negro Congress," 547; *Amsterdam News*, May 4, 1940. George Kennan provides a concise assessment of the policy implications for the West of the Hitler and Stalin non-aggression pact (*Russia and the West under Lenin and Stalin* [Boston: Little, Brown and Company, 1960)], 314-30).

5. Bassett, "The Third National Negro Congress," 548; Interview with Carlton Moss, 12 December 1989; A. Phillip Randolph, "The World Crisis and the Negro People Today," 14, A. Phillip Randolph File, Southern California Research Library; Ralph Ellison, unidentified feature article, 14 May 1940, Schomberg Clipping File, National Negro Congress Papers, UCLA Microfilms; A. Phillip Randolph, "Why I Would Not Stand For Re-election For President of the National Negro Congress," *The Black Worker*, 6 May 1940, 1.

6. *Daily Worker*, 25 July 1940; Bassett, "The Third National Negro Congress," 549; Bunch, *Programs, Ideologies, Tactics*, 356 and 365; *Defender*, 11 May 1940; *Defender*, 25 May 1940; Randolph, "The World Crisis and the Negro People Today," 30.

7. Negro National Congress Press Release, 7 May 1940, Negro National Congress Papers; *The CIO News* 3 (6 May 1940): 4; *Afro-American*, 18 June 1940; *Afro-American*, 29 June 1940.

8. *Pittsburgh Courier*, 11 May 1940; *The New Era* (Eunice, Louisiana), 3 January 1941; *Hearings, Communist Infiltration of Minority Groups*, 487

9. *Amsterdam News*, 20 April 1940; *Amsterdam News*, 18 May 1940; *Afro-American*, 25 May 1940; *Afro-American*, 8 June 1940; Bunche, *Programs, Ideologies, Tactics*, 370.

10. *A Generation of Lynching in the United States, 1921-1946* (New York: NAACP), 1-2; "Gains and Losses of Negro Labor Summarized," *Negro History Bulletin* 3 (February 1940): 71.

11. *Defender*, 4 May 1940; *Defender*, 11 May 1940; *Defender*, 18 May 1940; *Amsterdam News*, 1 June 1940; *Negro People Speak Out Against Jim Crow*, (Washington, D.C.: Negro National Congress).

12. There is an abundance of opinions on the Communist Party's sudden change of heart on American intervention. I will cite only two. Foster defends the Party position in *History of the Communist Party of the United States* (400-10) and Record attacks it in *The Negro and the Communist Party* (209-26). Max Yergan, *Democracy and the Negro People Today*, (New York: Negro National Congress, 1940), 9; Max Yergan, "Negro America and the War for Survival," (mimeo copy) CP Pamphlet File—1942, Southern California Research Library. The words of two more black Communist leaders tell the story of the Party's near comic turn. Henry Winston said, "The simple truth is that the purpose for which this armed force is being created is not for the defense of the

nation rather for the profits and empire to benefit the rich" (*Old Jim Crow Has Got To Go!* [New York: New Age Publishers, 1941], 10). Pettis Perry argued, "This is not a white man's war. This is a war on the part of the United States against international gangsterism" (*The Negro's Stake In This War*, Los Angeles, CPUSA, ca. 1942).

13. Doxey Wilkerson, "The Negro People in the National Front for Victory," in Rayford Logan, ed., *What The Negro Wants* (Chapel Hill: University of North Carolina Press, 1944), 210; Various issues of the *Daily Worker* between September, 1941-January, 1944; "Communists and the Labor Movement" (editorial), *The Black Worker*, August 1940, 4, A. Phillip Randolph, "The Communists and the Negro," *The Black Worker*, July 1942, 6; A. Phillip Randolph, "Communists: A Menace to Black America," *The Black Worker*, November 1945, 5. Gerald Horne, offers a fresh perspective on the ambivalence Davis had toward the Party's position on civil rights during the war in *Ben Davis—Black Liberation/Red Scare* (Unpublished Manuscript), 158-59. In his testimony at the Smith Act trials in 1948 Davis would confess "that on the whole we had not taken up the real militant struggles against the main enemy of the Negro People." Davis left the impression that he was sharply at odds with the Party hierarchy on civil rights: "Certainly I thought we had to get back to Marxism-Leninism, only then could we fulfill our duty to the American working class, to the Negro people, to fight for democracy" (Transcript of the Testimonies of the Smith Act defendants, 1948, 9 [mimeo copy], CP File—1948).

14. "Have Communists Quit fighting for Negro Rights?" *Negro Digest*, 56; Bunche, "Memorandum on Negro Organizations and the War," Miscellaneous Memorandum, Bunche Papers; *Negro People Will Defend America* (pamphlet), Negro National Congress File, Southern California Research Library.

15. "Join the March to Washington" (flyer), Negro National Congress Papers; National Negro Congress (appeal letter), 23 April 1945, Negro National Congress Papers; C. A. Leigh to James Anderson, 2 August 1934, Negro National Congress File, Southern California Research Library; W. Gerald Tuttle to Robert S. Robinson, 2 August 1940, Negro National Congress File, Southern California Research Library; Government survey on black employment in defense plants cited in Ottley, *New World A-Coming*, 289-90.

16. *Defender*, 28 September 1942; *Jim Crow* (pamphlet), 26-27, Negro National Congress File, Southern California Research Library; *Negro Workers after the War* (pamphlet), New York, Negro National Congress, April 1945, 3, 7, NNC File, Southern California Research Library; Robert Lacy, *Ford: the Men and the Machine* (New York: Ballantine Books, 1986), 234-35 and 387-97; *Pittsburgh Courier*, 6 July 1940; James S. Olson, "Organized Black Leadership and Industrial Unionism:

The Racial Response, 1936-1945," 480-84 in Jacobson, *The Negro and the American Labor Movement*; Christopher C. Alston, *Henry Ford and the Negro People* (pamphlet), Michigan Negro National Congress, Negro National Congress Files, Southern California Research Library.

17. Henry Winston, "Party Tasks Among the Negro People," *Political Affairs* 25 (April 1946): 361. On Winston's death in 1987, *Political Affairs* recapped his Party career (*Political Affairs* 56 [February 1987]: 3-25). "Planning notes on the National Negro Congress," Box 13, Robert Minor Papers, Columbia University.

18. *The Worker*, 27 April 1946; *The Worker*, 4 June 1946; *The Worker*, 9 June 1946; *California Eagle*, 30 May 1946; John Pittman, "The Negro People Spark The fight For Peace," *Political Affairs* 25 (August 1946): 724-25; *Summary Proceedings, Tenth Annual Convention, National Negro Congress,* 30 May-2 June 1946, Detroit, Michigan, 4, Negro National Congress Papers, Southern California Research Library. In a speech in Paris in 1949, Robeson allegedly said that black Americans would never take up arms against the Soviets. He was roundly condemned by black leaders for his remarks. But Martin Duberman says that Robeson was misquoted. Robeson's actual words were: "We shall not make war with anyone. We shall not make war on the Soviet Union" (*Paul Robeson* [New York: Alfred A. Knopf, 1989], 421).

19. *Summary Proceedings*, 5; *The Worker*, 18 June 1946; "A Petition," New York, National Negro Congress, 1946, 3, Negro National Congress Files, Southern California Research Library; *Summary Record of the Presentation of a Petition by Dr. Max Yergan, National Negro Congress,* 1-2, Negro National Congress Papers, Southern California Research Library; "A Petition," 2, 5; *Daily Worker*, 30 June 1946.

20. National Negro Congress (press release), 2 August 1946, Negro National Congress Papers, Southern California Research Library; *The Worker*, February 1947; *Summary Proceedings,* Continuation Committee on the Problems of Minorities and the United Nations, 8 February 1947, 1, 2, Negro National Congress Papers, Southern California Research Library; *Minutes,* Finance Committee, National Negro Congress, 15 May 1947, Negro National Congress Papers, Southern California Research Library.

21. *California Eagle*, 27 November 1947; *California Eagle*, 4 December 1947; "Statement on the Merger of the National Negro Congress with the Civil Rights Congress," 18 December 1947, Negro National Congress Papers, Southern California Research Library.

22. *The Worker*, 21 December 1947; Interview with Carlton Moss, 12 December 1947; *Hearings*, House Un-American Activities Committee, 489; *Fifth Report of the California Senate Fact Finding Committee on Un-American Activities,* Published by the California Senate, 1949, 341-42.

10 The Rediscovery of Civil Rights

Since the close of the war, Party membership had plummeted. Even worse, many blacks who once sympathized with the Communists now turned their backs completely on the Party. The task of winning them back fell on the shoulders of Doxey Wilkerson.

He confirmed the Party's low standing among blacks: "Many thousands of those who entered our ranks failed to find the answers they sought and thereupon produced the fluctuating Negro membership problem." This was an amusing understatement. By 1946, fewer than two thousand blacks remained in the Party, the smallest number in more than a decade.[1]

Davis and other Party leaders suddenly developed an acute case of political amnesia. They blamed Browder for their disarray. They accused the former general secretary of dissolving the Party in 1944 and sacrificing the civil rights struggle for the narrow expediency of war aims. They denounced his slogan "Communism is Twentieth Century Americanism" as a travesty. His punishment: expulsion and revilement. "It was only after the defeat of Browderism," Davis boasted, "that the Party could make such a giant stride on fulfilling its responsibility on Negro rights." Herbert Aptheker backed up Davis and admitted that the Party's civil rights policy was "pushed frequently far to excess."

Aptheker claimed that he was among the few who, through his "writings and actions," stood up to Browder. His claim gets some support from Dorothy Healey. The former Communist leader insists that "even though some members of the National Committee may have downplayed the issue, many regional leaders didn't go along with them and stayed active in local fights against such things as restrictive covenants in housing and union racism."[2]

195

But these local efforts did not halt the slide in black Party membership. So Davis did a bit of image cleansing. He announced that the Communists were making a comeback. In 1946, he noted that three blacks were elected to the National Board and ten were appointed to the National Committee. He claimed that there were black editors at the *Daily Worker*.

But Party leaders needed an issue to attract the attention of blacks. It did not take them long to find it. The year after Japan's surrender in August 1945, forty-one blacks reportedly were murdered by whites. When vigilantes in South Carolina gouged out the eyes of returning war veteran Isaac Woodward in February 1946, Paul Robeson was outraged. In July, when a white mob in Monroe, Georgia murdered four blacks, one of whom was a veteran, he took action. The popular black singer organized the American Crusade To End Lynching.

The Crusade drew support from black ministers, educators, and public officials. Party leaders jumped aboard quickly. The *Daily Worker* pounded away in editorials demanding that Truman and Congress pass legislation to "end southern lawlessness." Davis, a close friend of Robeson's, was usually present at Crusade rallies in New York. Davis and other Party members attended the Crusade's national anti-lynching conference in Chicago. Working through the still-existing National Negro Congress, Communists throughout the summer bombarded President Truman with letters, telegrams, and petitions demanding that he take action against mob violence.[3]

In September Truman agreed to meet with a Robeson-led delegation at the White House. Yergan joined the small group that entered the Oval Office. When Robeson left the meeting he was immediately surrounded by reporters. They seemed interested in only one question: Were he and other Crusade supporters Communists? He snapped that he was a "violent anti-fascist." That was not good enough. The reporters continued to pepper him with questions about whether he "followed the Communist line." Robeson did not hesitate: "Right now the Communist Party is against lynching. I'm against lynching." His cryptic answer did little to dispel suspicions that the Crusade was Communist-controlled.[4]

But Robeson was not about to back off. In March 1947 Truman's Labor Secretary, Lewis B. Scwellenback, proposed that the Communist Party be outlawed. The Party fought back. It organized the National Committee To Defend Negro Leadership and began collecting names on a petition addressed to Truman and Congress.

Instead of outlawing the Party, the petition demanded that Truman outlaw segregation and lynching. Robeson was the first to sign. The petition was circulated in more than a dozen black newspapers as a paid advertisement.[5]

Another Robeson creation also met with Party favor. In 1937 Robeson and Yergan cofounded the Council on African Affairs. The Council was a political lobby group that sponsored conferences and provided money and support for African independence struggles. Still a loyal Party man, Yergan served as Council Executive Director. At a conference on Africa in April 1944, Yergan called on the delegates "to aid in making the African people our full and equal ally in the struggle against fascism." He said that African freedom depended on the support of the British and American labor movements. Robeson suggested that Africans pattern their economies after the Soviet Union's. Council statements on labor and the African struggle closely mirrored Party positions on the same issues.[6]

Meanwhile, HUAC, gearing up for a new round of post-war anti-Communist probes, was hot on Robeson's trail. They got help from Yergan and Manning Johnson. After his break with the Communists in 1947, Yergan was more than willing to tell what he knew about Communist activities to government investigators. Yergan's target in December 1948 was Robeson. He told HUAC that Robeson was "part of the Communist-led core" in the Council. Johnson appeared before HUAC the following July and was even more specific than Yergan. He claimed that Robeson was a secret Party member and that the Communists "used him as a great artist to impress other artists." Neither Yergan nor Johnson produced a shred of evidence to corroborate their statements.

A Party veteran who worked in many CRC campaigns and who knew Robeson well maintains that no one could truly answer the sixty-four-dollar question about Robeson's alleged Party membership: "Nobody that I ever knew in the Party said that he was a Communist. Only Robeson could answer that." He did not, and the Council still wound up on the Attorney General's "subversive" list.[7]

The search for allies also led the Communists to take up the cause of black veterans. As long as Jim Crow barriers remained strong, black troops returning from Europe and the South Pacific could not totally share in the country's post-war euphoria. Black veterans were especially angry at the refusal of the American Legion and other veterans groups in the South to accept black members. Party leaders saw a good opportunity to turn that anger into civil rights protest by organizing the patriotic-sounding United Negro Veterans of America

In April 1946 *Afro-American* editor George Murphy Jr. claimed the title of National Commander of the group. Joe Louis agreed to be honorary national chairman, and Jackie Robinson was designated as the New York state commander. The organization was interracial and had chapters in Georgia, Alabama, Arkansas, South Carolina, and Oklahoma. The Party mostly stayed in the background. The demands of the veterans were relatively modest, centering on inequities in G.I. Bill benefits and job discrimination by the U.S. Employment Service. During the four years it lasted, several thousand black veterans joined. Party leaders were probably realistic in not expecting that the members would concern themselves with anything other than veterans' issues.[8]

The rediscovery by the Communists of civil rights was important for another reason. In the short space of two years, the Soviet Union had gone from war-time ally to cold war enemy. Americans once more were frightened by the Red menace. Davis and another ten top Communist leaders in 1948 were battling in a New York courtroom to stay out of jail. They were indicted under the 1940 Smith Act for conspiring to overthrow the government.

Despite the goodwill that Party leaders had struggled to build among blacks, the line of prominent blacks taking swats at the Communists grew longer. In 1949 Jackie Robinson took his turn at bat. Appearing before HUAC, the Major League's first black player took a few swipes at Robeson for his support of the Soviet Union. Robinson said he was a vigorous civil rights man, but "we can win our fight without the Communists and we don't want their help."[9]

The Civil Rights Congress

Even as their problems mounted, the Party still had some black friends. Many of them came together in Detroit's First Congregational Church on April 27, 1946. Their eyes were riveted on Robeson, who delivered the keynote address at the first national "Congress on Civil Rights." More than 600 delegates and observers had turned up in the city for what would be the founding convention of the Civil Rights Congress.

The Party dreamed of repeating the brief success it had during the 1930s working with black organizations. But this was a new era. The groups represented in Detroit were the National Farmers Union,

198

American Veterans Committee, National Council on American-Soviet Friendship, National Federation For Constitutional Liberties, and a handful of CIO unions. They were all heavily influenced by the Communists or either outright Communist fronts.

Before the convention closed, the Party formally merged the International Labor Defense, the NNC, and the Federation into the CRC. Party leaders felt that the civil rights issue would always draw some local black leaders, and they were right. A handful of black ministers, and representatives from NAACP chapters in Louisville, Philadelphia, South Carolina, and Texas, showed up in Detroit.[10]

In his speech, Robeson spoke of the dangers of fascism and the need for labor unity. Other speakers told harrowing stories of abuses by southern sheriffs and vigilante groups. The delegates were outraged over the plight of thirty-three blacks in Columbia, Tennessee who faced trial for attempted murder. The blacks had been arrested two months earlier following a night of violence in which white mobs had burned and looted black homes and businesses in Columbia. Two blacks died during the clash. The CRC demanded that the state drop charges against the thirty-three. Two of the defendants were delegates to the convention.

Lulu White, NAACP chapter leader from Texas, warned that "blacks would stay in the South and fight until democracy is made to work." Washington Congressman Hugh DeLacy, the only public official present, was aware that the Congress operated under a cloud. He warned delegates to "be alert against those who will try to divide us with the phony cry of communism." A black CIO organizer from Georgia brought the delegates to their feet, shouting that they would build "a mighty labor movement alongside of which will stand defense organizations like the Civil Rights Congress."

While the final resolutions touched most of the familiar bases—housing, job discrimination, voting rights—it was obvious the main CRC target would be physical violence. Protection from physical attack was at the heart of the civil rights program of the NAACP and other black organizations.

Party leaders needed no reminder that the Scottsboro case in the 1930s had done more to endear Communists to many blacks than all their resolutions and declarations on "Negro rights" combined. The choice was easy and expedient for Communists. The CRC would become a defense organization fashioned along similar but broader lines than the now defunct International Labor Defense.[11]

During the next few years, the CRC would focus national and international attention on a string of spectacular murder and rape cases involving blacks. Thousands of black and white Americans would march, stage rallies, and sign petitions for the release of Willie McGee, the Trenton Six, the Martinsville Seven, Warren Wells, and the Columbia Thirty-three. The CRC also had its hands full trying to fend off government assaults against its own leaders.

Federal prosecutors went after the Party with their full legal arsenal. Communist leaders were subpoenaed by congressional committees, blacklisted, deported, and jailed. The Party-run National Committee To Defend Negro Leadership worked closely with the CRC to try to get black leaders to support the indicted black Communists. Ford, whose Party career was in its twilight years, directed the committee. He and Patterson wrote appeal letters to black organizations nationally, asking them to protest Davis's and Winston's pending jail sentences. Patterson tried hard to sell the idea to black leaders that the Smith Act indictment of the eleven Communists was a "menace confronting the Negro people."

Robeson and DuBois responded to Patterson's appeal with yet another petition to Attorney General Tom Clark on behalf of the Communist leaders. In December 1948 a wary Clark sent an aide to meet with a delegation of blacks led by Robeson and Mary Church Terrell of the National Council of Negro Women. Insulted that Clark did not personally meet with the group, Terrell complained to Patterson that the government's policy toward blacks was "destroying the moral strength of white America."[12]

The CRC Campaign

Party leaders knew that an organization often rose or fell on the talents of one man. But in the growing anti-Communist hysteria of the late 1940s, individuals who were willing to lend their names and talents to the Party were few and far between. The leader they needed would have to be found within the ranks. Patterson got the call mostly because there was nobody else.

For twenty years, "Pat," as he was affectionately called by his friends, had mustered legal support for the Scottsboro boys, Angelo Herndon, Sacco and Vanzetti, and black army veterans arrested during disturbances at the Washington Bonus March in 1932.

He served short stints as an attorney for the Metal Workers Industrial Union and the National Miners Union. He rose to national attention as National Secretary of the ILD from 1932 to 1936. Friends admired him because he was a hard worker and tenacious fighter. Foes who crossed swords with him came away with a healthy respect for his razor sharp legal mind.[13]

Now he was the National Executive Secretary of the CRC. The Party expected him to turn the group into an effective civil rights organization. There were two things he had to do. He had to win the cooperation and respect of established black leaders and garner publicity for the CRC. With the prisoner-defense cases, he got the required media attention.

Getting established black leaders to work with the CRC was something else. Patterson knew it was crucial to get moderate black leaders to acknowledge the CRC. Whoever "has the leadership of the Negro people for their rights," he reminded one co-worker, "has the leadership of the whole struggle in this country for constitutional liberties, civil and human rights."

From past experience, Patterson knew there was only one place to start. "The NAACP crusade," he told CRC West Coast Director Margie Robinson, "offers us the possibility of sharpening this fight." Patterson referred to the NAACP-sponsored National Civil Rights Mobilization scheduled for Washington in February 1950. He wanted to send CRC representatives to the conference. Patterson made a pitch for unity. He reassured Wilkins that the CRC was a non-partisan organization, concerned only with civil rights and civil liberties. There was no issue in the country, Patterson wrote, "that takes priority over the Negro question."[14] Wilkins was not buying. In a thanks-but-no-thanks reply to Patterson, he reminded him about the bitter history of Communist attacks and mud slinging against the NAACP and other black organizations. He rebuked the Party for abandoning civil rights during the war. The NAACP board backed Wilkins.

At a press conference immediately following a meeting Mobilization leaders had with Truman at the White House, a reporter for the *Daily Worker* demanded to know why Communists had been excluded. Wilkins shot back: "You know very well why the *Daily Worker* wasn't invited." Patterson could hardly have been surprised by Wilkins's blasts at the Party. These were the opening days of the Red scare. It was simply too risky for Wilkins and White to identify with anything that carried even a hint of Communist influence.[15]

In April 1948 NAACP officials launched their own anti-Communist crusade by publicly reaffirming their political "nonpartisan status." The move was clearly aimed at the left-leaning Henry Wallace's third-party presidential movement. Board members were alarmed that many of the local branches had caught the Wallace campaign fever. The board feared that any identification with the Progressive Party candidate's message of foreign policy neutrality and accommodation to the Soviets would scare Truman Democrats away from supporting the organization's civil rights program.

Party leaders saw it just the opposite. Ford praised the NAACP locals for "coming out for Wallace and the Third Party." He fully expected that the militancy of the local branches would force the NAACP hierarchy to the Left: "There is no doubt that the NAACP at its next convention will have to adjust its political policy to correspond with the sentiments of the local branches." It was a spurious statement born of wishful thinking. Although many blacks approved of Wallace's progressive support of civil rights, they did not vote for him. Truman handily carried the black vote.

If Ford had any lingering doubts where the NAACP board stood on Wallace, in December *The Crisis* put them to rest: "It must have come as a shock to non-Communist Negro Wallace supporters that they had been merely used by a disciplined pro-Communist group." The NAACP board was just getting warm. In March 1949 *The Crisis.* warned all the NAACP locals "not to be deceived" by the words of the Communists. The following August, *The Crisis* saluted White for his "journalistic prescience" in exposing the Reds during the Scottsboro campaign. Calling it "must rereading" in light of the Red danger, *The Crisis* reprinted White's 1931 *Harper's* article, "The Negro and the Communists." The NAACP's labor secretary was more blunt. Herbert Hill branded the Communists "the enemy of Negro equality." He rehashed all the old NAACP accusations against the Communists from Scottsboro to their desertion of civil rights during the war.

Wilkins took aim at Paul Robeson. Wilkins said that he was sorry to see that the man whom millions idolized as a singer and actor had now fallen into Communist hands. In his view, Robeson had committed a litany of wrongs, including supporting Henry Wallace's Progressive Party, making numerous pro-Soviet speeches, and inciting race riots. The latter was a reference to the Peekskill riots of 1949, which broke out when American Legionnaires and right-wing vigilantes attacked concertgoers who had traveled to Peekskill, New York to hear Robeson sing. While he did not specifically name the Civil Rights Congress as one of the "half dozen communist fronts" that Robeson allegedly was

associated with, there was little doubt that he damned him for supporting the organization. Wilkins pronounced his verdict. Robeson "had
become a Communist propagandizer first, and a singer second."[16]

The NAACP board directed Wilkins and other officers to study
"Communist infiltration" in the NAACP locals. The report claimed
that there were Communists in locals in San Francisco, Richmond,
California, New York City, Indiana, and Iowa. To weed out the Reds,
the NAACP Board of Directors demanded that all officers, delegates to
meetings and conventions, and members chosen to serve on committees be rigidly screened. In the future, the board wanted all "resolutions and public statements adopted by the NAACP" to be theirs and
"not those of a group using our name for its own political purposes."

At its forty-first annual conference in Boston in June 1950, the
NAACP made it official. The Board of Directors henceforth would
have the full authority "to suspend and reorganize, or lift the charter
and expel, any unit" that was Communist influenced. Party leader Ed
Strong let loose with another string of invectives at the board. They
were "inseparable from the imperialists," "tied to a policy of pseudo
liberalism," and "supporters of Truman's reactionary, war-making foreign policy."[17]

Urban League Executive Director Lester Granger was also busy
warning against the Red threat. Granger assured HUAC probers that
the Urban League was no stranger to the anti-Communist fight: "We
have never been afraid of Communist infiltration, for there is no room
for anti-democratic influences in a movement which is wholly and con-
tinuously and effectively engaged with the business of building
Democracy." He told the congressmen how he would deal with Red
infiltration: "Sometimes I think it is better to let the Communists
move in and then chop off their heads after they move in."[18]

Patterson took the long view. The NAACP and Urban League were
only two doors closed to CRC; there were others to be knocked on.
The most promising belonged to the black church. During the Popular
Front days of the 1930s, Party leaders had courted rather than attacked
the church. For a short time, the strategy had worked. Many influential
black ministers zealously supported Party campaigns against segregation and unemployment. Black ministers often turned over their pulpits
to Patterson to make appeals for the Scottsboro Boys. He was optimistic that he could rekindle the interest of the ministers. He boasted
to Robinson, "The church is closer to us today than the trade unions."
Patterson sought to turn his exaggeration into a reality. He instructed

CRC locals to call conferences with church leaders, and to use the media to "reach church membership." Patterson's overtures to black ministers paid off in a way that he had not expected.[19]

On August 3, 1950, the House Committee on Lobbying Activities ordered him to appear and turn over all CRC records and membership lists to the government. He not only refused to comply, but proceeded to lecture Georgia Democrat Henderson Lovelace Lanham on his state's racial practices. What happened next could only be described as opera bouffe, if it were not for the serious consequences that befell the CRC leader.

Patterson: "Georgia is a state where the black man has no rights that can be compared with. . . ."
Lanham: "That is another lie."
Patterson: "And that statement is also a lie."

Obviously not used to such impudence by a black man, Lanham flew into a rage. He rushed from his seat shouting "You black-son-of-a-bitch!" and tried to pummel Patterson. Two policemen jumped in and restrained Lanham. The congressman's derogatory remark was stricken from the Congressional Record.[20]

Patterson was in hot water. The Committee cited him for contempt and a grand jury indicted him for failing to turn over the records. Patterson's trial in April 1951 resulted in a hung jury. In the meantime, the CRC mounted a national campaign to have the indictment quashed.

The campaign got its biggest boost from black ministers. The AME Bishops passed a resolution demanding the charges be dropped and that "Congressman Lanham be reprimanded and dismissed." The Baptist Ministers Conference of Philadelphia sent an appeal letter to Truman urging him to drop the indictment. Rev. Henry Patten, who signed the letter, thought Patterson was being prosecuted "because he is fighting against Jim Crow and in defense of the Bill of Rights."

The editor of the *Oklahoma Dispatch* outdid the ministers. Oscar Dungee called for dismissal of the charges and compared Patterson "to the Martin Luthers of their time." The case dragged on for nearly two years. After the government eventually dropped the charges, Patterson sent his personal thanks to the black church leaders who "were among the millions who united to free me."[21]

"We Charge Genocide"

Restless for more victories, Patterson felt that the CRC needed something dramatic to arouse the black masses. He realized he could not build or sustain a mass movement among blacks around the freedom of Communist Part National Council Members Ben Davis and Henry Winston, or any other black Communist. In the repressive climate of the early 1950s, free speech and civil liberties were issues too closely connected in the public's mind with the Communists. Blacks could personally identify with the plight of Willie McGee and the Martinsville Seven as victims of racial oppression, but that was it.

Another problem for the CRC was that these were individual cases that drained their meager resources without drawing in fresh recruits to the CRC or the Party. Patterson would have to sharpen the issue of black persecution if the CRC was to have a more meaningful impact on blacks. Patterson told one supporter that "present conditions in our country indicate definitely the national character of the persecution of the Negro people."[22]

He prepared to make some changes. In a symposium conducted by the *Harlem Quarterly Magazine*, he blamed the federal government for creating "an atmosphere of official government terror" against blacks. Davis, who also took part in the symposium got more specific: "These crimes against the Negro people must be laid at the door of both the Republican and Democratic parties."

The plan began to crystallize for Patterson. If Washington was responsible for the "official" persecution of blacks, then the government and not the individual perpetrators was the guilty party.

The post-war trials of Nazi and Japanese leaders established a precedent for holding governments culpable for crimes committed against its citizens. He was cognizant of past efforts by blacks to influence world opinion, since he had done a small bit of legal leg work for the National Negro Congress toward the end of its UN petition campaign. However, since critics quickly dismissed the plan as a Communist scheme, it had no political effect. Patterson believed that U.N. officials had taken the NAACP's "Appeal to the United Nations" more seriously.[23]

In 1944 the NAACP Board of Directors rehired DuBois to direct its Department of Special Research. DuBois took the job with the understanding that the board would allow him complete freedom to work the way he saw fit. DuBois intended "to concentrate on the study of colonial peoples and peoples of Negro descent throughout the world." Two years later, he began compiling figures on discrimination in housing, health, employment, and education. The NAACP findings would be presented to the United Nations as an "Appeal" for justice and equality. The study did not touch the more politically charged area of police and mob killings of blacks. The board viewed the document as more on the order of a statement of facts, and certainly did not intend for the "Appeal" to be a blanket condemnation of the United States government.

At the NAACP's annual conference in 1947, DuBois had given a fiery left-leaning speech attacking capitalism, the press, and political persecution. After bitter quarrels with White over policy—and some said personality—in September 1948, the NAACP board again unceremoniously dumped the aging scholar before he had a chance to present his "Appeal" to the U.N.[24]

But the NAACP "Appeal" gave Patterson more ammunition to use against the government. He set out to devise a credible campaign that would bring the CRC maximum visibility while short-circuiting the inevitable attacks by the press and government officials. Attorney General Tom Clark had already cited the CRC, along with the NNC, as "subversive" and "Communist" in separate letters to the Loyalty Review Board, released to the press on December 4, 1947 and September 21, 1948. Patterson counted on black support to deflect government assaults from the CRC.[25]

He was treading a thin line. He would have to distance the campaign from the Party. It would require cool-headed professionalism rather than emotional attacks. Patterson decided that the CRC 's indictment of the government must look and read like an indictment. In l951 he sounded out Party associates, local black leaders, and legal experts. Robeson was especially interested in his idea.

Robeson had been devoting more of his energies to the CRC. He had agreed to become one of the organization's ten vice presidents, and had returned to the CRC's 1947 national convention to give another address. In June 1950 Robeson spoke at a CRC-sponsored "Hands Off Korea" rally in New York, where he attacked American intervention in Korea as "the culmination of a wicked and shameful policy of government." The following year he told another CRC crowd protesting the Smith Act convictions that he was "proud to stand by the side of these great Communist leaders."

Over the years, Robeson had grown closer to Patterson. At a testimonial dinner in September 1948, he had credited Patterson with furthering his political education: "It is only through William Patterson that I am what I am today." According to a government informant, Patterson returned the compliment a few years later when he allegedly told a CRC leadership meeting, "Robeson is a Communist." When Patterson asked Robeson's advice, he was more than happy to help. The two men spent long hours together discussing the petition plans.[26]

Over the next several months Patterson compiled records on dozens of cases concerning blacks who had been killed by police or mobs from June 1945 to June 1951. He came up with 120 names and listed them in the order of their deaths, with a brief summary of the circumstances.

To find a statute that covered government acts of violence, Patterson combed through the trial proceedings of the Nazi generals and political officials at Nuremberg. The German leaders, prosecuted under the Geneva Accords, were convicted of crimes against humanity and received death sentences or long prison terms. Following the war, the U.N General Assembly adopted articles drafted by the Convention on the Prevention and Punishment of Genocide. The articles defined genocide as "acts committed with intent to destroy, in whole or in part, a national, ethnic, or religious group."[27]

To give the campaign more legitimacy, he quoted extensively from the report "To Secure These Rights," issued by the Truman-appointed Committee on Civil Rights in 1947. Patterson adroitly pulled out excerpts from the report that made it appear that the president's commission agreed with his petition: "The almost complete immunity from punishment enjoyed by lynchers is merely a striking form of the broad and general immunity from punishment enjoyed by whites." Even though the NAACP's "Appeal" did not attack the government directly, he felt there was enough circumstantial evidence in it to present a damning case. He cited, as an example, the passage in the "Appeal" that declared, "The government is compelled to admit its impotence" in protecting blacks." Patterson also quoted liberally from six recent NAACP annual reports that documented patterns of discrimination and violence against blacks.

What exactly did he expect the U.N. to do after he "proved" his case? The petition spoke vaguely of the demand that the U S government "stop and prevent the crime of genocide." But Patterson knew that the chance of the U N censoring the United States was nonexistent. Party leaders had repeatedly denounced the U.N. as a "tool of US imperialism." He was also aware that major U.N. policy decisions were made in the Security Council, not the General Assembly. The United

States would use its Council veto to block any administrative actions it opposed. He also knew that the U.S. had abstained from voting on the Genocide Convention articles. Anticipating rejection, Patterson said, "If the U.N. will not entertain our petition, that will be proof of its domination by those whose deeds we protest."[28]

Patterson publicly unveiled his petition on November 12, 1951. Several hundred supporters packed into the Riverside Plaza Hotel in New York and cheered loudly as poet Beulah Richardson read excerpts from the play, *Genocide*, that she had written especially for the evening. The crowd burst into a frenzy as she read the last lines: "Listen to him and learn, fight with him and live. We give Mr. William L. Patterson."

A jubilant Patterson stepped to the stage. He told the audience, "'We Charge Genocide' is to be a weapon against war and American fascism." Patterson said he would let the facts speak for themselves. He intended to show critics that Communists were capable of running an efficient and reasonable campaign, free of political mud-slinging.

He and Robeson regarded the media as crucial to their efforts. At the same moment, Patterson would present the petition to the General Assembly meeting in Paris, and Robeson would present a copy to the U.N. officials in New York. Robeson had to scrub his plans to join Patterson in Paris when the government refused his request for a special passport to leave the country.

With little fanfare, Patterson strode into the office of United Nations Secretary General Trygvie Lie on December 17 and deposited the document on his desk. Lie was not in his office at the time and no State Department official or member of the American delegation would meet with him. Eleanor Roosevelt, who headed the U.N. Human Rights Committee, also declined to see him. Patterson took a swipe at the former first lady. He pointed out that three years earlier, Mrs. Roosevelt, then an NAACP Board member, had strongly opposed DuBois drafting the "Appeal." When it was presented, she voted against placing it on the agenda at the Human Rights Committee meeting in Geneva. Mrs. Roosevelt later explained that she was only trying to follow approved procedures.[29]

The former first lady might have been indifferent to him, but the government was not. When he returned to New York, customs officials detained him for hours. They searched his bags and grilled him about his activities. Customs officers released him after briefly confiscating his passport. Authorities, however, could not stop the sale of copies of the document in the United States. A month earlier, the CRC had printed five thousand copies of the petition. An elated Patterson announced that the petition was moving so fast that the CRC ordered a second printing of ten thousand. He sent copies to the press, congressional leaders, and all nine Supreme Court justices. Patterson claimed that several members of the American U.N. delegation bought copies. With a push from Communist Parties throughout Europe, the petition was translated into several languages and sold well in France, Spain, and Germany.[30]

Robeson had better luck than Patterson. Accompanied by New York Congressman Vito Marcantonio, novelist Howard Fast, Rosalie McGee, and local trade unionists, he presented the petition to an official at the U.N. Secretariat. The U.N. official, apparently awestruck by the great singer, lingered for a few moments to talk. This gave him an opening. With the press hovering around, Robeson described his visit near the end of World War II to Dachau. His voice rising with emotion, he told the U.N. official, "I saw there the bones and ashes of the Jewish victims, and now not so long ago, we could see the bones and ashes of the Negro victims in the South."

The *Amsterdam News* was not as enthralled with Robeson as the U.N official. The paper tersely mentioned the visit in its general news coverage. Its only comment was that "Harlem leaders had not issued any statements on the charges." *The New York Times* briefly mentioned that the "Left Wing Civil Rights Congress" had presented its petition. The *Times* devoted more space to Yale University professor Raphael Lemkin, who refuted the CRC's charges of genocide.[31]

Neither Robeson nor Patterson was bothered by government harassment or black press indifference. The day after Patterson arrived back in New York, more than four thousand supporters gathered for a Welcome Home Rally at the Rockland Palace. Patterson basked in the spotlight as he listened to Robeson and a bevy of speakers congratulate him on his achievement.

Patterson had some good news of his own for the crowd. He announced that U.N. delegates from Egypt, Kenya, India, Haiti, and the British West Indies assured him they would bring the petition before the U.N. General Assembly. The crowd broke into loud applause when Patterson declared that "representatives of colored and colonial countries" would convene an "international conference for freedom and peace."

Since Robeson was by far the most glamorous figure in the CRC camp, Patterson's strategy was to keep him before the public's eye. He also hoped that he could get DuBois to play a role in the genocide campaign. But DuBois was in no position to help the CRC. He had his own legal problems. In February 1952 a Washington grand jury indicted the eighty-three-year-old DuBois for "failure to register as an agent of a foreign principal." The government decided that the Peace Information Center which he directed was a Communist front.[32]

Robeson was more than willing to take the lead. At a "labor symposium on Genocide" in January 1952, he blasted the government: "They have tried genocide against us for three hundred years." He painted a dire picture of imminent doom: "We are dealing here with the question of life and death of the Negro people—life or death for American democracy—life or death for the whole world." Patterson wanted to send Robeson on a CRC tour of several cities to speak on the petition.[33]

The counter-attack was swift. It was all a "pack of lies," raged syndicated columnist Drew Pearson. A commentator in the *New York Times* called Robeson and Patterson "un-American." The same week that Patterson presented his petition to the General Assembly, Ralph Bunche, also in Paris, was asked by the State Department to address the American Club of Paris.

He was uneasy about Patterson. He passed him several times in the halls of the Palais Chaillot where the General Assembly was meeting without speaking. Bunche told the Club that the petition was "fuel for America's enemies." However, he was not prepared to exonerate the government completely. He told the assembled officials that racism was still "a crack in our democratic armor."

Eleanor Roosevelt also broke her silence. She expressed regret to the *Times* that men like Patterson belittled the progress that blacks had made in the previous decade in voting and employment. She was convinced there were enough Americans of good will who believed that discrimination was "irreconcilable with the fundamental principles of humanity and justice in the Bill of Rights." Two months later, Mrs. Roosevelt evidently had some second thoughts about those "principles of humanity." She reversed herself when she told an interviewer that the petition "may do some good in focusing world attention on the bad situation in America."[34]

Patterson believed that public sympathy was swinging his way. He claimed that the State Department, nervous about adverse publicity, pressured MGM studios to cancel the European release of its film "Intruder in the Dust" because one scene showed a near lynching. To thwart the genocide campaign, he insisted that State Department officials rushed out their own pamphlet, "The Negro in American Life," presenting a rosy view of middle-class blacks in America.

The black press was generally noncommittal toward the CRC's petition drive. The only exception was the *Courier,* which opposed it: "There is no evidence," the *Courier* stated, "of any drive to exterminate the Negro." The paper picked up Mrs. Roosevelt's initial argument that blacks were living better in America than ever before: "If this is 'extermination' then let us have more genocide, and the rest of the world will demand it, too." But *Courier* columnist J. A. Rogers did not agree. He thought that the CRC had made a good case against the government. So good, Rogers declared, that the State Department "shivers" at any act of violence against blacks. He credited Patterson with throwing the floodlight of world opinion on civil rights abuses in the U.S.

Adam Clayton Powell Jr., now a congressman, agreed with Rogers. Back in New York after a four-month tour of Europe, Powell told a mass meeting of 2,000 supporters that the workers of Europe were saying, "We don't have any faith in America because of what she is doing to her Negroes."[35]

As in all their well-publicized campaigns of the past, the Communists kept a close watch on public opinion. When *Jet* magazine mistakenly defined genocide narrowly as the "deliberate killing of an entire race," CRC Organizational Director Emil Freed informed *Jet* publisher John H. Johnson that genocide had a broader definition. He cited all the articles adopted by the U.N. Genocide Convention to show that the U.N. defined genocide as "any act" intended to destroy a racial or religious group, including the transference of children from one group to another.

Peoples World, the Party's West Coast edition of the *Worker*, quoted extensively from any favorable review of Patterson's book that appeared in black newspapers. *Peoples World* declared that this "continued a trend of opinion among U.S. Negro leaders and newspapers." Under the title "Negro and White Leaders Hail 'We Charge Genocide' Petition," CRC compiled its own list of quotes made by church and civic leaders. Heading the list was Robeson.[36]

CRC Fails to Win Black Leaders

Since Wilkins and Granger had attacked the Communists, Patterson had generally written off their two organizations. In the first months after the petition campaign began, neither group had given him any reason to think they were any less hostile. In a debate with a CRC representative at Northwestern University, Chicago Urban League Director Fraser Love made it clear that the League would have nothing to do with the petition "because the name of Patterson is associated with it."

Patterson had every cause to expect that the NAACP would be even more adamantly opposed to the petition. But there was a small surprise. Despite strong reservations, White treated the petition with near scholarly dignity in a review. He dismissed the central CRC charge of genocide as not one of "the sins of the nation against the Negro."

White agreed with Bunche that the petition could be used by the "enemies" of the U.S "to destroy faith in American democracy." Then the NAACP Executive Secretary took his surprising turn. He admitted that "75 percent or more of the charges are carefully documented" and were not just Communist propaganda. White added this curious thought: "When all this is recognized, what remedial steps to off-set this body blow are possible? The most immediate and effective step is for the United States to plead guilty to the charges." It appeared White was hedging his bets by saying that the U.S. was guilty of genocide without actually using the CRC's charged words.[37]

Patterson was delighted. White seemed to be offering a small opening. In February he addressed "An Open Letter to the Leaders of the NAACP." The *Washington Afro-American* ran it as a paid advertisement. He played hard on the race card. "Let us end the pitting of Negro against Negro," Patterson said. He appealed to White to forget "political philosophies" and bring about "the unity of black men and women." Patterson made no mention of past conflicts. He told White he wanted only harmony to tackle the problems that "menaced all among black Americans."[38]

White did not respond, but Patterson was not discouraged. The CRC sent his letter to local black newspapers, hoping to put public pressure on the NAACP to recognize the CRC. He directed all CRC chapters to distribute the "Open Letter" to all "interested parties," with special emphasis "placed upon Negro communities." Black ministers and "the rank and file of the NAACP" topped the list of black leaders that Patterson was anxious to have receive the "Open Letter."

He cautiously played down the CRC's Communist links and kept the focus on the theme of racial unity. He demanded that local CRC chapters make a "rigid division of labor between white and Negro salesmen" of the genocide petition. In effect, he was ordering whites to "concentrate on Negro communities." Patterson also urged the locals to place their ads in black community and college papers. He continued to blitz local chapters with memos reminding them that "'Genocide' is not the monopoly of CRC, but must be the common property of all peace loving Americans—of the Negro people." CRC chapters approached black churches, fraternal organizations, and local political clubs in the black community with pleas to circulate the petition.[39]

On the next CRC press handout White's name headed the list of petition supporters. The NAACP was not moved. In March 1952 the NAACP held another leadership conference in Washington, D.C. and the CRC again was purposely excluded. This time neither White nor Wilkins bothered to reply to his request to be included.[40]

Even in the unlikely event that the NAACP or some other prominent black leader endorsed the CRC, the genocide campaign would still have been in trouble. Major problems plagued the CRC from the start. The first was money. Local chapters constantly criticized the national office for failing to provide sufficient funds for local operations, and felt that CRC officials were putting too heavy a squeeze on them for money. When the Los Angeles chapter neglected to send a forty-dollar contribution to the national office, Louise Thompson Patterson reminded the chapter's executive director Marguerite Robinson that all moneys raised "should be sent to us speedily."

The government had not relaxed its efforts to put the CRC out of business. Author Dashiel Hammett, Abner Green, and Dr. Alphaeus Hunton, the trustees of CRC's Bail Fund, served six-month jail terms for refusing to turn over to a federal prosecutor the names of contributors to CRC's Bail Fund. CRC leaders were routinely summoned to testify about CRC activities before various state and congressional investigating committees.

Some CRC leaders also had reservations about Patterson. They questioned whether he, as a well-known Communist, was not more of a liability than an asset to the CRC. Emil Freed felt that Patterson should have taken Rosalie McGee and Janice Grayson with him to Paris. The two women were the wives of defendants in cases that the CRC had supported. In his view, they were not as open to red-baiting as Patterson. Freed may have overstated the case against him. One CRC activist argued that they were generally able to submerge the question of their Communist connections: "Some people may have had a general idea that we had something to do with a radical group, but we always stuck to bread and butter issues and didn't get sidetracked."[41]

Despite criticisms within the organization, the CRC could stay afloat as long as it maintained some visible presence among blacks. However, by the summer of 1952 that was no longer the case. CRC activities had become nonexistent in most places.

In Los Angeles, some local black leaders sympathetic to the CRC were so frustrated with its organizational malaise that they decided to take matters into their own hands. "Some people ask us where is the CRC?" Genevieve Cox complained to Robinson. Cox and other CRC sympathizers did not wait for a response. They formed a "Provisional Committee Against Genocide," sold books, and sent their own speakers to talk at black churches, community organizations, and labor unions. When the CRC failed to send a representative to a Provisional Committee meeting, Cox exploded to Robinson, "Are we more interested in the campaign than the petition sponsor?" Others were not discouraged by the CRC's ineptitude either. At its August convention, The National Association of Colored Women praised the petition and urged its members "to know more about how it can be fought in the United Nations." It was a faint hope. By the start of the summer, the CRC's genocide campaign was virtually dead.[42]

The CRC continued to plod along. At CRC meetings and conferences, Patterson still talked of building "united fronts" with churches and other "progressives," but the strains inside the organization were growing. White Party members, who were never comfortable with the CRC's "emphasis" on black organizing, began to take shots at him.

One white critic lectured Patterson that the CRC was "not a Negro liberation organization" but "a defense organization." He felt that Mexicans, Jews, and other "political minorities" were being ignored. Another white CRC supporter insisted that the CRC should get more white workers involved in "quality work" in white neighborhoods. One critic clung tightly to Party orthodoxy and asked, "Where were the trade unionists?" Without a Negro-labor alliance," he argued, there could not be a "people's victory of any lasting character."

Still others felt that the CRC had strayed too far afield and forgot that its main duty was to defend "people's civil and human rights." This appeared to be their polite way of saying that the CRC should be a defense organization for Communists alone. Much of the carping from white CRC members only masked a deeper fear that the CRC was becoming a black organization. If the CRC was drifting toward a black

214

focus, where did that leave them? And if it became too "narrow," they wondered if Party ideology would get lost in the shuffle, thereby making the CRC indistinguishable from other "reformist" groups.

In an internal memo, Patterson acknowledged that these were valid issues of concern, but he also had some pointed questions of his own to raise. Were there some whites in the CRC who could not "recognize the abilities of the Negro people in the organization?" If that were true, he concluded, "some of our white leadership" were guilty of the very same racism that the CRC was supposed to be fighting. At a major organizational meeting in Chicago in August, he continued to hammer away at whites whom he felt were "taking the Negro people for granted."[43]

Patterson never got his answers. The CRC was barely hanging on as an organization. He assured supporters that he would present the genocide petition to the General Assembly at the end of 1952. He bravely spoke of new campaigns for an anti-genocide bill and anti-lynching legislation, but he knew it was over. The hammer blows of McCarthyism were taking a daily toll on the Party. The trials and jailings of Party members, congressional witch hunts, loyalty oaths, legislation, and defections were grinding the Party into the ground.

In 1954 the CRC officially closed down. Dorothy Healey chalked it up to government repression: "The Party was under extreme pressure to keep its leaders out of jail. It couldn't afford to keep giving CRC support." However, former CRC activist O'Neil Cannon is not so sure that explains the CRC's demise: "I don't think there was any conscious decision at the top to fold it up. The people involved in the leadership just ran out of steam."[44] Patterson was far less sanguine. The CRC, in his expansive view, "had a profound affect on U.S. history."[45]

Whether it was repression or inertia, the end result was the same. The CRC was gone and the Communist Party was now an outcast in America, left alone to feed on its own isolation with enemies too powerful to strike out at. And since Party leaders needed enemies, they did the only thing they could: they found them within. The Party once more turned inward.

Notes

1. Interview with Dorothy Healey, 16 December 1989; "Speech by Doxey Wilkerson," *Political Affairs* 24 (July 1945): 623. Glazer says that Foster wildly exaggerated the number of blacks in the Party (seven thousand) in 1946 (*The Social Basis of American Communism*, 175-76).

2. William Z. Foster, "On the Expulsion of Browder," *Political Affairs* 25 (April 1946): 339-48; Foster, "One Year of Struggle Against Browderism," *Political Affairs* 25 (September 1946): 771-77; National Board, Communist Party USA, "On the Recent Expulsions," *Political Affairs* 25 (November 1946): 1011-15; Foster, *History of the Communist Party*, 424; Herbert Aptheker, "Whose Dilemma?" *New Masses* 52 (23 July 1946): 12; Interview with Dorothy Healey, 16 December 1989.

3. *Daily Worker*, 8 September 1946; *Daily Worker*, 18 July 1946. Woodward became immortalized in folk singer Woody Guthrie's ballot "The Great Duststain," *Daily Worker*, 25 August 1946; *A Generation of Lynching in the United States, 1921-1946* (New York: NAACP, 1946) 1-3; *Daily Worker*, 29 September 1946; *Daily Worker*, 28 July 1946; Benjamin Davis, *Communist Councilman From Harlem* (New York: International Publishers, 1969), 165.

4. *Chicago Defender*, 28 September 1946; *Daily Worker* 28 July 1946; *Afro-American*, 5 October 1946.

5. David Caute, *The Great Fear*, 27; "Appeal letter from Robeson, DuBois, and Roscoe Dungee," 22 March 1947, National Committee to Defend Negro Leadership File, Southern California Research Library; "A Petition: To the President and Congress of the United States," National Committee to Defend Negro Leadership File, Southern California Research Library; *The Worker*, 16 March 1947; *The Worker*, 27 April 1947.

6. Davis, *Communist Councilman From Harlem*, 201; Adelaide Cromwell Hill and Martin Kilson, eds., *Apropos of Africa* (London: Frank Cass and Co., 1969), 209-12; *Conference on Africa, Proceedings*, 14 April 1944 (New York: Council of African Affairs, 1944), 1-12; *Daily Worker*, 25 August 1946.

7. *Hearings*, Committee on Un-American Activities, House of Representatives, 84th Cong. Second Session, 12 June 1956, Washington D.C., 1956, 4492-4510; House Committee, *Communist Infiltration of Minority Groups*, Hearings 81st Cong., part 2, 14 July 1949, 505-13; *New York Times*, 15 July 1949; *Hearings*, Committee on Un-American Activities, Ibid., 487; Interview with O'Neil Cannon, 4 December 1989.

8. For an idea of the changing racial attitudes during and immediately after the war see John Hope Franklin, *From Slavery to Freedom*, 592-600. *The Worker*, 18 May 1947; *The Worker*, 25 May 1947; Howard Johnson, "The Negro Veteran fights for Freedom," *Political Affairs* 26 (May 1947): 429-40; George B. Murphy Jr., "Negro Veterans on the March," unpublished manuscript; Wilson Record, *The Negro and the Communist Party*, 252-54.

9. A number of works have treated various aspects of McCarthy anti-Communist wave that swept post War America. Among the best are

Caute, *The Great Fear*; Fred J. Cook, *The Nightmare Decade: The Life and Times of Senator Joe McCarthy* (New York: Random House, 1976); Michael Paul Roggin, *The Intellectuals and McCarthy: The Radical Specter* (Cambridge, Mass.: MIT Press, 1967); Telford Taylor, *Grand Inquest: The Story of Congressional Investigations* (New York: Simon and Schuster, 1955); Jacob Solansky, The *Communist Trial in America* (New York: Macmillan, 1951); Davis, *Communist Council From Harlem*, 180-86; Committee on Un-American Activities, *Hearings*, 18 July 1949, 481. The Robeson-Robinson tiff was indeed an irony. On 3 December 1943 Robeson and the publishers of the major black newspapers met with baseball commissioner Kennesaw Mountain Landis and major league owners at the Hotel Roosevelt in New York City. The meeting was the culmination of a long standing campaign by Robeson and the publishers to break the color line in baseball. During the meeting Robeson took the lead and told the owners, "This is an excellent time to bring about the entry of Negro players into organized baseball." Of course, the black player who did enter baseball four years later was Robinson. As an interesting sidelight to the baseball integration fight, the Communists also could take some credit. They had been calling for integration since 1937 when *Daily Worker* sports editor Lester Rodney interviewed Satchel Paige (*Daily Worker*, 16 September 1937). Later, Wendell Smith, sports editor of the *Pittsburgh Courier*, praised Rodney "for your past great efforts in this respect" (*Daily Worker*, 20 August 1939). Evidently the Communist effort was not lost on some black players. Rodney claims that some years later at an old timers benefit game a well-known former black baseball star whispered to him, "You guys never got any credit for us did you?" (Interview with Lester Rodney, 5 December 1989; Rodney to author, 19 December 1989). Robeson took his own turn at the bat a few years later and reminded Robinson that one of the reasons he was in baseball was because of the pressure that he and other black leaders put on the baseball owners" (Open Letter to Jackie Robinson," *Freedom*, April 1953).

10. *California Eagle*, 25 April 1946; *California Eagle*, 2 May 1946; *Daily Worker*, 30 April 1946; Patterson, *The Man Who Cried Genocide* (New York: International Publishers, 1971), 156.

11. *Daily Worker*, 27 April 1946; *Daily Worker*, 29 April 1946; *Afro-American*, 11 May 1946; *Terror in Tennessee* (New York: NAACP, 1946); Wiiliam L. Patterson, Official U.S. Prison Statistics Bare Persecution of Negro People (flyer), Civil Rights Congress Papers, Southern California Research Library.

12. *Civil Rights Congress* (Los Angeles: Civil Rights Congress Papers), 1-5, Civil Rights Congress Papers; Patterson, "Official U.S. Prison Statistics Bare Persecution of Negro People," 156-68; Interview with Dorothy Healey, 16 December 1989; Patterson to William Bidner, 5 August

1948, Civil Rights Congress Papers; Patterson to Marguerite Robinson, 11 November 1949, Civil Rights Congress Papers; Patterson to Robinson, 5 October 1951, Civil Rights Congress Papers; Patterson to Mary Church Terrell, 10 December 1948, Terrell Papers; Terrell to Patterson, 22 December 1948; Terrell Papers, Library of Congress.

13. Interview with Don Wheeldin, 2 December 1989; Interview with Carlton Moss, 12 December 1989; Interview with Louise Thompson Patterson, 10 December 1989; Patterson, Ibid. 42-112; Michael Gold, "William L. Patterson: Militant Leader," *Masses and Mainstream* 4 (February 1951): 36-43; Interview with Dorothy Healey, 16 December 1989.

14. Patterson to Anne Shore, 1 September 1948, Civil Rights Congress Papers; Patterson to Robinson 17 November 1949, Civil Rights Congress Papers.

15. NAACP Board of Directors Minutes, 22 June 1950, NAACP Papers; Record, *Race and Radicalism*, 154-55; *New Leader* 32 (24 December 1949): 1; Wilkins, *Standing Fast*, 209.

16. *New York Times*, 20 March 1948; *James W. Ford Newsletter*, 1 April 1948, 1; *The Crisis* 55 (December 1948): 361; *The Crisis* 56 (March 1949): 72; *The Crisis* 57 (August-September 1950): 502; Herbert Hill, "The Communist Party—Enemy of Negro Equality," *The Crisis* 58 (June-July 1951): 365-71 and 421-24. Wilkins wrote under the pseudonym of Robert Alan ("Paul Robeson—the Lost Shepherd," *The Crisis* 58 [November 1951]: 569-73). Martin Duberman, has meticulously traced Robeson's political battles with the government and black leaders during the 1940s and 1950s in *Paul Robeson* (New York: Alfred A. Knopf, 1989), 421. American Civil Liberties Union, *Violence in Peekskill* (New York: ACLU, 1950); Howard Fast, "Peekskill," *Masses & Mainstream* 2 (October 1949): 3-7. Randolph probably best reflected the hostility mainstream black leaders felt toward Robeson: "We believe that Paul Robeson is not only naive but that he is the wrongest good-able Negro in the United States" (*Black Worker*, 9 August 1949).

17. Walter White, *A Man Called White* (New York: Viking Press, 1948), 344-45; *Resolutions*, NAACP Annual conference, Boston, 24 June 1950 (New York: NAACP, 1950), 1, NAACP Papers; Warren D. St. James, *The NAACP* (New York: Exposition Press, 1958), 152-54; Edward Strong, "On the 40th Anniversary of the NAACP," *Political Affairs* 29 (February 1950): 26-27.

18. *Hearings*, Communist Infiltration of Minority Groups, 466. A *Freedom* newspaper editorial later ridiculed Granger, Wilkins and other moderate black leaders as "Cadillac leaders" (*Freedom*, March 1952).

19. Patterson to Robinson, 17 November 1949, Civil Rights Congress Papers; Patterson to Robinson, 20 December 1949, Civil Rights Congress Papers.

20. Gold, "William L. Patterson: Militant Leader," 34-35; Interview with Carlton Moss, 5 December 1989

21. *People's Champion*, 1 June 1951; *Daily Worker*, 1 February 1952; *The National Guardian*, 26 March 1952; *The Black Dispatch*, 29 March 1952.

22. There is strong evidence that a considerable number of Harlemites did rally to the defense of Ben Davis. During the trial, spirited rallies were held at the Rockland Ballroom in Harlem. When Davis was released on bail nearly five thousand supporters gathered at the Hotel Theresa in Harlem to hear him make a fighting balcony speech. A torchlight march through Harlem followed which turned into a near riot when club swinging police attacked some of the marchers. *Afro-American*, 12 November 1949; *Daily Worker*, 4 November 1949; Gerald Horne, *Black Liberation/Red Scare; Benjamin Davis and the Communist Party*, unpublished manuscript, 414; Virginia Simpkins to Patterson, 12 October 1949, Civil Rights Congress Papers; Patterson to Robinson, 17 November 1949, Civil Rights Congress Papers.

23. [William Patterson], "Are Negroes Winning Their Fight for Civil Rights?" *Harlem Quarterly* 1 (Winter 1949-1950): 23; Continuation Committee on the Problems of Minorities and the United Nations, National Negro Congress, 8 February 1947, 3, Negro National Congress Papers.

24. W. E. B. DuBois, *The Autobiography of W.E.B. DuBois* (New York: International Publishers, 1968), 326-38; Shirley Graham DuBois, "Why was DuBois fired?" *Masses & Mainstream* 1 (November 1948): 19-21; *The Worker*, 6 July 1947.

25. *A Statement on the Denial of Human Rights to Minorities in the Case of Citizens of Negro Descent in the United States of America and an Appeal to the United Nations for Redress* (New York: NAACP, 1947); *The Worker*, 19 October 1947; *The Worker*, 2 November 1947: *Hearings*, Committee on Un-American Activities, 487.

26. Patterson, *The Man Who Cried Genocide*, 175-76 and 179; *Daily Worker*, 6 December 1971; Report of Melvin A. Thompson, 7 March 1951, File # 100-12304-226, FBI-Robeson File; *Daily Worker*, 30 June 1950; March 22, 1952, File #100-12304-255, FBI-Robeson File; *Daily Worker*, 28 June 1952; January 13, 1953, File # 100-12304-279, FBI-Robeson File; File #12304-282, February 11, 1953.

27. *We Charge Genocide*, 58-125; *The Convention on the Prevention and Punishment of the Crime of Genocide*, article II ratified by the general Assembly of the United Nations, 9 December 1948, (New York: U.N. Printing Office, 1948).

28. *To Secure These Rights, The Report of the President's Committee on Civil Rights* (New York: Simon and Schuster, 1947); *We Charge Genocide*, 172, 176 and 196; *The Worker*, 19 October 1947; William L. Patterson, "We Charge Genocide," *Political Affairs* 30 (December 1951): 47.

29. Patterson, "We Charge Genocide," 42 and 43; Beulah Richardson, "Genocide," 11, Civil Rights Congress Papers; *Daily Worker*, 17 December 1951; *Daily Worker*, 18 December 1951; Patterson, *The Man Who Cried Genocide*, 186; *Daily Worker*, 2 November 1947.

30. *The National Guardia*n, 30 January 1952; Patterson, *The Man Who Cried Genocide*, 209-10; Internal Memo, 20 November 1951, Civil Rights Congress Papers; *Daily Worker*, 2 December 1951.

31. *Daily Worker*, 18 December 1951; *Amsterdam News*, 22 December 1951; *New York Times*, 18 December 1951; *The National Guardian*, 26 December 1951.

32. Patterson, *The Man Who Cried Genocide*, 211-12; *Daily Worker*, 28 January 1952; W. E. B. DuBois, *In Battle For Peace* (New York: Masses and Mainstream, 1952), 51-61.

33. *Daily Worker*, 14 January 1952; Patterson to Marguerite Robinson, 10 February 1952, Civil Rights Congress Papers.

34. Quoted in *The National Guardian*, 26 December 1952; Patterson, *The Man Who Cried Genocide*, 190-91; *Pittsburgh Courier*, 15 December 1951; *Amsterdam News*, 12 January 1951; Internal memo, 10 February 1952, Civil Rights Congress Papers; Civil Rights Congress Papers Chapter Bulletin, 7 December 1951, 4, Civil Rights Congress Papers.

35. *Pittsburgh Courier*, 15 December 1951; *Pittsburgh Courier*, 19 January 1952; *Amsterdam News*, 12 January 1952.

36. *Jet*, 10 January 1952; Emil Freed to John H. Johnson, 31 January 1952, Civil Rights Congress Papers; *People's World*, 24 April 1952; Internal Bulletin, Civil Rights Congress Papers.

37. *Daily Worker*, 20 February 1952. White's review was reprinted in the Civil Rights Congress Papers Chapter Bulletin, 7 December 1952, Civil Rights Congress Papers.

38. *Washington Afro-American*, 15 February 1952; *The San Diego Lighthouse*, 8 March 1952.

39. Patterson to District leaders, 19 February 1952, Civil Rights Congress Papers; Special Bulletin Supplement, "Plan of Work," Civil Rights Congress Papers.

40. Provisional Committee Against Genocide (flyer), Los Angeles, 30 January 1952, Civil Rights Congress Papers; Freed to Angie Dickerson, 30 January 1952, Civil Rights Congress Papers; Wilson Record, *Race and Radicalism*, 180-82.

41. Robinson to Angie Dickerson, 17 January 1952, Civil Rights Congress Papers; Patterson to Marguerite Robinson, 14 February 1952, Civil Rights Congress Papers; Louise Thompson Patterson to Marguerite Robinson, 19 July 1951; *Daily Worker*, 28 January 1952; Emil Freed to Angie Dickerson, 3 January 1952, Civil Rights Congress Papers.

42. Odessa Cox to Marguerite Robinson, 21 January 1952; Robinson to Cox, 24 January 1952; Report to the President to the Ninth Biennial

Conference of the National Association of Colored Women, 20 August 1952, Civil Rights Congress Papers.

43. Civil Rights Congress Papers Chapter Bulletin, 20 March 1952; [Emil Freed], Internal Memo, "Pre-Board Discussion on Patterson Report" 6 July 1952, 2, 7, Civil Rights Congress Papers; Abridged Report of the National Organizational Secretary, 7 July 1952, 10, Civil Rights Congress Papers; Executive Secretary Report, Minutes of the Civil Rights Congress Papers Board of Directors, Chicago, 13 August 1952, Civil Rights Congress Papers; Civil Rights Congress Papers National Board Meeting, 10-12 June 1952, 9, Chicago, Civil Rights Congress Papers.

44. Interview with Dorothy Healey, 17 December 1989; Interview with Louise Thompson Patterson, 10 December 1989, Interview with O'Neil Cannon, 4 December 1989.

45. William L. Patterson to Earl Ofari Hutchinson, 7 July 1971.

11 The Enemy Within

Party leaders could not rid the country of McCarthyism so they decided to rid themselves of the malignant forces among themselves. To outsiders it may have seemed ridiculous that a party facing so many enemies and with so much to lose should pick that moment to clean house. But to Communist leaders the attack on racists within made good sense: "They had this notion," Dorothy Healey explains, "that fascism was just around the corner, and that the Party would be driven underground. So they figured it was necessary to purify the Party so that only the most dedicated members would remain."[1]

In July 1945 Ben Davis was stern: "We have relaxed our vigilance against white chauvinists even in our own ranks, for which we are paying dearly." Davis, a Communist Councilman from Harlem, also warned Negro workers not to "weaken the fight against misguided Negro nationalists." His admonition to the Party members was meant as more than just a cautionary note. He was firing the opening salvo in the Party's war against itself. Davis maintained that white racism and Negro nationalism were spreading like cancerous sores through the Party. Both, if left unchecked, would pit blacks against whites and undermine the fight for internationalism and working class solidarity within Party ranks.

While he relentlessly attacked black nationalism, Party leaders regarded white racism as the far greater danger. Party leader John Williamson criticized the Party for dragging its feet on promoting blacks into "posts of specific responsibility."[2] He did not say it, but the truth was Party leaders were trapped in a contradiction. They insisted on a color-blind party and a color-blind revolution. Yet, Party practice and actions subtly reinforced racial differences by making

223

color an all-consuming issue within the Party. The contradiction was often glaring in the locals.

Party leaders supposedly promoted members into leadership positions on the basis of loyalty, service, and dedication to Communist principles. While blacks were fairly represented on the Party's National Committee, whites had greater numbers, were better educated, and had more political experience. This gave them a slight edge in competition for Party leadership posts. It was not unusual for whites to be leaders of Party locals working exclusively in black communities.

On the surface, the Party gave the appearance that rank was based on merit, not color. However, to many blacks, the prospect of whites leading blacks was not appealing. It seemed that the Party did not have enough confidence in blacks to train and elevate them into middle- or even lower-echelon posts. Williamson demanded that the Party "abandon the practice of having Negro comrades serve an apprenticeship" before the Party deemed them fit to be leaders.[3]

Davis and Williamson pressed Party leaders to be more sensitive to black needs if they hoped to wipe away the war-time perception that Communists had "betrayed" civil rights. Ford put the burden of proof squarely on the shoulders of white Communists: "The Communist Party places upon its white members, and seeks to convince all white workers, that they should be in the front ranks against white chauvinism." Ford challenged them to show the public that they could once more be the "champions of the struggle for Negro rights and national liberation." Davis simply warned: "White chauvinism is not tolerated in the Communist Party."[4]

Communists were determined to put the "Negro Question" back on their front burner. For nearly eighteen months they searched for the right strategy to make the Party appealing to blacks. The debate was intense and often confused. The turmoil was evident at a Plenary meeting in December 1946. Party leaders could not seem to make up their minds whether they should fight for civil rights, revive the old notion of a separate "Negro nation" in the South, or strive for some combination. Foster tried to put the best face on the discussion: "One thing that must strike all of us here is the high level of this discussion on the question of self-determination." But Foster was a realist and acknowledged that blacks were "not moving in the direction of becoming a nation." Davis also hedged: "This is now the policy of the Communist Party, although not a slogan of immediate action."[5]

What Foster and Davis seemed to mean was that the slogan was explosive enough to serve as the attention-getter the Party desperately needed but had little practical value beyond that. The NAACP was the accepted leader in civil rights and the Party had absolutely no chance of weaning significant numbers of blacks from that organization. For the Party to tilt toward black nationalism would require compromises that would leave Party members even more confused. Communists had to find the middle ground to distinguish themselves from the NAACP "Negro reformists" while not alienating the blacks who supported their program.

Party leaders also had another compelling but less apparent reason for shifting directions. It gave them a new weapon to attack dissenters in the Party as white chauvinists or Negro nationalists. In his report, Davis drew the demarcation line for the Party: "The question of the Negro people as an oppressed nation is in the center of all the problems today facing the American working class." Remembering the tumult that previous internal house-cleansing campaigns caused, Party leaders moved cautiously. Communists were in a shaky position and could ill afford to lose members needlessly. For the time being, Party leaders would sheathe the sword and rely on persuasion.[6]

The National Committee decided that the rank and file had to be educated on how to recognize and fight white chauvinism. In 1949 the Party's National Education Department issued an official study guide to all Party schools, classes, and study groups. The first lesson was that "the party member's personal life cannot be divorced from his or her political life." The next lesson: "One's past and present services to the Negro Liberation Movement are no guarantee against white chauvinist manifestations."

After refreshing members on the Party's "proud history" of struggles for blacks, the department gave the state and local committees their marching orders. Party members had to read and study all Party literature on racism, books on black history, and Lenin's writings on colonialism. District officials were instructed to comb the ranks for potential black candidates for Party leadership spots. To do that they were advised to "establish comradely and proletarian social relations with Negro comrades." Local committees were also encouraged to form study groups, develop their own materials, and conduct their own educational programs. The southern California section was so eager to please that it gave its members an eighteen-question quiz. If they flunked the test, they were given a reading list to help them pass.

For Communists who were particularly thick-headed, the Party had a more persuasive educational weapon. The department cited Article VIII, Section 4 from the Party's constitution: "The practice or advocacy of any ground of racial, national or religious discrimination shall be grounds for expulsion from membership."[7] The National Committee prodded local leaders to expose racist practices in the Party chapters and report on the progress they were making in eliminating them.

Rose Chernin, Los Angeles Organization Secretary, sent in her complaints. They ranged from petty annoyances like whites correcting blacks when they spoke, to the larger problems of whites not fighting for blacks in unions and not supporting blacks for leadership positions. She called on whites to show their sincerity by "opening their homes to Negro comrades, and inviting them to our social functions." Chernin pointed to one peculiar habit that many white Communists shared with most white Americans of the day. "Comrades living in restrictive communities must lift the restrictive covenants from their own houses." She referred to property-owner deeds that barred blacks from buying their homes.

Before the War, Party leaders rarely questioned restrictive covenants. There was little mystery why. Many Party officials either personally signed or left intact restrictive covenants on their own property. During the day, white Party members may have organized in black neighborhoods, but at night they returned home to neighborhoods that were lily-white. Restrictive covenants were legal until the Supreme Court ruled in 1948 that they were unenforceable. The decision drew national attention to the problem. In the Party, it became a major scandal and source of embarrassment.[8]

Party leaders expressed their righteous indignation over the practice. Memos flew back and forth between the National Committee and the locals. The word filtered down: "No party member, as a matter of Communist principle, may sign a restrictive covenant." The California state chairman directed all the state's chapters to devise a "specific program" to combat restrictive covenants. Party members were ordered to fight "to move Negro families into all white neighborhoods." In New York, Communists publicly disclosed that more than forty Party members had not only signed restrictive covenants but knowingly moved into housing projects that barred blacks. One Party member had gone out of his way not to move into a black housing project in Harlem. When questioned, he admitted he felt the project was a "bad environment" for his kids. All the members charged were expelled.

226

It did not end there. Some of their friends protested the expulsion. A Party member who also belonged to a union executive committee was so enraged that he threatened to resign if the 'comrades' weren't reinstated.[9]

The crusade against Party deviators had to have a leader. The old guard would not do. Ford and Haywood were too closely identified with the failed practices of the past. Many still remembered Wilkerson's vigorous defense of the Party's discredited war-time domestic policies. Patterson was busy with the CRC, Briggs and Moore were long gone, and Davis and Winston were preoccupied with their fight to stay out of jail. Needing a fresh black face, Communists turned to their ranks.[10]

A Man from the Ranks

It was hard not to like Pettis Perry. Friends and associates always talked about the infectious grin he possessed. Perry was a big, good-natured sort who appreciated a sly joke and who could poke fun at himself and others. Perry was a true son of the working-class. Born near a plantation in Marion, Alabama, Perry got his first taste of the rigors of working class life in California's agricultural fields.

During the 1920s Perry picked crops from the hot, dry Imperial Valley in the south to the Sacramento Valley in the north. Tiring of the back-breaking grind, he took to the rails. As a hobo, he roamed the West, traveling from Montana to Arizona.

Perry might easily have finished his days as a casual worker or tramp if it had not been for a fellow worker. In September 1932 Perry was working at a cottonseed mill in Los Angeles. One day a machine operator sidled up to him and pressed a copy of the *Daily Worker* in his hand. The machinist did not know that Perry had never attended school and could not read, but Perry took it and thumbed through the pages. He was fascinated by the pictures of blacks and whites demonstrating for the Scottsboro Boys. When the machinist asked him to come to a picnic of the International Labor Defense at a Los Angeles park, Perry eagerly accepted.

There were about four thousand people and maybe fifty blacks at the outing. But that was fifty too many for the local sheriff. He ordered the blacks to leave the park. Perry was dumbfounded at what happened next: "A delegation of whites told the sheriff, 'If you throw out the Negroes, you'll have to throw out the rest of us too, and we don't think you can do it.'" Perry was so astonished at the sight of whites "standing together for Negro rights" that he joined the ILD on the spot.[11]

For the next fifteen years, Perry was a Party devotee. Dorothy Healey, a prominent southern California Communist during those days, remembers that the Party "assigned a comrade" to help him with his reading. But Perry did most of the work. Once he could read, he digested a steady diet of books from *The Communist Manifesto* to DuBois' *Souls of Black Folks.*

The now-literate Perry began his steady ascent in the Party. He held a variety of local and national Party posts. He ran for political office in California four times, wrote several pamphlets and articles on minorities and farm labor, and was involved in most of the Party's major protest campaigns during the Depression.

Now his superiors assigned him to lead. As part of the build-up, Foster called Perry one of the "true leaders of the Negroes." In April 1949 Perry gave a wide-ranging report to the Party's National Committee, detailing all the wrongs that the Party had committed against blacks, especially its black members. Perry accused the whites on local and district committees of subtly trying to derail the Party's campaign against racism. The campaign was so ineffectual that black Communists "are not recruiting Negro workers into the party," he said. Perry also questioned whether black workers would join even if they were recruited, since "they do not see the party waging a sufficiently sharp and sustained struggle on behalf of the Negro people."[12]

He kept a close watch on the locals to see what kind of "fight" they were really putting up. A few chapters made sincere attempts to involve more blacks at the top levels. That August, the Party's California State Chairman directed all county districts to raise funds to hire a full-time black state organizer. The State Chairman ordered the Districts to develop "a systematic educational program" to prepare black members for leadership posts. The districts were given a December deadline to comply.

But California was an exception. During the next few months, Perry grew more impatient with the local districts. Expelling a few members, removing a leader or two, and conducting an occasional "educational" was hardly Perry's idea of a serious campaign against racism. As far as he was concerned, the weak local campaign only "served to drive white chauvinism underground."

Perry needed a weapon to go after the offenders. The National Committee ruled out 1930s-type mass show trials as "ineffective."

Considering the precarious condition of the Party in 1950, they were impractical as well. He decided to play on the guilt of white Party members. At an "ideological conference" in January 1950, Perry read off a numbered list of racist "expressions" and "acts of white chauvinism" that he claimed white Communists committed. He was particularly troubled that white members continued to live "very comfortably" in all-white neighborhoods. He also was disturbed by the number of Party members who belonged to racist unions or worked in plants that discriminated against blacks without "opening their mouths." Personally, he was always on guard against any racial affront, no matter how seemingly trivial.[13]

A young *People's World* staff writer found out how vigilant Perry could be: "I was typing a story about Negroes—we called them Negroes then—well, Pete happens to walk through the pressroom. He stops at my desk, glances down at the paper, and sees that I didn't capitalize Negro. He took the page out of my typewriter and lectured me about five minutes about why the word should be capitalized. I got the message."[14]

Guilt did not work any better. Perry reported to the National Committee in September 1950 that there were "re-emerging chauvinist tendencies" in the Party. He ticked off another list of abuses by the district committees and ended with a pep talk to the party not to "relax" or "depart" from the struggle.[15] Sobered by Perry's words, the National Committee badgered and harassed white members to do more to bring blacks into Party leadership positions. Henry Winston had one idea how to eliminate white chauvinism. He would subject Party members to a withering shake-down of "criticism and self-criticism." Only through Winston's test of fire could they "develop Communist methods, habits, and qualities of Party leadership."

Next, he wanted Communists to talk less esoteric theory and more about the daily concerns of blacks. He suggested the Party start by organizing block clubs in black neighborhoods and focusing on the "small issues" of police abuse, jobs, welfare rights, and city services. These were bread-and-butter issues that moved blacks. The block club Winston had in mind would operate as a combination social fraternity, service agency, and political cell.[16]

The National Committee still was not satisfied. A memo on "The Party in the Negro Communities" was dispatched to all the district and state committees. Party leaders again repeated that "Negro work must now become a way of life." They demanded "a better, bolder, and more serious effort" to involve blacks in the locals. They directed the state committees to "check up" on the districts to make sure they did not shirk their duty.

None of this really pleased Perry. He wanted whites to change not only their racist practices but also their attitudes. Perry argued that whites should not expect blacks to rubber-stamp decisions made by whites. "There is this idea that Negro leaders must always say 'yes' to their white co-workers." He threw in a little hyperbole, saying that the outlook of many white Party members "borders on the attitude of the Southern plantation owner."[17]

Putting on the Brakes

While the National Committee directed its main fire at the "white chauvinists" in the Party, they had not completely forgotten the "second evil." Any black Communist who sounded a little too exuberant on racial issues was automatically suspect. Samuel Henderson said the Party had a sworn duty to insulate black workers from "the contamination" of Negro nationalism.

He warned black Party members not to be swayed by the "racial reformist" ideas of middle-class black leaders. He spread his net wide. The black middle class included all businessmen, politicians, ministers, and educators. They were the black "privileged class," Henderson claimed, who believed in "gradualist solutions of the Negro question."[18] With the blessing of the National Committee, he directed black Party members to oppose them as forcefully as they opposed the capitalists. If they did not, they might find themselves hauled before a Party tribunal and charged with the crime of "Negro nationalism."

A woman the southern California district chose only to call "Comrade E" probably thought that she was following the correct Party script when she enthusiastically wrote a few articles in support of the "Negro Nation" program. After all, Comrade E reasoned, it was the official policy of the Party. She was wrong. State Committee leaders reprimanded her for creating "disruption" and "factionalism" within the Party. Being the loyalist that she was, Comrade E was properly contrite: "I slipped first of all into the incorrect position of being a Negro first and a Communist second."

Comrade E had a friend in the Party who also had some misguided notions. "Comrade F," as he was called, did not think that Comrade E was wrong and he said so. He complained that the Party made scapegoats of blacks like Comrade E while showing an "ostrich policy" toward the white racists in the Party. Comrade F did not repent and consequently was removed from the leadership post he held in his local club.[19]

During the summer of 1952, the grumbles from black and white Party members began to grow louder. The campaign against racism and nationalism was fast sinking into a quagmire of pettiness. At one meeting, Eslanda Robeson saw two young black women chattering noisily. A white woman, who was a long-term Party stalwart, turned and told the women to shut up. The meeting broke up in pandemonium when the young blacks accused her of being a white chauvinist. Siding with the two women, the chairman severely reprimanded the woman for her alleged racist act and kicked her out of the meeting. Robeson could not believe it. "Now I submit, this was carrying things too far." The floodgates were opening. In every district, Party members told tales of woe about being harassed for saying or even thinking something that was contrary to the Party's view.

Healey recalls the damaging impact a minor incident had on one Party member: "This one white comrade served coffee to a black member in a cracked cup. Next thing she knew she was being brought up on charges of being a racist. She was censured. Now how can anybody defend themselves against that?"[20]

Harry Haywood asked what it was all accomplishing. It smacked to him of an intramural match where victory was determined by how many members were disciplined or expelled. Haywood wanted to know what happened to the struggle against segregation in housing, jobs, schools, and voting. The Party needed to stop "psychoanalyzing" itself, Haywood said, and get on with the serious business of building mass struggle around these issues.

His anger may have been due less to ideology than the way in which the Party had treated his wife. Belle, who was white, was a cashier at the Party's Jefferson School. During one lunchtime, she mistakenly gave a black student the wrong change. When the student questioned her she casually pointed to his hand and asked him to show her the change. A minor mishap that might have passed unnoticed suddenly became a major act of racism. Belle was summoned before the district committee and charged with "seventeen separate incidents of white chauvinism." It took eight months before she was finally "cleared." Years later Haywood, after he quit the Party, bitterly called the campaign the "Party's phony war against white chauvinism."

More Party leaders agreed with him. Scapegoating the Belles of the Party was self-defeating and stupid. "Fighting within our Party to rid comrades of white chauvinism," Jefferson observed, "was not nearly enough." He insisted that the Party "create an atmosphere" where blacks would "feel free" to help the whites become more sensitive to racism. Jefferson conveniently did not say that Party leaders themselves bore a large responsibility for helping to pollute the atmosphere. The myopia of the leaders was so bad that even some blacks wondered whether the Party had any future. A former Party member says "Many blacks would privately tell me that what the Party was doing was ludicrous, and that it was just cutting its own throat."[21]

By 1953 Foster was ready to call a halt. Party members were dropping out and the reputations of many loyal comrades were being discredited. Foster shook his head at the silliness: "No white comrade should ever do anything to offend a Negro. This idea is sheer nonsense." Foster ridiculed the way whites were required to talk. White members, he said, were forbidden to say "boy," "girl," "black," "dark," or even "blackmail." Foster wanted the blood-letting to stop because it "confused and weakened" the Party. Stopping the brawl was not that simple.[22]

Reports flowed into New York that the weakening and confusion that Foster referred to was evident in every district. On Chicago's southside, a Communist leader noted that "the Party is still isolated from the mainstream of the life of the people." Whites, he said, refused to organize in black areas because they thought it was "of little or no importance."

Horace Fleming bemoaned the fact that there were fifteen blacks in his Party section and not one belonged to any community organization or attended any community meetings. In the past, he said, Party members had routinely joined the local chapter of the NAACP. Now they did not. Another "party reporter" wanted the National Committee to explain why *Political Affairs*, the Party's official journal, had not printed any articles by whites commenting on racism since 1951. The observer was especially alarmed at hearing many white Party members remark that the fight against racism was "overemphasized."[23]

For the next two years, Communists continued to flail about in a vain effort to right the Party ship. "Many times we gave the impression," Brooklyn Communist Howard Johnson confessed, "that we only supported civil rights struggles which were led by those who agreed with us on foreign policy." He felt the Party should be ashamed that it branded Randolph, Wilkins, Bunche, and Powell "Uncle Toms." Communists, said Johnson, needlessly made enemies and further alienated themselves from black organizations: "This fed thinking that we regarded civil rights as secondary matters."

Davis admitted that the Party had erred in rejecting the desegregation campaign pushed by the black press during World War II. He ended with a promise that the Party would mend its ways. "I hope we shall have done for all time with zigging and zagging in the mass struggle for Negro rights."

Party leaders were even ready to dump one of their oldest and most sacred icons. Writing under the pseudonym "Bernard," a Party official said that Communists had never had the right to demand self-determination for blacks. He called the idea of a "Negro nation" in the South arrogant and presumptuous. "Bernard" came to the belated conclusion black leaders reached thirty years earlier: "Self-determination gave the appearance of a desire on the part of the CP for such separation of the Negro people." Since "Bernard's" rebuke appeared in the *Worker*, presumably the writer spoke with the approval of the National Committee.

It was open season on all past and present Party policies. Everyone seemed to have an opinion on how the Party had gone astray. Local leaders dredged up every imaginable failure, from the refusal to campaign for more black representatives in Congress to ignoring Negro History Week.[24]

Perry thought it was healthy for the Party to bare its soul. In fact, he had his own criticisms. In October 1957 Perry opened the Communist-sponsored Conference on Negro Affairs with a sharp attack on the Party for "isolating itself from the masses." Perry had some specific suggestions on how the Party could "reconnect itself" with the black community. Communists should join civil rights groups, fraternal organizations, and social clubs, and "not try to impose our opinions upon them." Failure to take decisive action, Perry warned, would cost the Party "our good reputation."

It was costing the Party more than reputation; it was costing it members. Claude Lightfoot, Party Chairman in Illinois, reported that in one decade party membership had dropped from 80,000 to 10,000. In 1956 alone, more than 7,000 had quit the Party. Lightfoot warned that the Party was losing some of its best people: "They represented workers in the basic mass production industries and, especially, Negro workers."

Cyril Briggs had another explanation for the high drop-out rate for blacks. They left, Briggs said knowingly, when they discovered that black churches and organizations were "conducting a far more militant and meaningful struggle for Negro freedom than their own Party." He had rejoined the Party in 1948, but the years he drifted in the political wilderness did not diminish the old Communist fighter's willingness to do combat with Party higher-ups. Briggs thundered: "It is imperative that we take immediate steps to correct our shortcomings."[25]

But the Party was not through creating victims. In 1958 it made one more. "I can still make a contribution to the party." They were pathetic words to hear coming from the man who had done more than any other Communist to purge the Party of its deviators. Now Perry was accused of being one himself. He faced expulsion from the Party for doing "narrow and sectarian work."

It came at an especially bad time for Perry. He was on the rebound from his own Smith Act ordeal. In January 1953 Perry and fourteen other Party leaders were convicted under the Smith Act. Perry was fined $5,000 and sentenced to three years in prison. He would serve two and a half years.[26]

Perry had given the Party more than a quarter century of faithful service. He asked for forgiveness. A contrite Perry began by listing all the honors and posts that he had held in the Party. He recounted the work he had done in political and civil rights campaigns. Then he admitted his guilt. To atone for his sins, he pledged that he would master Marxism-Leninism, accept criticism from coworkers, and have a "better relationship" with his comrades.

Spared by the National Committee, a rejuvenated Perry returned to Party work with a new zealotry. Anyone who did not recognize that the Party was the hardest fighter against racism would incur Perry's wrath. When the NAACP made a veiled criticism of the Communists following the school integration battle in Little Rock in 1957, Perry dashed off an "Open Letter" to Wilkins.

He denounced the NAACP's red-baiting tactics and challenged Wilkins to "name one Communist that participated in a lynch mob." If he could, Perry swore that the Party would rent Madison Square Garden, Yankee Stadium, or the Coliseum in Los Angeles hold a public trial, and summarily expel the offender.[27]

By 1958 McCarthyism was on the wane and the nation began to center attention on civil rights. The Supreme Court's Brown school desegregation decision, the Montgomery bus boycott, and racial violence in Southern cities had energized blacks. Southern Christian Leadership Conference (SCLC), Congress of Racial Equality (CORE), and the NAACP were preparing to launch massive campaigns against segregation. Party leaders felt an even greater sense of urgency to not be left behind.

They looked for any sign that the NAACP had softened its hard line anti-Communist policy. Wilkerson thought he spotted the beginning of a thaw as early as 1955 at the NAACP's annual conference. "Not one national leader of the Association made a red-baiting speech at Atlantic City."

At their national convention in 1957, Party leaders passed a resolution promising not to establish any more "separate organizations to steer the Negro people's movement." But Wilkins let them know there were no cracks: "We reject their support and do not need it. What the party seeks is confusion, not solution."

It was not so much confusion as another attempt by Party leaders to right a tottering ship. When Paul Robeson's autobiography, *Here I Stand* was published in 1958, Davis thought he had an anchor. He sought to capitalize on Robeson's still considerable popularity with blacks and liberal whites. When he learned that Othello Associates planned to publish 100,000 copies of the book he urged the National Committee to "give every assistance" to the publisher.

The realists on the National Committee recognized that Robeson's book could hardly make-up for the continued erosion in their black support. They scored the leadership for not holding conferences, failing to revive the moribund Negro Commission, and "not tackling in any organized way theoretical questions" regarding blacks.[28]

To pull the shattered pieces together, the National Committee would have to perform major ideological surgery. The committee began the operation by deciding to take care of a piece of unfinished business. With barely any dissent, Party leaders in September 1958 announced they were dropping the program for a separate Black Belt nation.

James Jackson sent a letter to all districts announcing the shift. Jackson, designated the Party's new secretary for Southern and Negro Affairs, had become the Party's theoretician on integration. Using a maze of facts, figures, and revamped political analysis, he took the rank and file through the entire tortured history of the "Negro Nation" concept. Jackson did not do it just for discussion purposes but to prod Party members into supporting the "Negro freedom struggle." He called the NAACP the "spokesman for the entire 18,000,000 Negro people." Communists, Jackson said, had no other recourse but to support the NAACP slogan "Free by '63." At the Party's seventeenth convention, delegates rubber-stamped the resolution that pronounced the NAACP "the pivotal center" of the "National Negro Freedom Front."

Careful not to make it seem that he was directly challenging the committee's decision, Perry thought that other civil rights groups should also be supported: "It is known that King, Abernathy, and many other prominent ministers in the South are the most authoritative spokesmen for this movement."[29]

Race First

If Perry chose to be circumspect, Briggs had no such constraints. He was willing to defy the National Committee even at the risk of being expelled again. During the war years, Briggs had moved to Los Angeles, where he worked as an editor for the *California Eagle* newspaper. Once back in the Party, he kept a low profile, mostly working on local black community activities for the Southern California District. However, he had not forgotten the past.

Briggs still believed Communists should not identify with the "Negro reformists" but should support the world revolutionary movement. He argued that the only "permanent solution" to racism was to defeat "white supremacy on a world scale." Taking as his models for revolutionary heroes Egypt's Nasser and China's Mao, he contended that blacks must "sympathize and identify with the freedom struggles of the colonial people."

Jackson's integrationist views prompted him to launch his own personal campaign against the National Committee. He started by reminding the Party of its history. Communists, he said, did not become "the party of the Negro people" by supporting middle-class black leaders. The Party had earned that distinction, he railed, "on the basis of our revolutionary position on the Negro question that we led the mass struggles (Scottsboro, unemployed) and won the respect of the Negro masses."

For Communists to "trail behind the NAACP," Briggs felt, was to opportunistically accept the "legalistic, kitchen door approach of the Negro bourgeoisie." He conceded that the NAACP had "won great victories in the courts," but they had resulted, he immediately added, in only "token integration."[30]

236

Briggs was alert to another trend among blacks that the Party was missing. "There is occurring today a veritable mushrooming of Negro nationalist movements, particularly the Negro Moslem movement and neo-Garveyite groups." He argued that the Party was making a critical mistake by ignoring the black nationalists. "It is necessary that we give serious thought to the nationalist trend in the Negro movement." The aging warrior believed that race, not class, would dominate the 1960s and that the black nationalists soon would become major players in the struggle.[31]

To Party leaders, these were the utterances of a bitter and disillusioned old man whom the times had passed by. Communists had firmly charted their course for the 1960s and would sail into the turbulent waters of the new decade on the winds of the civil rights movement.

Communists agreed that the student sit-ins, protest marches, freedom rides, and voter registration campaigns were the ultimate battles for American democracy. It could only be won by blacks and whites linking hands together. National Committee member Hyman Lumer echoed the sentiment: "If ever Negro-white unity was imperative, that time is now." Claude Lightfoot closed the debate: "Our Party's view is to secure to the Negro people the complete realization of equal economic, political, and social status with all other Americans."

Whether Briggs approved or not, Lightfoot reiterated that the Party would back the NAACP because "It deserves the continued support and attention of all progressive forces." He called for a "Negro Leadership" summit to discuss "unity of purpose and methods" in the civil rights movement. Since black Communists, he claimed, "have given so much to build" the movement, he hoped that the NAACP, SCLC, and the southern Negro student movement would reserve a place at the conference table for them.

Party General Secretary Gus Hall was equally insistent that the Party would make no concession to nationalism: "We also oppose narrow nationalist views in the Party and thereby work for the firmest unity of Negro and white."[32]

The pill was too distasteful for Briggs to swallow. He would continue to vent his anger against Party leaders for appealing to "middle-class leaders" who "accommodate and betray the Negro masses." He strongly defended the black militants, particularly the Black Muslims, and warned Party leaders that attacking them served only "to feed the white chauvinism" of the capitalists.

237

In October 1966 he came full circle back to where he had started fifty years earlier and made his final peace with the racial militants: "Black Nationalism, with its advocacy of Black self-assertion, evokes the fear and hatred of the white ruling class." Briggs had no more battles to fight. A forgotten man by the Party, he died of a heart attack in 1967.[33]

The Communist Party had survived the internal turmoil and the McCarthyite repression of the fifties. Now it was time to regroup. Communists would try to put the shattered pieces of their Party back together and move ahead. But by failing to heed the warnings of men like Briggs, they would soon find themselves on a collision course with new foes.

Notes

1. Interview with Dorothy Healey, 16 December 1989.
2. *The Worker*, 22 July 1945; John Williamson, "A Program for Developing Communist Cadres," *Political Affairs* 24 (March 1945): 365.
3. Interview with Don Wheeldin, 2 December 1989; Williamson, "A Program for Developing Communist Cadres," 365.
4. James Ford, "Champion Fighter For Negro Rights," *Political Affairs* 28 (June 1949): 47; Benjamin Davis, "Why I Am a Communist," *Phylon* 8 (Second Quarter 1947): 117.
5. The faction that wanted to scrap the "Negro Nation" scheme in favor of integration presented their case in Francis Franklin, "The Status of the Negro People in the Black Belt," *Political Affairs* 25 (May 1946): 448 and Doxey Wilkerson, "The Negro and the American Nation," *Political Affairs* 25 (July 1946): 660. The diehards who held out for the old line argued their case in Harry Haywood, "Toward a Program of Agrarian Reforms for the Black Belt," *Political Affairs* 25 (October 1946): 932 and James Allen, "The Negro Question," *Political Affairs* 25 (December 1946): 1150. Foster straddled the fence between both sides (Foster, "Self-Determination for the Negro People," *Political Affairs* 25 [June 1946]: 553-54). *The Communist Position on The Negro Question* (New York: New Century Publishers, 1947), 14 and 15; "Resolution on the Question of Negro Rights and Self-Determination, *Political Affairs* 26 (September 1947): 155-58.
6. Davis, *The Path of Negro Liberation* (New York: New Century Publishers, 1947), 8 and 11.
7. "The Struggle Against White Chauvinism" (New York: National Education Department, CP, 1949), 15 and 16, Communist Party File— 1949, Southern California Research Library; "The Struggle Against

white Chauvinism," *Discussion Guide*, December 1950, 7, CP File—1950, Southern California Research Library. Interview with Charles Morgan, 6 December 1989.

8. Rose Chernin, "Party Building and the fight for Negro Rights," *Pre-convention Discussion Bulletin* no. 2, 25 May 1948 1-2; Clement Vose, *Caucasians Only: The Supreme Court, the NAACP and the Restrictive Covenant Cases* (Berkeley: University of California Press, 1959); Richard Kluger, *Simple Justice* (New York: Alfred A. Knopf, 1976), 246-55. Dorothy Healey says that the use of restrictive covenants was such a widespread practice in the 1940s that many Party members were not aware that they were written into the deeds on their homes (Interview, 6 December 1989).

9. "Memorandum on the Struggle Against Restrictive Covenants," 7 CP File—1949; "Memo to all Districts," CP File—1950; Bob Thompson, "Strengthen the Struggle against White Chauvinism," *Political Affairs* 28 (June 1949): 19 and 20; Pettis Perry, "Destroy the Virus of White Chauvinism," *Political Affairs* 28 (June 1949): 3.

10. Gerald Horne gives solid background on the disarray in the Party during this period of intense political repression in *Black Liberation/Red Scare; Benjamin Davis and the Communist Party,* " 496-521. Speech by Doxey Wilkerson," *Political Affairs* 24 (July 1945): 620-22.

11. Interview with Don Wheeldin, 2 December 1989; Interview with Charles Morgan, 6 December 1989; Interview with Dorothy Healey, 16 December 1989; Richard O. Boyer, "Pettis Perry," New York, Published by the Self-Defense Committee of the 17 Smith Act Victims, April 1952, CP File—1952; *Pettis Perry Speaks to the Court* (New York: New Century Publishers, 1952), 4-7.

12. *Political biography of Pettis Perry*, CP Files—1954; Dorothy Healey, *Tradition's Chains that Bind Us* (Los Angeles: UCLA Oral History Program, 1982), 208; Boyer, "Pettis Perry,"; Pettis Perry, "Destroy the Virus of White Chauvinism," 12.

13. Memo to County Chairmen, "On the Struggle Against White Chauvinism," 26 August 1949, 4, CP File—1949; Perry, "A Consistent Struggle Against White Chauvinism," *Our Party*, 1950, 1, CP File—1950.

14. Interview with Charles Morgan, 6 December 1989.

15. Brooklyn Communist Party, "Ideological & Political Conference," 27 and 28 January 1950, 3, CP File—1950; Pettis Perry, "Further Strengthening of the Fight Against White Chauvinism," *Political Affairs* 29 (October 1950): 53 and 55.

16. Henry Winston, "The Club in the Negro Community," *Our Party*, 1951, 1, CP File—1951; Interview with Deacon Alexander, 16 December 1989. Winston had his own harsh view of the effect "criticism and self-criticism" should have in building what he called "disciplined

party cadre" (Henry Winston, *What It Means To Be A Communist* [New York: New Century Publisher, 1951], 10-11).

17. The Party in the Negro Communities (memo), CP Files—1951; Internal Discussion Bulletin, "Notes on Party organization," 5, 7, CP Files—1952; Pettis Perry, "Certain Prime Aspects of the Negro Question," *Political Affairs* 30 (October 1951): 16.

18. Samuel T. Henderson, "White Chauvinism and Negro Bourgeois Nationalism 2," *Political Affairs* 32 (June 1953): 52 and 54.

19. Interview with Dorothy Healey, 16 December 1989; Memo to District Chairmen, April 1953, 5-6, CP File—1953.

20. *National Guardian*, 21 August 1952; various memoranda and reports in CP File—1952, 1953; Interview with Dorothy Healey, 16 December 1989; Interview with Charles Morgan, 6 December 1989.

21. Harry Haywood, "Sectarian Purism Blocks Fight Against Chauvinism," *Negro Affairs Quarterly* 1 (Spring 1953): 8; Harry Haywood, *Black Bolshevik*, 590-91; Don Jefferson, "On the Fight Against White Chauvinism," *Political Affairs* 32 (June 1953): 29; Interview with Don Wheeldin, 2 December 1989.

22. William Z. Foster, "Left Sectarianism in the fight for Negro Rights and Against White Chauvinism," *Political Affairs* 32 (July 1953): 24 and 26.

23. Horace Fleming, "Forge Ties to Negro People through a Mass Policy," *Negro Affairs Quarterly* 1 (Spring 1953): 7; "Report from Chicago," *Negro Affairs Quarterly* 2 (Spring-Summer 1954): 5; Party reporter, "Peace Is the Key Issue in Negro Freedom Fight," *Negro Affairs Quarterly* 2 (Summer-Fall 1954): 6; *Negro Affairs Quarterly* 2 (Negro History Week-1954): 3; Interview with O'Neil Cannon, 4 December 1989.

24. Howard Johnson, "Work among Negroes Suffered from Left Sectarianism," *The Worker*, 24 June 1956 ; Benjamin Davis, "Left sectarianism: Our Biggest Fight," *Party Forum* 1 (2 October 1956): 5; *The Worker*, 15 July 1956; "Lagging behind Negro Rights Struggle," *Party Forum* 1 (10 September 1956): 6.

25. Pettis Perry, "The Framework of the Negro Liberation Movement Today," 11 October 1957, Pettis Perry Papers, Southern California Research Library; Report to Illinois State Committee, September 1957, CP File—1957. The odyssey of Briggs from his fall from Communist grace in 1942 to his readmittance in 1948 can be traced in Cyril Briggs, *On the Negro Question*, (unpublished manuscript), Dorothy Healey Papers, California State University, Long Beach; Robert Hill, ed., *Marcus Garvey and the UNIA Papers*, vol. 2 (Berkeley: University of California Press, 1983), 526-27; and Briggs, undated, untitled manuscript, ca. 1957, Cyril Briggs Papers, Southern California Research Library.

26. Former Communist Party members I interviewed had no recollection of Perry's being disciplined by the Party. However, Perry's confessional

tone in his "political biography" dated "after 1958" indicates that Party leaders took some disciplinary action against him during this period. Pettis Perry Papers, Southern California Research Library; Pettis Perry, *The Communist Party* (New York: New Century Publisher, 1953); David Caute, *The Great Fear*, 197-98.

27. Perry, "Political Biography," Pettis Perry Papers; Perry, "Open Letter to the Men and Women of the NAACP From a Negro Communist," Pettis Perry Papers.

28. Doxey A. Wilkerson, "The 46th Annual Convention of the NAACP," *Political Affairs* 34 (August 1955): 1 and 3; *Daily Worker*, 19 February 1957; Memo to Bill Taylor, 14 April 1958, Taylor Papers, Southern California Research Library.

29. James E. Jackson to All National Committee Members, 23 September 1958, CP File—1958; Draft Resolution on the Negro Question in the United States, CP File—1958; Pettis Perry Comments on Draft Resolution, 5, 10, Pettis Perry Papers, Southern California Research Library.

30. Briggs to *Daily Worker*, 28 April 1957 Briggs Papers, Southern California Research Library; Briggs to Pat Alexander, 9 May 1957, Briggs Papers; Briggs to Alexander, ca. May 1957, Briggs Papers; Response to Harry Haywood, unpublished manuscript, ca. 1958, Briggs Papers.

31. Briggs, "On the Negro Question," November 1959, 13, published by the Southern California District, CP, CP File—1959; Briggs, "Discussion Article on the Negro Question," January 1959, *District Bulletin*, Briggs Papers.

32. Gus Hall, "The United States in Today's World," *Political Affairs* 41 (February 1961): 36-40; Hyman Lumer, "Notes of the Month," *Political Affairs* 40 (April 1960): 5; Claude Lightfoot, "On the Negro Question in the United States," *Political Affairs* 40 (April 1960): 54; Lightfoot, "The Negro Liberation Movement Today," *Political Affairs* 41 (February 1961): 66.

33. Briggs, "A Critique," Southern California Viewpoints, 6, Southern California District, CPUSA, CP File—1963; Briggs, "American Neo-Colonialism," *Liberator* 7 (January 1967): 17.

12 A Time of Storm

The civil rights movement fixed the eyes of the nation on the dramatic events in the South. The great moral struggle fought by Martin Luther King, Student Non-violent Coordinating Committee (SNCC), SCLC, CORE, and thousands of black and white activists against segregation had produced massive changes in the South. With the NAACP hammering away in the courts, legal segregation was nearly dead. A host of new civil rights laws would put the final seal on it.

Civil rights leaders confidently predicted that integration would soon become a reality for the nation's blacks. James Farmer, director of the Congress of Racial Equality, cheerily pronounced that the worst was over: "They are opening up jobs previously closed to Negroes. They are cracking barriers in northern housing. The mask of hypocrisy has been ripped off northern school segregation." The NAACP's "Free by '63" slogan appeared to be prophetic.[1]

Less visible to the nation were thousands of blacks who did not fit neatly into the scenario of integration. Largely poor and working class, they remained trapped in dozens of Northern ghettoes from Watts to Harlem. They lived in rotting tenements and tumbledown shacks. Their kids went to inferior schools or dropped out. The ghetto poor suffered the highest crime and health mortality rates. Many scraped by on the bare essentials that welfare could provide. Each year, they grew more discontented and disillusioned. The right to vote, eat at a lunch counter, sleep in an integrated motel, or move into an all-white neighborhood had not altered their marginal existence.

They listened as civil rights leaders spoke glowingly of their white liberal allies and how important they were to the success of the civil rights movement. However, the only whites they saw were police, landlords, and store owners. In their view, they were not benevolent benefactors but oppressors.

The story was the same on the job. Black workers were still the last hired, first fired. More often than not unions still excluded them. Where they did work side by side with whites, an uneasy truce existed that ended only at the finish of the work day, when blacks went to their neighborhoods and whites went to theirs.[2]

While poor blacks revered King for the courageous sacrifices he made for justice, they were also listening to Malcolm X. He seemed to speak their language and understand their problems. Malcolm was a fast-rising star who spoke on behalf of the Nation of Islam, or the Black Muslims, as they were commonly called. Under the tutelage of their frail, brown-skinned leader, Elijah Muhammad, the Muslims were outcasts and rebels. And blacks in the ghettoes reveled in it. The Muslims did not speak of love for the white man, or require that blacks join integrated organizations. They called whites "the devil." Like Marcus Garvey, they called for black unity, black pride, Black Power and control. The Muslims demanded that blacks reject any calls from the left to unite with white workers. They called for blacks to ally with Africans and other oppressed colored peoples of the world.

Ironically, it was a chance crack Malcolm made about communism that first brought him to the attention of the FBI. "I have always been a Communist," a young, frivolous Malcolm wrote to a friend from his Massachusetts prison cell in 1950. "I had tried to enlist in the Japanese army, now they will never accept me in the U.S. army." Other than a short visit with a member of the Crispus Attucks Club of the American Youth for Democracy in 1952, he had no other contacts with the left. When the FBI visited him five years later Malcolm swore he was not a Communist. His nationalist beliefs were so strong that at a Harlem rally in 1954, he held up a copy of the *Daily News* and shouted, "The Chinese Reds are not Communists but black people." To the roars of the audience, he added, "They told all the white devils to get out."

Words like that endeared the Muslims and Malcolm to the black poor. Their battle was against the white man, no matter whether he was capitalist or worker. Without exception, Muhammad considered all whites the slave-master's children.[3] He shared Garvey's admiration of the capitalists. They had the wealth and power that Muhammad felt blacks needed. The Muslims frantically tried to emulate them by opening a string of bakeries, markets, and service enterprises. *Muhammad Speaks*, the Muslim newspaper, approvingly quoted speeches by corporate businessmen and government leaders that attacked the Communists. In 1962 *Muhammad Speaks* praised the National Association of Manufacturers and Wall Street investment firms for criticizing the government for "wasting foreign aid dollars on the 'Commies'." The paper was not impressed with the civil rights efforts of the Communist Party. "No communists have been lynched; only so-called Negroes," a *Muhammad Speaks* editorial dryly noted.

Black Muslims did make some allowances for good Communists, but they had to be non-white. Picking up on Malcolm's earlier quips, China was "colored China" not "Communist China." The Eastern European nations and the Soviet Union, in Muhammad's view, were Socialists second and whites first. *Muhammad Speaks* correspondent Gordon Hancock observed: "The white West and White Russia, in the last analysis, will stand together in a crisis against the colored world."[4]

With the Black Muslims, Communists were now faced with a vibrant new movement unwilling to compromise with the white Left. In 1961 Party leaders prepared to fight back. As always, when the Party took the offensive against a foe or prepared a policy shift, it searched the ranks for a leader.[5] This time Claude Lightfoot got the call.

Portly, with penetrating eyes, the Illinois State Party Chairman had a reputation as a no-holds-barred in-fighter. A Party activist and leader since 1934, Lightfoot was a good choice to take on the nationalists for another reason. He had some leanings in that direction himself. His aunt was a dedicated Garveyite, and the young Lightfoot had attended Garvey rallies. But that was all past. As secretary of the Party's Negro Commission—Patterson was the chairman—he had to develop a strategy for attack. At first he dismissed the Black Muslims: "The Moslem movement is divisive of Negro-white unity and will lead not to Negro freedom but to just the opposite." But Lightfoot quickly realized that the Muslims were not fading, they were gaining in strength.[6]

A CBS documentary special produced by Mike Wallace in July 1961 had given them instant national recognition. For the first time, white Americans were shocked to find there were blacks who denounced integration and called them "evil." The Muslims were suddenly a hot media item, with newspapers falling over each other to gather sensationalist news on this strange and menacing new organization.

Party leaders scrambled to find a position that would not feed the anti-Muslim hysteria of the mainstream press, nor endorse the Muslims. Lightfoot tried to walk the tightrope: "The Muslims are not the main danger" to the freedom struggle. "The bankers, industrialists, and big brass that support the racists," he declared, were the real "enemy of the people." He quickly added that the Party could not approve of the Muslims' "go-it-alone policy." Excluding whites from the black struggle, he insisted, would "only throw them into the lap of the common enemy."[7]

With Malcolm X steadily drawing more press coverage, the Nation of Islam rode higher on the crest of their publicity. By 1962 thousands of blacks had flocked to the organization. Lightfoot's criticisms had done nothing to blunt their appeal. At a Party forum in February 1962 he admitted, "The Muslim organization is a phenomenon which must be examined and assessed from the point of view of its impact in meeting the major problems of the Negro people." He conceded that the Muslims were now "national in scope and have become a tremendous mass movement." Badly inflating the Muslims' strength as "perhaps as many as one quarter million members," he explained that they had grown not because blacks hated whites, but because of the "long historical" oppression of blacks. He blamed the Muslims' popularity on white liberals and black moderates. When they failed to deliver on their promise of economic reform and social change, he said, blacks became more frustrated, embittered, and discouraged. He also cited African and Third World struggles as another significant factor that enhanced the Muslims' appeal.

While Lightfoot stretched his analysis to the limits of Party dogma, he did not cross the line: "Nationalism, as expressed today in the United States, unlike in Africa and other places, is an obstacle in the path toward freedom." He concluded that the only hope for blacks was "a movement which would actively seek and promote Negro unity in the context of an alliance with labor." In July 1963 the National Committee notified its district committees to be on alert against the "sharpening danger of the counter-revolutionary role being played by the Muslim organization."[8]

New Party Dilemma

Party leaders watched the dramatic events of 1963 unfold with a mixture of apprehension and joy. It was the year that the civil rights movement would make its greatest strides. The March on Washington, Birmingham demonstrations, and the Mississippi voter registration campaign had aroused the conscience of America. The Communists were determined to match strides with the civil rights leaders.

Davis found it "disappointing" that the NAACP did not push harder on its "Free by 63" pledge. He reminded civil right leaders that it was the Communist Party that demanded that President John F. Kennedy issue a "Second Emancipation Proclamation" and "abolish the whole Jim Crow system in one fell swoop." He accused the White House of tokenism and gradualism. It was a mild rebuke. Davis could barely contain himself in praising the "militant spirit" of the NAACP delegates at their summer convention. He even congratulated Wilkins for "being responsive to the will of the delegates and the Negro masses generally." Convinced that a breakthrough of sorts had taken place, he urged all the "civil rights supporters" to contact the NAACP national office for copies of the resolutions passed at the convention. "It is important," Davis insisted, "to be thoroughly familiar with the program of the major Negro civil rights organization."[9]

Party leaders did not want to tip the boat. On the eve of the March on Washington in August 1963, James Jackson declared that even Kennedy was a friend. He "has properly judged the temper of the rebellion that has been set aflame." Lightfoot went a step further and extended the Party's seal of approval to the Democratic Party: "There is nothing in the cards which would suggest that the great masses of workers, black and white, are about to leave the Democratic Party." Since that was the case, he urged Communists to help them "find immediate solutions right where they are."[10]

Lightfoot and Jackson apparently misjudged the deep anger welling just beneath the surface in the blighted urban slums. During the civil rights demonstrations in Birmingham during the spring of 1963, angry young blacks stoned the police and set fires to businesses. Civil rights leaders were heckled and ignored when they tried to stop the violence. It was an ominous warning. Events were moving with breakneck speed. More young blacks, fired by the anti-white rhetoric of the black nationalists, denounced integration and ridiculed civil rights leaders as "Uncle Toms." African and militant Third World leaders became their heroes.

Since Malcolm X replaced King as their idol, the young militants did not make any distinctions between the white capitalist and the white worker. They were both regarded as the enemy of blacks. In 1964 writer A. B. Spellman asked Malcolm X "Can Negroes do it alone?" Malcolm X responded, "Yes. They'll never do it with working class whites. The history of America is that working-class whites have been just as much against not only working-class Negroes but all Negroes."

247

A National Black Student conference in Nashville in May 1964 drew a diverse group of students from southern black colleges and northern universities. The students unanimously agreed that white workers were "racist and reformist." A final resolution proclaimed that the black movement had to be led by "black radicals, not opportunistic white Marxists." The same year, a shadowy group with the incendiary name of RAM—Revolutionary Action Movement—issued a "Manifesto" that called on blacks to wage a "war with white America." RAM leader Max Stanford, a college drop-out, painted a fantastic scenario of black armies conducting guerrilla warfare and urban terrorism, spreading death and destruction to America's cities. He defined RAM's philosophy simply as "revolutionary nationalism, black nationalism, or just plain blackism." His revolution would "create a new world" for blacks. Whites were excluded.[11]

Stanford 's mentor was an escaped fugitive from North Carolina. After serving a stint in the Marines during the Korean war, Robert Williams returned to his home in Monroe, North Carolina in 1955. He revived the local NAACP chapter and soon became president. Williams put the pressure on Monroe whites. He led marches and rallies demanding complete integration of the city's public accommodations. His protests not only angered city officials, the Klan, and local police, but also Roy Wilkins. The NAACP chief was upset that he had advocated black self-defense against the Klan and bounced him from the local presidency. Following a shoot-out with the Klan and local police, Williams fled to Havana in 1960. He declared Cuba "a liberated base," and nightly beamed inflammatory appeals over his "Radio Free Dixie" for a black uprising against the "white oppressors." Williams also published a monthly newsletter, the *Crusader*, in which he called on black revolutionaries to "eliminate the puppet master and the whole gaudy show will close."[12]

At first he seemed to welcome white support. In Monroe, he called himself an "Inter-Nationalist" to distinguish himself from the black nationalists. In the earliest editions of the *Crusader*, he was careful to distinguish "white savages" from "white progressives." By 1965 Williams had stopped making fine distinctions among whites: "The racist American ofay has deceived the world into accepting him as a democrat, a humanitarian, a Christian, an equalitarian, a universal philantropist, and even sometimes as a Marxist."[13]

It became highly fashionable for black writers to challenge the Marxists. And Harold Cruse was not bashful in taking his shots at them.

A former *Daily Worker* correspondent, Cruse claimed he quit the Party in the late 1940s because it manipulated blacks. With the nationalist wave rising, Cruse sharpened his criticism of the Marxists. He charged that white Communists only pretended to be the allies of blacks: "This 'alliance' is meant to build the Marxist party, not the Negro movement, in order to rescue the Marxists from their own crisis."

Meanwhile, Cuban-born black writer Carlos Moore was so enraged at what Castro had done to his native land that he asked, Were "Marx and Engels White Racists?" He pulled bits and pieces from the early writings of Marx and Engels on Africa and Asia to make his case that Marxists had always held non-whites in contempt. Moore argued that racism was still rampant in his country despite the Socialist preachments of Castro and Che Guevarra: "It is self-evident that the role of black people in today's 'revolutionary' Cuba is confined to pawns on an all-white chessboard." His point was that Marxists could not free blacks, so it was foolish for blacks to expect them to.[14]

James Boggs was not quite ready to call Marx a racist, or say that his philosophy had no meaning for blacks. He was not a student activist, nor a middle-class professional. During his many years in the auto plants of Detroit, Boggs daily witnessed the tension and conflicts between black and white workers. The experience convinced him that organized labor would not make trustworthy allies for blacks. Boggs argued that capitalists had "bought" the loyalty of unions by showering them with secure jobs, good wages, and consumer goods. He also insisted that being white conferred additional "skin privileges" on them that they jealously protected against blacks. It was silly, he asserted, for white Communists to hoist the slogan "workers of the world unite," since black and white workers had nothing in common.

Maulana Karenga also had little use for Marxists. Karenga, a local college lecturer in Los Angeles, formed his black nationalist US organization immediately after the Watts riot in 1965. US attracted hundreds of young blacks in Los Angeles and in northern cities. He urged his followers to return to African traditions. Echoing DuBois nearly a half century earlier, Karenga declared that communism was an outdated theory because whites were too blinded by racism to unite with blacks: "We do not accept the idea of a class struggle."

"You have to remember the mood then," he later noted. "To young blacks the Communists were like an alien force. They never pushed black Marxists like Kwame Nkrumah or Amilcar Cabral, and these were the people the young blacks wanted to hear about."[15]

The black militants found a friendly home for their anti-Marxist attacks in the pages of the New York-based *Liberator* magazine. No pure ideologue, editor Dan Watts took his heroes from everywhere. At one time or another, he urged blacks to adopt as their models Castro, Nkrumah, Mao, and Ho Chi Minh. However, Watts was mindful that all of them were also fervent Marxists, so he cloaked them in Third World garb rather than Communist cloth.

In 1964, Watts turned his magazine's crusade against the white Left into a full-blown vendetta. *Liberator* editor C. E. Wilson charged that the white radicals had made a career out of worming their way into black movements and trying to control them. "The white radical Left, when it joins black movements, often shows itself more white than radical Left." He said they used their superior organizational skills, resources, and contacts to direct the black movement. No less obsessive than Wilson about the power white Communists supposedly had over blacks, Odell Sykes warned, "There is too much dependence on white money and white conscience." Watts was less charitable than his writers. He called the Marxists "the most acrobatic of whites," continually "hustling their pro-Peking and Pro-Cuba slogans" while trying to set up "phony store-front offices" in black communities.[16]

Following the assassination of Malcolm X in February 1965, *Liberator* went after Marxist critic Frank Kofsky, who dared suggest that "Malcolm X was, or was becoming, an international socialist." The Reverend Albert Cleague scoffed at Kofsky's assertion: "Brother Malcolm is in danger of being lost in a vast tissue of distortions."

Cleague's Shrine of the Black Madonna church in Detroit had drawn national attention with its black-painted statues of Jesus, Mary, and the angels. He vehemently denied that Malcolm was about to become "a Marxist and join the Socialist Workers Party." In a later debate with a leader of the Trotskyite Socialist Workers Party, Cleague also blasted the Communist Party for being the "custodian of DuBois." He referred to the Party's being the sole publisher of DuBois's writings after he became a Communist in 1963.[17]

Despite the fulminations of Cleague and other nationalists, Kofsky had a credible argument. Before his death, Malcolm had shown signs of political change. He had done much soul searching after his break with the Black Muslims in 1963. Malcolm had traveled to Africa and the Middle East and had extensive talks with whites, many of whom were Marxists. He believed they were genuinely opposed to racism. When he returned, Malcolm shelved his "whites as Devils" talk. He readily accepted invitations to speak at the Militant Labor Forum, sponsored by the Socialist Workers Party. To the delight of his leftist audiences, he took huge swipes at the capitalists and even threw in a favorable plug for socialism. Everything was up for grabs as he continued his troubled search for a new ideology and a place for himself in the civil rights struggle. At a press conference at the Park Sheraton Hotel in New York in March 1964, a reporter asked him if he would accept help from Communists. The question touched off this quixotic exchange:

> Malcolm: "If I was a prisoner of a wolf I would accept release from any source."
> Reporter: "Does that mean yes?"
> Malcolm: "I only told you a story of a wolf."

But Communists were not quite as willing to forget his past. A Party leader in Chicago called Malcolm "a phony adventurer." Jackson's *Daily Worker* editorials against him were so caustic that even some members of the National Committee wondered if the Party was not going to far. Dorothy Healey recalls one stormy National Committee meeting where she tried to get Jackson to stop the attacks: "I thought it was incongruous for the *Daily Worker* to come out with editorials denouncing Malcolm without any recognition of his potential revolutionary significance."

Healey spoke alone. No other National Committee member backed her, even though she maintained that "there were others who objected to this and felt it was an outrageous thing to do." She suspected another reason for Jackson's hostility: "Malcom appealed to the 'lumpen-proletariat'—the street hustler, the unemployed—and somehow this was seen as a threat to the Party's line that the working class must be organized."

Although he made no personal attacks against the Communists, members of his new organization, the Organization of Afro-American Unity, were cautioned to be on guard against Communist infiltration. To insure they did not, OAAU organizers, probably with Malcolm's approval, welcomed Communists as members but stipulated they could not hold leadership positions in the group.

Even after his assassination in February 1965, *The Worker* still could not completely absolve him. "Our difference with Malcolm X on many points does not in any way qualify our condemnation of the brutal act of murder." Although National Committee member Charlene Mitchell did not think the Party was guilty of any political impropriety in relation to Malcolm X, she later admitted, "We were slow in recognizing that Malcolm was changing." Despite the nationalist fervor, Party General Secretary Gus Hall still kept faith that the best hope for blacks was a "Negro-labor alliance."[18]

Black Power!

Meanwhile, the rumblings of discontent in black America had moved to the flash point. A routine traffic stop by Los Angeles police of two blacks on a hot August day in 1965 was no different than countless others the police made on young blacks. However, when the smoke cleared five days later, the nation was reeling. The Watts uprising left 34 dead, 1,032 injured, 3,952 arrested, and over $40 million in property damage. It took martial law and a massive show of force by the National Guard to quell the violence.

The nation was now faced with a frightening new horror. Black rage had spilled out of the ghetto. While government officials searched for answers, Party leaders claimed that they knew that Watts-style eruptions were coming. Bill Taylor, a member of the Party's California State Committee, said that the burning and looting was not revenge against whites but was aimed at greedy landlords and storeowners, "whether owned by Negroes, Japanese, whites, etc."

Taylor patted Communists on the back for "initiating activity in the white communities to understand the explosion." Taylor did not say exactly what the Party had done to make whites understand, other than distribute free copies of the *Peoples World*. In Taylor's prosaic view, Watts was part of the class struggle and had no racial implications. That left him with only one conclusion: "Negro-white unity is developing on a more healthy basis than ever before."[19]

Hall also ignored the changed racial climate. In his report to the Party's eighteenth convention in 1966, the General Secretary continued the fiction that the "Negro freedom struggle" was only "a specialized part of the general class struggle" against "the reign of the monopolists." He reassured the rank and file that the "labor-Negro alliance" was alive and well. To prove it, Hall announced that the National Committee had made history by elevating Winston to the post of Party Chairman. This was the first time a black had ever held the exalted position.

With Winston at the helm, the Party felt secure in touting its Negro-white labor unity line. His appointment was an effort to diffuse racial tensions that were stirring in the lower ranks. Black members complained that they were isolated and ignored by local Party leaders. One black Party worker described the frustration he felt at one district meeting: "Not once did anyone raise the problem of black and white people working together in any kind of community. If we're serious about getting black working-class folk together then I say we had better start getting down to the real nitty-gritty."[20]

If Winston and Hall had trouble recognizing the problems in their own Party, they were even more at a loss trying to make sense out of the drama that was being played out on a dusty highway in Mississippi. When James Meredith decided to take his stand against fear and violence in his native state in May 1966, neither he nor the nation could have known what would follow.

Already well known as the first black student to enroll at the University of Mississippi in 1962, he intended his march down Highway 51 that wound from Jackson through Mississippi's impoverished black delta as one man's personal statement for racial justice. He got only a few miles before he was wounded in an ambush.

As Meredith lay in a hospital, King, CORE's new National Director Floyd McKissick, Urban League Executive Secretary Whitney Young, and James Farmer rushed to the state to continue his march. They were joined by a tall, ebony-complexioned young activist who a few months before had taken over as SNCC national chairman.[21]

Stokely Carmichael had gained a small measure of fame in 1965 when SNCC launched a voter registration drive in Lowndes County, Alabama with the aim of ousting the county's lily-white Democratic officials from office. SNCC called their organization the Black Panther Party. Carmichael openly declared that blacks should seek power and control, not integration. Rejecting King's nonviolence, SNCC leaders advocated self-defense against racist attacks. Like other black nationalist groups, their heroes were Malcolm X and other Third World revolutionaries. Whites, who had played a significant role in the early days of SNCC, were moved further to the edge of the organization. Soon they would be out completely.

As the marchers trudged down the road under the broiling Mississippi sun, a chant rose from the rear of the line. It was only two words but they were catchy. Soon more and more of the marchers were shouting BLACK POWER. Carmichael and the SNCC leaders had started the chant. King, Young, and Farmer were uncomfortable with the words. King even suggested to him that he chant "Black Equality" instead, but it was too late. The media had picked up on it and the two words soon rang through the living rooms of America.[22]

Black Power drew a hard threshold that whites could not cross. The white Left especially took the rejection hard. It was one thing for blacks to brow-beat white liberals for their patronizing attitudes. Now Communists and white radicals were coming under fire, too. In his first public statement on Black Power, Carmichael taunted white radicals for their "paternalistic attitude." He found it "ironic" and "curious" that white radicals could cheer Africans and Asians demanding self-determination, but when American blacks demanded the same they were "racists and anti-white." In his increasingly jaundiced view, the white leftists may have been well meaning but they still "furthered white supremacy" with their paternalism.[23]

Carmichael's shrill words grated on the ears of Party leaders. If blacks did indeed want to do things for themselves, as he and the black militants proclaimed, where did that leave Communists? Black Power was hardly compatible with the Party's plan for a Negro-labor alliance. Party leaders needed to come up with a quick response to the new challenge. They realized it was fruitless to hurl invectives at Carmichael and SNCC since they clearly had the upper hand for the moment. They decided, instead, to do a little image remaking, to repackage what the black militants were saying and send it back to the public as their product.

Winston chose to give Carmichael a brief history lesson. He would show him that Black Power was nothing new. Communists had been saying the same things years before he came along. At his suggestion, *Political Affairs* reprinted the chapter from Robeson's 1958 autobiography *Here I Stand*, titled "The Power of Negro Action."

Robeson stated, "The Negro people's movement must be led by Negroes" and that white control "reduced the power and effectiveness of Negro leadership." He actually used the term "Negro Power" and criticized those black leaders that "relied upon white power."

Jackson took his turn and pointed to the resolution on the "Negro Question" adopted at the Party's 1959 convention. He argued that the resolution "corresponds" to many of the same demands that the Black Power advocates were making. He claimed that the Party had always supported black political organizing and economic control by the black working class. But Jackson and Winston were too closely identified with the old guard to be much good in the type of image sprucing the

Party needed. Only someone younger and more attuned to the thinking of the young black militants could effectively counter Carmichael.[24]

Party leaders made a feeble attempt to stay in step with the times by spinning off a national network of W.E.B. DuBois clubs in June 1964. Designed to draw young black and white activists into the Party, the clubs were largely a flop. Young black activists were more excited by Malcolm X, Africa, and dashikis than by Marxism—which many considered outdated and even racist. However, a small nucleus of blacks did move through the ranks of the clubs into the Party leadership. Roscoe Proctor was one.

He could work both sides of the street. At Party gatherings, Proctor argued that Communists should listen closer to what the black militants had to say: "This growth of Negro nationalism is a reflection of Negro political maturity." To the young Communist leader, nationalism was positive in that it was a valid expression of black "political independence" and the "organization of the Negro masses."

Unlike older Party leaders, he was not troubled by the slogan "Black Power." He disagreed with those Marxists who thought it was "divisive" and wanted to substitute "people's power" or "human power" instead. Once he had established himself as a "friend" to the black militants, he moved quickly to put the Party back into the hunt. "Marxists-Leninists should help to put more flesh and bone on the "Black Power" slogan."

He found some support from Lightfoot, who evidently had been having some second thoughts about the Party's one-dimensional approach to the black movement. In a report to the National Committee, Lightfoot did not feel that black nationalism was "anti-white." Quite the contrary, he thought that "the main content of black nationalism is of a progressive character."[25]

Their views did not sit well with Jackson. He believed that Proctor had conceded too much to the nationalists. Jackson still considered Carmichael's philosophy a threat to class unity: "One cannot foretell a decade of Negro isolation without at the same time prophesying a decade of defeats for the working class as a whole."

Which of these men spoke for the party? In truth, both did. Proctor only said that the Party should understand the nationalists. He did not say that the Party should endorse their views. Jackson said that the Party should not "sacrifice" the "Negro-labor alliance." Jay Thomas, in his summary of the positions of Proctor and Jackson, showed how specious the debate was: "I don't think we can write off many of these nationalist-oriented groups as we tended to do several years ago; nor can we go along with their incorrect, though understandable, anti-white expressions."

The debate spilled over at the Party's annual convention in June. Younger Party activists wanted the National Committee leaders to adopt the old concept of black self-determination instead of integration. Party leaders quashed that fast. "The unity of struggle of Negro and white is the key," the Committee forcefully declared, "not segregation and separation."[26]

Agony over Black Power

The massive riots that rocked Newark, Detroit, and dozens of other northern cities during the summer of 1967 seemed to prove that the black militants were right. Blacks wanted power and control. They did not want integration with whites. In "all my life," James Baldwin said, he had "never known a Negro who was not obsessed with Black Power." Even King began to edge cautiously toward the black militants: "The Black Power slogan did not spring full blown from the head of some philosophical Zeus. It was born from the wounds of despair and disappointment. It is a cry of daily hurt and persistent pain."[27]

Party leaders were not moved. They clung desperately to their sanitized view of black-white relations. Patterson carried his racial blindness to absurd lengths. He explained Detroit as "an upsurge of the poor which featured the united and fraternal action of the Negro and white together!" The old fighter's prescription for curing urban ills was not much better: "Only continued united struggles by a people, black and white, who understand their mutual interests can bring such profound and fundamental changes as will introduce harmony into our cities."

Tired of getting caught short on this issue, the National Committee decided to act. In November 1967 the Committee instructed its Negro Affairs Commission to assemble top Communist leaders from around the country. For two days, they barnstormed at their "special conference" to find a plausible approach to the black movement. At the end, they seemed no further along than before. Winston merely repeated the official line: "Armed uprisings cannot successfully be undertaken by the black community alone." Few would dispute that, but that was only a preface to his main point: "They require powerful allies above all in the ranks of the working class, white and black."[28]

The "special conference" was partly inspired by another event during the bloody summer of 1967. In July, with the white hot fires of the Newark riot still raging, over one thousand blacks met in the city for the first annual Black Power Conference. A year earlier, Harlem Congressman Adam Clayton Powell had suggested the idea during the unveiling of a seventeen-point Black Position Paper in Congress. Powell insisted that the conference be all black, and nonpartisan.

He got his wish. Black businessmen, workers, educators, and Democratic and Republican politicians attended. The NAACP, Urban League, RAM, and even the Communist Party sent representatives. During the three days they met, they were able to submerge their wildly varied political differences and conflicting interests in the name of black unity.

The delegates were especially angry over the killings, beatings, and jailings in Newark and other cities. They blamed Congress and the administration of President Lyndon Johnson for failing to put forth new initiatives to resolve the urban crisis. Most of all, they wanted whites out of the movement for good. The conference closed with the issuance of a Black Power Manifesto that included a top-heavy list of proposals for black political and economic power.[29]

But the proposal that caught the public's attention had been penciled in at the end of the conference almost as an afterthought; indeed, it was even inserted in the "Miscellaneous" category. It called for "a national dialogue on the desirability of partitioning the U.S. into separate and independent nations" for blacks and whites.

It became the headline story in the major press. By appearing to call for a separate nation, the delegates had taken Black Power to its ultimate end. It was a frivolous proposal that few delegates really took seriously, but the debate was on.

Robert Browne, an economics professor at Fairleigh Dickinson, gave it an air of respectability in *Ramparts* and the *New York Times*. He gave the "new black nation" the less than imaginative name of "New Africa." Browne strung whites along with a series of elaborate recommendations for tourism, trade, and diplomatic relations between "New Africa" and the United States. While the separation proposal was mainly a media debate, the other issues the delegates raised were real and reflected the deep distrust blacks had of whites.[30]

Black Communist Douglass Archer worried about this. Archer was in Newark to cover the conference for *The Worker*. He attended all the workshops, listened to the speeches, and carefully noted each resolution

257

passed. Unlike the rest of the mainstream press, Archer agreed with many of the proposals. Many of them he felt were not out of line with proposals the Party's Negro Commission had already put forth on police abuse and political organizing.

Archer, however, quickly parted company with the delegates who brought a "separatist tone" to the conference. He criticized the "questionable resolutions" for black economic development, "black bonds," "black financial institutions," and "cooperative economic ventures." To Archer, they were nothing but updates of the old "Buy Black" schemes that Communists had opposed when Garvey and the Harlem nationalists proposed them during the 1930s. He also dismissed these resolutions as the "provocative and unyielding demands by a few of the more vocal sects."

What disturbed Archer the most was that those "vocal sects" threatened a cherished dream of the Communists. "The greatest casualty was the clear recognition of the need of black and white unity." Karenga, who was a chief planner of the conference, thinks that the Communists misread the signs: "Most of the people there were students and young people. They weren't anti-working class. As far as we knew there were no Marxists there anyway. Our main concern was promoting 'blackness'."[31]

Party leaders were going to do all they could to prevent the black militants from slaying "Negro-white unity." In October 1967 Communist leaders huddled at a two-day conference to plan a fresh counterattack. Rather than confront the Black Power advocates head on, they decided on a flanking strategy. Carmichael had repeatedly hammered away at the idea that white radicals should organize in their own neighborhoods. "Whites who come into the black community with ideas of change seem to want to absolve the power structure of its responsibility." The Communists would take him at his word.

Conference participants agreed that they had to fight harder in labor unions, anti-war groups, and Jewish organizations against racism. Party leaders had a long memory. Remembering the success they had with defense campaigns around Scottsboro and the Civil Rights Congress, they proposed a national defense organization to "build truly honest Negro-white unity on the basis of the self-interest of white working people."

In February 1968 Party leaders publicly aired their views on Black Power. It was obvious that the National Committee intended to keep the pressure on white members. The only way that blacks could ever

trust whites, Hall maintained, was for whites "to burn out the influence of racism from white Americans."

Betty Gannett exhorted the whites to remember the campaigns for
the Scottsboro Boys and Herndon. She also reminded them about the
role white Communists had played in the fight against the poll tax,
lynching, segregation, and racism in the labor movement. White
Communists could do it again, Gannett insisted, if they were willing to
"go where the problem is—among whites" and "to enlist white support for Negro freedom."

Peoples World editor Carl Bloice believed that whites could be more
effective if they better understood Black Power. It was incorrect, he
said, to interpret Black Power as a "separatist slogan." Black Power was
really an attempt by blacks to "marshall their resources" for more political and economic gains. In Bloice's palatable definition, Black Power
came off as nothing more than another legitimate challenge to the capitalists. There were no winners or losers in the debate.[32]

At their June national convention, Party leaders had little choice but
to ride the nationalist tide: "Separation is derived from the frustration
of Black people with the seeming impossibility of achieving any form of
equality." Those Party leaders who saw Black Power as a menace to
their "labor-Negro alliance" would take little comfort in the events of
the next few months.[33]

Following the murder of Dr. King in April 1968, dozens of cities
again felt the torch from black rioters. Twenty-one thousand federal
troops patrolled streets in Washington, Chicago, and Baltimore.
Property damage was placed at $45 million. There were forty-six
deaths. Not only were the black militants talking tough, but the moderates were, too.

Whitney Young, who had long held the dike against the Black
Power advocates, finally capitulated. Appearing at CORE's summer
convention in July in Columbus, Ohio, Young said, "America does not
respond to people who beg on moral grounds." When he added that
blacks "were no longer enchanted with being near white people" and
that he was for Black Power, too—albeit a gentler version than
Carmichael's—the delegates cheered wildly.

Wilkins, who also showed up at the convention, was not quite prepared to go as far as Young. But he was there and that in itself said
something about the times.[34]

A statement by Chinese leader Mao Tse-Tung immediately after
King's death calling for blacks to "deal a telling blow to U.S. imperialism"

gave the appearance that America was at war with itself. As many black moderates began to shift toward black nationalism and self-defense, more black militants became infatuated with "the teachings of Mao." Mao buttons appeared on lapels and "little Red Books" containing Mao's revolutionary declarations shone from the pockets of black militants. But it did not mean that the militants were any more sympathetic toward Marxism.

SNCC's new chairman was a case in point. H. Rap Brown gave every sign of being even more inflammatory than Carmichael. And he proved it by promptly getting himself shot during disturbances in Maryland and later indicted by the government for carrying firearms on an airplane. Although Brown may have thought that America was ripe for revolution, he did not think socialism was the answer. "To talk socialism to black people at this point is ridiculous. Black people think a communist is someone who does not go to church." Brown had another motive for opposing the Socialists: "when it's white controlled, it can foster just as much racism as anything else."[35]

Former SNCC leader James Forman, now on the outs with the organization, was free-lancing his "revolutionary Black Power" concept all over. In April 1969, he issued a "Black Manifesto" to the white Christian churches and Jewish synagogues, demanding $500 million as reparations for black suffering. Not satisfied with that, Forman upped the stakes. In an address at the National Black Economic Development Conference in Detroit, he made a new demand on white America: "We say think in terms of total control of the U.S. We must prepare ourselves to seize state power." If the government did not yield power, Forman once more threatened Americans with the nightmarish specter of black guerrilla warfare. A few churches took him at his word and invited him to depict his horrific vision before their frightened congregations. Party leaders tried to treat Forman's fanciful scheme with an air of seriousness. The *Daily World's* Ted Bassett called it "a just demand. "[36]

The fact that Forman and the others got any consideration from Party leaders did not mean that they had changed their minds, only that black militancy had become too compelling a force to ignore. A *Newsweek* poll in June 1969 found that an alarming twenty-one percent of blacks agreed that a separate nation was desirable. If the numbers were correct, there were millions of blacks who would reject any appeals for "Negro-white unity," whether they were made by white liberals or Communists.

Some Party leaders did believe the separatist sentiment was as strong as *Newsweek* reported. Lightfoot felt the Party should face the reality head on. He suggested that a plebiscite be held among blacks to determine "whether they want to remain in the general commonwealth, or to establish another nation within the continental United States." He may have had a few lingering memories of the old black belt slogans from the Party's past.

However, Jackson did not. As far as he was concerned, Lightfoot's idea was his own and not the Party's. "We think the approach toward accommodation with nationalism and separatism, which comrade Lightfoot has surfaced, must be rejected." He felt strongly that Lightfoot was flunking his basic Marxism. He urged him to reread Lenin and he would discover that "bourgeois nationalism and proletarian internationalism are two irreconcilably hostile slogans."

Party leaders were not through lambasting him. Bassett got in his licks too: "What Lightfoot has done is to confuse the Marxist-Leninist concept of self-determination with the popular connotation of the black nationalists." Both Bassett and Jackson demanded that Lightfoot stop confusing the Party's "non-black labor and liberal allies."[37]

The debate was really no debate. Lightfoot had constructed a straw man that the Party could easily shootdown. He undoubtedly knew that the notion of "plebiscites" or "secession" would never fly with the leadership. However, by appearing to give credence to the nationalist demands, Communists could straddle the political fence. Party leaders would continue to bide their time waiting for the black militants to run out of steam. By the summer of 1969, there were signs that that would happen.

Carmichael, also on the outs with SNCC and following a brief fling with the Black Panthers, had moved beyond Black Power. His new philosophy was Pan-Africanism. He contended that blacks must have land and power, not just in America but in Africa. Carmichael dreamed of Pan-Africanist armies, governments, and corporations that would end European and American domination of the black world. In his apocalyptic racial vision, whites and Marxism were still excluded: "For me, to always look to Marx is once again to give the credit for everything good to Europe. Once again I continue to stress my inferiority as an African."[38]

A Moment of Hope

Just at the point where Communist political fortunes had seemingly reached their lowest ebb since the 1950s, some bright spots appeared. In May 1968 a small band of young black workers at the giant Dodge River Rouge plant in Detroit, frustrated over working conditions and union discrimination, walked off the job. They formed the Dodge Revolutionary Union Movement. DRUM stepped up its organizing among black workers at the plant. Their efforts bore some fruit.

In an election for union trustee at Dodge River Rouge, DRUM defeated the United Auto Workers candidate. The movement caught fire at other auto plants. Within a few months, Ford and General Motors plants also had their own "Revolutionary Union Movements."

Buoyed by their momentary victory, the black dissidents banded together into the League of Revolutionary Black Workers. Borrowing ideas from the nationalists and the Marxists, the League declared itself a "Black Marxist-Leninist Organization" that would organize black workers at the "point of production."[39] The League distanced itself from Carmichael and the black militant's race-baiting and called for a "dialogue" with white workers. While they agreed that much of white labor "retained white consciousness as opposed to class consciousness," they also believed that white labor "faced many of the same problems that black workers face."

John Watson, the fiery editor of the *Inner City Voice* which served as a sounding board for League views, took on Carmichael and the nationalists. He told an interviewer, "To say socialism or communism is irrelevant is foolish and we oppose this." The *Daily World* hailed the League as "valiant young black auto workers battling" the auto giants and the corrupt UAW leadership. For a while, whatever the League did was news and received feature coverage in the Party press.[40]

It did not last. The League's Marxist enthusiasm waned fast under the harsh attacks from the UAW and the hostility of most white auto workers. In 1970 the league withdrew its olive branch to the white workers. Instead of a "revolutionary alliance" between whites and blacks, the League now called for a "black united front." Watson now spoke of working class revolt only in terms of non-whites and Third World revolutionaries. With the UAW firmly in the saddle at Dodge and Ford plants, the League was finished. It limped along for a while as the Black Workers Congress, attracting few black workers and no coverage from the *Daily World*.[41]

Meanwhile, two thousand miles away in Oakland, California, two young black college drop-outs had a different idea of how to combat racism. From the time they burst onto the national scene in 1966 with their shotguns, black berets, and tough talk, the Black Panthers, under the lead of Bobby Seale and Huey Newton, kept the nation transfixed with a mixture of fear and awe.

The Panthers preached self-defense and anti-capitalist revolution. An amalgam of street hustlers, ex-convicts, and disenchanted student radicals, the Black Panthers were the tough guys of the black revolution. Newton became the first casualty. An early morning street confrontation in August 1967 left one police officer dead and a severely-wounded Newton facing the gas chamber. But the Panthers spread quickly. Chapters were formed in more than twenty cities. Raids and shoot-outs with police further enhanced their street-tough reputation within the radical movement.[42]

With Newton off the scene, Eldridge Cleaver took over. Fresh out of San Quentin and with a best-selling book about prison life, *Soul On Ice*, under his belt, Cleaver set out to give the Panthers a new political direction. Assuming the title of Minister of Information, Cleaver made the first item on his agenda a rapprochement with whites. "We have always maintained that it is sheer stupidity for black people to pick up the white man's burden of racism."

In 1968 the Black Panthers formed coalitions with the Peace and Freedom Party and the Students for a Democratic Society. Cleaver, perhaps with a backward glance at the nationalists, explained why he felt the Panthers should read whites back into the black movement: "We recognize that there is a valid white radicalism on the American scene today and we say it is in the best interests of black people to have a functional working relationship with white radicals."

In staking out a position to the left of the black nationalists, the Panthers realized they were bucking the political tide. Roundly criticized by black nationalist groups for selling out to the Communists, violent clashes ensued. The culmination was a bloody shoot-out at UCLA in January 1969 between the Panthers and Karenga's US organization. Two Panthers were killed. "The whole thing was unfortunate," Karenga insists. "We thought we had good relations with them, even though we did think they were too dependent on the white left."[43]

But the Panthers held firm. They would not abandon their Marxism or their white allies. Seale was adamant: "The cultural nationalists talk about the Third World. We talk about the colored peoples of the world, but at the same time there are going to be white people who want to change the system." The Panthers dissolved their brief alliance with Carmichael, in which they had intemperately made him their "Prime Minister." Carmichael could not stomach the Panthers' Marxism, and the Panthers in turn could not take his Pan-Africanism.

In bidding him good-by, Cleaver gave him a parting lecture: "If you look around the world you will see that the only countries which have liberated themselves are precisely those countries that have strong Marxist-Leninist parties." If they were going to be true to their Marxist faith, the Panthers could not ignore the workers. Writing from his jail cell, Newton concluded: "All members of the working classes must seize the means of production. This naturally includes black people."[44]

His words gave Party leaders their opening. In a *Political Affairs* article Patterson cautiously held out the olive branch. First, he gently chided them for their gun-toting, violent posturing. They were "grave ideological weaknesses." However, since they did not reject labor, Marxism, or whites, he was willing to chalk up their faults to political immaturity. Patterson then turned on the political flattery: "The Panthers are the first black-led organization to understand the menace of anti-Communism and unqualifiedly to express opposition to it."

Next, he urged the Panthers to talk with Party leaders to "iron out the differences that exist between us." Whether the Panthers agreed to the dialogue he had in mind or not, he assured them that the Party "solidly supported" them. Supported, that is, as long as the Panthers worked to "defeat racism and bring about the unity of the black and white working class." Lightfoot moved to solidify the relationship Communist leaders imagined they could have with the Panthers. He introduced a resolution at the Party's nineteenth national convention in June 1969 urging the Party to "initiate cooperation" with the Panthers for "the victory of the working class."

With the Panther death toll mounting from assaults and shoot-outs with the police, Hall and Winston pressed the district committees to send letters, telegrams, and petitions to the Justice Department protesting the killings. "Nobody in the country was more supportive of them than the Party," Charlene Mitchell says, obviously feeling no need to apologize for the actions of the Communists. "We criticized them when we thought they were wrong, but we didn't try to manipulate them."[45]

264

But the Panthers were not as pristine in their belief in Marxism and the working class as the Communist leaders wanted to believe. The Panthers, often wrapped more in cult than ideology, sent off confused messages. Newton may have called the Panthers "Marxist" but he did not fully buy the idea that communism was the magic tonic for blacks: "I would say that it wouldn't work, I would say that until you get rid of racism, no matter what kind of economic system you have, black people will still be oppressed."

Newton further confounded the Marxists, and perhaps himself as well, when he sent a "message of greetings" to Robert Williams. In September 1969 Williams had given up his forced exile in China and returned to the United States. Settling in Detroit, he began a lengthy fight against extradition to North Carolina. He busied himself politically, taking over as the president of the Republic of New Africa, an avowedly black separatist group that demanded a secessionist nation in the South. Newton agreed with him that the RNA was "perfectly justified in declaring their right to secede from the union." Newton compared blacks to a "colonized" nation occupied and controlled by a white ruling class. Newton included white workers as part of that ruling class: "We're exploited not only by the small group of the ruling class, we're oppressed and repressed by even the working class whites in the country."

Seale was equally unreassuring to the Panthers' hopeful white allies: "We are not a front for white radicals." Panther Minister of Education Raymond "Masai" Hewitt picked up on Carmichael's theme that white radicals should organize whites, not blacks. "To assume that the black workers don't have enough brains to take care of themselves is really a racist fallacy." If white workers really wanted to help, Hewitt suggested that "they fight racism, ignorance, and political backwardness in their own community."[46]

If Patterson had paid closer attention he would have known that when the Panthers spoke of alliances with white radicals they did not mean the Party. Cleaver made a sharp distinction between the "Old Left," which was another way of saying the Communist Party, and the "New Left." Cleaver told the Communists that the Panthers would "not allow them to function in the black community." He called them "interlopers" and urged blacks to "escort them to the borders of the black community" with a warning "not to return with their literature and propaganda." Cleaver accused the Communists of trying to "dictate" to the Panthers and black organizations.

By 1970, the Panthers were on a downhill slide. Police attacks and internal factional feuds between Newton and Cleaver had taken their toll. Winston did not shed any tears. He called the Panther leaders "pseudo militants" who "made their own party vulnerable to genocidal assaults and frame-ups." But that was not their greatest sin. "It is apparent that neither Newton nor Cleaver have ever based their tactics on the working class and Marxism-Leninism." Party leaders believed that time, once more, had proven them correct.[47]

Reds in the Civil Rights Movement?

But it was not a time for gloating. Although Communists found little common ground with the black movement during the decade, they did share one ominous and disturbing fate. Both were the targets of a relentless government repression. The irony was that while the Party failed miserably to make any connection with the black movement, government officials often made the connection for them. Appearing before the Eisenhower Commission, set up by President Johnson in September 1968 to investigate campus and ghetto violence, Hoover blamed Moscow Communists for spawning "vicious, hate-filled black extremists."

Not to be outdone, California legislators went after the Panthers: "The Panthers are being controlled by the Communist Party to serve as its shock troops on the front line of the revolution." That was the contention of the California State Senate Subcommittee on Un-American Activities in August 1970.

While the Panthers were an easy and obvious choice to tie into the Left, it was not as simple to brand as a Communist the man who held the esteem of much of the nation and whose moderate credentials were seemingly beyond reproach. But there were those who were willing to try. With the blessing of both the Kennedy and the Johnson administrations, the FBI and the Justice Department persistently tried to link Martin Luther King with the Communist Party.[48] "There were, at the top, no fewer than fourteen men with high-ranking positions who not only never objected to the investigation of King, but because of Hoover's pressure were vigorously behind it." Despite what Assistant FBI Director William Sullivan said, there was no personal vendetta on the director's part.

Since his first days as head of the Bureau of Investigation, the precursor to the FBI, Hoover harbored deep suspicions about the patriotism of black leaders and their organizations. He could never prove it, but he was convinced there was a Red hand lurking somewhere behind their protests. To Hoover, King was not just another black leader. He was a powerful symbol of the black movement. If King was indeed a Red, then he would at long last have bagged his prey.[49]

It started off innocently enough. During the Labor Day weekend in 1957, King and Abernathy had traveled to the Highlander Folk School in Tennessee. Highlander was celebrating the twenty-fifth anniversary of its founding. For years, the school had a favorable reputation with blacks for its pioneering work in civil rights and economic reform. To King, Highlander was a school with "noble purpose that did creative work." A number of black activists had attended training workshops and classes at the school. Because of that, Highlander was a special target of outrage for southern whites. From time to time, southern legislators investigated the school for Communist activity. Mississippi Senator James O. Eastland called Highlander "a front for a conspiracy to overthrow this country." During the McCarthyite years, the Tennessee state legislature even passed a statute abolishing the school. But it survived.

King was at the school just long enough to sing a few songs, greet a few friends, and get his picture taken. That was enough. The picture showed King seated next to Aubrey Williams, President of the Southern Education Fund, and Abner Berry, a member of the Communist Party's National Committee. Warning bells went off throughout the South and in Washington.

For the next few years, the Highlander picture would be circulated widely by right-wing groups with the caption "Martin Luther King. . . At Communist Training School." In 1963 Karl Prussian, a paid FBI informant, signed an affidavit that he had attended five Communist Party committee meetings in California during King's alleged Highlander training years. At each meeting, Prussian said, King "was always set forth as the individual to whom Communists should look and rally around." Letting his imagination take complete flight, Prussian stated that King belonged to more than "sixty Communist fronts." The FBI thought so little of Prussian's fantasies that even Hoover took pains to assure anxious inquirers that the informant spoke only for himself and was not a Bureau agent.[50]

Still, he firmly believed that the Communists were pulling invisible strings behind King and the civil rights movement. He reminded his agents that the Kennedy administration had taken his warnings about

Castro's "communist influences" lightly and the country paid the price when Castro, after taking power, turned to the Soviets for aid. He would not make the same mistake with King.

Hoover was convinced that he had already uncovered King's Communist influences through extensive electronic surveillance of King and the SCLC. He named several SCLC organizers and financial supporters that he felt had direct Communist ties. He labeled two of them "top" Party leaders. In August 1963 he ordered Sullivan to draw up a plan to expose the Communist Party's hold over the SCLC.

Sullivan, like Hoover, also saw the larger picture. He assessed King as a leader who "stands head and shoulders over all other Negro leaders when it comes to influencing great masses of Negroes." Sullivan was ready "to mark him" as the "most dangerous Negro of the future in this nation." He came to the same conclusion that Hoover had long since reached: "Nineteen million Negroes constitute the greatest single racial target of the Communist party, USA."

The plan to counter King was still fuzzy. Sullivan and other top FBI officials had set up a "Seat of Government" committee "for the purpose of exploring this entire matter." FBI intelligence until then was confined to collecting surveillance and wiretap information on King and his alleged Communist supporters.[51]

By December, they decided on more. Sullivan called a Washington meeting of his "Seat of Government" committee and agents from the Atlanta office. He repeated the FBI's view that "it was necessary for us to continue obtaining evidence of the CPUSA's influence on King and, through King, influence on the Negro people." The FBI unveiled a sweeping plan to conduct surveillance on all SCLC employees, monitor SCLC funds, and track down its contributors. He also hinted that the FBI would target the SCLC office for full-scale monitoring. That same month Hoover told the Brotherhood of the Washington Hebrew Congregation, "Some individuals exploit the tension for purposes not confined to the equality of human rights under the Constitution." *The Worker* knew exactly who Hoover meant, and called on Attorney General Kennedy to "do something about this all-powerful, seemingly sacrosanct police chief."[52]

What the *Worker* did not know was that Hoover had moved the campaign against King into high gear. In April 1964 a FBI official even asked Sullivan for permission to prevent Yale and Springfield College from conferring honorary degrees on King. He indicated that the FBI had successfully stopped Marquette University from honoring King.

Hoover convinced a reluctant Robert Kennedy to approve wiretaps on King and his associates. Kennedy believed that the Communists were ineffectual in the civil rights movement. But Hoover was persuasive. On April 15, the *New York Herald Tribune* reported that Hoover had told a House subcommittee in January, "We do know that the Communist influence does exist in the Negro movement and it is this influence which is vitally important."[53]

Hoover's campaign had the immediate effect of putting King and the SCLC on the defensive. Arriving at San Francisco International Airport the following day, King handed the press a prepared statement denying Hoover's charges. He accused Hoover of aiding and abetting "the fallacious claims" of southern racists and right-wingers.

King also wanted to talk about his own organization's position on communism. Calling communism "crippling totalitarianism" and a "denial of human freedom," he announced that the SCLC had a standing policy that Communists could not join nor give advice to the organization. He had not forgotten that the specific issue was his alleged ties with the Party. "Our struggle each day is to achieve the American Dream, a concept which is alien to those who espouse the cause of the Communist Party."

King was determined not to give the FBI chief any more oil to pour on the flames. In his statement, he crossed out the word "legitimately" and substituted the word "easily" in a sentence on potential Communist influence on blacks. The original read: "The more significant truth is the amazing lack of success that communism has met in attracting the Negro, who legitimately might be tempted to some other discipline to gain respite from his desperate plight."

Reporters threw more questions at King. He seemed genuinely relieved to get the issue out in the open. He denied that he had ever heard of the informant Prussian. He assured them that the SCLC would drop anyone from the organization who had "Communist leanings." In fact, he said, the SCLC had already dismissed one person who in the past belonged to the Party.

However, he did not silence the critics or Hoover. They insisted that he still maintained close contacts and accepted funds and advice from the men that the FBI named as Communists. Later, the FBI identified the two alleged Communists as Jack O'Dell, a former editor at *Freedomways* magazine, and Stanley Levinson, an attorney and SCLC fund-raiser.[54] King had to go over the same ground again in May when he appeared on "Face the Nation." The reporters questioned him sharply on Hoover's charges. King made the same points again. No, there were no known Communists in SCLC. Yes, they would get rid of them if they were discovered; communism was incompatible with the civil rights movement.

King realized that the stakes involved in the communism debate were great. When the FBI questioned his integrity, he knew they were really questioning the integrity of the black movement. King confronted the issue directly when he rhetorically asked: "Why is this issue being used now to smear and attack the civil rights movement and the SCLC?"

The debate over who was or was not a Communist within the black movement was a hollow issue. The FBI in truth knew that Communist influence within civil rights organizations was nil. In November 1963 one of their informants reported on a talk that Ben Davis gave to the Marxist Discussion Group at New York City College. Davis stated flatly that there was "no communist leadership in the Negro revolution." The informant, in a personal aside, expressed surprise that the "CP has done nothing during the greatest social reform in American history." On the other side, both civil rights leaders and black nationalists, for personal and political reasons, shared every ounce of white America's Red phobia. Despite what the FBI wanted the public to believe, Communists had nowhere to go in the black movement.[55]

Even without the burdens of white backlash and government probing, the Party would have continued to slide. The young black militants of the 1960s had decisively rejected Marxism as outdated and unsuited to black needs. The NAACP, Urban League, and other established black organizations were just as anti-Communist, and black workers were indifferent to Communist appeals for a "labor-Negro alliance." But Party leaders such as Lightfoot still plugged away: "The building of a Negro and labor alliance is the cornerstone for the building of an anti-monopoly coalition." He spoke as if the 1960s had never happened.[56]

As the decade ended, there was good reason to expect that the Communist Party would enter the 1970s reduced to a minor footnote in American history. But history is full of the unexpected. Unbeknownst to Party leaders, the daring but foolish act of a seventeen-year-old was about to give Communists a momentary respite from oblivion.

270

Notes

1. Floyd B. Barbour, ed., *The Black Power Revolt* (Boston: Porter Sargeant, 1968); Harold Cruse, *The Crisis of the Negro Intellectual* (New York: William Morrow, 1967); Robert L. Allen, *Black Awakening in Capitalist America* (New York: Doubleday, 1969); James Farmer, *The New Jacobins and Full Emancipation*, in Robert A. Goldwin, ed., *100 Years of Emancipation* (Chicago: Rand McNally and Co., 1964), 101.

2. For background on the deteriorating economic plight of urban blacks during the 1960s see Daniel R. Fusfield, *The Political Economy of the Ghetto* (Carbondale: Southern Illinois University, 1984); Hollis R. Lynch, *The Black Urban Condition* (New York: Thomas Y. Crowell, 1973); [*Fortune* Magazine editors], *The Negro and the City* (New York: Time, Inc., 1968).

3. Malcolm X with Alex Haley, *The Autobiography of Malcolm X* (New York: Grove Press, 1965); C. Eric Lincoln, *The Black Muslims in America* (Boston: Beacon Press, 1963); E. U. Essien-Udom, *Black Nationalism* (Chicago: The University of Chicago Press, 1962); Elijah Muhammad, *Message to the Blackman* (Chicago: Muhammad Mosque of Islam No. 2, 1965); FBI—Racial Matters, 29 June 1950; FBI—Racial Matters, January 1952; FBI—Racial Matters, December 1954; FBI—Racial Matters, 10 January 1955, Freedom of Information release, Microfilm, A.C. Bilbrew Library.

4. E. U. Essien-Udom, *Black Nationalism*, 181-89; *Muhammad Speaks*, February 1962; *Muhammad Speaks*, March 1962; *Muhammad Speaks*, August 1963.

5. Communist leaders were hardly unaware of the profound influence of nationalist thought on nineteenth-century black leaders; see Foster *The Negro People in American History* (New York: International Publishers, 1954); Herbert Aptheker, "Consciousness of Negro Nationality: An Historical Survey, *Political Affairs* 28 (June 1949): 95.

6. A short Party-written biography of Claude Lightfoot is on the dustjacket of his book *Ghetto Rebellion to Black Liberation* (New York: International Publishers, 1968). Lightfoot also had his share of hard times in the Party. In 1940 he was hauled before the Dies Committee and ordered to turn over names of Illinois Communist members. He refused (*Afro-American*, 27 April 1940). In 1955 he was tried and convicted under the Smith Act. His sentence was overturned on appeal "The Case of Claude Lightfoot and Junius Scales," October 1955, CRC Papers; David Caute, *The Great Fear*, 207; Lightfoot, *Ghetto Rebellion to Black Liberation*, jacket; Claude Lightfoot, "The Negro Liberation Movement Today," *Political Affairs* 39 (February 1961): 90.

7. E. U. Essien-Udom, *Black Nationalism*, 86; "An Open Letter to the Negro People" (Negro Commission, CPUSA), June 1961, 3-4, Dorothy Healey Papers, CSULB.

8. Lightfoot, "Negro Nationalism and the Black Muslims," *Political Affairs* 41 (July 1962): 4, 13, 20; "To All Districts," CPUSA, 11 July 1963, CP File—1963.

9. Ben Davis, "Tokenism and Gradualism in the Negro Struggle," *Political Affairs* 43, (February 1963): 21; *The Worker*, 28 July 1963; *The Worker*, 30 July 1963; *The Worker*, 4 August 1963.

10. *The Worker*, 7 July 1963; Lightfoot, *Negro Freedom* (New York: New Currents Publishers, 1964), 44.

11. David Garrow, *Bearing the Cross* (New York: William Morrow and Co., 1986), 260-61; A. B. Spellman "Interview with Malcolm X," *Monthly Review* 16 (May 1964): 19-20; Don Freeman, "Nationalist Student Conference," *Liberator* 3 (July 1964): 18; Max Stanford, "We are at War with White America," *Black America* (Fall 1964): 12; (Editors) "Colonial war at Home," *Monthly Review* 16 (May 1964): 5-8.

12. Williams gives his version of the events in Monroe in, *Negroes with Guns* (New York: Marzani and Munsell, 1962); Robert C. Cohen, *Black Crusader*, (New York: Lyle Stuart, 1972); *The Crusader* 4 (February 1963): 6.

13. Williams, *Negroes with Guns*, 120; *The Crusader* 5 (March-April 1964): 4; *Crusader* 6 (October 1965): 9; Quoted in *Socialist Workers Party Discussion Bulletin* 25 (29 July 1965): 22.

14. As a Party man in the late 1940s, Cruse drew on his own military experiences to deliver a biting attack on Jim Crow practices in the army during world War II (*Daily Worker*, 7 December 1947). *Marxism and the Negro Struggle* (New York: Pioneer Publishers, 1963), 6; Carlos Moore, "Cuba: The Untold Story" (original copy in author's possession), 216-17. Moore claims that Marx and Engels "employed those racist epithets coined by the slave traders in designating the enslaved and subjugated Black peoples" (*Were Marx and Engels White Racists?* [Chicago: Institute of Positive Education, 1972], 26).

15. James Boggs, "Black Power," *Liberator* 6 (April 1967): 6-7. Boggs covers much of the same ground in his essay, "Liberalism, Marxism, and Black Political Power," in *Racism and the Class Struggle* (New York: Monthly Review Press, 1970), 26-32 and in "The American Revolution," *Liberator* 8 (October 1968): 4-9. Maulana Karenga, *The Quotable Karenga* (Los Angeles: US Organization, 1967), 24; Interview with Maulana Karenga, 17 December 1989.

16. C. E. Wilson, "Here We Go Again," *Liberator* 4 (June 1965): 9; Odell Sykes, The New Left Acceptance of Responsibility," *Liberator* 4 (July 1965): 23; "The White Liberal" (editorial), *Liberator* 5 (August 1966): 3.

17. Frank Kofsky, "Malcolm X," *Monthly Review* 18 (September 1966): 51; Albert Cleague Jr., "The Malcolm X Myth," *Liberator* 6 (June 1967): 4 and 6; "The Future of the Negro Struggle," (symposium) *International Socialist Review* 24 (Spring 1963): 60; A. B. Spellman, "The Legacy of Malcolm X," *Liberator* 4 (June 1965): 13. Historian John Henrik Clarke who knew Malcolm personally claims that Malcolm never agreed with the left: "Malcolm X considered the Communist Party and Socialist Party as just another bunch of white people seeking control over Black People" (Clarke to Hutchinson, 24 January 1990). Finally, two researchers even went so far as to attempt to "quantify" Malcolm's shift toward whites. Predictably, they concluded the results were "not clear cut" (Raymond Rodgers and Jimmie N. Rogers, "Evolution of the Attitude of Malcolm X Toward Whites," *Phylon* 44 [June 1983]: 114).

18. Malcolm X, *The Autobiography of Malcolm X*, 348-88. Malcolm's speech at the Militant Labor Forum, and interview with the *Young Socialist* were published in Malcolm X, *By any Means Necessary* (New York: Pathfinder Press, 1970), 14-32 and 157-66; FBI File, "Racial Matters," 18 June 1964, FBI File, FBI File #105-8999, 20 January 1965; *Tradition's Chains That Bind Us,* vol. 2, 671; Interview with Dorothy Healey (author), 16 December 1989; *The Worker*, 28 February 1965.

19. *Violence in the City—An End or a Beginning?* (Los Angeles, Governor's Commission, 1965); Anthony Oberschall, "The Los Angeles Riot of August 1965," *Social Problems* 15 (Winter 1968): 322-41; Robert Blauner, "Whitewash over Watts," *Transaction* 3 (March-April 1966): 9; Della Rossa, *Why Watts Exploded* (Los Angeles, Socialist Workers Party, 1966); William Taylor, "Storm over Los Angeles," *Political Affairs* 44 (October 1965): 14, 15.

20. Gus Hall, "Our Work Begins," *Political Affairs* 45 (August 1966): 9; C. D. "Party Life and the Negro Comrade," *Discussion Bulletin*, 18th Convention CPUSA, 22-26 June 1966, CP File—1966.

21. Martin Luther King, *Where Do We Go From Here: Chaos or Community?* (Boston: Beacon Press, 1968), 23-32; Forman, *The Making of Black Revolutionaries*, 456-60; Benjamin Muse, *The American Negro Revolution From Nonviolence to Black Power, 1963 to 1967* (Bloomington: Indiana University Press, 1968).

22. The following works were the most useful for understanding SNCC and Carmichael's conversion from non-violent resistance to militant Black Power: Allen J. Matusow, "From Civil Rights to Black Power: The Case of SNCC, 1960-1966," in *Twentieth Century America: Recent Interpretations* (New York: Harcourt, Brace and World, 1969); Clayborne Carson, *In Struggle: SNCC and the Black Awakening of the 1960's* (Cambridge: Harvard University Press, 1981); Stokely Carmichael and Charles V. Hamilton, *Black Power: The Politics of Liberation* (New York: Random House, 1967), 86-120; and King, *Where Do We Go From Here*, 31.

23. *Black Power: SNCC Speaks for Itself* (Ann Arbor, Michigan: Radical Education Project, 1966), 5. Carmichael gave his first public explanation of Black Power in a speech at the University of California, Berkeley on 29 October 1966 (*New York Times,* 30 October 1966). Carmichael, "Toward Black Liberation," *Massachusetts Review* 7 (Autumn 1966): 639-51; Stokely Carmichael, "Power and Racism," in Floyd Barbour, *The Black Power Revolt* (Boston: Porter Sargeant, 1968), 69.

24. Paul Robeson, "The Power of Negro Action," *Political Affairs* 46 (August 1967): 33 and 35; James Jackson, "The Meaning of Black Power," *Political Affairs* 45 (September 1966): 7.

25. *The Worker*, 30 June 1964; Roscoe Proctor, "On the Slogan and Concept of Black Power," *Internal Discussion Bulletin*, 19, CP File— 1967; Proctor, "Notes on the 'Black Power' Concept," *Political Affairs* 46 (March 1967): 49, 51; Claude Lightfoot, "Report to National Conference," CPUSA, 14-15 October 1967, 9, Dorothy Healey Papers.

26. James Jackson, "National Pride Not Nationalism," *Political Affairs* 46 (May 1967): 44; Jay Thomas, "Negro-White Unity and the Communists," *Political Affairs* 46 (May 1967): 52; *Minutes of the 1966 Convention*, CPUSA, 12, CP File—1966.

27. The most comprehensive report on the destructive violence that hit Northern cities during the summer of 1967 remains the *Report of the National Advisory Commission on Civil Disorders* (New York: Bantam Books, 1968). *St Petersburg Times,* 3 March 1968; King, *Where Do We Go from Here*, 33.

28. *The Worker*, 30 July 1967; *The Worker*, 8 August 1967; *People's World*, 2 December 1967.

29. Adam Clayton Powell, "My Black Position Paper," in Barbour, *The Black Power Revolt*, 305-9; *The Worker,* 30 July 1967. There were no official minutes or proceedings kept by Conference officials. My sources are newsman Chuck Stone's report which was published in *The Black Power Revolt* (189-98) and the recollections of a major planner of the conference, Maulana Karenga, Interview, 17 December 1989.

30. Interview with Maulana Karenga, 17 December 1989; Robert S. Browne, "The Case for Black Separatism," *Ramparts* 6 (December 1967): 51; Robert S. Browne, *Should the U.S. Be Partitioned?* (New York: Merit Publishers, 1968).

31. *The Worker*, 30 July 1967; Interview with Maulana Karenga, 17 December 1989.

32. Carmichael, "Power & Racism," in *The Black Power Revolt*, 68; Conference on Strategy and Tactics in the New Stage of Struggle for Negro Liberation, 14-15 October 1967, 2, Dorothy Healey Papers; Betty Gannett, "The Stench of Racism," 63; Carl Bloice, "Status of Black Liberation," 71.

33. Gus Hall, "New Stage of Struggle," *Political Affairs* 47 (February 1968): 28.

34. *The Guardian,* 13 April 1968; *The Guardian,* 20 April 1968; *New York Times,* 7 July 1968; *The Worker,* 14 July 1968. For Young's and Wilkins's views on Black Power see Whitney Young Jr., *Beyond Racism: Building an Open Society* (New York: McGraw-Hill, 1969), 236-55. Roy Wilkins, "Whither 'Black Power'?" *The Crisis* 73 (August-September 1966): 353-54.

35. "Maoism" was harshly attacked by American Communists as a distortion of the "authentic" doctrine of Marxism-Leninism, see Winston, *Strategy for a Black Agenda* (New York: International Publishers, 1973), 107-76. Mao Tse-Tung, "Statement in Support of the Afro-American Struggle Against Violent Repression, 16 April 1968," *World Revolution* 5 (Summer 1968): 75-76; *Guardian,* 15 June 1968. Although Brown did acknowledge the need for socialism, like other black nationalists he still saw the struggle as strictly a showdown between "the colored oppressed" and the "white West." The Marxists he did pay homage too were Frantz Fanon, Mao Tse-tung, and Regis Debray. Their Third Worldism for him always took precedence over their Marxism (*Die Nigger Die!* [New York: The Dial Press, 1969], 128-30).

36. Various black leaders and churchmen give their views on Forman's reparations demand in Robert S. Lecky and H. Elliot Wright, *Black Manifesto* (New York: Sheed and Wright, 1969). Forman, *The Making of Black Revolutionaries,* 543-53; "Manifesto: To the White Christian Churches and the Jewish Synagogues in the United States," presented at the Black Economic Development Conference, Detroit, 26 April 1969, 5 (copy in author's possession); *Daily World,* 7 May 1969.

37. "The Struggle for Black Liberation," *Internal Discussion Bulletin,* 1968, CP File—1968; *Newsweek,* 30 June 1969. Newsweek sampled black opinion in 1963, 1966, and 1969; each time the editors noted a significant rise in black separatist sentiment. See Peter Goldman, ed., *Report From Black America* (New York: Simon and Schuster, 1970); Claude Lightfoot, "The Right of Black America to Create a Nation," *Political Affairs* 47 (November 1968): 8 and 9; James Jackson, "Separatism—A Bourgeois Nationalist Trap," *Political Affairs* 48 (March 1969): 38; Ted Bassett, "Slogan of Self-Determination Unwarranted," *Political Affairs,* 48 (March 1969): 39 and 40.

38. Stokely Carmichael, "Pan-Africanism—Land and Power," *Black Scholar* 1 (November 1969): 10-20; Carmichael, "We Are All Africans," *Black Scholar* 2 (May 1970): 15-19. In an odd role reversal, Carmichael found himself under attack for vigorously defending socialism in a panel debate at a SNCC reunion in April 1988 (*Radical Historian's Newsletter,* 55, May 1988, 7.

39. A. Geschwender, *Black Marxist-Leninist Worker Movements: Class or National Consciousness?* (mimeo copy in author's possession) 1973, 1-10; Robert Dudnick, *Black Workers in Revolt* (New York: Guardian, 1968), 3-5; League of Revolutionary Black Workers, *General Policy Statement and Program*, 5, 11 (copy in author's possession).

40. *General Policy Statement*, 15; "Interview with John Watson," *Radical America* 11 (July-August 1968): 38; *Daily World*, 28 March 1969; *Daily World*, 20 March 1969.

41. *Liberated Guardian*, 1 May 1971; *Manifesto of the Black Workers Congress* (Detroit: Black Workers Congress), 6. The author surveyed the entire run of the *Daily World* for 1971.

42. Bobby Seale, *Seize the Time: The Story of the Black Panther Party and Huey Newton* (New York: Random House, 1970); Gene Marine, *The Black Panthers* (New York: New American Library, 1969); Phillip S. Foner, ed., *The Black Panthers Speak* (Philadelphia: J.B. Lippincott, 1970).

43. *The Black Panther*, 15 March 1968; *The Black Panther*, 4 May 1968; *Guardian*, 13 April 1968; Interview with Maulana Karenga, 17 December 1989.

44. *The Black Panther*, 3 March 1969; *People's World*, 24 February 1968; *The Black Panther*, 16 August 1969; *The Black Panther*, 23 August 1969.

45. William Patterson, "The Black Panther Party," *Political Affairs* 49 (November 1969), 12 and 14; Claude Lightfoot, "Panel 4. Black Liberation," *Party Affairs*, 30 June 1969, CP File—1969; *Daily World*, 18 December 1969.

46. *The Black Panther*, 16 March 1968; *The Black Panther*, 18 May 1968; Cohen, *Black Crusader*, 356-61. The fact that Williams was never extradited prompted some militants to speculate that a deal had been worked out in which Williams would drop his hard line rhetoric against the government in exchange for his freedom (*The Black Panther*, 6 December 1969; *The Black Panther*, 4 May 1969).

47. *The Black Panther*, 20 July 1967; *The Black Panther*, 28 June 1969. The story of the FBI's war of subversion against the Panthers from 1967 to 1970 broke when NBC newsman Carl Stern made public memos he obtained from the FBI after a threatened lawsuit. The documents known as COINTELPRO are excerpted in Baxter Smith, *FBI Plot Against the Black Movement* (New York: Pathfinder Press, 1974) 14-23. Henry Winston, "The Crisis of the Black Panther Party, " *Political Affairs* 50 (August 1971): 10.

48. Kenneth O'Reilly, "The FBI and the Politics of the Riots, 1964-1968," *Journal of American History* 75 (June 1988): 108; *Los Angeles Times*, 4 August 1970; *Los Angeles Times*, 10 August 1970; *Time Magazine* 96, 17 August 1970.

49. William Sullivan, *The Bureau, My 30 Years in Hoover's FBI* (New York: W.W. Norton, 1979), 137. For another view of Hoover's early obsession with black radicals and the left see, William Gid Powers, *Secrecy and Power: The Life of J. Edgar Hoover* (New York: Free Press, 1987).

50. Highlander Folk School, an Adult Education School With a Purpose," *Negro History Bulletin 21* (May 1958): 170 and 185-87; Taylor Branch, *Parting the Waters*, 121-22, 263-64, 289-90 and 853-54; C. Alvin Hughes, "A New Agenda for the South: The Role and Influence of the Highlander Folk School, 1953-1962," *Phylon* 46 (September 1985): 243; FBI File # 100-106670, ND, Section 7; *The Augusta Courier*, 8 July 1963; FBI File # 100-106670, Section 13, 22 July 1964, (affidavit dated 28 September 1963).

51. Sullivan to August H. Belmont, 30 August 1963, FBI File #100-106670; *New York Times,* 27 July 1963; *New York Times,* 30 July 1963; David Garrow, *The FBI and Martin Luther King, Jr.* (New York: Penguin Books, 1983), 56-77; FBI File # 100-5586, Atlanta Serial, Section 7, 1-13 FBI File #; Sullivan to Belmont, 30 August 1963.

52. Belmont to Sullivan, 24 December 1963, FBI File # 100-106670 Section 7; *The Worker,* 10 December 1963.

53. Fred J. Baumgardner to Sullivan, 2 April 1964, FBI File # 100-106670-348, Section 10; *New York Herald Tribune*, 15 April 1964.

54. SCLC Press Release, 23 April 1964; FBI File # 100-10670, Section 11 FBI File # 100-106670, Section 10, 30 April 1964.

55. Milton A. Jones to Catha DeLoach, 11 May 1964, FBI File # 100-106670-361, Section 11; FBI File #10-106670, Section 6, 4 November 1963. On 22 November 1989, the author queried FBI Director, William Sessions as to his knowledge of FBI intelligence directives against King. He received the following response: "As you may know, J. Edgar Hoover was the Director of the FBI during the period which you inquire. Therefore, Director Sessions would have no first hand recollections regarding specific FBI operations during that time" (Assistant Director, Milt Ahlerich to Earl Ofari Hutchinson, 22 December 1989).

56. A Party official who penned his signature, "Lefty" also sharply attacked the black militants for "writing off the working class forever" (Lefty, "James Boggs: The New Left and the American Revolution," *Party Affairs* 3 [7 February 1969]: 24). Claude Lightfoot, "The International Significance of Black Liberation," Lecture at Karl Marx University, Leipzig, GDR, 13 August 1969, 12, CP File—1969.

13 Free Angela

If there was ever a candidate least likely to be a world-wide *cause cele-bre,* it was Angela Davis. She was hardly cast in the mold of such black militant firebrands as H. Rap Brown, Stokely Carmichael, or Eldridge Cleaver. A tall, elegant woman, Davis spoke in a ponderous, measured tone, which was quite fitting since she was very much a child of the black middle class. Her parents were respected professionals in her native Birmingham, Alabama. Because of their position, they were able to shield their daughter from some of the worst racial abuses in the segregated city during her childhood years in the 1950s.

To her later regret, she was out of town when King and the SCLC brought their civil rights crusade to Birmingham in 1963. At the time, she was living in Brooklyn at the home of a white minister and attending Brandeis University on scholarship. Afterwards, she traveled in Europe and pursued her graduate degree at the Sorbonne in Paris and Heidelberg University in Germany. During this period most of the civil rights movement passed her by.[1]

But like many young blacks who came of age in the 1960s, she was deeply touched by the spirit and intensity of the protests. She desired to do more. As the civil rights movement turned more militant, with new leaders emerging and radical politics beginning to dominate their actions, Davis's thinking began to change. After careful study, she embraced Marxism because it seemed to provide ready answers to the problems of black poverty and oppression.

As Communists explained, capitalism created giant class schisms in Western society. Wealth and power became concentrated in the hands of a small group of industrialists and landlords. Government, the police, and the armed forces served as tools manipulated by the capitalists to preserve their economic interests. Meanwhile, the working class and the poor were consigned to a permanent existence of low wages, job insecurity, and political powerlessness.

Davis agreed with the Communists that the only solution was a Socialist revolution. Armed with her new enlightenment, Davis returned to America, anxious to play a role in building the new Socialist society that would free blacks from their oppression.

In 1967, she moved to the West Coast to pursue her doctoral studies in philosophy at the University of California, San Diego. Davis worked under the tutelage of Herbert Marcuse, a widely read, iconoclastic philosophy scholar. Marcuse's writings, which blended Marx with Freud, had become an instant hit among New Left student radicals. In the meantime, Davis discovered the radical movement in Los Angeles.

On weekends she would drive up to Los Angeles to attend SNCC and Panther meetings. Her troubles began the following year when she accepted a job as a part-time lecturer at UCLA. She might have been just another of the many young, social activist professors prevalent on college campuses during the 1960s. Most of them occasionally walked the picket line for a radical cause and then returned to the cozy, theoretical confines of Academia. But there was the letter.[2]

An anonymous letter-writer asked UCLA Chancellor Charles Young if he knew that one of his faculty members also belonged to the Communist Party. While Young did not know, it did not take him long to find out that Davis was the Communist Party member in question. The Chancellor dug out a resolution passed by the University of California Regents during the McCarthyite loyalty oath days that stated: "The Regents direct that no member of the Communist Party shall be employed by the University."

Young demanded that Davis tell whether she was a Communist. She did not skirt the issue. In a letter to Young, she cited numerous successful legal challenges to various loyalty statutes. She accused Young of violating her privacy and "constitutional freedom" to belong to any political grouping that she so chose. "It would seem that you are without authority to require answers concerning mere membership in the Communist Party or to deprive me of employment on such grounds." Davis was not ashamed to admit that she was a Party member. She told Young why: "I want you to know that as a black woman I feel an urgent need to find radical solutions to the problems of racial and national minorities in the white capitalist United States."

280

That was enough for Young. On September 19, 1969, the Board of Regents fired her. As a sop to quiet protest, Young allowed her to teach one non-credit class with the innocuous title of "Recurring Philosophical Themes in Black Literature."[3]

For the next few months, Davis was in the glare of the media spotlight. Professors, students, and black and women's groups rallied to her defense. Davis came off as the innocent black female professor under attack. Now that the public knew that she was a Communist, Davis plunged even deeper into radical organizing.

The Party had not stood still. Sensing the possibility for a comeback in the black community, Party leaders in 1968 organized the Che-Lumumba club as a "black Marxist-Leninist collective." By layering the club's program with Black Power and Pan-Africanist slogans, Party leaders hoped to turn a sufficient number of young black activists into Communists. None of this came easy for the old-timers on the Party's National Committee. "This was really something frowned on in the party," Dorothy Healey remembered. They were adamant, she said, that blacks and whites had to be together, since Communists "always had to show internationalism." Healey also pointed to the continuing dilemma that plagued Communists when they tried to avoid what they considered the odious stigma of nationalism. "If there hadn't been this all-black formation, I don't think that Angela Davis would have joined the Party."

Whether Party leaders liked it or not, the fact remained that many young blacks—even the Marxist converts—plainly regarded whites as intruders and did not feel as comfortable around them. At Che-Lumumba meetings, new recruits barely heard a word about Marx, and the Communist Party was never mentioned. Club leaders nearly always focused their planning and strategy on immediate issues that appealed specifically to blacks, such as police abuse or unemployment. Often forgetting that the enemy was supposed to be the capitalist, club members heaped as much scorn on the "white man" as the Muslims and SNCC had done. A former Che-Lumumba leader confirms that they did this more from expediency:" I joined the Che-Lumumba club, not the Communist Party, because I believed in what Che-Lumumba was fighting against, like police abuse and high rents in the community."

Davis also preferred to talk about these issues with black audiences. When the inevitable question was asked about her Marxist beliefs, she couched her answer in a way that made it more palatable to blacks: "It

281

is significant that many of the organizations are beginning to see that socialism has worked in many countries all over the world."[4]

In 1970 Davis began a correspondence with George Jackson. By then, Jackson had become the symbol of the alienated and tormented black prisoner who finds his political soul through the revolutionary ideas of Marx, Lenin, and Mao. His poignant letters and prisons essays, collected into the best-selling book *Soledad Brother*, transformed him into an internationally acclaimed author and hero to black and white militants. To Davis, Jackson was the quintessential symbol of the romantic outlaw, political hero, and downtrodden prisoner. Many of her letters found their way into Jackson's *Soledad Brother* and ranged over subjects from politics and revolution to romance.

She became a passionate defender of Jackson and the Soledad Brothers, organizing rallies and marches for their defense committee. A newspaper photo vividly captured Davis on camera, spiritedly marching in front of the Federal Office Building in Los Angeles with a picket sign. Behind her marched Jonathan Jackson, George's younger brother. He held a sign that read "Free the Soledad Brothers."[5]

The Campaign to Free Angela

Jonathan Jackson would do more than march. His plan was simple: he would rescue the convicts and hold the judge as a hostage until authorities released his brother. On August 7, 1970 he was cut down by a hail of police bullets outside the Marin County courthouse near San Francisco. Killed with him were two black convicts and a judge. A third convict, Ruchell Magee, was wounded.

This was an act that could only have been conceived by a very young man, blind to the reality of life. George was too well-known and too dangerous for authorities to ever release. A year later, George met his death during an outbreak of prison violence at San Quentin.

But Jackson's desperate act touched off a stunning chain of events. After Marin County authorities discovered that the two guns Jonathan Jackson used were registered to Davis, a warrant was issued for her arrest. She fled. On October 13, 1970, Davis was captured by the FBI in New York. Following a two-month extradition fight she was returned to California on December 22, 1970, to stand trial on charges of murder and kidnapping. With the stage set for what promised to be the most spectacular and most watched trial in recent American history, the National Committee went to work.[6]

Because she was an avowed Communist, Party leaders had to devise a strategy that would not alienate potential supporters, especially blacks. They would have to use every ounce of political skill they had to sanitize the image of Davis as the victim of state persecution. First, they needed to dispel public fears that they were violent, gun-toting anarchists out to destroy the country. Party leaders had gone to great lengths to disassociate themselves from the violent rhetoric of the Panthers and the other young black militants. During the late 1960s, Party leaders issued numerous statements denouncing the urban riots and condemning Robert Williams's and Rap Brown's calls for guerrilla warfare. Immediately after the Marin shoot-out, Hall and Winston issued a public statement: "The Communist Party has always made clear its opposition to acts of desperation or resort to gunplay on the part of individuals." Winston characterized Jackson's action as "a desperate act" that had set the black struggle back. "The revolutionary process," Winston argued, "is never advanced by actions which fail to strengthen militant mass struggle."[7]

Party leaders were prepared to draw on the long history and experience they had in organizing mass defense movements since the 1930s. The safest model remained the Scottsboro case. Party leaders decided to reach back and recycle the strategy that had worked then. They would get the best attorneys, raise thousands of dollars for defense; and stick to the narrow legal issues.

Outside the court, they would conduct a nonpartisan national and international campaign, with the major focus on mobilizing the black community. This would include black educators, ministers, professionals, and workers. Party leaders knew from their experience with Scottsboro that for the plan to be effective they would have to play down Davis's Communist Party membership. It was essential not to allow the media or government to pigeon-hole the defense as nothing more than Communists trying to save one of their own.[8] To do otherwise would scare away the black middle class and white liberals who were crucial to provide the money, publicity, and prestige the defense campaign needed. The cagey veteran of many past Party-run legal battles geared up once again for the fight. Patterson knew how to play all the angles. "He who raises the question of Angela's philosophy and ideological outlook seeks, consciously or unconsciously, to make the constitution null and void."

The Party's Political Committee decided not to raise the demand for Davis's freedom. It sounded too radical and might frighten liberals and black moderates who were not convinced that Davis was completely innocent. The committee instead settled on the less threatening demand for bail. "It was crucial that we make this the issue; there were too many people who wouldn't go any further than that," said Charlene Mitchell, who headed the Party's Black Liberation Commission and was generally credited as being an architect of the Davis defense strategy. The Party formed the Angela Davis Legal Defense, and the cry became "Bail For Angela." The committee instructed all Party members to raise the slogan "wherever people gather," and to urge organizations to "adopt resolutions urging bail for Angela Davis."

In November 1970 Party leaders drew up an "organizational plan" for a national network of "Committees To Free Angela Davis." The plan was practically a carbon copy of the Scottsboro defense campaign. The Committees were assigned the task of building maximum community support without the Communist label. The strategy committees would organize block clubs. Once the clubs were established, Party members would recruit ten other community persons into the clubs.

Party leaders planned on conducting an intense advertising campaign in the black press. They would try to get black editors at *Jet*, *Ebony*, and black newspapers to endorse the "bail for Angela" appeal. They also urged them to reprint a Party brochure "exploding the myth of a fair trial." Local committees were directed to flood the black press with newsletters, press releases, reprints of Davis's UCLA lectures, and copies of favorable articles, endorsements, and statements of support.

Communists did not want to ignore completely the political implications of the case, so they also outlined specific steps to develop "community awareness" of the problems "relative to oppression" of black and brown prisoners. But care had to be taken here. Calling all blacks in jail political prisoners was risky. Party leaders pointed out that the Che-Lumumba Club in Los Angeles collapsed after making police abuse its only organizing issue. Patterson strongly resisted Davis's pleas for the committee to link her case with Magee's. Eventually the two cases were severed.

To give the defense campaign more visibility and respectability among blacks, local defense committees sent thousands of letters to black ministers appealing for support.[9] In New York the local defense committee formed Black Women for Freedom. One Sunday the women visited every church in Harlem, urging support for Davis. The women were persuasive. More than four thousand persons wrote letters to Governor Nelson Rockefeller imploring him not to extradite Davis to California.

The Party's strategy seemed to be working. A *Los Angeles Times* poll found that more than eighty percent of blacks sympathized with Davis. But it was not brilliant strategy alone that made the defense campaign effective. It was Davis herself. She was the Party's best asset. Her infectious charm and courtly demeanor appealed to Americans across political bounds.

Middle-class blacks and whites could easily identify with her life. She fit perfectly the American ideal of the well-bred young professional. When they looked at Davis they did not see a wild-eyed Communist revolutionary but a career person struggling to rise up the social and economic ladder. If the state could jail her for capital crimes, then who was safe? Her plight also was a grave reminder to the newly emergent black middle class of their precarious position within American society.[10]

On a cold night in Brooklyn in February 1971, two thousand persons gathered in the auditorium of Brooklyn College to show their support for Davis. The mostly black crowd included ministers, educators, businessmen, radical activists, and local officials. They stomped and cheered as the light-skinned man in a black suit and bow tie harangued "America's white rulers" for "persecuting black leaders." Louis Farrakhan, then Minister of the Nation of Islam's Muslim Mosque #7 in New York, compared Davis's battle against the government to Paul Robeson's. Farrakhan made it clear that he was "concerned" about Davis because she was black, not because she was a Communist.

A month later, the SCLC's Ralph Abernathy brought more than 4,000 persons to their feet at the Manhattan Center in New York when he accused the "American system" of "kidnapping black people daily and putting them in prison." Abernathy promised that the SCLC would do its part to build a "massive united movement" to free Angela "and all twenty-five million black Americans."[11]

In Chicago, Mrs. Christine Johnson, director of the African-American Heritage Association, announced plans to form a local Free Angela committee. She said that the views of her group would be "in line with the views of other outstanding Americans such as Jesse Jackson and William Patterson." Mrs. Johnson apparently saw no irony in linking the political ideas of a prominent minister and a prominent Communist together. The match became less incongruous when

Jackson visited Davis at the Marin County Jail and declared that he was one of her "spiritual advisers." Few blacks thought to question the notion that a Communist had need of heavenly guidance.

If Davis's bail request were granted by the court, one person was anxious to contribute. "I have the money," popular soul singer Aretha Franklin stated. "I got it from black people." Whatever it cost, Franklin said she would be happy to foot the bill. In case any of her fans wondered why she was doing it, Franklin assured them that she felt such generosity "not because I believe in communism but because she's a black woman and she wants freedom for black people."[12]

Although the NAACP would never describe the justice system as vicious and oppressive, as the black militants did, the Board of Directors gave local branches the green light to support the Davis campaign. In outlining a "general policy" on the case, the NAACP board avoided taking a position on her guilt or innocence. The board called on the government to do what was necessary to insure that she receive a fair trial. Many local branches did not share the board's restraint. They passed strong resolutions demanding her freedom and contributed funds to the local defense committees.

While the NAACP Board of Directors tiptoed lightly around the case, the Urban League did not. League officials closed the national office in New York and joined in with local black activists to celebrate "Black Solidarity Day" for Davis. Two hundred delegates at a League conference in New York unanimously opposed her extradition from New York. The League's Board of Trustees sensed the strong pro-Davis sentiment in the ranks and issued a statement assailing the government: "We all know that the system of criminal justice in America often discriminates against black people." Questioning whether she could get a fair trial, the trustees blamed the media for "prejudicial and sensationalist" coverage of her case which, in effect, "presumed her guilt."[13]

The black press, usually a reliable barometer of the mood of blacks, fell into line. Davis was a hot item not because of anything the Party did. A former Party organizer and defense committee leader admitted, "The black press was never scared off by the communism issue because they took Angela's case on as their own cause. They projected the image that they wanted and kept us out." As one black editor noted, black readers were ready to "cast aside the labels of Communist" when it came to supporting her bid for freedom. Black editors soon developed their own unique terminology to describe her. The *Afro-*

American called her "Joan of Arc." *The Los Angeles Herald Dispatch* dubbed her "Sweet Sister Courage." The *Amsterdam News* compared her political daring to "Patrick Henry." To most black editors, it was purely a matter of whites railroading another black to prison. The question of communism was ignored.[14]

Despite the mushrooming national support that Davis had garnered, there were a few bumps in the road. Party leaders had scarcely got their defense campaign under way before they began hearing complaints from blacks that they were "using" Angela for their own purposes. Almena Lomax was sure it was true. Lomax, who at one time edited the *Los Angeles Tribune*, a small tabloid that specialized in "expose" stories concerning local blacks, claimed that sources told her that Angela had "quarreled incessantly" with Party leaders over their racial policies. Lomax speculated that Davis was captured after someone in the Party "fingered" her to the FBI. Even though she offered no evidence to back up her charge, the damage had been done. The story was repeated often and caused more blacks to wonder about the Communist's motives.

Pat Alexander would not go quite as far as Lomax, but she came close. The publisher of the *Los Angeles Herald Dispatch* was convinced that Communists were "beating their breasts" to raise money not for Davis's defense but for the Party's coffers. Alexander charged that Davis was only the latest in a long line of black victims stretching back to the Scottsboro boys that Communists used to "dupe" the black community.[15]

It was easy for Eldridge Cleaver to accept Lomax's and Alexander's allegations. He never had trusted the Communist Party anyway. Cleaver languished in self-imposed exile in Algeria after jumping bail in 1968 rather than face sentencing on charges stemming from an Oakland shoot-out. Cleaver warned that the Party and the government were in "active collusion" to turn her case into "a smoke screen to obscure the real issues."

Cleaver was peeved that Bobby Seale was not getting the same publicity as Davis. Seale was then on trial in Chicago on conspiracy charges stemming from the demonstrations at the 1968 Chicago Democratic convention. Predictably, whatever Cleaver said, Huey Newton would quickly rebut. Newton fired off a statement declaring his support for Davis as a "unifying factor in the struggle of black people." Newton made no mention of the Communist Party.[16]

Black or Red?

Black mistrust of the Party burst into the open in January 1971. A *Muhammad Speaks* canvasser walked the streets of Harlem asking blacks what they would like to ask Davis if they had the chance. Topping the list of questions was, "Why are you a Communist?" The questions were relayed to Davis by her attorney and her answers were tape-recorded and printed in *Muhammad Speaks*.

Davis defended her membership in the Party. Perhaps with an eye on the paper's largely black readership, she added: "Before anything else, I am a black woman. I dedicated my life to the struggle for the liberation of black people—my enslaved people." Davis tinged her answers with strong nationalist appeals for black unity and support for Third World struggles.

Davis waltzed around the role of whites by ascribing to the Party a dubious position at best: "The Communist party acknowledges the need for white people to accept the leadership of blacks, especially white workers." In an earlier interview with the radical *Guardian* newspaper, Davis showed even more ambiguity on whites when she said that they had "actively perpetuated racism" and had permanently "embedded it in the fabric of the country." She did not limit her indictment to white capitalists. Rankled by accusations that she was a pawn of the Communists, Davis threw the charge back at her critics. Anyone, she said, who believed such "flagrant lies" were themselves "terribly deceived" by the "Nixon-Hoover clique."

Her denial did not stop the rumors. Following a benefit concert in which Sammy Davis Jr. and Barbara Streisand performed at the L.A. Shrine Auditorium, a reviewer for the *Los Angeles Free Press,* the city's "underground" newspaper, expressed skepticism that the money raised would actually get to her defense committee. Davis was outraged. Charlene Mitchell remembers how angry she was: "I was sitting with her in her cell and she was practically in tears as she wrote a letter denying the accusations." The letter Mitchell referred to was quickly issued as an official statement by the National Defense Committee: "I want to assure everyone that all funds are directly channeled to my defense needs."

The second charge, that she was being manipulated by the Communists, remained the more damning to many blacks. Davis leveled her sharpest blast at this accusation: "It is an example of racist slander historically aimed at black people who are best capable of determining for themselves their political affiliation."[17] While Party leaders were pleased with the way she handled her detractors, they were less happy with the way she explained her political beliefs. In press statements and interviews, she repeatedly described herself as a "black woman and a Communist." During her first court appearance in Marin County, she insisted on acting as co-counsel because only she could speak "as a black woman and a Communist." To some Party leaders her "and" sounded as if she was apologizing for being a Party member. Privately, Party leaders questioned her thinking. Later, Mitchell denied that there was any racial rift. She said it was "only a few older members who saw everything in terms of class" who ever raised any questions.[18]

But at the time, Mitchell was far less confident. As the Party leader seemingly most in touch with the feelings of blacks, she explained the political facts of life to Communists. Blacks were supporting Davis, Mitchell observed, "because she is black, and often, contrary to what we say, not because she's a Communist." She cautioned Party leaders not to underestimate the "red-baiting taking place in the black community." She realized that this was causing a serious problem in the defense campaign. "There are people who come into the office in New York and who refuse to sit down and talk with the white people in the office." Mitchell said she could understand their feelings. She blamed white Communists for creating the cool attitude of many blacks toward the defense committee. Mitchell cited examples where whites in the Party refused to push the issue of Davis's freedom in plants and neighborhoods. She saw blacks wearing buttons, passing out literature, and circulating petitions for Davis. She asked why the whites were not doing the same. Her tongue-lashing of the Party ended with the rebuke: "There are few Party members who are willing to go out as Communists and speak on behalf of Angela's freedom." Mitchell tactfully refrained from calling their actions racist, but her meaning was clear.

James Tormey did not hesitate to say what Mitchell did not. Tormey, a white Party member, was a leader in the National Free Angela Davis Defense Committee. He bluntly asked, "Is it possible that among the many commitments our Party has, we have not given this struggle a high enough priority?" Tormey proceeded to answer his own question. The Party's National Committee, he said, often acted as if it regarded Angela's defense as a "black people's problem."

Tormey noted that nearly everyone the Party assigned to speak on the case was black, yet when it came to choosing leaders in the committees there was "a resistance to black leadership and initiative." His political eyesight was as good as Mitchell's. He also claimed to have seen few white Communists wearing "Free Angela" buttons. Tormey demanded that whites in the Party "carry the fight" against racism by becoming more aggressive in their defense of Davis.[19]

Acting fast to head off the brewing crisis, the National Committee passed the word down that the Davis defense must be given the highest priority. For the duration of the campaign, all districts would be required to submit in writing a plan of action and send weekly reports directly to the National Committee. The districts were put on notice that committee members would review their reports to insure that they were giving the defense the right "communist initiative and leadership."

It would take more than weekly reports to bring all Party members around. As the trial neared its end, Elaine Mann, identified only as "a white comrade" by *Political Affairs,* still had harsh words for her white comrades. She ticked off a list of "incidents" of racism that occurred in various local defense committees. In one case, Mann said, whites pressured a black woman to serve on the entertainment committee. The implication she drew was that "whites should do the thinking while blacks provide the singing and dancing." When a black man volunteered to scout out halls for a fund-raising party, a white blurted out, "Oh, Bob, he knows the inside and outside of bars." Mann was incensed when a white member did an "Amos n' Andy" mockery of an older black woman. Many blacks caught the drift and left the local defense committees in droves. Mann felt that the "older, experienced" Party members should do more to correct the problem.[20]

But could they? Were they too shell-shocked by the internal Party battles against "white chauvinism" in the 1930s and 1950s that had left their legacy of bitterness and division among Communists? Perhaps most Party members of that era found it too painful to protest racism within the Party, so they kept silent. Or could it have been that many of the older members themselves still had not come to grips with their own racism? Fortunately, Party leaders did not have to answer these questions. They were forgotten in the euphoria of Davis's acquittal in June 1972.

Patterson regarded the verdict as vindication of the Party's defense strategy: "The Angela Davis case is indeed history-making. It demonstrates the invincible power of black-white unity." Basking in the reflective glow of Davis's triumph, Patterson took a last whack at an old adversary: "Angela fought not as a black nationalist obsessed with a desire to put the ghettos of blacks under the control of their own bourgeoisie of color." Patterson had a much loftier, more majestic role in mind for Davis: "She wanted all segments of the population, black and white alike, freed from class exploitation."[21]

The Party had its hero and its victory. But Patterson had been through enough past struggles to know that fame can be very elusive. Without the sheen of new victories, it can swiftly dull. With the Davis acquittal, there were no new mass struggles on the immediate horizon for Communists.

Their work done, the defense committees soon disbanded. The blacks that proudly wore their "Free Angela" buttons went back to their busy lives and daily routines. They did not join the Party. Marxism remained just as enigmatic and threatening to them as before the Davis case.

Although the memories of Davis's fight receded into history, time did not wash away the suspicions that blacks held about the Communist Party. In 1986 an interviewer would still tell Davis, "Many black people have criticized you for being a member of the Communist Party." She replied, "The notion that to be a communist is to be associated with European ideas is, unfortunately, used against the interests of black people."[22] Many blacks remained stubbornly certain that Davis had it backward—that it was precisely the interests of blacks that Communists sought to use for their own ends and ultimately betrayed. Still, black Communists like Davis would hold to the faith. What the critics could not deny was that the Party had successfully mounted yet another major multi-racial campaign to save a black political activist. But it would be their last.

Notes

1. Angela Davis, *Angela Davis: An Autobiography* (New York: Random House, 1974) 78-113; Angela Moreland Jackson, "Angela Davis: What She's Rapping About," *Soul* 4 (15 December 1969): 2; *Newsweek*, 26 October 1970, 20.

2. *Newsweek*, 26 October 1970, 20-21; Angela Davis, *An Autobiography*, 158-76; Interview with Charlene Mitchell, 18 December 1989. Of the countless works on Socialism and Communism including those by Marx and Lenin, the British Marxist Maurice Cornforth perhaps gives the most concise explanation of how Communism is supposed to work in *Historical Materialism* (New York: International Publishers, 1954), 110-29. Interview with Deacon Alexander, 18 December 1989.

3. Charles E. Young to Angela Davis, 26 August 1969; Charles J. Hitch to Angela Davis, 20 September 1969; Resolution Adopted by the Board of Regents (Executive Session) 11 October 1949, reaffirmed 19 September 1969; Angela Davis to Charles E. Young, 5 September 1969, Angela Davis Defense Committee Papers, Southern California Research Library.

4. Joel Gardner, Interview with Dorothy Healey, *Tradition's Chains Have Bound Us*, vol. 3, UCLA Oral History Program, 1982, 1029, 1030, 1031; Interview with Dorothy Healey, 16 December 1989; Interview with Deacon Alexander, 16 December 1989; Interview with Emily Gibson, 22 December 1989; *The Black Panther*, 1 November 1969.

5. *Los Angeles Times*, 7 August 1970; *Los Angeles Times*, 8 August 1970; *Los Angeles Times*, 9 August 1970; *Los Angeles Times*, 14 October 1970; George Jackson, *Soledad Brother* (New York: Bantam Books, 1970) 212-21, 227-30, 230-32 and 234-36; *Newsweek*, 26 October 1970, 21.

6. A sense of Jonathan Jackson's devotion to Jackson as brother and mythic figure can be gleaned from George Jackson's letters of 25 September 1969, 28 December 1969, and 9 August 1970 reprinted in *If They Come in the Morning* (New York: The Third Press, 1971), 148-51. Interview with Deacon Alexander, 16 December 1989.

7. *Daily World*, 28 August 1970; Henry Winston, *Strategy for a Black Agenda* (New York: International Publishers, 1973), 246-53.

8. *Party Affairs* 5 (October 1971): 13-15; *Daily World*, 5 February 1971; Draft Proposal for Fund Raising Program, 1-2, ADDC Papers; Interview with Charlene Mitchell, 18 December 1989.

9. "Suggested Organizational Plan for Local United Committees to Free Angela Davis," November 1970, 1, 3; Draft Proposal for Fund Raising Campaign, 3, ADDC Papers; Interview with Deacon Alexander, 16 December 1989; Westside Angela Davis Defense Committee to Clergy, ADDC Papers; Rev. C. L. Dred to Westside Angela Davis Defense Committee, ADDC Papers.

10. *Daily World*, November 20, 1970; Cited in *Daily World*, October 23, 1970; Daily World, February 4, 1971; Interview with Dorothy Healey, December 16, 1989.

11. Anonymous interview, December 15, 1989; *Daily World*, January 9, 1971.

12. *Daily World*, October 30, 1970; Kenneth Lamont, "In Search of the Essential Angela," *West*, May 30, 1971, 27; *Peoples World*, December 5, 1970.

13. *Los Angeles Herald Dispatch*, February 25, February 18, 1971; *Daily World*, January 30, 1971; Kenneth Lamont, "In Search of the Essential Angela," 28; *Daily World*, November 7, 1970;

14. Interview with Deacon Alexander, December 16, 1989; *Amsterdam News*, October 22, 1970; *LA Herald Dispatch*, January 26, 1971; *LA Sentinel*, December 31, 1970; *Baltimore Afro-American*, November 7,

10; *Norfolk Journal and Guide*, November 21, 1970; *Jet Magazine*, January 24, 1972: *Nommo*, October 27, 1970.

15. *LA Sentinel*, November 26, 1970; *LA Herald Dispatch*, October 15, 1970.

16. *The Black Panther*, January 23, 1971; Bobby Seale, *Seize the Time*; *The Black Panther*, March, 13, 1971.

17. Joe Walker, "Angela Davis—What's On Her Mind?" *Muhammad Speaks*, January 1, 1971; *Guardian*, December 26, 1970; *Los Angeles Free Press*, March 10, March 17, 1972; Interview with Charlene Mitchell, December 18, 1989; National United Committee to Free Angela Davis and All Political Prisoners (press release), 14 March 1972, ADDC Papers.

18. *Los Angeles Times*, 6 January 1971; *If They Come in the Morning*, 209-10; Interview with Charlene Mitchell, 18 December 1989.

19. Charlene Mitchell, "Report on the Angela Davis Case," part 2, March 1971, 2-4; James Tormey, Report on the Angela Davis Case, part 1, March 1971, 4, ADDC Papers.

20. *Party Affairs* 5 (July 1971): 10; Elaine Mann, "The Fight a gainst Racism and the Angela Davis Campaign," *Political Affairs*, 51 (May, 1972), 19-20, 26.

21. William Patterson, "Some Features of the Angela Davis Case," *Political Affairs* 51 (September 1972): 25-26

22. Interview with Deacon Alexander, 16 December 1989. Even worse then failing to win new recruits, some of the black Party members lost interest and dropped out after the campaign. Some even accused whites in the Party of "patronizing" blacks. A former Che-Lumumba Club organizer recalls: "They seemed so happy to have an articulate black who was not afraid to speak. They sent me to the Soviet Union and East Germany; set up speaking engagements for me, but when I began to speak out on some things I didn't like, the attitude changed" (Interview with Emily Gibson, 23 December 1989). *Essence* 10 (August 1986): 142.

14 Faded Memories

By 1976 the warning signs were pronounced. The civil rights and Black Power movements were well on their way to becoming nostalgic remembrances in American history. Four years later, as historians were busily revising the 1960s, they dismissed the radical activism of the times as an aberration. It was easy to do. Ronald Reagan was in the White House, and young Americans had long since left the communes and headed for suburbia. They had traded in their battered VWs for BMWs, and children of the next generation had changed their college majors from sociology and political science to business administration. Individualism and self-indulgence had returned to America with a vengeance.

Despite major public employment and social service cuts under the Reagan administration, the black middle class steadily grew in numbers. This new generation of black professionals was better educated, better housed, and more economically secure than its predecessors. Its members were determined to enjoy the fruits of American prosperity. They had never been forced to sit at the rear of a bus, did not know what it was like to be refused service at a lunch counter or to be denied a hotel room. Some lived in integrated neighborhoods and sent their freshly scrubbed kids to integrated schools. Some even called themselves black conservatives and felt more at home in the GOP than in the Democratic Party.

A *Washington Post-ABC* poll in 1986 confirmed the changing mood. More than fifty percent of the 1,000 blacks surveyed said they were satisfied that racial conditions had improved. Many had never heard of Scottsboro, Angelo Herndon, or Angela Davis. They knew nothing of the struggles of the Depression years. Councils for the unemployed,

295

rent-strike committees, bonus marches, and anti-lynching campaigns had never existed for them. Unlike the black middle class of the 1930s, they would not debate the merits of Marxism or the Communist Party.

Of course, there was another side. Millions of blacks remained trapped in a vicious cycle of poverty and neglect, with crime and drug use their only escape. But they were not politically active, so policy-makers could ascribe their problems to the rigors of ghetto life and suffer no pangs of conscience about their plight.[1]

As America headed toward the twenty-first century, the Communist Party members were like athletes running a race backward—congratulating themselves for outdistancing the other runners as they watched their backs recede into the distance. But like the errant runners, Communists would still maintain their illusion that victory was in sight.

"We can roll up a powerful vote, larger than at any previous time in the sixty-year history of our Party." The speaker was not Ronald Reagan but Gus Hall. The Party's General Secretary was prepping his troops at the Party's twenty-second convention in Detroit in August 1979. Hall was going to be the Party's presidential candidate during the 1980 election. Hall's vice presidential running mate also fired up the Party faithful with visions of fresh triumphs. Angela Davis believed that "a permanent third party" could "be victorious over both" the Democrats and Republicans.[2]

Party leaders may have lost touch with political reality, but they were still full of the old fight. Hall and Winston talked bravely of uniting with Chicanos, Asians, Indians, and the "additional millions from Asia and Latin America" against capitalism. But above all, Communists still yearned for "the historic alliance of labor and the black people's movement." The years had not dimmed the Party's expectation that black workers would still lead the fight. *Political Affairs* editor Ted Bassett was even certain that black workers were poised "to exercise leadership over the black liberation movement." The National Committee drew up an ambitious "Draft Program" for the 1980s. Hall called it "People vs. Monopoly." He envisioned millions of blacks joining with women, consumers, environmentalists, and minorities in one giant movement of "resistance to corporate power."[3]

There was only one problem. "The struggle against racism," Hall announced, "has emerged as a requisite for working-class unity and people's victories." The old bugaboo was back. By the time Hall spoke, Communists had been wrestling with the issue among themselves for nearly two years.

In April 1980 the California state committee sponsored a conference on racism. Black and Latino Party members gave Party leaders a thorough bashing. They accused them of fostering segregation by forming separate black and white Party clubs. They charged that white Communists failed to take part in integrating the schools in their own neighborhoods, were reluctant to accept blacks or Latinos as leaders, and refused to fight against "white chauvinism" within the Party. White Party members were asked, "Have you ever critically examined your club life to assess if oppressed comrades felt comfortable there, or asked yourself why they don't like to attend meetings?" The dissidents blamed Party leaders for the high drop-out rate among black and Latino members.

But how could the blacks and Latinos feel comfortable in the Party, when the whites ignored their needs? Davis was upset with the way white members of the "party clubs" in Oakland and Los Angeles treated blacks. "They pay no attention to them—just as if they don't exist." According to Davis, they had been doing this for fifteen or twenty years. She stopped short, however, of blaming her leaders. Davis was satisfied that they were doing everything in their power to combat the racism of the white Party members. "Our Party has done the best of any organization, not only in fighting racism as it is expressed in society but in purging the organization itself of racism."[4]

Affirmative action was another obstacle that sent Party leaders back to the drawing board. While they issued ringing declarations in support of affirmative action, they knew that most white workers were opposed to it. They had to figure out how to convince white Party members, many of whom belonged to trade unions and were sensitive to the feelings of white workers, to support affirmative action.

In 1981 the National Committee decided to conduct racial sensitivity training for white Party members. Communist leaders wanted them to be "clear themselves on the centrality of black equality." In his keynote address, Winston pointed to two problems. The whites, he said, were not actively trying to change the racist attitudes of white workers. He urged them to challenge any "racist jokes, remarks, and acts" of the whites. What disturbed the Party chairman even more was that the whites were not battling hard enough to get more blacks involved in the activities of their union locals.[5]

Meanwhile, Hall was preparing to fight a two-front battle. At the same time that he exhorted Party members to "remake" America, he was trying to convince them to "remake" themselves. Hall must have wondered if there would ever come a time when the Party would not have to fight new battles against "white chauvinism." within its ranks. Hall trudged ahead and demanded that Party members "burn out" the "racism and chauvinism in our own ranks." Winston was even more anxious to set the fires. He figured the best way to cleanse the Party of the racist taint was to bring in fresh bodies. Davis and Hall were appointed to a committee to "initiate" a three-month special recruiting drive.

Winston had good reason to be irked at racial attitudes within the Party. Some of the actions were blatant. *Political Affairs* writer Bruce Kimmell said, "It is common for the Party to give Afro-Americans manual tasks that nobody wants to do." He was disturbed that white Party members would interrupt blacks when they were speaking or talk or go to the bathroom. He noted that blacks were "pounced on" for making the least little mistake while mistakes made by whites were overlooked. If the Party was really serious about "purging" racism from within, it would take more than once-a-year "soul-searching" seminars.[6]

Charlene Mitchell had another concern. She was hopeful that "Communists could find the way that will help bring labor together with the black people's movement." She thought that Jesse Jackson's Rainbow Coalition might be a good place to start. It was a short-lived hope. Mitchell was soon criticizing Jackson for not making it an "imperative" of his 1984 presidential campaign to organize white workers. She apparently ignored the polls that showed that blue-collar whites were the backbone of the "Reagan revolution." They gave him overwhelming support during his election landslide victory over Democratic candidate Walter Mondale in 1984. Jackson could do little to counter this.

Communists diligently searched for someone to blame for the failure of white workers to respond to the "progressive movement." They quickly put the finger on Reagan and the corporations. According to James Steel, big business and the Reagan administration colluded "to conceal the self-interest of white workers in opposing racism."

To avoid criticizing white labor for opposing affirmative action, Steele stretched the bounds of credulity: "There is widespread evidence that white workers have not only accepted affirmative action but are willing to fight for it." He made no mention of the hundreds of lawsuits and legal test cases brought by contractor associations, craft unions, police, fire and public employee groups throughout the country to eliminate affirmative action programs. To admit the truth would have required that Party leaders face the painful reality that most white workers were not prepared to give up their status, security, or union seniority rights for the sake of class unity. It was much simpler for Communists to repeat their standard position of black and white unity and brand as a nationalist any black who argued "that white workers benefit from racism."[7]

Close of an Era

No matter how grim the news under Reagan, Hall found ways to make events seem cheery. At the Party's twenty-fourth convention in 1987 he claimed that the people "were winning." The General Secretary assured the delegates that racism was on the decline and that prospects were never better for blacks and labor to join forces.

As the 1988 election approached, Michael Zagarell, *Political Affairs* editor, got out his political crystal ball and predicted a bright future. He argued that it was "black-labor unity" that put black mayors in office in seventeen cities across the country. Political analysts might ponder over what precinct tally sheets he read.

It was true that white support was crucial for the election triumphs of Harold Washington in Chicago in 1985 and Wilson Goode in Philadelphia in 1988. But the white voters who supported both men were not blue-collar workers but rather reform-minded white professionals and business leaders.

Zagarell's political myopia was really the Party's way of reminding blacks that they needed alliances with whites to achieve any political or economic gains. Jarvis Tyner was brutally direct: "Black people constitute a racial minority but they are a strategic and inseparable part of the working-class majority." Any thought of "Go it alone-ism, black-only strategies," he declared, "have never won majority acceptance among Afro-Americans because they don't correspond to the real interests of the oppressed."

With Reagan's departure from the White House in 1989, Party leaders were ecstatic. Hall spoke as if all it would take was just a little nudge to make "unity between labor and the Afro-American people" a reality.[8] A *People's World* editorial put a favorable spin on George Bush's presidential victory in 1988. The paper contended that the "labor-Afro-American alliance" put enough Democrats in Congress to prevent Bush from continuing the harsh social policies of Reagan. The editors fully expected that black and white workers would continue to gain strength during the Bush years.

299

But even as pro-democracy movements gained strength in Eastern Europe and the Soviet Union, Party leaders tried to maintain the political status quo. In 1990 a prominent Party leader still insisted "that the American Communist Party didn't go out of business in the 1940s and it will remain an important institution in the 1990s among blacks."[9]

It was wishful thinking. A year later, the Soviet Union would dissolve, and democratic governments would replace Communist regimes in Eastern Europe. By the end of 1991, the American Communist Party had broken up into competing factions, with the Old Guard still refusing to concede that times had changed and democracy had won out. Perhaps with the passage of even more time, American Communists will honestly confront their racial past—both the bad and the good. If they do, what will they find?

During the last century, many Communist Party members believed deeply in racial equality. Their campaigns against segregation, political repression, and economic equality resulted in many landmark decisions that advanced the cause of civil rights and racial justice in America. But despite their efforts, black leaders have repeatedly asked Communist leaders two questions. First, did they fight for black freedom because they sincerely believed in it? Second, given the volatile mix of racism and anti-communism in America, could blacks afford to be Red, too?

DuBois, Randolph, Garvey, King, Wilkins, Malcolm X, Carmichael, the Panthers and the Black Muslims have not been satisfied with the answers Communists have given to either question. But how could they be? With the exception of one short moment in American history—the Depression years—Marxists have never had the type of mass following that would allow them to offer blacks an ironclad assurance of their sincerity or their security.

Thus, while blacks could at times throughout recent history applaud them for their civil rights efforts, and even rally behind black Communist leaders when they were under fire, they could never really embrace the Reds. It has been that way because wherever the two groups have met, there has been a clash of race and ideology that more than a century of struggle has not resolved—and now, perhaps, never will.

Notes

1. Political analysts are well into presenting their pros and cons on the Reagan years, see Hodding Carter, *The Reagan Years* (New York George Braziller, Inc., 1988); Gary Wills, *Reagan's America* (New York:

Doubleday, 1987); Gary Gerstle, "The Changing Shape of Power: A Realignment of Public Policy," in Steve Fraser, ed., *The Rise and Fall of the New Deal Order, 1930-1980* (Princeton New Jersey: Princeton University Press, 1988); *Washington Post* Poll cited in *Los Angeles Times*, 19 January 1986.

2. Gus Hall, "The Communist Campaign," *Party Organizer* 13 (December 1979): 3.

3. Ted Bassett, "Draft Resolution on Afro-American Liberation," *Party Organizer* 13 (July 1979): 38; "Draft Program CPUSA: The People vs. Monopoly," *Political Affairs* 59 (April 1980): 33.

4. Gus Hall, "Keynote Report to the Second Extraordinary Conference of the Communist Party, USA," Milwaukee, Wisconsin, 23-25 April 1982, 5, CP File—1982; "Report Given to the Conference on Racism," 20 April 1980, 8, 9, CP File—1980, Southern California Research Library; Angela Davis, "It's Happening All Over the Country," *Party Organizer* 15 (July 1981): 25; *World Magazine*, 24 September 1981.

5. *Report form the Black Liberation Seminar*, (Communist Party of California), held 25-26 April 1981, 43, CP File—1981.

6. Gus Hall, *1981—Mandate For Fightback* (pamphlet), New York, New Outlook Publishers, January 1981, 27, CP File—1981; Hall, "Mastering the Interconnections of the Struggle Against Racism," *Political Affairs* 59 (November 1980): 17; Henry Winston, "Party Building," *Party Organizer*, 14 (April 1981): 10; Bruce Kimmel, "For Sensitivity in Black-White Relations," *Political Affairs* 62 (February 1983): 14.

7. *Black Liberation Journal* 8 (Summer 1984): 10 ; Charlene Mitchell, "The Sharpened Edge of Racism," *Political Affairs* 64 (August 1985): 21; James Steel, "Affirmative Action," *Political Affairs* 67 (February 1988): 33. David W. Bishop provides a sound analysis of the racial impact of the Supreme Court cases in "The Affirmative Action Cases: Bakke, Weber, and Fullslone," *Journal of Negro History* 67 (Fall 1982): 229-45.

8. "Black Representation, the Labor Movement and the 1988 Elections," *Political Affairs* 67 (April 1988): 26-27; Jarvis Tyner, "Prospects for Afro-Americans," *Political Affairs* 67 (April 1988): 13; *Political Affairs* 67 (July 1988): 10-11.

9. *Peoples Daily World*, 10 November 1988; Interview with Charlene Mitchell, 18 December 1989.

Bibliography

Manuscript Collections

Angela Davis Defense Committee Papers, Southern California Research Library, Los Angeles.

A. Phillip Randolph Papers, Southern California Research Library, Los Angeles.

Bill Taylor Papers, Southern California Research Library, Los Angeles.

Charlotta Bass Papers, Southern California Research Library, Los Angeles.

Civil Rights Congress Papers, Southern California Research Library, Los Angeles.

Countee Cullen Papers, Amistad Research Center, Tulane University.

Cyril Briggs Papers, Southern California Research Library, Los Angeles.

Dorothy Healey Papers, California State University, Long Beach.

Kelly Miller Papers, Library of Congress, Washington, D.C.

Langston Hughes Papers, Schomberg Research Library, New York.

Mary Church Terrell Papers, Library of Congress, Washington, D.C.

NAACP Papers, Library of Congress, Washington, D.C.

National Negro Congress Papers, Schomberg Research Library, New York.

National Urban League Papers, Library of Congress, Washington, D.C.

Pettis Perry Papers, Southern California Research Library, Los Angeles.

Ralphe Bunch Papers, University Research Library, UCLA, Los Angeles.

Robert Minor Papers, Columbia University.

Socialist Workers Party Papers, Southern California Research Library, Los Angeles.

W. E. B. DuBois Papers, University of Massachusetts, Amherst.

Abbreviations of Magazines and Newspapers

DW   *Daily World*
DW   *Daily Worker*
IPC   *International Press Correspondence*
JNH   *Journal of Negro History*
JNE   *Journal of Negro Education*
NYT   *New York Times*
LAT   *Los Angeles Times*
MS   *Muhammad Speaks*
PW   *Peoples World*
PA   *Political Affairs*

Abbreviations of Manuscript Collections

CPF   Communist Party File—1949, 1950, 1951, 1952, 1953, 1957, 1960, 1965, 1966, 1967, 1968, 1969, 1980, 1981, 1982
CPCF Communist Party Campaign Files
NNC   National Negro Congress Papers

Abbreviations for Manuscript Collections in Libraries

ARC   Amistad Research Center, Tulane University
LC   Library of Congress
SCL   Southern California Research Library
UMass University of Massachusetts
CU   Columbia University

Abbreviations for Microfilm Files

FBI Racial File—Malcolm X
FBI Racial File—Martin Luther King
FBI Racial File—Paul Robeson

Interviews

Charles Morgan, 6 December 1989
Donald Wheeldin, 2 December 1989
Dorothy Healey, 16 December 1989
Lester Rodney, 5 December 1989
Louise Thompson Patterson, 10 December 1989
Mariam Sherman, 6 December 1989
O'Neil Cannon, 4 December 1989
Charlene Mitchell, 18 December 1989
Deacon Alexander, 16 December 1989
Emily Gibson, 22 December 1989
Carlton Moss, 12 December 1989

Correspondence

John Henrik Clarke to author, 24 January 1990
Milt Ahlerich to author, 22 December 1989
William L. Patterson, 8 July 1971

Unpublished Manuscripts

Briggs, Cyril. On the Negro Question. Dorothy Healey Papers, California State University, Long Beach.
Geschwender, James A. Black Marxist-Leninist Worker Movements: Class or National Consciousness? Copy in author's possession.
Hathaway, Clarence. The American Negro and the Churches. Copy at the Southern California Research Library, Los Angeles.
Horne, Gerald. Black Liberation/Red Scare: Benjamin Davis and the Communist Party. Copy in author's possession.
Moore, Carlos. Cuba: The Untold Story. Copy in author's possession.
Murphy, George B. Negro Veterans on the March. Copy in author's possession.
Pettis, Perry. Political Biography. Pettis Perry Papers, Southern California Research Library, Los Angeles.

Journals and Periodicals

Black Liberation Journal
James Ford Newsletter

Harlem Quarterly
Journal of American History
Journal of Negro Education
Journal of Negro History
Negro History Bulletin
Negro Affairs
Phylon
World Revolution
Workers Council

Newspapers and Magazines

1919-1945

Afro-American
Amsterdam News
Blackman
California Eagle
Crisis
Chicago Defender
Communist
Daily Worker
Harlem Liberator
Labor Defender
Negro Liberator
New Masses
New York Age
New York Herald
New York Times
Opportunity
Party Organizer
Phylon
Pittsburgh Courier

1945-1960

Black Dispatch
Daily Worker
Freedom
Jet
Masses & Mainstream

National Guardian
New Leader
Peoples World
San Diego Lighthouse
Washington Afro-American

1960-1970

Black America
Black Panther Newspaper
Crusader
Guardian
International Socialist Review
Monthly Review
Muhammad Speaks
Newsweek
Political Affairs
Progressive Labor
Ramparts
World

1970-1990

Amsterdam News
Baltimore Afro-American
Black Panther
Daily World
Essence
Los Angeles Free Press
Liberated Guardian
Los Angeles Herald Dispatch
Los Angeles Sentinel
Los Angeles Times
Liberated Guardian
Muhammad Speaks
Newsweek
New York Herald Tribune
Nommo
Norfolk Journal
Party Affairs
Party Organizer
Political Affairs

Books

Allen, James S. *The Negro Question in the United States*. New York: International Publishers, 1936.

Allen, James S. and James W. Ford. *The Negroes in a Soviet America*. New York: Workers Library Publishers, 1935.

Allen, Robert L. *Black Awakening in Capitalist America*. New York: Doubleday, 1969.

Aptheker, Herbert. *A Documentary History of the Negro People in the United States*. Seacaucus, New Jersey: Citadel Press, 1973.

Agarwal, N. N. *Soviet Nationalities Policy*. Agra, India: Sri Ram Mehra & Co., 1969.

Anderson, Jervis. *A. Phillip Randolph*. New York: Harcourt Brace Jovanovich, Inc. 1972.

Barbour, Floyd, B., ed. *The Black Power Revolt*. Boston: Porter Sargeant, 1968.

Bell, Howard. *A Survey of the Negro Convention Movement, 1830-1861*. New York: Arno Press, 1969.

Berry, Mary Francis. *Black Resistance/White Law*. New York: Merdeity Corp., 1971.

Bimba, Anthony. *History of the American Working Class*. New York: International Publishers, 1927.

Bloor, Ella Reeve. *We Are Many*. New York: International Publishers, 1940.

Browder, Earl. *Communism in the United States*. New York: International Publishers, 1935.

Bunche, Ralph. *The Political Status of the Negro in the Age of FDR*. Reprint. Chicago: University of Chicago Press, 1973.

Calverton, V. F., ed. *Anthology of American Negro Literature*. New York: The Modern Library, 1929.

Carmichael, Stokely, and Charles V. Hamilton. *Black Power: The Politics of Liberation*. New York: Random House, 1967.

Carson, Clayborne. *In Struggle: SNCC and the Black Awakening of the 1960s*. Cambridge: Harvard University Press, 1981.

Carter, Dan T. *Scottsboro: A Tragedy of the American South*. New York: Oxford University Press, 1971.

Carter, Hodding. *The Reagan Years*. New York: George Braziller, Inc., 1988.

Caute, David. *The Great Fear*. New York: Simon and Schuster, 1976.

Cayton, Horace R. and Sinclair Drake. *Black Metropolis.* Vol. 2. New York: Harper & Row, 1967.

Charney, George. *A Long Journey.* New York: Quadrangle, 1968.

Claudin, Fernando. *The Communist Movement, From Comintern to Cominform.* New York: Monthly Review Press, 1976.

Cohen, Robert. *Black Crusader.* New York: Lyle Stuart, 1972.

Communist Party Soviet Union. *The History of the Communist Party of the Soviet Union.* New York: International Publishers, 1939.

Cook, Fred J. *The Nightmare Decade: The Life and Times of Senator Joe McCarthy.* New York: Random House, 1976.

Cooper, Wayne F. *Claude McKay.* Baton Rouge: Louisiana University Press, 1987.

Cornforth, Maurice. *Historical Materialism.* New York: International Publishers, 1954.

Cruse, Harold. *The Crisis of the Negro Intellectual.* New York: William Morrow, 1967.

Davis, Angela. *Angela Davis: An Autobiography.* New York: Random House, 1974.

Davis, Benjamin. *Communist Council from Harlem.* New York: International Publishers, 1969.

DeReid, Ira. *Negro Membership in American Labor Unions.* New York: Alexander Press, 1930.

Deutscher, Isaac. *Ironies of History.* Berkeley: Ramparts Press, 1971.

Dilling, Elizabeth. *The Red Network.* Chicago: Elizabeth Dilling, 1934.

Dimitrov, George. *For Unity of the Working Class against Fascism 1935.* Reprint. Sofia, Bulgaria: Sofia Press, 1969.

Draper, Theodore. *The Roots of American Communism.* New York: Viking Press, 1957.

———. *American Communism and Soviet Russia.* New York: Viking Press, 1960.

Duberman, Martin. *Paul Robeson.* New York: Alfred A. Knopf, 1989.

DuBois, W.E.B. *The Autobiography of W.E.B. DuBois.* New York: International Publishers, 1968.

———. *In Battle for Peace.* New York: Masses & Mainstream, 1952.

Essien-Udom, E. U. *Black Nationalism.* Chicago: The University of Chicago Press, 1962.

Foner, Phillip. *Organized Labor and the Black Worker, 1619-1973.* New York: Praeger, 1974.

———. *The Black Panthers Speak.* Philadelphia: J.B. Lippencott, 1970.

Ford, James. W. *The Negro and the Democratic Front*. New York: International Publishers, 1938.

Forman, James. *The Making of Black Revolutionaries*. New York: The Macmillan Co., 1972.

Foster, William Z. *History of the Communist Party of the United States*. New York: International Publishers, 1951.

Fox, Stephen R. *The Guardian of Boston*. New York: Atheneum, 1971.

Franklin, John Hope. *From Slavery to Freedom*. New York: Vintage Books, 1969.

Garrow, David. *Bearing the Cross*. New York: William Morrow, 1967.

———. *The FBI and Martin Luther King, Jr*. New York: Penguin Books, 1983.

Glazer, Nathan. *The Social Basis of American Communism*. New York: Harcourt, Brace & World, 1961.

Gordon, Eugene and Cyril Briggs. *The Position of Negro Women*. New York: Workers Library, 1935.

Gosnell, Harold F. *Negro Politicians: The Rise of Negro Politics in Chicago*. Chicago: University of Chicago Press, 1935.

Hamilton, Charles V. *Adam Clayton Powell, Jr*. New York: Atheneum, 1991.

Harris, Abram L. and Sterling D. Spero. *The Black Worker*. New York: Atheneum, 1968.

Harris, William H. *Keeping the Faith*. Urbana: University of Illinois Press, 1991.

Haley, Alex. *The Autobiography of Malcolm X*. New York: Grove Press, 1962.

Haywood, Harry. *Black Bolshevik*. Chicago: Liberator Press, 1978.

Healey, Dorothy. *Tradition's Chains that Bind Us*. Los Angeles: UCLA Oral History Program, 1982.

Herndon, Angelo. *Let Me Live*. New York: Arno Press, 1969.

Hill, Robert, ed. *Marcus Garvey and the UNIA Papers*. Vol. 2. Berkeley: University of California Press, 1983.

Hooker, James R. *Black Revolutionary*. London: Praeger, 1967.

Horowitz, ed. *Containment and Revolution*. Boston: Beacon Press, 1967.

Hughes, Langston. *I Wonder as I Wander*. New York: Hill & Wang. 1964.

Jackson, George. *Soledad Brother*. New York: Bantam Books, 1970.

Jacobson, Julius, ed. *The Negro and the American Labor Movement*. New York: Anchor Books, 1968.

Johnson, Manning. *Color, Communism and Common Sense.* New York: Alliance Inc., 1958.

Kellogg, Charles F. *NAACP, A History of the National Association for the Advancement of Colored People 1, 1909-1920.* Baltimore: Johns Hopkins Press, 1967.

Kennan, George F. *Russia and the West under Lenin and Stalin.* Boston: Little, Brown & Company, 1960.

King, Martin Luther, Jr. *Where Do We Go from Here: Chaos or Community?* Boston: Beacon Press, 1968.

Kornweibel, Theodore, Jr. *No Crystal Stair.* Westport, Connecticut: Greenwood Press, 1975.

Kluger, Richard. *Simple Justice.* New York: Alfred A. Knopf, 1976.

Kirby, John B. *Black Americans in the Roosevelt Era.* Knoxville: University of Tennessee Press, 1980

Lecky Robert S. and Elliot H. Wright. *Black Manifesto.* New York: Sheed and Wright, 1969.

Lincoln, C. Eric. *The Black Muslims in America.* Boston: Beacon Press, 1963.

Lightfoot, Claude. *Ghetto Rebellion to Black Liberation.* New York: International Publishers, 1967.

———. *Negro Freedom.* New York: New Currents Publishers, 1964

Locke, Alain, ed. *The New Negro: An Interpretation.* New York: Albert and Charles Boni, 1925.

Logan, Rayford. *Howard University: The First Hundred Years, 1867-1967.* New York: New York University Press, 1969.

Logan, Rayford, ed. *What the Negro Wants.* Chapel Hill: University of North Carolina Press, 1944.

Malcolm X. *The Autobiography of Malcolm X.* New York: Grove Press, 1964.

———. *By Any Means Necessary.* New York: Pathfinder Press, 1970.

Mann, Peggy. *Ralphe Bunche: U.N. Peacemaker.* New York: Coward, McCann & Geoghegan, Inc., 1975.

Markosch, F. *The Negroes in the United States of North America.* Berlin: MOPR-Verlag, 1930.

Martin, Tony. *Race First.* Dover, Massachusetts: The Majority Press, 1976.

Marine, Gene. *The Black Panthers.* New York: New American Library, 1969.

McKay, Claude. *Harlem: Negro Metropolis.* New York: Harcourt Brace and Jovanovich, 1968.

311

————. *A Long Way from Home*. New York: Lee Furman, 1937.

Myrdal, Gunnar. *An American Dilemma*. New York: Harper & Bros., 1944.

Muhammad, Elijah. *Message to the Blackman*. Chicago: Muhammad Mosque of Islam No. 2, 1965.

NAACP. *A Generation of Lynching in the United States, 1921-1946*. New York: NAACP, 1946.

Nahaylo, Bohdan and Victor Swoboda. *Soviet Disunion*. New York: The Free Press, 1989.

Naison, Mark. *Communists in Harlem During the Depression*. New York: Grove Press, 1984.

Ottley, Roi. *New World A Coming*. Boston: Houghton Mifflin Company, 1943.

———. *Lonely Warrior*. Chicago: Henry Regnery Company, 1955.

Padmore, George. *Pan-Africanism or Communism*. New York: Doubleday & Company, 1971.

Parris, Guichard P. and Lester Brooks. *Blacks in the City: A History of the National Urban League*. Boston: Little Brown & Co., 1971.

Patterson, William. *The Man Who Cried Genocide*. New York: International Publishers, 1971.

President's Committe on Civil Rights. *To Secure These Rights*. New York: Simon and Schuster, 1947.

Powell, Adam Clayton, Jr. *Marching Blacks*. New York: Dial Press, 1945.

Powers, William Gid. *Secrecy and Power: The Life of J. Edgar Hoover*. New York: Free Press, 1987.

Rampersad, Arnold. *The Life of Langston Hughes*. Vol. 1. New York: Oxford University Press, 1986

———. *The Life of Langston Hughes*. Vol. 2. New York: Oxford University Press, 1988.

———. *The Art and Imagination of W. E. B. DuBois*. New York: Schocken Books, 1990.

Record, Wilson. *Race and Radicalism*. Ithaca: Cornell University Press, 1964.

———. *The Negro and the Communist Party*. New York: Atheneum, 1971.

Report of the National Advisory Commission on Civil Disorders. New York: Bantam Books, 1968.

Roggin, Michael Paul. *The Intellectuals and McCarthy: The Radical Specter*. Cambridge: M.I.T. Press, 1967.

Schlessinger, Arthur M., Jr. *The Politics of Upheaval*. Boston: Houghton Mifflin Company, 1960.

Schuyler, George. *Black and Conservative*. New Rochelle, New York: Arlington House, 1966.

Seale, Bobby. *Seize the Time: The Story of the Black Panther Party and Huey Newton*. New York: Random House, 1970.

Sitkoff, Harvey. *A New Deal for Blacks*. New York: Oxford University Press, 1978.

Smith, Dennis Mack. *Mussolini's Roman Empire*. New York: Viking Press, 1976.

Sullivan, William. *The Bureau, My 30 Years in Hoover's FBI*. New York: W.W. Norton, 1979.

Webb, Constance. *Richard Wright*. New York: G.P. Putnam's Sons, 1968.

Wesley, Charles. *Negro Labor in the United States*. New York: Vanguard Press, 1927.

White, Walter. *A Man Called White*. New York: Viking Press, 1948.

Whitney, R. M. *Reds in America*. New York: Beckwith Press, 1924.

Wills, Gary. *Reagan's America*. New York: Doubleday, 1987.

Winston, Henry. *Strategy for a Black Agenda*. New York: International Publishers, 1973.

Wolter, Raymond. *Negroes and the Great Depression*. Westport, Connecticut: Greenwood Press, 1970.

Williams, Robert. *Negroes with Guns*. New York: Marzani & Munsell, 1962.

Wright, Richard. *Native Son*. New York: Harper & Bros., 1940.

———. *American Hunger*. Reprint. New York: Harper & Row, 1977.

Articles

Aptheker, Herbert. "Whose Dilemma." *New Masses* 52 (23 July 1946): 10-15.

———. "Consciousness of Negro Nationality: An Historical Survey." *Political Affairs* 28 (June 1949): 92-96.

Allen, James. "The Communist Way Out." *Crisis* 42 (May 1935): 140-54.

Bassett, Theodore. "The Third National Negro Congress." *The Communist* 19 (June 1940): 540-48.

———. "Slogan of Self-Determination Unwarranted." *Political Affairs* 48 (March 1969): 39-42.

Berry, Abner. "A Step toward Negro Liberation." *The Communist* 16 (October 1937): 960-69.

Bishop, David. "The Affirmative Action Cases: Bakke, Weber and Fullslone." *Journal of Negro History* 67 (Fall 1982): 229-45.

Blake, George. "The Party in Harlem." *Party Organizer* 11 (June 1938): 14-18.

Blauner, Robert. "Whitewash over Watts." *Transaction* 3 (March-April 1966): 2-9.

Bloice, Carl. "Status of Black Liberation." *Political Affairs* 47 (February 1968): 69-74.

Browne, Robert S. "The Case for Black Separatism." *Ramparts* 6 (December 1967): 5054.

Browder, Earl. "Tasks of Our Party." *The Communist* 12 (March 1933): 235-45.

Briggs, Cyril. "American Neo-Colonialism." *Liberator* 7 (January 1967): 15-18.

Bunche, Ralph. "A Critical Analysis of the Tactics and Programs of Minority Groups." *Journal of Negro Education* 4 (July 1935): 310-15.

———. "Black Capitalists." *New Masses* 17 (10 November 1936): 19-25.

———. "Triumph? or Fiasco?" *Race* 1 (Summer 1936): 90-99.

Carmichael. Stokely. "Pan-Africanism—Land and Power." *Black Scholar* 1 (November 1969): 10-20.

———. "Toward Black Liberation." *Massachusetts Review* 7 (Autumn 1966): 639-51.

———. "We Are All Africans." *Black Scholar* 2 (May 1970): 15-19.

Clarke, John Henrik. "The Early Years of Adam Clayton Powell." *Freedomways* 7 (Summer 1967): 199-211.

Cleage, Albert, Jr. "The Malcolm X Myth." *Liberator* 6 (June 1967): 4-7.

Davis, Angela. "It's Happening All Over the Country." *Party Organizer* 15 (July 1981): 23-26.

Davis, Benjamin. "Why I Am a Communist." *Phylon* 8 (June 1947): 105-20.

Davis, John P. "A Black Inventory of the New Deal." *Crisis* 42 (May 1935): 141-42.

Drake, St. Clair. "Communism and Peace Movements." *Crisis* 43 (February 1936): 40-47.

Dubois, Shirley Graham. "Why was DuBois Fired?" *Masses and Mainstream* 1 (November 1948): 19-21.

Eisenberg, Bernard. "Only for the Bourgeois? James Weldon Johnson and the NAACP, 1916-1930." *Phylon* 60 (June 1982): 114-25.

Fleming, Horace. "Forge Ties to Negro People through a Mass Policy." *Negro Affairs Quarterly* 1 (Spring 1953): 3-7.

Frazier, E. Franklin. "Some effects of the Depression on the Negro in Northern Cities." *Science and Society* 2 (Fall 1938): 490-500.

Finkle, Lee. "The Conservative Aims of Militant Rhetoric: Black Protest during World War II." *Journal of American History* 40 (December 1973): 690-705.

Ford, James. "The United Front in the Field of Negro Work." *The Communist* 14 (February 1935): 162-71.

———. "The Negro People and the Elections." *The Communist* 16 (January 1937): 70-75.

———. "Development of Work in the Harlem Section." *The Communist* 14 (April 1935): 312-25.

———. "Build the National Negro Congress." *The Communist* 15 (June 1936): 550-58.

———. "Political Highlights of the National Negro Congress." *The Communist* 15 (May 1936): 458-64.

Foster, William Z. "On the Expulsion of Browder." *Political Affairs* 25 (April 1946): 339-48.

———. "One Year of Struggle against Browderism." *Political Affairs* (September 1946): 771-77.

———. "Left Sectarianism in the Fight for Negro Rights and against White Chauvinism." *Political Affairs* 32 (July 1953): 22-26.

Frazier, E. Franklin. "Some Effects of the Depression on the Negro in Northern Cities." *Science and Society* 2 (Fall 1938): 491-92

Gannett, Betty. "The Stench of Racism." *Political Affairs* 47 (February 1968): 60-65.

Gold, Mike. "At Last, a Negro Theater?" *New Masses* 18 (10 March 1936): 15-20.

———. "William L. Patterson: Militant Leader." *Masses and Mainstream* 4 (February 1951): 36-43.

Granger, Lester. "The Negro—Friend or Foe of Organized Labor?" *Opportunity* 13 (May 1935): 142-44.

Hall, Gus. "The United States in Today's World." *Political Affairs* 41 (February 1961): 36-40.

———. "New Stage of Struggle." *Political Affairs* 47 (February 1968): 25-29.

Harris, Abram L. "Negro Labor's Quarrel with White Workingmen." *Current History* 21 (September 1926): 900-10.

———. "The Negro and Economic Radicalism." *Modern Quarterly* 2 February 1925): 195-211.

———. "Lenin Casts His Shadow upon Africa." *Crisis* 31 (April 1926): 265-75.

Haywood, Harry, "The Leninist Position on the Negro Question." *The Communist* 12 (September 1933): 885-97.

———. "Sectarian Purism Blacks Fight against Chauvinism." *Negro Affairs Quarterly* 1 (Spring 1953): 8-10.

Henderson, Samuel T. "White Chauvinism and Negro Bourgeois Nationalism." *Political Affairs* 32 (June 1953): 50-55.

Hill, T. Arnold. "Communism." *Opportunity* 8 (September 1930): 275-79

———. "The Plight of the Industrial Workers." *Journal of Negro Education* 5 (January 1936): 44-47.

———. "Building New Roads." *Opportunity* 12 (December 1934): 372-77.

Hines, Linda O. "White Mythology and Black Duality." *Journal of Negro History* 62 (April 1977): 170-80.

Jackson, Angela Moreland. "Angela Davis: What She's Rapping About." *Soul* 4 (15 December 1969): 2-5.

Jackson, James. "The Meaning of Black Power." *Political Affairs* 45 (September 1966): 3-8.

———. "National Pride Not Nationalism." *Political Affairs* 46 (May 1967): 42-45.

———. "Separatism—A Bourgeois Nationalist Trap." *Political Affairs* 48 (March 1969): 34-38.

James, C. L. R. "George Padmore." *Radical America* 2 (July-August 1968): 18-29.

Jefferson, Don. "On the Fight against White Chauvinism." *Political Affairs* 32 (June 1953): 28-32.

Kimmel, Bruce. "For Sensitivity in Black-White Relations." *Political Affairs* 62 (February 1983): 10-20.

Kofsky, Frank. "Malcolm X." *Monthly Review* 18 (September 966): 47-53.

Lamont, Kenneth. "In Search of the Essential Angela." *West* (30 May 1971): 26-29.

Lightfoot, Claude. "Negro Nationalism and the Black Muslims." *Political Affairs* 41 (July 1962): 3-28.

———. "On the Negro Question in the United States." *Political Affairs* 40 (April 1960): 50-57.

———. "The Negro Liberation Movement Today." *Political Affairs* 41 (February 1961): 60-68.

———. "Negro Nationalism and the Black Muslims." *Political Affairs* 41 (July 1942): 4-20.

———. "The Right of Black America to Create a Nation." *Political Affairs* 47 (November 1968): 4-10.

Lumer, Hyman. "Notes of the Month." *Political Affairs* 40 (April 1960): 38-41.

Mann, Elaine. The Fight against Racism in the Angela Davis Campaign." *Political Affairs* 51 (May 1972): 13-27.

Marks, Carol. "Black Workers and the Great Migration North." *Phylon* 46 (June 1985): 150-56.

Martin, Charles H. "The International Labor Defense and Black America." *Labor History* 26 (Spring 1985): 170-84.

———. "Communists and Blacks: The ILD and the Angelo Herndon Case." *Journal of Negro History* 64 (Spring 1979): 128-40.

Miller, Kelly. "Should Black Turn Red?" *Opportunity* 11 (November 1933): 325-30.

———. "The Negro as a Workingman." *American Mercury* 10 (November 1925): 310-17.

Miller, Loren. "The Negro Middle Class." *New Masses* 18 (7 April 1936): 19-22.

———. "One Way Out—Communism." *Opportunity* 12 (July 1934): 210-18.

Minor, Robert. "The Negro and His Judases." *The Communist* 10 (July 1931): 625-34.

Moon, Henry Lee. "A Negro Looks at Soviet Russia." *The Nation* 138 (28 February 1934): 240-47.

Murray Hugh T. "The NAACP versus the Communist Party: The Scottsboro Rape Cases, 1931-1932." *Phylon* 28 (Third Quarter 1967): 276-87.

Naison, Mark. "Harlem Communists and the Politics of Black Protest." *Marxist Perspectives* 1 (Fall 1978): 20-45.

Oberschall, Anthony. "The Los Angeles Riot of August 1965." *Social Problems,* 12-17.

Olson, James S. "Organized Black Leadership and Industrial Unionism: The Racial Response, 1936-1945." *Labor History* 10 (Summer 1969): 475-86.

Padmore, George. "The Bankruptcy of Negro Leadership." *Negro Worker* 1 (December 1931): 2-11.

Painter, Neal and Hosea Hudson. "Hosea Hudson." *Radical America* 11 (July-August 1977): 2-11.

Patterson, William L. "Are Negroes Winning Their Fight for Civil Rights?" *Harlem Quarterly* 1 (Winter 1949-50): 23-24.

———. "The Black Panther Party." *Political Affairs* 49 (November 1969): 10-16.

———. "Some Features of the Angela Davis Campaign." *Political Affairs* 51 (May 1972): 18-27.

Perry, Pettis. "Destroy the Virus of White Chauvinism." *Political Affairs* 28 (June 1949): 1-13.

Randolph, A. Phillip. "The Communists and the Negro." *The Black Worker* (July 1942): 3-7.

———. "Communists: A Menace to Black America." *The Black Worker* (November 1945): 3-6.

Robeson, Paul. "The Power of Negro Action." *Political Affairs* 46 (August 1967): 30-36.

Rodgers, Raymond and Jimmie N. Rogers. "Evolution of the Attitude of Malcolm X Toward Whites." *Phylon* 44 (June 1983): 110-18.

Rosenzweig, Roy. "Organizing the Unemployed, 1929-1933." *Radical America* 10 (July-August 1976): 40-51.

Ryan, Eleanor. "Toward a National Negro Congress." *New Masses* 4 (June 4 1935): 14-16.

Sanford, Max. "We Are at War with White America." *Black America* (Fall 1964): 10-13.

Spellman, A. B. "The Legacy of Malcolm X." *Liberator* 4 (June 1965): 11-14.

Sykes, Odell. "The New Left Acceptance of Responsibility." *Liberator* 4 (July 1965): 20-23.

Thomas, Jay. "Negro-White Unity and the Communists." *Political Affairs* 46 (May 1967): 50-53.

Turner, Burghardt W. "The Richard B. Moore Collection and Its Collector." *Caribbean Studies* 15 (April 1975): 135-45.

Tyner, Jarvis. "Prospects for Afro-Americans." *Political Affairs* 67 (April 1988): 10-14.

White, Walter. "The Negro and the Communists." *Harpers* 64 (December 1931): 62-69.

Wilkerson, Doxey A. "The 46th Annual Convention of the NAACP." *Political Affairs* 34 (August 1955): 1-5.

Winston, Henry. "Party Tasks among the Negro People." *Political Affairs* 25 (April 1946): 352-65.

——. "Party Building." *Party Organizer* 14 (April 1981): 8-11.

Witmer, Lawrence. "The National Negro Congress: A Reassessment." *American Quarterly* 22 (Winter 1970): 878-90.

Wright, Richard. "Blueprint for Negro Writing." *New Challenge* 2 (Fall 1937): 50-65.

——. "Two Million Black Voices." *New Masses* 4 (25 February 1925): 10-16.

Zangrando, Robert. "The NAACP and a Federal Anti-Lynching Bill, 1934-1940." *Journal of Negro History* 50 (April 1965): 106-17.

Pamphlets

Alston, Christopher C. *Henry Ford and the Negro People.* Michigan National Negro Congress, n.d.

Browder, Earl. *Build the United People's Front.* New York: Workers Library Publishers, 1936.

Brown, William M. *Why I Am a Communist Lecture No. 12.* Gallion: Ohio: Brown Educational Co., 1932.

Browne, Robert S. *Should the U.S. Be Partioned?* New York: Merit Publishers, 1968.

Communist Party USA. *The Communist Position on the Negro Question.* New York: New Century Publishers, 1947.

——. *Pettis Perry Speaks to the Court.* New York: New Century Publishers, 1952.

——. *Race Hatred on Trial.* New York: CPUSA, 1931.

Davis, Benjamin. *The Path of Negro Liberation.* New York: New Century Publishers, 1947.

Davis, John P. *Let Us Build a National Negro Congress.* Washington, D.C.: National Negro Congress, 1935.

Hall, Gus. *1981—Mandate for Fightback.* New York: New Outlook Publishers, January, 1981.

Haywood, Harry, and Robert Minor. *The Road to Negro Liberation.* New York: Workers Library Publishers, 1935.

Herndon, Angelo. *You Cannot Kill the Working Class.* New York: International Labor Defense, 1935.

Johnson, Tom. *Reds in Dixie.* New York: Workers Library Publishers, 1935.

Lightfoot, Claude. *Negro Freedom*. New York: New Currents Publishers, 1964.

Moore, Carlos. *Were Marx and Engels White Racists?* Chicago: Institute of Positive Education, 1972.

NAACP. *A Statement on the Denial of Human Rights to Minorities in the Case of Citizens of Negro Descent in the United States of America and an Appeal to the United Nations for Redress*. New York: NAACP, 1947.

National Negro Congress. *Jim Crow*.

———. *Negro Workers After the War*.

Perry, Pettis. *The Communist Party*. New York: New Century Publishers, 1953.

Rossa, Della. *Why Watts Exploded*. Los Angeles Socialist Workers Party, 1966.

SNCC. *Black Power: SNCC Speaks for Itself*. Ann Arbor, Michigan: Radical Education Project, 1966.

Trotsky, Leon. *On Black Nationalism and Self-Determination*. New York: Merit Publishers, 1967.

Doctoral Dissertations

Finkle, Lee. "Forum for Protests: The Black Press During World War II." New York University, 1971.

Hunter, Gary Jerome. "Don't Buy Where You Can't Work: Black Urban Boycotts during the Depression, 1929-1941." University of Michigan, 1977.

Kellogg, John Peter. "Northern Liberals and Black America: A History of White Attitudes, 1936-1952." Northwestern University, 1971.

Government Publications

U.S. Congress. *Senate Foreign Relations Subcommittee. Hearings*. 68th Cong., pt. 1, 1st sess. Washington, D.C., GPO, 1924. 135.

U.S. Congress. House Special Committee on Communist Activities. *Investigation of Communist Propaganda in the United States*. 71st Cong., 2nd sess., 26 and 27 September 1930. 200, 243, 244.

U.S. Congress. *House Report of the Hearings, House Un-American Activities Committee*. Vol. 1, no. 3. October-November 1938. 2148.

U.S. Congress. House Un-American Activities Committee. *Communist Infiltration of Minority Groups.* 81st Cong., 2nd sess. 14 July 1949. 497-539.

U.S. Congress. *House Un-American Activities Committee Report.* 84th Cong., 2nd sess. 12 June 1956. 4492-510.

Subversion in Racial Unrest. Public Hearings of the State of Louisiana Joint Legislative Committee. Part 2. Homer, Louisiana *Guardian Journal,* 1957, 143-48.

California Senate. *Fifth Report of the California Senate Fact Finding Committee on Un-American Activities,* 1949.

Official Proceedings/Conference Documents

American Negro Labor Congress. *First National Conference, Manifesto, Resolution, Constitution.* Chicago, 28 June 1925. Chicago International Labor Defense.

Proceedings of the American Writers Congress. New York: International Publishers, 1935.

Proceedings of the Fourth National Convention of the International Workers Order. Pittsburgh: International Workers Order, 1938.

Proceedings of the National Negro Congress. Chicago: National Negro Congress, 1936.

Proceedings of the Second National Negro Congress. Philadelphia: National Negro Congress, 1937.

Proceedings, Conference on Africa, 14 April 1944. New York: Council of African Affairs, 1944.

Proceedings, Summary, Tenth Annual Convention, National Negro Congress, May 30-June 2, 1946.

Proceedings of the Second Congress of the Communist International. Washington, D.C.: GPO, 1920.

Miller, Kelly. *The Negro Sanhedrin: A Call for a Conference.* Washington, D.C., 1923.

Index

A

325